PRESS CENSORSHIP IN
CAROLINE ENGLAND

Between 1625 and 1640, a distinctive cultural awareness of censorship emerged, which ultimately led the Long Parliament to impose drastic changes in press control. The culture of censorship addressed in this study helps to explain the divergent historical interpretations of Caroline censorship as either draconian or benign. Such contradictions transpire because the Caroline regime and its critics employed similar rhetorical strategies that depended on the language of orthodoxy, order, tradition and law, but to achieve different ends. Building on her two previous studies on press censorship in Elizabethan and Jacobean England, Cyndia Clegg scrutinizes all aspects of Caroline print culture: book production in London, the universities, and on the Continent; licensing and authorization practices in both the Stationers' Company and among the ecclesiastical licensers; cases before the courts of High Commission and Star Chamber and the Stationers' Company's Court of Assistants; and trade regulation.

CYNDIA SUSAN CLEGG is Distinguished Professor of English at Pepperdine University. Her books include *The Peaceable and Prosperous Regiment of Blessed Queene Elisabeth* (2005), *Press Censorship in Jacobean England* (2002) and *Press Censorship in Elizabethan England* (1997), both published by Cambridge University Press. She has published widely on the subjects of Renaissance literature and print culture, and her articles have appeared in many publications including *Renaissance Quarterly* and *Shakespeare Quarterly*.

PRESS CENSORSHIP IN CAROLINE ENGLAND

CYNDIA SUSAN CLEGG

Pepperdine University, Malibu, California

CAMBRIDGE
UNIVERSITY PRESS

CAMBRIDGE UNIVERSITY PRESS
Cambridge, New York, Melbourne, Madrid, Cape Town, Singapore,
São Paulo, Delhi, Dubai, Tokyo, Mexico City

Cambridge University Press
The Edinburgh Building, Cambridge CB2 8RU, UK

Published in the United States of America by Cambridge University Press, New York

www.cambridge.org
Information on this title: www.cambridge.org/9780521182850

First published 2008
First paperback edition 2010

A catalogue record for this publication is available from the British Library

ISBN 978-0-521-87668-1 Hardback
ISBN 978-0-521-18285-0 Paperback

Contents

Acknowledgments

In the world of early modern English print culture, one of the charming claims that epistles to the readers made was that books did often "take printed wings, and fly about" – purportedly quite free from the expectations and knowledge of authors, printers, and official censors. While few writers today would embrace the careless flurry of activity this trope implies, most of us hope the product of our scholarly labors indeed will take wing. This one will do so, however, not because it has sprung from some platonic conception of itself, but because I am deeply indebted to so many people and institutions for their help along the way. Research for this book, carried out at the Public Record Office (now the National Archive), the Bodleian Library, the British Library, Lambeth Palace Library, Harvard University's Houghton Library, and the Huntington Library, was supported by fellowships from the Huntington Library, the British Academy, the Bibliographical Society of America, and by a research grant from the dean of Pepperdine University's Seaver College, David Baird. This project would not have come to fruition without the knowledge, help, and patience of all of the library staff at the Huntington, but especially the curators of early manuscripts and books, Mary Robertson, Alan Jutzi, and Steve Tabor. The Huntington Library's Director of Research, Robert C. Ritchie, generously provided me with a room of my own in the library's new Babcock Scholars Suite to complete the book. Working at the Huntington Library has allowed me to participate in a community of scholars who have offered me their encouragement, support, suggestions, observations, and the gems of their knowledge; among those who have been so enormously helpful are David Cressy, Lori Anne Ferrell, Heather James, Mark Kishlansky, Peter Lake, Alan Nelson, and Kevin Sharpe. I have also been privileged to participate in two conferences on the Jacobean Printed Book at Queen Mary, University of London, where Maria Wakely and Graham Rees have brought together some of the best scholars working in the history of the book – one among them, Ian Gadd, kindly provided me with a copy of "'Being Like a Field': Corporate Identity in the Stationers' Company 1557–1684," his DPhil dissertation. Debora Shuger's generous gift of an early copy of *Censorship and Cultural Sensibility* also proved invaluable.

Working on this book with the excellent people at Cambridge University Press – who assure that nothing will ever merely "fly about" – once again has been a privilege. I am as ever indebted to Sarah Stanton, who combines vision with common sense. Rebecca Jones has brought to this project her fine editorial sense. Zachary Lesser, a sensitive and informed reader, has significantly improved this book by his fine comments and suggestions. This study quotes extensively from seventeenth-century manuscripts and printed books. I have not modernized their spelling although I have regularized spelling that reflects manuscript contractions employing ∼ and printing-house font choices that interchange the letters I and J and U and V (both upper and lower case). A version of chapter 3, entitled "The Court of Star Chamber and Press Control in Early Modern England," appeared in the Spring 2005 issue of *Journal of Modern European History*.

I am enormously grateful to all of these people who have given this book wings. Please accept my heartfelt thanks – and also to my husband, Michael Wheeler. I so appreciate his unwavering encouragement and great faith in me.

CHAPTER I

Censorship and the law:
the Caroline inheritance

William Prynne, who was tried in the court of Star Chamber in 1634 for several charges (including sedition and perjury) in relation to the duly authorized book he had written denouncing actors and the theatre (*Histrio-mastix*, 1633), looms so large in the historical imagination of Caroline England, that however often his story has been told, any effort to come to terms with the relationship between the government of Charles I and print culture must contend with Prynne and his place in the historical imagination. I begin here with Prynne's name not to ground my study of Caroline press censorship in the encounter between Prynne and the Caroline regime, but to suggest the complex investments that have attended even the most astute studies of England between Charles I's accession in 1625 and his execution in 1649. However cautiously scholars have sought to navigate the troubled waters of seventeenth-century historiography, the events of the 1640s and 1650s – whether "Civil War," "Rebellion," or "Revolution" – inevitably impinge upon the ways in which stories like Prynne's have been told. It may appear to be an artificial exercise to attempt to place press censorship during the reign of Charles within its prevailing economic, political, and religious contexts, looking back to historical precedents rather than forward to the Civil War, as this study seeks to do. Considering a few of the narratives that have attached to Prynne's trial, however, should suggest the desirability (indeed the necessity) of such an approach. Each of the following accounts tells a quite different story about Prynne's offense and the nature of censorship in Caroline England.

F. S. Siebert's *Freedom of the Press in England, 1476–1776*, published in 1952, has for some time been regarded as the acknowledged authority on the history of press censorship in England. In *Censorship and Interpretation* (1984), Annabel Patterson insists that her own interest in the hermeneutics of censorship may justifiably focus "only occasionally" on the mechanisms and institutions of "state control" because "The legal history of censorship in relationship to all aspects of the printing trade has been well covered by F. S. Siebert."[1] In *The Trouble with Ownership* (2005), Jody Greene still cites Siebert's book as the authoritative survey of "the wide variety of press controls in place in the period."[2] For Siebert, Prynne's case served to illustrate how "early Stuart kings continued on their way, extending the repressive measures as their efforts to convince by argument and exhortation failed."[3] Prynne was an idealistic Puritan who "was irritated into action by what he considered the Stuart defection from the Protestant cause":

He espoused the central ideal of Calvinism in his first book published in 1627. In succeeding works he attacked both Presbyterianism and Romanism and then went on to castigate the social foibles of the times. For condemning such "immoralities" as dancing, hunting, play-acting, and public festivals in his *Histrio-Mastix* (1632), he was haled before the Star Chamber (1633) and was sentenced to be pilloried, to lose both ears, to be disbarred from his profession, and to be fined £10,000.[4]

Despite its tone of historical objectivity, Siebert's account illustrates Kevin Sharpe's assessment of the resonance of Prynne's trial, that for many historians the "power of the basic story . . . has often led to a suppression of the details."[5] The very real Star Chamber charge of seditious libel disappears entirely from Siebert's account, implying that the Star Chamber arbitrarily enacted Caroline ideological repression.

   Even though Annabel Patterson defers to Siebert's authority on the mechanisms of press control, she appreciates the representative value the culture ascribed to Prynne's loss of his ears, which "stands as a symbol for the whole ghastly area of the sensational public trial and dismemberment."[6] While she admits such trials were exceptions, Prynne's experience served as a sign "that the codes governing sociopolitical communication had broken down, that one side or the other had broken the rules."[7] From Patterson's perspective early modern English writers had to adapt to a political environment in which censorship prevented open political discourse. Writers "gradually developed codes of communication, partly to protect themselves from hostile and hence dangerous readings of their work, partly in order to be able to say what they had to publicly without directly provoking or confronting the authorities."[8] William Prynne's case embodies a

ritualism . . . which lies at the very center of everything we could possibly mean by the theater of state . . . In this case both sides broke the rules; Prynne, by attacking one of his culture's main media of indirection, the public (and private) drama; Charles I and Laud, by disallowing Prynne's own use, however scanty, of the time-honored protective devices of analogy and "authority."[9]

Charles and Laud, from this perspective, sacrificed "the power of illusion" so that they might "preserve the illusion of power." According to Patterson, "By making Prynne a martyr, Charles took an irrevocable step toward civil war and a polarized culture."[10]

Like Patterson, Kevin Sharpe recognizes the symbolic value of Prynne's trial but not as a sign of a disintegrating political regime. In depicting the reign of Charles I as a time of consensus and moderation, Sharpe regards Prynne's 1634 trial, as well as the notorious 1637 trial of Prynne together with Henry Burton and John Bastwick for writing against the Church, as a "miscreant's" due.[11] Even though Prynne's attorneys argued that the charges of committing scandal against the Queen and suggesting that it was "lawful to lay violent hands upon a prince" resulted from "incriminating interpretations" being "imposed on the text," according to Sharpe, "there was no disagreement among the judges. Sir John Coke, Attorney Heath, Justice Richardson and the Earl of Pembroke, men of strong Protestant convictions, all agreed with Cottington, who branded Prynne a dangerous man."[12] From Sharpe's perspective, Prynne, who wrote "vituperative treatises against the church," was a renegade intent on discrediting the Caroline regime. He was someone who aroused little pity: "neither his trial nor punishment was the subject of public attention or sympathy."[13] Prynne may have verbally assaulted the Caroline regime, but he posed no real threat. The real foes in Sharpe's account are the historians who have made Prynne, Burton, and Bastwick into *"causes célèbres"* – those for whom, as noted above, the "power of the basic story ... has often led to a suppression of the details."[14] The "graphic stories" told about trials and terrible punishments "have besmirched the court of Star Chamber and the episcopate and government of Caroline England."[15]

While Sharpe slights the significance of Prynne's trial for anything other than its power over the historical imagination, Debora Shuger finds in the proceedings the best intent and practice of censorship in early modern England. She sees "particular value" in Prynne's trial "because the sole issue under dispute was that of intent": "Had Prynne's words been ambiguous, the law would have allowed them a favorable construction."[16] His words, however, were not found by the judges to be ambiguous, and Prynne was held accountable. Prynne's transgression, according to Shuger, did not reside in the content of his "tirade" against stage plays:

Accused of writing "a most scandalous, infamous libel," Prynne was tried in the Star Chamber in 1632–33. The indictment charges him in general terms with libeling "his Majesty's royal queen, lords of the counsel, &c." whom Prynne "well knew" had been "spectators of some masques and dances," and with "stir[ring] up the people to discontent, as if there were just cause to lay violent hands on their prince" (*State Trials* 3:563) – charges which, taken alone, make one wonder if Prynne's offense was simply to have criticized something the queen liked, and why this would be considered inciting rebellion.[17]

Prynne's language was the transgressor and the sole witness to the malice of his intent:

What made *Histrio-mastix* intolerable was not Prynne's wholly conventional argument that playgoing fostered immorality but rather his rhetoric of divine wrath, hellfire, devils, and damnation, because such language worked upon tender consciences of God-fearing men and women to instill dark suspicions of rulers who patronized "Devil's Chapels."[18]

From Shuger's perspective Prynne's *Histrio-mastix* participated in the conventional polemics of "Protestant militants of the earlier seventeenth century" that relied on "defamation, malicious conjecture, and fearmongering."[19] While Elizabethan censorship had been directed at such abuse among both Catholic and Protestant polemicists, the end of both Jacobean and Laudian censorship was to "mute this rabidly paranoid antipopery that formed the core of the political worldview of mainstream evangelical Protestantism and which, in the end, brought down the Stuart monarchy."[20]

David Cressy challenges Sharpe's contention that in its time Prynne's trial was relatively unimportant. Like Patterson, he regards Prynne's trial as symbolic, but less of an abusive regime than of the "rising tensions and changing fortunes of the years 1633 to 1641" that were marked by "rising political temperature, an escalation of vituperative rhetoric, and a sharpening of cultural divisions."[21] From Cressy's perspective Prynne was an effective polemicist who, like his "tormenters," "understood the importance of propaganda and symbolism, and turned the suffering of the body and the manipulation of text into a fine political art."[22] Far less sympathetic to Laudianism than Shuger, Cressy reminds us that in 1633 Prynne, a conforming member of the Church of England, was so alarmed by Arminianism and aggrieved by England's sins that he sought to rebut contemporary charges "that puritans and precisians" were "seditious, factious, troublesome, rebellious persons, and enemies both to the state and government" by demonstrating his concern for England's moral and spiritual health.[23] He did so in his book by condemning "all popular, festive, and dramatic entertainments that furthered the work of the Devil."[24] Prynne's misfortune in the case of *Histrio-mastix*, from Cressy's perspective, was that "William Laud, at this time still bishop of London, and still smarting from Prynne's earlier attack on Arminianism, was determined to make the writer suffer."[25] By writing not only against stage plays but also against "'hunting, public festivals, Christmas-keeping, bonfires and maypoles', and even 'against the dressing of a house with green ivy'," Prynne made himself vulnerable to "an extreme application of reader response" from his "enemies at Whitehall," who saw the book as "an attack on the honour of those closest to the king, as a challenge to royal authority, and as an assault on the entire public, festive, celebratory, and recreational life of the country and the court," even though "there was nothing new in *Histrio-Mastix*," a book that had been printed with ecclesiastical approbation.[26] According to Cressy, the effort to control public opinion was not Prynne's alone. The judgments rendered in the Star Chamber trial were as intemperate and vituperative as Prynne's prose, and the punishments Star Chamber imposed – disbarring, imprisonment, an excessive fine, disfigurement, and public humiliation in the pillory (an indignity gentlemen rarely suffered) – far exceeded anything that had been done before, especially considering that Prynne made a submission to the King and begged for "pardon and grace."[27] Prynne's trial contributed to a growing political and cultural divide within England, and reactions to it reflected the division: "Some observers were delighted by Prynne's come-uppance, others were appalled by the savagery of his mistreatment."[28] For Cressy, "Prynne's experience, and the contest among contemporaries to control and interpret it, undermines any notion that the personal rule of Charles I was an era of order, consensus, and moderation."[29]

The cultural divisions that marked Caroline England, it would appear, still persist – although now in the historiography of the period. While it is tempting at this point to sort out the widely divergent accounts of Prynne's trial and its cultural implications, this must wait for later chapters. Prynne's fate and that of printers and other writers whose work was regarded as somehow transgressive must be seen within the context of the practices of press regulation in early modern England. To be able to understand whether Prynne's trial is exemplary or extraordinary, the remainder of this chapter will describe the various institutions in England under the Tudor and early Stuart monarchs that circumscribed the printed word. Some of these are the mechanisms of censorship that all of the above accounts of Prynne's trial seem to take for granted: the regulation of language by English law, the use of the court of Star Chamber to punish offending authors, and the vetting of texts prior to printing to assure their acceptability (authorization).[30] Besides pre-print censorship, the courts, and the law, other interests in Tudor and Stuart England affected what did and did not appear in print: the monarch, Parliament, the Church, the printing trade, and, curiously enough, custom. In England, the past, recent and distant, was invoked to allow, justify, restrict, and redefine the present. As Charles M. Gray reminds us, England in the late sixteenth and early seventeenth centuries was a traditional society where material change was slow and both secular and religious intellectual habits were grounded in respect for the authority of the past: "England was peculiar . . . mainly for concretizing the established and the ancestral in the common law."[31] Because of this, all the institutions that impinged upon the printed word were in flux. To understand the sometimes subtle, sometimes dramatic changes that affected print, we will consider the accumulation of precedents that shaped the relationship between the various English institutions and the printed word.

THE ROYAL PREROGATIVE

In the not disinterested pamphlet *The Original and Growth of Printing*, dedicated to Charles II, Richard Atkyns wrote, "Printing belongs to your Majesty, in Your publique and private Capacity, as Supream Magistrate and Proprietor."[32] By Atkyns's account the first printing press was set up in Oxford ten years before any printers or printing houses appeared on the Continent, and King Henry VI, readily receiving the printers, swore them as "the king's Servants": "Thus was the Art of Printing, in its Infancy, nursed by the Nursing Father of us all."[33] Tudor monarchs, Atkyns contends, saw fit to control printing when they saw it become abusive. While Atkyns frames his discourse in the customary language of censorship (abuse and control), he is actually more concerned with the monarch's prerogative to confer on individuals not necessarily members of the printing guild (the London Company of Stationers) the right to print and market a book or given categories of books. (By asserting the King's prerogative authority over printing, Atkyns was seeking to legitimate his royal patent to print common law books.) Since Atkyns's pamphlet, as Adrian Johns reminds us, is virtually the first history of the printing trade, it may have contributed to the understanding of the monarch's relationship to printing that finds expression in this opening sentence of Siebert's *Freedom of the Press*: "The authority to control and regulate the printing press in England was claimed for two centuries by the Crown as one of its prerogative rights."[34]

  G. R. Elton observes that "'Prerogative' was the great Tudor word, stressed in particular by Henry VII and Elizabeth, by Henry to restore the Crown and its finances and by Elizabeth to oppose her subjects' interference in matters of policy."[35] Prerogative, granted to the monarch by the laws of the realm, enabled the Crown to "discharge the task of governing."[36] Among most of the lawyers, according to Elton, the most important aspect of the King's prerogative arose from the King's "feudal overlordship," authority in war and peace, in coining money, in dispensing the laws, and in conferring dignities and offices (and the properties associated with them).[37] The making of laws was reserved to Parliament and the monarch's prerogative action could not "abrogate, repeal or suspend any act of Parliament."[38] In his list of the monarch's prerogatives in the sixteenth-century political treatise, *De Republica Anglorum*, Thomas Smith makes no mention of the monarch's prerogative to control printing.

From the advent of printing English monarchs, recognizing the printed word's extraordinary power to achieve religious, political, and cultural ends, engaged with the press at many levels but never with the sense of the prerogative right to control it that Atkyns and Siebert envision. Rather, it was in their position as feudal overlords that English monarchs first exercised control over printing. From the time of the Magna Carta an essential focus of English law was ascertaining the right to property and its transmission, and, for several reasons, early printed texts participated in complex notions of property. Authorship, unimportant and often ignored in the medieval world, was an unstable concept, in part because so many of the earliest books printed – law books, missals, Bibles, miscellanies – actually lacked authors, in part because the early Protestant writers who used the press extensively often concealed their identities. Thus authorship, though it might be identified with agency, provided no link to material property. The printed book, however, possessed material value. It represented both the costs of the publisher's investment in his shop and all its material accoutrements – press, letters, paper, print, and labor – and the means by which he could assure his continued interest in this property. Under English common law property was something that could be held in an estate, but books had to be disbursed – sold – to assure economic return. This condition, of course, also existed for other material goods, but print's distinctive feature, its ease of replication, allowed relatively inexpensive access of one man to the product of another. Such appropriation – unrestricted printing – violated the principle of property. Recognizing the need to identify the material object of the printed text as "real" property, title pages and colophons were imprinted with printers' names, printing house locations, publishers' and booksellers' names, and shop signs (depending on who owned the copy). Without some form of enforcement, however, this was an insufficient measure to assure the printer or publisher his sole right to the benefit of his investment and labor. Printers and publishers sought and received protection from the Crown in the form of a royal privilege to print generally issued under the Privy Seal as a patent. Hence when a Tudor monarch granted a patent – for printing or anything else – the monarch essentially transferred to the subject those property interests that by feudal rights belonged to the Crown. In this respect, printing privileges (patents) were like the Crown's grant of licenses to acquire or alienate lands, to hold fairs and markets or to import or export goods. They were entered in the patent rolls as "licenses," with the words "license" and "privilege" used interchangeably. Books so privileged included imprints identifying the publisher's sole property right in the text (or later, bearing the words "*cum privilegio regiae ad imprimendum solum*"), the violation of which gave the privilege holder protection in the royal courts.[39]

Such privileges, granting to their recipients the right to enjoy the economic benefits derived from printing, proliferated during that reign of Henry VIII but ceased to be the principal means of protecting printers' rights to copy after 1557, the year in which the Company of Stationers of the City of London received its charter. Even so, Elizabeth continued to grant lucrative printing patents for entire classes of books (law books, primers, catechisms, school books) to favored printers like John Day, who received a patent for a given term for anything he printed, and to individual authors like Christopher Saxton for his English atlas. Additionally, from the time of Henry VII patents created the office of Printer to the King, the holders of which printed not only official documents like proclamations, but the Book of Common Prayer and some editions of the Bible. When James I came to the throne in 1601, he rescinded all Elizabethan patents by a royal proclamation that denounced monopolies and patents – although this did not extend to the office of King's Printer or the trade monopoly of the Stationers' Company. Furthermore, he issued letters patent that granted the Stationers' Company rights in the formerly patented titles. Despite his announced objection to patents and monopolies, James still bestowed patents on political favorites (rarely printers) – sometimes to assure the printing of books in which he had a vested interest and sometimes to secure revenues for the Crown.[40]

The charter Mary granted in 1557 to the London Stationers was also a form of property protection that derived from the Crown. Issued as a grant of privilege extended through a patent under the Privy Seal, the charter conferred on the Company of Stationers privileges and practices common among the older guilds: rights of property ownership, self-regulation, keeping apprentices, and engaging in searches to protect the trade from "foreigners" (non-members) and poor workmanship.[41] It allowed the Stationers to petition the City of London for the right to have a livery (granted in 1560), which assured the Company voting rights in London and parliamentary elections, participation in London governance, and status among London livery companies. Further, the charter provided for the Company's government by a master and two wardens, who shared their authority with the Company's court of Assistants, whose members were elected from among the livery.[42] In these respects, the Stationers were no different from other city companies. One unique benefit the printers of the Stationers' Company procured in their charter was the exclusive practice of their trade of printing.[43] In principle, this monopoly, like those created by individual printing patents, provided a means by which the right to print a text or have it printed could be construed as a property right, although one to be conferred and administered by the Company rather than the Crown. The Stationers' Company's principal task, besides admitting new members and administering routine Company business, lay in recognizing and protecting the integrity of its members' textual property rights. To this end they conducted searches for presses printing a Company member's copy or for presses of non-company printers – for presses engaging in "disorderly" printing – and they seized books that were "illegal," i.e., printed against Company ordinances.[44]

The Stationers' Company has been often misunderstood to be merely a creature of royal authority, formed to administer the state surveillance of print. Although the language Queen Mary employed in the 1557 patent for the charter reveals her intention that the Company serve as a "suitable remedy" to the Protestant press,[45] when Elizabeth confirmed the charter in 1558, she ignored Mary's intentions altogether. Elizabeth let stand the language of Mary's patent even though she would not have shared Mary's interest in protecting "Mother Church." This is not to say, however, that the Stationers' Company did not participate in print control. Explicit in the Stationers' Company's Charter was the notion that the exercise of their privilege could not be "repugnant or contrary to the laws or statutes of this our kingdom of England, or to the prejudice of the commonwealth of the same."[46] To assure the continuity of their monopoly, it was in the Company's best interest to prevent the publication of texts that violated the law of the land, whose central interests in regard to the printed word were protecting the monarch from treason, the aristocracy from scandal, and whatever church settlement that existed at the time from opposition.[47]

Another area in which a Crown prerogative may be misconstrued as evidence that printing "belonged" to the monarch appears in royal proclamations that addressed printing and printed texts in multiple ways. A proclamation was a royal legislative order whose legal authority was confirmed in 1539 by the Act of Proclamations. According to G. R. Elton, this act grounded royal prerogative in parliamentary authority, but the nature and scope of proclamations derived from practice, tradition, and the common law.

Since they emanated from king and Council they were regarded as inferior to statute and common law. They could not (and did not) touch life or member; though they might create offences with penalties, they could not create felonies or treasons. Nor could they touch common law rights of property . . . Their [Tudor] proclamations covered administrative, social and economic matters – though they included religion, as the sphere of the supreme head's personal action – but never matters which both the judges and Parliament would regard as belonging to law and statute.[48]

Since proclamations issued from the monarch and Privy Council, the common law courts could not enforce them, and the task of enforcement "was left to the Council, sitting as a court in Star Chamber."[49] According to Paul L. Hughes and James F. Larkin, a royal proclamation's real power resided in its value as propaganda; it was "a literary form psychologically gauged to elicit from the subject an obedient response, favorable to the interests of the Crown."[50]

The earliest Tudor proclamations that related to printing suggest the manner in which they might be misconstrued as evidence of a royal prerogative governing print. In 1529 in the monarch's role as defender of the faith and protector of the realm's peace, Henry VIII issued a proclamation prohibiting writing anything "contrary to the Catholic faith," maintaining any person writing or publishing such a book, or importing or owning one. Any transgressive books were to be delivered to the bishop or ordinary within fifteen days. A list of fifteen prohibited books that threatened the realm with "pestiferous, cursed, and seditious errors" appeared at the end of the proclamation. The books were seditious because by the "procurement" of Luther and other heretics, "an infinite number of Christian people were slain."[51] In 1530 Henry issued another proclamation that similarly prohibited five additional texts "sent into this his said realm . . . to the intent as well to pervert and withdraw the people from the Catholic and true faith of Christ, as also to stir and incense them to sedition and disobedience against their princes."[52] After Henry VIII had broken ties with Rome, he saw as his own "the great cure

and charge ... over all the congregation of the ... Church of England,"
and speaking from this position, in November 1538 he issued a proclamation that prohibited printing scripture without official approbation,
deprived married clergy, exiled Anabaptists, and declared Thomas
Becket no longer a saint. This proclamation has often been regarded as
the origin of ecclesiastical licensing (a matter considered later in this
chapter), but its language suggests that Henry's effort here to control
the press derived not from a prerogative authority over printing but from
his interest in ridding the kingdom of "all wicked errors, erroneous
opinions, and dissention" bred by "sundry and strange persons called
Anabaptists and Sacramentaries" and assuring that printed books upheld
the traditional (Roman) rites and ceremonies. In 1539 to assure the quality
and consistency of printed Bibles, Henry VIII gave Thomas Cromwell,
the Keeper of the Privy Seal, full authority to determine what editions of
the Bible could be printed. The sole Henrician proclamation that in any
way regulated printing was issued in 1546 and required the printer of "any
manner of English book, ballad, or play" to "put his name to the same,
with the name of the author and day of the print, and shall present the
first copy to the mayor of the town where he dwelleth." This, however,
was one of several means the proclamation proposed "to purge his
commonwealth of such pernicious doctrine, as by books in the English
tongue hath been of late divulged abroad in this his grace's realm" – books
by Continental Protestant reformers.[53] Essentially, the proclamation prohibited any book in English not printed in England, unless the person
who imported it had special license to do so. Here again Henry is more
concerned with the oversight of religion than with printing per se. Besides
his proclamations restricting religious books, Henry issued proclamations
requiring a single book of English grammar and authorizing an English
primer and giving Richard Grafton and Edward Whitchurch a monopoly
for its printing and sale. Henry never issued a proclamation directly
regulating the printing trade, even though trade regulation was within
the scope of his prerogative power. This is apparent since his proclamations regulated wool cloth manufacture (one of England's most important
industries), pricing wines, prohibiting unlicensed shipping, requiring
export licenses for exporting butter and cheese, and requiring alien
artisans to register. If an English monarch were to regulate printing, it
was not because of the particular character of printing, but because trade
regulation generally came within the monarch's prerogative. That Henry
did not exercise such authority indicates that he did not envision printing
as "belonging" to him.

Henry VIII's heirs showed little more inclination to "own" printing than their father had. Proclamations from the reigns of both Edward VI and Mary I, however, do suggest that their governance met with resistance and unrest. Edward faced rebellious assemblies in the west and rioting over enclosures. Vagabonds disturbed the peace in London. Edwardian proclamations sought to silence debate and discussion of the Eucharist, outlawed controversial and seditious sermons in favor of prescribed homilies, and repeatedly tried to quell unsettling rumors – once of military defeat; once that after Somerset was apprehended, the country would abolish the "good laws" of the Edwardian Reformation. Edward's interest in print was subservient to these larger concerns. A 1551 proclamation called for enforcing statutes against vagabonds and rumormongers. As part of the effort to secure a greater respect for law, he issued a proclamation requiring that plays and books be vetted by government officials to assure that "every man" would love the King, fear his sword, and live "within the compass of his degree, contented with his vocation, every man to apply himself to live obediently, quietly, without murmur, grudging, sowing of sedition, spreading of tales and rumors, and without doing or saying of any manner of thing that may touch the dignity of his majesty." "Printers, booksellers, and players of interludes," the proclamation says, "do print, sell, and play whatsoever any light and fantastical head listeth to invent and devise, whereby many inconveniences hath and daily do arise."[54] Even though the proclamation does not spell out the standards by which writing and playing might be judged, its emphasis on lawfulness and order suggests as much of an interest in controlling the output of the press for politics as for religion.

Political and religious ends coincided for Mary. She contended that Protestant books were "Filled both with heresy, sedition, and treason."[55] One month after she came to the throne, she issued a proclamation that prohibited both printing without official sanction and the "playing of interludes and printing of false fond books, ballads, rhymes, and other lewd treatises in the English tongue concerning doctrine in matters now in question and controversy touching the high points and mysteries of Christian religion."[56] Two years later a proclamation called for enforcing a 1401 statute against heresy and prohibited any book "containing false doctrine contrary and against the Catholic faith and the doctrine of the Catholic church."[57]

Elizabeth issued eleven proclamations which, although they did not impose regulations on printing generally, imposed censorship on particular texts: six addressed Catholic texts that issued from continental presses, one a principally political work, and four radical Protestant texts. The first proclamation, issued in 1569, described the books by continental Catholic controversialists as being "repugnant to truth, derogatory to the sovereign estate of her majesty, and stirring and nourishing sedition in this realm" because "they usurped jurisdiction of the Papistical See of Rome" and argued against the legitimacy of the doctrine of the Church of England.[58] A 1570 proclamation calling for the discovery of people bringing into the realm "seditious books" and "traitorous devices" was principally concerned with any writing supporting Mary Stuart's right to the English throne.[59] In 1573 copies of the scandalous Catholic libel against Lord Burghley and the Earl of Leicester, *A Treatise of Treasons*, was ordered destroyed by proclamation. A 1584 proclamation condemned William Allen's *A True, Sincere And Modest Defence, of English Catholiques that Suffer For their Faith*, and two books advancing Mary Stuart's right to succession, John Leslie's *Touching the Right, Title, and Interest of the Most excellent Princesse Marie Queen of Scotland* and *The Copie of a Letter*, commonly referred to as *Leicester's Commonwealth*. In 1588 Allen's *Admonition to the Nobility and People of England*, a book justifying Spanish invasion and libeling Elizabeth, was the target. The radical Protestant books targeted by four different proclamations were *An admonition to the parliament* and books defending it (1572), books advancing the "heretical" sect known as the Family of Love (1580), books by the Congregationalists, Robert Browne and Robert Harrison, containing "very false, seditious, and schismatical doctrine" (1584),[60] and the Martin Marprelate pamphlets (1589) "containing in them doctrine very erroneous, and other matters notoriously untrue and slanderous to the state."[61] The political book condemned by proclamation was John Stubbs's *The Discovery of a Gaping Gulf* (1579), an outspoken attack on Elizabeth's intended marriage with Francis, Duke of Alençon and Anjou. Stubbs was tried and convicted in King's Bench for writing a "seditious libel" in violation of the statute passed during the reign of Mary (1&2 Phil. & Mar., ca. 3), which prohibited scandalous words against the Queen's husband, and specified that any one who wrote or published such words would lose his right hand in the market place.[62] Of the eleven proclamations, then, four sought to rout out books that were doctrinally unsound – the principal end of Henry VIII's proclamations. Two prohibited books written on the succession, a topic proscribed by statute and deemed traitorous writing. The remainder censored books that participated in some way in maliciously attacking the Queen, her ministers, her clergy, or the church settlement. Henry VIII and Mary issued proclamations that called upon their subjects to observe the statutory laws against specific kinds of religious writing. Edward called for his subjects to respect the statutes, including those prohibiting rumor, and to honor his authority. Elizabeth's proclamations variously prohibited printing, importing, and possessing books that either violated statutory definitions of treason and sedition or contained unsound religious doctrine.[63]

Elton remarks the common observation that "one of the major differences between the Tudors and Stuarts lay in their treatment of the royal prerogative."[64] While Elizabethan proclamations account for most of the efforts taken to censor texts during her reign, James I only occasionally employed proclamations for the purpose of censorship. James issued only three proclamations that directly sought to control printed texts: in 1610 for John Cowell's *The Interpreter* (1607),[65] and in 1623 and 1624 in an effort to quell opposition to his pro-Spanish policy. *The Interpreter*, a dictionary of legal terms, appeared in 1607 in response to appeals within the legal community for developing some "method" for common law practice. Among its vast catalogue of legal terms were sections on "Parliament," "Prerogative," and "Subsidy" that some members of Parliament, especially common law lawyers, saw as infringing parliamentary privilege and demeaning the common law. Before either house could proceed in the matter, the King intervened, emphasizing his respect for Parliament and the common law, as well as his desire that nothing like Cowell's book, which might be seen to suggest the contrary, should become part of the historical record. The language of the proclamation indicates that James censored Cowell's book both to defer to the interests of the common lawyers and to distance himself from Cowell's restrictive definitions.

The outbreak of the Thirty Years War led to a proliferation of printed texts, some of which were news books on continental affairs that expressed sympathy for the international Protestant cause and for the war's potential martyrs, Frederick and his wife Elizabeth (James I's daughter), and criticized James's foreign policy. Rather than commit to the war, James pursued a diplomatic solution with Spain, including a marriage alliance. In 1620 James issued a proclamation against licentious speech on matters of state that, while it did not mention printing, was clearly interpreted to do so. The proclamation commanded his subjects, "every of them, from the highest to the lowest, to take heede, how they intermeddle by Penne, or Speech, with causes of State and secrets of Empire, either at home, or abroad."[66] This was reissued the following July. In September 1623 in response to printed texts that reflected eroding public support for his foreign policy, a proclamation appeared that directly addressed the press by declaring, among other things, that the 1586 Star Chamber decrees for order in printing, which according to James had required official "licens-ing" (authorization), should be "from henceforth strictly observed." The proclamation complained of the proliferation of "seditious, schismaticall, or other scandalous Bookes, or Pamphlets"[67] and charged the Stationers' Company officials to search for, seize, and suppress such works. James's final effort to use a proclamation to increase official oversight of printed books came in response to a parliamentary effort to suppress Catholic writing. In a 1624 anti-Jesuit pamphlet, *The Foot out of the Snare*, John Gee included a list of 150 Catholic books that had been "vented" by priests and their agents in the two previous years. The Commons employed this list as the basis of their May 28 grievance against recusant books to the King. A Proclamation was drawn up to prevent the publication of such books by requiring that all books "concerning matters of Religion, Church govern-ment, or the State" be "perused, corrected, and allowed" by the Archbishop of either Canterbury or York, the Bishop of London, or the Vice Chancellor of either Oxford or Cambridge. James refused to sign the proclamation, however, unless it also included "Puritanicall" books and pamphlets as equally "scandalous."[68]

Only James's final proclamation resembles those of his predecessors, Henry VIII and Mary, by making a special case for employing pre-print authorization to control religious printing. The 1623 proclama-tion, like Elizabeth's proclamation against Stubbs, sought to restrain political opposition, but unlike Elizabeth's, the proclamation does not refer to statutory definitions of treason or seditious writing. Instead it seeks to strengthen the effects of pre-print censorship (as does the 1624 proclamation). In the proclamation against Cowell's *Interpreter* and those of 1620 and 1621, James is more concerned with reserving to the Crown alone the privilege to speak or write about political matters, even though these proclamations do virtually nothing to enforce such a restriction.[69]

This survey of proclamations relating to printing suggests that neither James I nor his Tudor predecessors regarded the control of printing as an inherent part of the prerogative. These royal proclamations, as we have seen, enforced other parts of the prerogative, especially the monarch's duty to protect the Church and "to dispense with laws made."[70] Nearly all the Tudor proclamations called for adherence to statutes, while James's pro-clamations tended to reinforce the *arcana imperii*. Elton accounts for this divergence in his observation on the different conceptions of prerogative: "Tudor royal prerogative was a department of the law which conferred on the ruler certain necessary rights not available to the subject. The Stuarts saw their prerogative very differently . . . Their prerogative was not part of the law: it was over and above it . . ."[71]

For both James and the Tudors, however, proclamations clearly served as a tool of propaganda, employing highly charged language to denounce the regime's enemies and commend good subjects' best behavior. Debora Shuger sees the language of the proclamations as a key to understanding early modern language regulation's principal motive – suppressing injurious language or "hate speech."[72] According to Shuger, in the "early modern West" there are only two forms of language control: "one primarily concerned with the regulation of ideas, the other with relations among persons."[73] In England "virtually all substantive law dealing with the regulation of language concerned defamation," the regulation of language among persons.[74] Language regulation consisted of "a system of formal and informal controls that regulated permissible expression in the interests of truth, charity, respect, and order . . ."[75] While Shuger makes an important contribution to understanding some of the intent of language regulation, the censorship proclamations argue that the message as well as the medium was the object of royal concern. That books condemned by proclamations upheld papal authority, contained contrary religious teaching, wrote about the succession, or encouraged subjects to take arms against their ruler indicates that these monarchs regarded the ideas to be more important than the language in which they were expressed.[76]

Besides employing proclamations, the customary tools of royal administration, on occasion monarchs took special actions with regard to the printed word. Most of the time, these interventions were put in the hands of the Privy Council, but not always. On several occasions James I ordered books burned in public places, an action usually taken more to display his royal opinion about the contents than to actually remove the books from circulation.[77] He also called for the suppression of books about Scottish and English monarchs. He refused license to John Selden's *Mare Clausum*, a treatise on trade, because of his concern about relations with the Dutch, a concern that also motivated his suppression of Richard Mockett's *Doctrina et Politia Ecclesiae Anglicanae* (1616). On one occasion, however, James vigorously sought only continental suppression for a book – this for *Corona Regia* (1615), a stinging mock encomium of James's pretensions to piety and learning and an exposé of his sexual prowess with men and women. While his agents relentlessly sought the book's author and printer abroad, James took no domestic action that might call his subjects' attention to the book.

One other prerogative action a monarch could employ was imprisonment. Elizabeth imprisoned Thomas Wentworth for writing a tract on the succession, which although not printed, was widely circulated in Parliament. In 1614 James imprisoned George Wither in the Marshalsea prison for writing *Abuses Stript and Whipt* (published in 1613 with ecclesiastical authorization), probably because the book was regarded as attacking the Earl of Northampton. The 1621 publication of George Wither's *Withers Motto* without official sanction landed its author in the Marshalsea, with, according to Reverend Joseph Mead, "the king threatening to pare his whelp's claws."[78] According to Mark Kishlansky, "Imprisonment by special command of the king or council had binding precedents going back as at least as far as the reign of Edward III."[79] This prerogative was generally used as an expedient for a limited amount of time to restrain a subject in a matter of controversy. The imprisoned subject's recourse was usually submission and petition for grace.

THE PRIVY COUNCIL AND THE PRESS

Another agent of press control was the monarch's Privy Council, which though it acted on the ruler's behalf, possessed distinctive agency. The Privy Council's primary role was to "advise the king on matters of state and hold the reins of government."[80] Its actions responded to the press on many levels – religious, economic, and political – but it took "particular interest in criminal investigation, especially in matters touching treason, public order, or misdemeanours of a kind which were currently troubling the government."[81] During the reign of Elizabeth, the Privy Council frequently employed pursuivants to search for illegal Catholic writing – sometimes for illegal presses but more often for books and religious articles that might provide evidence of illegal Catholic worship. During the reign of James the most diligent monitoring of Catholic writing belonged to the early years, especially under Robert Cecil's supervision. Between 1605 and 1610 Cecil frequently received letters notifying him that a press had been found or that books had been seized, often by customs officials. Even before the discovery of the Gunpowder Plot in November 1605, Cecil actively sought intelligence on Jesuits in hiding by identifying Catholic writing and discovering printers who might have information on the Jesuits. Cecil employed regular informers like Henry Tailor, a printer who formerly had been arrested, and a Mr. Udall. (Printing especially prompted Udall's interest since he was rewarded with the revenues brought by the sale of any confiscated presses and letters.) Although the Privy Council continued to take interest in any writing that elicited the government's attention, close scrutiny of Catholic writing and printing subsided a few years after the Gunpowder Plot.

The Privy Council also responded to problems within the printing trade. In the 1570s, for example, a challenge to royal printing patents emerged and challengers and patentees alike petitioned the Privy Council for a redress of their grievances. The Privy Council responded by creating an investigative commission whose report led ultimately to one of the most important regulatory measures for the printing trade: the 1586 decrees in Star Chamber for order in printing, which will receive consideration below.

The Privy Council also enacted censorship. Twice during Elizabeth's reign the Privy Council stayed the sale of books and demanded their revision. In 1577, it objected to Richard Stanyhurst's account of the Irish rebellion during the reign of Henry VIII that appeared in Holinshed's *Chronicles*' "Historie of Ireland." In 1587 the Privy Council ordered a more sweeping review and revision of the second edition of Holinshed's *Chronicles*. The object of its concern was the "continuation" covering the years between 1577 and 1586, which had been supervised and largely written by Abraham Fleming. The censorship and reformation was carried out in three stages over the course of less than a month and reflected official anxiety about the *Chronicles*' account of sensitive issues affecting international diplomacy. Among them were England's involvement in Scottish politics following the Earl of Arran's coup in 1583, the Duke of Anjou's 1577 trip to England to court Elizabeth, the Earl of Leicester's campaign in the Low Countries, and events surrounding the treason trials of Edmund Campion and the Babington conspirators. Variant extant states of the text printed in facsimile in *The Peaceable and Prosperous Regiment of Blessed Queene Elisabeth* offer evidence of how the government's concern about its representation directed the censorship.[82]

Looking at these examples, we can understand Privy Council actions regarding print to be consistent with the royal prerogative generally and not with a special prerogative over printing. In its role as agent for the Crown, it responded to economic issues in the printing trade, routed out books contrary to the religious settlement, and protected the English government's international reputation. Sometimes, however, Privy Councilors pursued special interests. Such was the case in 1600 when a few members of the Privy Council questioned and imprisoned John Hayward, whose book, *The first part of the life and raigne of king Henrie IIII*, had been burned by command of the Bishop of London in 1599. Neither Hayward nor his book received any further attention until the following year, when Star Chamber proceedings were initiated against the Earl of Essex for his misconduct in Ireland. A few months later interrogatories seeking to establish a connection between Essex, Hayward's book, and contemporary resistance theory were prepared for Hayward. On May 17, 1600 Hayward was enjoined "to give his attendance upon theire Lordships in theire syttings to answere that which might be objected against him,"[83] but what transpired in the meeting between Hayward and a skeleton council went unrecorded in the official minutes, even though the session is noted.[84] On July 11, 1600 Hayward answered the interrogatories. Two days later the Privy Council issued a letter to Sir John Peyton, Lieutenant of the Tower, to receive Dr. John Hayward into his custody, "and see him safely kept . . . untill you shall receave other dyreccion."[85] Rather than being tried in Star Chamber, judged, and imprisoned for writing *Henrie IIII*, as is often surmised,[86] Hayward was imprisoned by the will of the Privy Council for an indefinite term, while a few members of the Privy Council were trying to build a case of treason against the Earl of Essex.

THE HIGH COURT OF PARLIAMENT AND PRESS CONTROL

Parliament's engagement with print culture can best be understood by considering the nature of Parliament in Tudor and Stuart England. Elton observes that "By the early sixteenth century Parliament was an accepted part of the constitution, a known and established element in the king's government, though not as yet a regular or necessary part." It is thus wrong to speak of "Parliament"; according to Elton, "there were only Parliaments, each meeting, called and ended by the Crown, having its own identity."[87] While scholars have not always agreed on the role of Parliaments, it is noteworthy that whether Parliaments are seen as lively political assemblies or courts of law occupied with the necessary business of making laws, granting taxes, and issuing pardons, controlling the press rarely appeared as a parliamentary interest. Once during the reign of Elizabeth a bill to control the press was prepared but not read in Parliament, and on one occasion during the reign of James a similar bill was read once and then tabled. Besides a few early measures for economic regulation, the statutes addressed books and printing only if the contents engaged in treason or seditious libel, or related to the established religion. During the reign of Richard III a statute allowed the importation of foreign books, in both print and manuscript (1 Ric. III, ca. 9). When the book trade became well established in England, Parliament repealed this statute and prohibited importing books for resale in England or buying books in England from foreign merchants for the purpose of resale. It also authorized the Lord Chancellor to control book prices (1 Ric. III, ca. 9).

The earliest statutory definition of the case of treason came during the reign of Edward III (25 Edw. III, ca. 2), and while under various monarchs Parliament added to it (and some rescinded these additions), the defining character of treason by words included compassing or imagining the monarch's death and adhering to or giving comfort or aid to the monarch's enemies. A statute (21 Ric. II, ca. 3) added to this intending to depose the king and raising people against him, and while these additions were rescinded during the reign of Henry VIII, under Mary Parliament revived them. Even though Richard II's definitions were annulled during the reign of Henry VIII, several statutes added other dimensions and penalties, and it was during this time that "wrytyng" or "impryntyng" were first added. Further addition to treason by words came during the reign of Mary, when it became treason to pray for the Queen's death (1 Phil. & Mar., ca. 9), and slandering either the Queen or King became treason on the second offense. Elizabeth's Parliaments expressly continued the Marian treason statutes, and made major additions to the definitions. Treason was extended to upholding the jurisdiction of Rome "by writing, ciphering, printing, preaching, or teaching" or by defending "the aucthoritee jurisdiction or power of the Bushoppe of Rome" (5 Eliz., ca. 1). A later statute made it treason to "publish, declare, holde, opinion, affirme or saye" that the Queen "is not or ought not to be Queene" or name her as "Heretyke, Schesmatyeke, Tyraunt, Infidell, or Usurper" (13 Eliz., ca. 1). This statute also included a provision against writing about the succession.

Statutes also criminalized slander and libel, the earliest definition of which appeared during the reign of Edward I in the Statutes of Westminster. While this did not exactly criminalize *Scandalum Magnatum*, it created a definition that became a basis for subsequent common law practice and later statutes. This statute commanded the people to refrain from telling or publishing "any false News or Tales" that would breed discord between the King and his people or between the King and the nobility. While this is often understood as prohibiting false rumors *about* the nobility, the statute's language focuses on the danger false rumor posed to the government: it divides the King from his people or from powerful landholders.

Forasmuch as there have been oftentimes found in the Country [Devisors] of Tales, whereby discord [or occasion] of discord, hath many times arisen between the King and his People, or Great Men of this Realm: for the Damage that hath and may thereof ensue; It is commanded, That from henceforth none be so hardy to tell or publish any false News or Tales, whereby discord, or occasion of discord or slander may grow between the King and his People, or the Great Men of the Realm; and he that doth so, shall be taken and kept in Prison, until he hath brought him unto the Court, [which was the first Author of the Tale.][88] (3 Edw. I, ca. 34)

It was not until the reign of Richard II that *Scandalum Magnatum* was more precisely defined as "false News, and of horrible and false Lyes, of Prelates, Dukes, Earls, Barons and other Nobles and Great Men of the Realm, and also of the Chancellor, Treasurer, Clerk of the Privy Seal, Steward of the King's House, Justices of the one Bench or of the other, and of other Great Officers of the Realm" (2 Ric. II, ca. 5). This also expands the relationship between rumor and sedition ("discord between the king and people"): rumor caused "Debates and Discords . . . betwixt said Lords, or between the Lords and the Commons, which God forbid, and whereof great Peril and Mischief might come to all the Realm, and quick Subversion and Destruction of the said Realm" (2 Ric. II, ca. 5). The penalty for spreading rumor remained imprisonment until the rumor's author was brought to the court. These statutes sought to quell rumor not just by punishing its authors but by detaining those who spread rumor until the author was discovered.

A statute passed in the first Parliament of Philip and Mary extended the principle of *Scandalum Magnatum* to the monarch and added to false rumor, writing, printing, publishing, and setting forth "sedicious and sclanderous Writinges Rimes Ballades Letters Papers and Bookes, intending and practicing therby to move and stir sedicious Discorde Disention and Rebellyon within this Realme." Once tried and convicted, the author of such lies "shall for every first Offence in some Market Place within the Shire Citie or Boroughe . . . be set openly upon the Pylorye by the Sheryffe or his Ministers . . . and ther to have bothe his eares cutt off, onles he paye One hundrethe powndes to the King and Quenes Highnes use." The sentence for merely repeating slander was the pillory and loss of one ear. Earlier statutes had confined the definition of transgressive language to untruth, but this statute prohibits "Slander, Reproche and Dishonor of the King and Quenes Majesties . . . or to the encouraging stirring or moving of any Insurrection or Rebellion within this Realme" (1 & 2 Phil. & Mar., ca. 3). Elizabethan Parliaments raised the stakes for speaking against the monarch. By 1580–81 Parliament recognized that the Marian statutes were not serving as sufficient deterrents for language that attacked the queen but did not constitute treason. The Act against Seditious Words and Rumors increased the penalties for seditious words but specified that they must be spoken or written "advisedlye and with malicious Intent" (23 Eliz., ca. 2). Fines for a first offense were set at £200; the second offense represented a felony that would be tried in the court of King's Bench or the Assizes.

The only statutes relating to the printed word, besides those that protected the monarch's authority and dignity, sought to defend religion.

During the reign of Henry VIII, a statute for "thadvauncement of true Religions and for thabbolisshment of the contrarie" banned William Tyndale's translation of the Bible and "all other bookes and wrytinge" of Protestant doctrine (34 & 35 Hen. VIII, ca. 1). Such books were to be "clerely and utterlie abolished extinguished and forbidden to be kepte or used in this Realme." Violators would be judged as heretics. During the first Jacobean Parliament, the Lords passed a bill "for Reformation of divers Abuses in bringing into this land, printing, buying and selling, seditious, popish, vain and lascivious books," but it failed in the House of Commons.[89] Following the discovery of the Gunpowder Plot, however, Parliament did pass a statute that made words or deeds treasonable that sought to "reconcile the king's subjects to the Pope or Sea of Rome" (3 Jac., ca. 4).

While parliamentary concern about the printed word was subsumed into these larger concerns about religion, treason, and verbal attacks on the monarch, on a few occasions individual books gained parliamentary attention. It was at Parliament's request that Elizabeth censored Arthur Hall's *A letter sent by F. A. touchyng the proceedings in a priuate quarell and vnkindnesse betweene Arthur Hall, and Melchisedech Mallerie,* and that James I censored Cowell's *Interpreter* by proclamation. In 1604 the Commons complained to the Lords about a book on the union by John Thornborough, Bishop of Bristol, because it tended "to the derogation and scandal of the proceedings of the house."[90] Thornborough, like Hall, had made privileged parliamentary proceedings public by publishing a book. Following a conference of both houses, Parliament summoned the printers and publishers to confirm the author, and the Bishop apologized for having erred "in presuming to deliver a private Sentence in a Matter so dealt in by the High Court of Parliament."[91] At the end of James I's reign parliamentary attention became focused on Richard Montagu's book, *A gagg for the new gospell? No: a new gagg for an old* because of a petition from some Calvinists who objected to the book on theological grounds. In this instance, the Commons turned to Archbishop George Abbot, who met with Montagu and recommended changes. As these occasions suggest, while Parliaments might become concerned with individual books that touched their privileges, they had little interest in controlling the press per se.

THE COURTS OF HIGH COMMISSION AND STAR CHAMBER

Lesser courts than Parliament did exercise some measure of control over the printed word. During the reign of Elizabeth, jurisdiction for press control devolved to the courts of High Commission and Star Chamber, the first as part of the Elizabethan religious settlement and the second as a prerogative court. During the reign of Charles I these courts acquired some notoriety for their exercise of press control, but this was not always the case, as we can see by considering their history.

The 1559 Act of Supremacy (1 Eliz., ca. 1), which gave the Queen the authority to both visit and reform the "ecclesiastical state," authorized the Queen to employ royal letters patent to create an ecclesiastical commission to administer this authority. Sometime before June 19, 1559, based on this authority, Elizabeth issued letters patent for an Ecclesiastical Commission for London, which came to be known as the High Commission. The letters patent named the Archbishop of Canterbury and the Bishop of London as first among the Commission's seventeen members. The Commission was charged "to put in execution throughout the realm the Acts of Uniformity and Supremacy and to INQUIRE touching all heretical opinions, seditious books, contempts, false rumours and the like and hear and determine the same." While these powers may appear all-encompassing, visitation and reform were restricted by the Act of Supremacy to "the Visitation of the Ecclesiastical state and persons, and for reformation, order and correction of the same."[92] The Queen's 1559 Injunctions, which set forth to the clergy the form and substance of the Elizabethan church reform, included one item (Item 51) that called for the Ecclesiastical Commissioners to approve books for print.[93] While pre-print authorization will be considered more fully below, it is notable here that the High Commission's press oversight was conceived entirely as a means to secure conformity to the Elizabethan Settlement. The High Commission could imprison and impose fines to secure compliance, but only for persons who sold or disseminated texts contrary to the Queen's 1559 Injunctions. In practice, press control occupied little of the High Commission's time. On one of the few occasions it intervened with the press, the High Commission appealed to the court of Star Chamber to issue an order that would restrict the flow of Catholic books into England and define as illegal writing against any statutes or the Queen's injunctions or ordinances.[94] First and foremost, as Philip Tyler has shown us, the courts of High Commission at London and York were properly constituted law courts whose procedure derived from other ecclesiastical courts.[95] According to John Guy the High Commission's principal activity at both London and York was depriving clergy who refused to take the oath to Elizabeth's supremacy or to conform to the Act of Uniformity and the Queen's 1559 Injunctions.[96] A few years after the High Commission's creation at London, the Archbishop of Canterbury and the Bishop of London assumed the High Commission's responsibility for authorizing books for print. In this capacity they came to serve as liaisons between the government and the London printers. (An illustration of this role appears in the Privy Council's order to the Archbishop of Canterbury to stay the sale of Holinshed's *Chronicles*.)

During the latter years of Elizabeth's reign the High Commission drew considerable criticism both for its efforts to procure conformity and for the extension of its jurisdiction beyond ecclesiastical matters. Attacks on the High Commission came from two sides. The Puritans objected to the High Commission's procedures, especially its practice of imprisoning perceived offenders until their trials, its use of the oath *ex officio mero* (an oath that obliged the accused to answer a libel of articles that he had not previously seen), and its trial without a jury.[97] The common law judges and lawyers viewed the Commission's exercise of its authority, loosely defined by its letters patent, as an unrestrained infringement on the customary prece- dence of parliamentary statute and the common law.[98] Beginning in the 1590s, common law judges sought to restrain the High Commission by issuing prohibitions.[99] The Puritans waited until James came to the throne and then voiced their concerns about the High Commission at the Hampton Court Conference. While James listened to the Puritans, he took no immediate action to reform the court. In 1611 James issued new letters patent that redefined the High Commission's jurisdiction and procedures.[100] Newly empowered by the King's letters patent, and further strengthened by the abolition in 1610 of the southern diocesan commission, the High Commission under Archbishop Abbot became a vital institution. According to Kenneth Fincham, Abbot was a "rigorous disciplinarian" who was quick to deprive clergy for corruption or negligence.[101]

As for press control, the 1611 letters patent specified that the High Commission was to look into "apostacies," "heresies," and "great errors" and into books that wrote "against the doctrine of religion, the Book of Common Prayer, or [the] ecclesiastical state." The High Commission was called upon to "inquire and search for ... all heretical, schismatical and seditious" books, libels and writings, together with their "makers," "devisers," printers, and publishers, and to apprehend and imprison offenders and seize their presses.[102] Not only did this authority extend beyond that conferred by earlier letters patent, but the nature of trans- gressive writing became more clearly defined.

Although the High Commission received considerable power over the press from the 1611 patent, only a few documented cases of censorship exist.[103] On April 30, 1611 the High Commission issued instructions to Rich Bratie and Walter Salter, Messengers of the King's Chamber, to search for and seize papists, Jesuits, and seminary priests, and popish books and relics. In 1621 the High Commission questioned the minister, William Whately, regarding his book *A bride-bush*, which had appeared in 1617 as a wedding sermon, and again in 1619 in an expanded version. Whately submitted to the High Commission, recanting his published views that desertion and adultery dissolved the bonds of matrimony. (The High Commission here appears to have taken a rather singular interest in a doctrinal matter, although a more likely explanation for their interest may have been the book's political overtones.)[104] A few years later, the High Commission imprisoned the "poor man" who printed *Votivae Angliae*, which opposed James's foreign policy and displeased King James "exceedingly."[105] About the same time, the publisher Nathaniel Butter and printer William Stansby got into trouble for their unauthorized and unlicensed corantos (news books) about the Thirty Years War, which the King found offensive.[106] Such actions, however, constitute only a fraction of the High Commission's business. Between 1611 and 1640 private litigants brought 95 percent of cases (many of which sought to remove immoral or eccentric clergymen) while only 5 percent came from commissioners, as would be requisite for matters of censorship.

Between 1603 and 1625, the High Commission's jurisdiction over the press appears more frequently in its adjudication of cases relating to printing patents and monopolies. Members of the Stationers' Company brought cases before the High Commission when either their own company court (the court of Assistants) could not resolve a problem, or the defendant was not a Company member. Non-Stationers used the court to challenge both Stationers and royal patent holders. An example of how the court operated in this respect can be seen in the 1603 publication of James I's *Basilikon Doron*. On March 28, only four days after James was proclaimed King, the Stationers' Company's master, wardens, and three other members entered *Basilikon Doron* as their copy in the Company Registers.[107] At the same time that the edition licensed by the Company was being printed, Edward Aldee and Edward White, both Stationers, printed another edition without license or entry, for which the court of Assistants subsequently imposed a prohibition and a fine. These sanctions did not deter them from printing a second edition, probably because the demand for the King's book was considerable.[108] This time the Stationers' Company took the matter to the High Commission, which issued a bond for Aldee and White and sent an order to the Stationers' Company's master and wardens that they should seize Aldee's "presse and letters."[109]

That the High Commission would be the venue for cases relating to the regulation of the printing trade appears contradictory to prevailing wisdom that maintains that the court of Star Chamber held jurisdiction over printing. Among the papers of Sir Thomas Egerton, Lord Keeper and from 1596 to 1617 Lord Chancellor, appears a summary of the kinds of cases that historically came within Star Chamber jurisdiction and "disorders in printing and uttering of books" is among them.[110] According to Siebert, "The Star Chamber, the judicial offshoot of the Council, was the instrument most frequently employed in the control of the press in the later sixteenth century."[111] "The prerogative court of Star Chamber," Adrian Johns maintains, was the "overseer" of press regulation.[112] Such convictions, I suspect, derive from several things: in part from Star Chamber's ordinances and decrees regulating the printing trade issued in 1566, 1586, and 1637; in part from its influential decisions regarding slander and libel; in part from the Star Chamber trials like Prynne's during the reign of Charles I. We can better understand Star Chamber's "regulatory" and legal jurisdiction over language and printing by seeing these functions within the history and general practices of the court.

Star Chamber began, as Sir John Baker observes, as "the name of a room rather than an institution."[113] It was the chamber room in the palace of Westminster where the Privy Council sat during term time. According to Baker, the Privy Council possessed "long-standing" jurisdiction in civil and criminal causes. During the reign of Henry VIII the influx of business made it necessary for the council to sit in Star Chamber as a court two days a week, when most of its suits were brought by private litigants either in matters of property or for abuses of judicial procedure. Only on occasion did the Crown use the court for prosecutions and then only for misdemeanors, although it prosecuted breaches of proclamations.[114] Richard Crompton's 1594 *L'authoritie et iurisdiction des courts de la Maiestie de la Roygne* indicates that while the principal business of the Elizabethan Star Chamber involved perjury, riot, and fraud (especially in the courts of law), on occasion actions of *Scandalum Magnatum* were brought there. My survey of Star Chamber reports for nearly two hundred cases during 33–34 Elizabeth, found the causes of most actions to be disputes over title and copyhold, perjury, counterfeiting, and judicial errors, although there is one suit for scandalous words and one for *Scandalum Magnatum*.[115] During the reign of James 80 percent of Star Chamber cases had property at the base of the litigation. Crimes against public policy and the state comprised less than 3 percent. Abduction and defamation, which Thomas Barnes describes as "crimes in denigration of status," represented only 2 percent of cases.[116] Of the seventy Star Chamber cases reported for the first three years of the reign of Charles I, one third were for perjury or forgery, one fifth for riot or mayhem, and one seventh for some form of abuse in a court of law. Aside from four cases brought for killing a deer, five for conspiracy, and two for marriage without consent, actions were brought once each for whipping women, rebellion, libel, scandal, and practice. Only three of these actions were brought by the Attorney General, one for a libel against the Duke of Buckingham, the others in non-criminal matters.[117]

According to Barnes, "The law which Star Chamber implemented was the common and statute law of England, primarily the law of misdemeanors because Star Chamber could not touch life or limb."[118] Furthermore, "the [written] pleadings (pleas, demurrer, replication, rejoinder) sacred to the common law on its civil side were observed scrupulously in Star Chamber."[119] Trials in Star Chamber consisted of three elements:

1) the pleadings, the prosecution's bill and the defendant's answer or demurrer, sometimes also replication and rejoinder; 2) the proofs, gathered by interrogation on oath of the defendant and then of witnesses on both sides; 3) the final proceedings, publication of the proofs at the hearing before the body of the court in which the counsel on both sides argued the points of law involved and the court delivered judgment ... At each stage of the proceedings, all public, the defendant and his counsel were apprised of the prosecution's case, which was restricted wholly to matters raised in the bill.[120]

Barnes says that ordinary procedure was abridged only when a defendant confessed freely during examination to the matters charged. In this case the Attorney General could bring the prosecution *ore tenus* (verbally or orally), without a written bill.[121] For most of its history the court's membership was confined to members of the Privy Council and the two chief justices. Its usual sentences were fine and imprisonment, although it could order a party to undergo public humiliation like the pillory or losing ears. Barnes observes that a favored punishment was "to have the convict publicly confess his crime, either at the local assizes or quarter sessions (if the case had considerable local import) or before all the courts in Westminster Hall (if the case involved contempt of court or abuse of legal procedure)."[122]

The first occasion on which the court of Star Chamber exercised any jurisdiction over the press was in 1566 when it issued "Ordinaunces decreed for reformation of divers disorders in pryntyng and uttering of Bookes." According to an early seventeenth-century discourse on Star Chamber procedure, Star Chamber could issue injunctions in cases where another court's decision was contested or when a party requested a judgment on a point of law. In these circumstances the plaintiff filed a bill in response to

which the court of Star Chamber immediately reached a decision and
"published" its judgment as an "Injunction" or ordinance.[123] In 1566 the
High Commission initiated such a procedure when it asked Star Chamber
to refine the definition of illegal writing, to uphold privileged printing, and
to outlaw Catholic books. According to the ordinances Star Chamber then
issued, it was illegal to print or import books "against the fourme and
meaning of any ordinaunce, prohibition, or commaundement" contained
in the statutes or "lawes of this Realme" or in any of the Queen's injunctions, letters patents or ordinances.[124] By including letters patent, the
ordinance upheld both the Stationers' Company's printing monopoly
and the authority of royal printing privileges. Publishing these refinements
as a Star Chamber ordinance created a legal precedent to serve as a ground
upon which legal action could be initiated in the courts (including but not
exclusively the court of Star Chamber). While this "decision" created a
precedent according to which subsequent actions could be brought in the
court of Star Chamber in matters relating to printing, it did not represent
an exercise per se of Star Chamber's role as "overseer" of press regulation.
Indeed, it does not appear that the court of Star Chamber took any further
action regarding printing until 1586 when it issued decrees for order in
printing in response to several actions brought in court, including one in
1577 by the Queen's Printer, who filed complaints against members of the
Stationers' Company who were printing against his patent.[125] In 1582 John
Day brought a bill of complaint in the court of Star Chamber against non-
Stationers Roger Ward and William Holmes for their failure to comply
with the 1566 "Decrees" by printing books licensed to Company members.[126] Several other cases followed (all well documented in Edward
Arber's transcription of the Stationers' Company Registers), and all of
which appealed to the precedent established by the 1566 Star Chamber
Ordinances.[127]

The court of Star Chamber could have decided these cases on patent
violations on an individual basis had discontents with the printing establishment not spread to other venues. In 1577 and again in 1582 journeymen
printers complained to the Privy Council of economic hardships resulting
from privileged printers' abuses, and in 1581 John Wolfe, a member of the
Fishmongers' Company, attacked the Stationers' monopoly by setting up
his printing business in London and printing copies owned by Company
members and royal patentees.[128] His actions emboldened other non-
Company members to do the same, provoking the Privy Council's intervention. It summoned Wolfe to appear and created a commission to
investigate printing privileges.[129] In summoning a defendant to physically

appear and in creating a commission to establish evidence, the Privy Council was following Star Chamber procedures.

The 1586 decrees for order in printing – commonly referred to as the "1586 Star Chamber Decree" and viewed as having considerable impact on printing and licensing practices well into the seventeenth century – set forth nine ordinances governing printing and placed their execution in the hands of the "Archebysshop of CANTERBURY and the righte honorable the lordes and others of her highenes pryvye councell."[130] Of the nine items in this decree, eight sought to remedy the problems that had arisen from a proliferation of printing presses, many of which were being used to print works that violated royal patents and Company licenses. The 1586 decrees sought to protect the printing establishment and placed the administration of that protection in the hands of the Stationers' Company. Item one required anyone involved in printing to register with the master and wardens of the Stationers' Company, and items six and seven designated that Stationers' Company's wardens or their deputies could search for and seize illegal presses and books. Item four reiterated the 1566 Ordinances and reserved printing to patentees and the Stationers; it also called for pre-print allowance by ecclesiastical officials.[131] While Elizabeth's 1559 Injunctions had called for ecclesiastical authorization (by the Queen's allowance in writing, by six Privy Councilors, by the chancellors of the universities, or by the Ecclesiastical Commissioners) the means proposed by the 1586 decrees – by either the Bishop of London or the Archbishop of Canterbury – streamlined ecclesiastical authorization. Furthermore, the decrees authorized the Stationers' Company to search for and deface illegal presses or presses printing patented books or books privileged by the Stationers' Company's license and called upon it to present offenders to the High Commission or three Commissioners one of whom was required to be either the Archbishop of Canterbury or the Bishop of London.[132]

A genuine triumph for the Stationers' Company and the privileged printers, the 1586 decrees were extraordinarily conservative in the sense that they reaffirmed old practices. They unequivocally upheld the rights and prerogatives of the Company and the privileged printers in the face of recent challenges and sought to insure both adequate work and adequate employment within the Company. By placing pre-print authorization in the hands of two individuals, and by giving the court of High Commission final jurisdiction for enforcing the regulations, Star Chamber's decision made press regulation more efficient, but the decrees neither intensified regulation nor extended Star Chamber's authority over the printing industry. Indeed until the reign of Charles I the court of Star Chamber rarely served as a venue for cases relating to the print trade or to the control of print unless a case was filed by private parties.[133]

The presence of the court of Star Chamber as a venue for printing disputes thus derived from the court's regular procedures and practices rather than from any special "jurisdiction" over censorship and the press. The same thing may be said of its role in regulating other forms of language. Shuger contends that in its procedures and jurisdiction the court of Star Chamber played a major role in effecting the only kind of language regulation in which early modern governments and people were genuinely interested: restricting injurious language (defamation). Individuals, indeed, could bring Star Chamber actions for slander and libel, but, as Barnes's study of Jacobean proceedings and my own survey of Elizabethan and Caroline Star Chamber reports suggest, the work of enforcing decorous language occupied few of the court's proceedings. Most cases of slander and libel were heard in other courts.

According to Martin Ingram, during the Elizabethan period slander cases flooded both the ecclesiastical and the temporal courts to such a degree that "the rush to take legal action to clear sullied reputations has been called 'a phenomenon of the age'."[134] Some sense of this phenomenon's scale, within the ecclesiastical courts at least, appears in Ronald Marchant's study of the consistory court records in Elizabethan York.[135] Early in Elizabeth's reign (1561–62), of the court's 213 cases only one was for defamation, or less than one half of 1 percent. In 1591 defamation accounted for 48 percent of the cases (170 of 357). According to Laura Gowing, after 1600 more than half of the London consistory court's cases concerned defamation.[136] While these statistics lend credibility to Shuger's conclusion that censorship grew out of cultural anxiety about honor and credibility, they also caution against seeing Star Chamber as having principal jurisdiction in defamation actions. We should, I think, greet skeptically the assessment of the 1630 editor of selections from Crompton's *L'authoritie et iurisdiction des courts de la Maiestie de la Roygne.* "Libellers," he says, "be oftentimes dealt with in Starchamber, as offenders not sufficiently provided by the Lawes otherwise."[137] While defamation may well have been an important area in which Star Chamber decisions effected legal transformation, when the court of Star Chamber issued its ordinances in 1566 and decrees in 1586, its definition of illegal writing concerned far more than railing libels. Writing was transgressive that opposed the statutes ("the law of the land") and the Queen's injunctions and letters patent, particularly with regard to the settlement of the ecclesiastical state.[138] To be able to assess Star Chamber in the reign of Charles I, as this study will do, we need to be quite clear about the fact that before that time any actions that the court of Star Chamber took with regard to the regulation of language, printed or written, derived not from any special jurisdiction of the court, but from its regular business that included, among other things, disputes over title and ownership, and clarification of points of law.

LICENSE AND AUTHORITY

The mandate that a text receive some form of official approval prior to printing was, as the earlier consideration of proclamations has shown, an old one. Indeed, the governments of Henry VIII, Edward VI, and Mary had ordered either by statute, decree, or proclamation some form of "licensing" (pre-print authorization).[139] Elizabethan pre-print censorship, born of her religious settlement, became institutionalized by the 1586 Star Chamber decrees, which, because they appeared as a law court's judgment, remained in place until they were redefined or repealed – or, as was the case in the 1640s, the court itself was dissolved. Thus, neither James I nor Charles I had to specifically institute particular "licensing" practices, although each of them seemed to hold his own distinctive vision about how licensing did or should operate.

Beyond this fundamental definition, the question of licensing is vexed. As Adrian Johns observes, "Modern historians have debated the role of the licensing regime as a system of censorship with extraordinary intensity."[140] Among the unresolved issues are its nature, its practice, its intention, its compliance, and, often, its effectiveness. Johns represents the influential view that licensing represented a single practice that "linked the Company's procedures immediately to wider mechanisms of political governance."[141] According to Johns, this form of regulation, "by the state and by the Stationers' Company in tandem, found support not just for its suppression of heresy and sedition, but as a positive bulwark for Protestantism and property."[142] One of the greatest difficulties in accounting for this regulatory form comes with the word "licensing" – this, because for all practical purposes, as Joseph Loewenstein makes clear, two systems of licensing were in place at the same time: one was ideological, the other proprietary. The first was instituted by royal authority, the second by custom in the printing trade. Following Peter Blayney's work on the Stationers' Registers, Loewenstein makes a useful distinction between "license" and "entrance": "Licensing, originating outside the printing industry, was complemented by an internal institution, 'entrance,' the institution from which modern copyright is the direct descendant."[143]

Although convenient, Loewenstein's discrimination between license and entrance does not attend sufficiently to contemporary use of the language. A discrepancy exists between official use of the word "licensing" and the language employed in the Stationers' Registers. When courts, monarchs, and Privy Councillors employed the word "licensing," they consistently meant pre-print approbation by designated church or government officials. Well into the seventeenth century, however, when Stationers entered their "license" to print in the Register book, the records of these "entries" refer to them as licenses, a practice that also appears in the Company's accounts and court transactions. In the Registers, pre-print approbation by ecclesiastical or government officials is either not specifically named or is referred to as "authority," as may be seen in this October 30, 1587 entry on John Harrison's behalf:[144] "Receaved of him for printynge three bokes of Colloquies concernyne shooting in great ordonance and small peeces ... Auctorised to the print under the archbishop of CANTERBURIES hand."[145] Even though by 1600 entries are regularized "Entered for his/their copie" with notice of approval as being "under the hand," conditional entries frequently awaited "authority." The court of Assistants' judgments also distinguished between the company's "licence" and the approval by authority. A typical record read: "It is ordered that William Barley shall pay xl[s] for printing 3 ballades and a booke disorderly without licence or aucthoritye."[146] Given this usage, it is problematic to accept Loewenstein's "license" as referring to official approbation and "entry" as the record of ownership.

Peter Blayney more accurately describes licensing as tripartite: official approbation, which he calls "authorization"; the Stationers' Company's "license," which was generally but not always issued contingent upon authorization; and "entry," the record of the license made by the Company clerk in the Stationers' Registers.[147] The Company's license provided the equivalent of modern-day copyright protection for the licensee. If anyone else printed a "licensed" copy without the owner's permission, the owner had recourse in the Stationers' Company court of Assistants if the violator was a Company member or if not a member, then in the court of High Commission. Obviously, the license was a necessity; entry, however, according to Blayney was not. Indeed, some texts might not be worth the cost of the added assurance of having a record of the license. The fee a Stationer paid for entering his license with the Company was sixpence; for recording the license's entrance in the Register, the Company clerk received an additional four pence.[148] In my correlation of Register entries with the *Short Title Catalogue*,[149] I could find no consistent rationale for unentered works, outside of works printed on the Continent or by presses concealing their identity by using a continental imprint. Some groups of works, civic pageants or masques for example, are less likely to be entered than plays – though some plays are not entered, and some pageants and masques are. Most, but not all, sermons are entered, but all the sermons by one preacher may not be entered. Foreign news books are largely entered, local news may not be. Some poetry is entered, some not. Carefully eyeing their competition, Stationers probably speculated that some titles were unlikely candidates for piracy. Given this, and the fact that books protected by royal patents or printed by the King's or Queen's Printers, as well as any book previously printed with a Company license, were not entered in the Registers, that more than half the books printed were not entered should not necessarily be seen (as it so often is) as an effort to evade press controls.

Even though they do not accurately reflect Company licensing, the Stationers' Registers serve as the only record we have of ecclesiastical or government authorization. Do these, however, accurately reflect the number of titles that were actually officially approved for print? The answer is both yes and no. We know from the 1586 Star Chamber decrees that authorization was required for one class of books not entered in the Registers; law books printed by the King's or Queen's Printers were to be perused by members of the judiciary. Royal printers also printed Bibles, and though it is unlikely these were formally vetted prior to printing, church officials attended carefully to the finished products. Only one patent – John Day's 1559 seven-year patent for everything he printed – required that the texts be perused and allowed. When the patent was renewed, however, the requirement disappeared. Even if patented books were not regularly perused, the quasi-official nature conferred by royal privileges probably means that at some point an official looked closely at the text to see if this was the kind of book that should properly be printed "*cum privilegio.*" On the other hand, it seems unlikely that Latin school books garnered much official attention.

While the existence of significant numbers of books issued with royal patents or from the King's or Queen's printers argues that "no," the Stationers' Registers do not accurately reflect the number of books that received official scrutiny, it seems likely that the record of official authorization that appears in the Registers should correspond to the number of non-patented texts actually licensed. This is because the decisions of the master and wardens of the Stationers' Company whether or not to require official authorization as a condition for license appear fairly intentional. The masters and wardens apparently felt comfortable issuing the Company's license for educational books on such topics as writing, cooking, and husbandry without requiring official allowance. Most ephemera, especially ballads, went unauthorized. Company officials' refusal to license other titles unless "sufficient" authorization was secured, however, shows their discomfort with issuing the company license for the kinds of texts that might be potentially provocative or transgressive. For example, during the reign of James I, the license was contingent upon the licensee securing official approval in 129 entries. Seventy-four of these still-extant titles were certainly printed, while no record exists for fifty-five of them. The categories of books conditionally licensed were consistent whether or not the book was ultimately printed, but whether or not a book was printed had little to do with its category. The Stationers' Company officials were reluctant to enter without notice of authorization anything political – news, pageants, poems, or literature – or any continental religious writings. Forty-five percent of texts that received conditional licenses were political and 16 percent addressed international religious matters. Company officials were particularly sensitive about writings that either concerned Jesuits or addressed matters raised in King James's controversy about the oath of allegiance. Interestingly, all the controversial materials received approval for print, while those on Jesuits clearly depended on their content, with only half being eventually printed. A book on the history of the Papacy was printed; one on the history of the Church was not. Nine percent of the conditional licenses show Company officials displaying sensitivity on domestic religious matters as well. Two books of Biblical commentary received approval; a synopsis of the doctrine of the Bible did not. One sermon was; another one was not. A catechism by a Calvinist went into print, but a treatise favoring divorce did not. A book offering instructions on receiving Communion was not printed. Of the five histories whose licenses were conditional, four were printed; the one that was not bore the curious title "The history of the Three heroical sons of the Three kinges of England Fraunce and Scotland. wherein the Aucthors fiction agreinge with one of Merlines prophecies" – a title which invites speculation on whether this may not have been more political than historical. Conditional licenses also considered Stationers' proprietary interests in titles at least eight times. Four more, issued for printed plays, may simply have been concerned with matters of licensing protocol: John Marston's plays, *The Dutch Courtesan* and *The Fawne*, and Shakespeare's *Troilus and Cressida* were entered in the Register with the requirement that they receive "sufficient" authority, presumably permission from the acting company that owned the play. A like condition attached to *Westward Hoe*, however, may have derived from a consciousness of the furor a play with a similar title had provoked in 1605. (A performance of *Eastward Hoe* brought its authors to the attention of James's Privy Council.)

Besides revealing the kind of texts that were or were not perceived to be of concern in Elizabethan and Jacobean England, these conditional entries show the Stationers' Company officials at work. The Registers first and foremost served to protect the members' rights in copy, but they also show the master and wardens protecting the integrity of the Company by assuring that any book which might conceivably contain material against the Church or the government be approved by the Church or the government. Keeping an accurate record of this was important. If ever a book might subsequently come into question, the master and wardens would want a record showing that the responsibility for allowing the text to be printed rested not with them but with the Church or government official who approved it. In the same way that Company officials would desire evidence that they were not allowing books to be printed that were contrary to the spirit of Elizabeth's 1559 Injunctions or the Star Chamber decrees which invoked them, it seems reasonable that individual Stationers would want the same. In the closed world of the London Stationers it may have been sufficient to have the Company's license without entering it, but what value would there be in obtaining (and paying for) official allowance, without being able to provide a record of it should a problem arise? Some unentered books may have been licensed (we have no way of knowing), but it seems unlikely. Given the intentionality the master and wardens exercised in determining the kinds of books that did not require allowance, and in issuing conditional licenses for those that did, we can, I think, accept that the number of titles entered in the Registers with a record of official authorization correlates highly to the number and kinds of texts actually "seen and allowed."

The Registers' evidence of official authorization counters widely accepted views that most books in early modern England were officially "licensed." Both Shuger and Loewenstein, for example, assume a high degree of compliance. Although Elizabeth's 1559 Injunctions and the 1586 Star Chamber decrees seem to indicate that authorization requirements applied to all newly printed matter, as Arnold Hunt reminds us, this was not the case. "In practice," according to Hunt, "the rules were interpreted very flexibly," so flexibly, indeed, that "the system was routinely disregarded."[150] My data supports Hunt's assessment.[151] During the 1560s only 3 percent of the entries in the Company's Registers record ecclesiastical authorization; during the 1570s this increased to 7 percent, and in the

1580s to 42 percent. Even the Star Chamber decrees' provision for ecclesiastical authorization did not create a universal system of pre-print censorship. In 1585 only 13 percent of Register entries identified authorizers. This rose to 45 percent in 1586 but declined in 1587 to 22 percent. In the final two years of Elizabeth's reign fewer than 60 percent of the entries evidenced authorization.[152] The number of Stationers' Register entries identifying official authorizers rose by 20 percent between 1605 and 1606, from 64 to 84 percent, and throughout James's reign notice of authorization was maintained at a much higher level than existed during Elizabeth's reign. During James's reign an average of 80 percent of entries notes the authorizer, and in only two years does this drop below 80 percent. Particularly notable are the high authorization rates in the 1620s, a period when James issued the series of proclamations restricting speech in matters of state and reiterating demands that anything printed be allowed by official authority. In 1623 and 1624, years in which royal proclamations prohibited unauthorized printing, evidence of compliance appeared in 98 and 94 percent of entries respectively. In one respect, however, all of these numbers suggest greater compliance than actually existed, since entries in the Company Registers never represented more than half of the books printed in a given year – between 1603 and 1625 the average rate of entry was 44 percent.

Hunt maintains that the disregard for authorization, which he refers to as "licensing," derived from the system's intent: "The express purpose of the licensing system was to prevent 'heretical and seditious' texts from getting into print," and since the "vast majority" of books were not objectionable "the approval of the licenser was merely a formality."[153] Such an assessment of practice, although widely accepted by most recent scholarship, including Loewenstein's and my own, has also met with challenges. In "Licensing, Censorship, and Religious Orthodoxy in Early Stuart England," Anthony Milton demonstrates how in the early seventeenth century both Calvinist and Laudian authorizers engaged in "tactful editing." It is to this practice that Milton credits "the absence of potentially volatile discussion of church government and attacks on church ceremonies" on the one side, and "downplaying anti-popery" on the other.[154] Shuger agrees that the authorizers were editors, but she sees their role as more extensive than merely removing provocations to religious contentiousness. She sees them as assuring a text's truth and authority: "factual accuracy was a standard criterion in the licensing of religious texts"; it was the "principal criterion in the licensing of secular ones, where censorship *primarily* targeted 'fardles of falsehood.'"[155] By assuring the accuracy of a text, she says that the

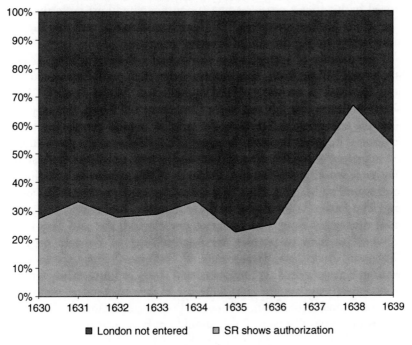

Books printed in London with ecclesiastical authorization 1630–39

■ London not entered   ▢ SR shows authorization

Figure 1

"licenser" conferred a distinction upon authors: "Writers did not object to pre-publication censorship because they desired the legitimacy – the authority – it bestowed by peer review."[156] Furthermore, from Shuger's perspective, because ecclesiastical licensing institutionalized the values of a society intent on Christian civility and good will, books printed in England could not engage in injurious attacks on persons. Hunt, Milton, and Shuger make a valuable contribution to understanding the practice of official authorization, especially between 1620 and 1635, but I think that Hunt's assessment that licensing was a formality was more true between 1559 and 1603 – indeed, probably until the early 1620s – than throughout the period. Furthermore, prior to 1630 the few accounts of how authorizers proceeded may be unreliable because their practices were being scrutinized. It is thus unwise to take as exemplary (as Shuger does)[157] claims like Daniel Featly's in *Cygnea Cantio* that he approved only fifty-two pages of Edward Elton's *Gods Holy Minde*, which then "took the libertie to flie out of the Presse without licence,"[158] or Samuel Harsnett's that he licensed John

Hayward's *First Part of the life and raigne of Henry the IIII* "sodeinlie as moved by his friend never reading (upon his salutation) more then one page of the hedlesse pamphlet."[159] There is evidence as well that suggests some variety among the official licensers' practices.

If the practice of authorization was indeed a form of editing, as both Shuger and Milton insist, then authors rather than publishers would have been involved in securing official approbation. While Featly's *Cygnea Cantio* indicates that this was so for Crompton and Elton, this may have been the exception rather than the rule. A regular correlation in the Stationers' Registers between the name of a publisher and a given author-izer suggests that publishers sought out authorizers, usually on the basis of a long-term working relationship. Evidence of this appears in a Stationers' court record on March 1, 1602: "It is orderd the master waterson shall pay x^s unto Tho Pavier for his clayme to the Irish newes. And that Jo hardy shall stand discharged from Tho pavier of the x^s which the said Tho Pavier delyvered to hym to procure the Aucthorisinge of the said copy."[160] (Waterson, Pavier, and Hardy were all Stationers.) Since the onus for securing licenses rested on Stationers, and since, as Loewenstein reminds us, proprietary authorship came quite late in the early modern period, the kind of intimate consultation between licensers and authors that Featly reports in *Cygnea Cantio* probably should not be seen as typical.

While during the reigns of Elizabeth and James licensing (official and Company) generally sought to prevent seditious and heretical writing, in some cases obtaining official approbation may be seen more as a means of promoting the publication of certain texts than vetting or restraining them. This appears, for example, in Thomas Goad's imprimatur for Eliza Jocelin's "The Mothers Legacie to her unborne child," which takes the form of a lengthy introduction that includes the following,

In this legacy left *In prosusus* whereout whosoever taketh yet leaveth no whit the lesse for others. In remainder wherefore upon the very first view I willingly not only subscribed my approbate for the registry [of] this will among the most publique monuments the rather worthy because proceeding: from the weaker sex but also as bound to doe right unto knowne vertue undertooke the care of thee publication thereof.[161]

Before Daniel Featly set his imprimatur to the manuscript for "Panegyrique a Tresgrand et trespuissant Prince Charles Prince de Galles," William Alexander first wrote, "I have read over this book by direction from his Majestie and doe conceave that it is worthie to be published."[162] This is followed in another hand by the Judgment of Sir William Alexander to whome this booke hath bin referred deserves to give it approbation. I have suddainely (at the request of the Author) looked over the heade and doe find nothing to give improvement to the publishing of it; And therefore doe humbly recommend it to my Lorde Grace of Canterbury's examination and priferenc. [signed] C L W CVNMY.[163]

In *Cygnea Cantio* Featly says, "The first thing to my remembrance questioned touching M. *Cromptons* booke, was a clause in my written defence, that I was rather induced to license the booke out of a respect to my Lord D. his Grace, to whom the book is dedicated."[164] These examples suggest a greater variety in the kinds of recommendations an official approbation entailed than Shuger's proposition that "books licensed by the state obtain a quasi-official status."[165] Certainly some official "licenses," like those for the law books Shuger considers, might confer an official status, but Alexander's assessment looks more to a French historical biography's worth or merit. The practice of approbation based on the stature of a dedicatee to which Featly refers may have been fairly common as well, given the complimentary trope in dedicatory epistles that the person's worth will enable the book's publication.

While some official licensers assured that a book's contents had been "seen and allowed" and others provided patronage, some were simply careless. Such was the case with Thomas Worrall, who authorized 119 works during the last three years of the reign of James and continued to serve as an ecclesiastical licenser during the reign of Charles. Andrew Marvell in *The Rehearsal-Transposed* (1672) observed that "Doctor Woral, the bishop of London's Chaplain, Scholar good enough, but a free fellowlike man, and of no very tender Conscience," was apt to approve and subscribe his name "hand over head" to any copy submitted to him.[166]

As the example of Worrall suggests, of as great an importance as the intention of ecclesiastical licensing were the men themselves. Prior to the 1586 Star Chamber decrees, a variety of London clerics saw and allowed books. Subsequent to the decrees, the Archbishop of Canterbury, John Whitgift, initiated the bureaucratization of ecclesiastical licensing by appointing a panel of authorizers. When Whitgift died in 1603, the idea of a "panel" of authorizers disappeared, and chaplains to the Archbishop of Canterbury and the Bishop of London and prebendaries of St. Paul's Cathedral assumed much of the responsibility for approving texts for print. This concentration of responsibility, however, did not preclude other clerics from approving books for print. In 1605, for example, 36 percent of the authorizations noted in the Registers came from outside the immediate circle of London and Canterbury. In 1608 and 1609 Richard Etkins, the vicar of St. Mary Abbotts, Kensington, licensed more books than members of either the Archbishop of Canterbury's or the Bishop of London's households. The records also suggests that once anyone served as an ecclesiastical authorizer inside of the Archbishop's or Bishop's household, he could continue licensing books even though the episcopal office holder changed. Gabriel Powell, chaplain to Bishop Vaughan of London (who died in 1607), continued to license books until 1623. Between 1604 and 1610, when the principal responsibility for authorization rested with Archbishop of Canterbury Richard Bancroft, the names of an average of fifteen different authorizers appear in the Stationers' Register. When George Abbot succeeded Bancroft in 1610, although he did not personally approve books for the press, he concentrated authority for licensing in his own household and that of John King, Bishop of London.[167] In 1611 the households of Abbot and King accounted for half the authorizations, and in 1612 two thirds. Between 1617 and 1625 Abbot's chaplains, Daniel Featly, Richard Mockett, and Thomas Goad, served as the principal authorizers, although political texts soon became the purview of a government appointee. In 1622 the Privy Council delegated the licensing of new books to Francis Cottington, whose name also appears as official authorizer for other political writing. Furthermore, John Taverner, secretary to Bishop King and Professor of Music at Gresham College, oversaw literary, educational, and moral writing, and while he occasionally reviewed political writing, he gave his imprimatur for only one religious book. Even during the years when Abbot and King held the reins of their authority on the press the tightest, the presence in the records of other authorizers' names indicates some give and take in the process of authorization. In practice, throughout the reigns of both Elizabeth and James, publishers, printers, and authors were free to seek the approval of any authorizer they knew would be sympathetic. The practice of individual authorizers, as much as the bishops and archbishops who oversaw them, thus could give to "official" licensing a peculiarly unofficial tenor – or at least an official tenor that was multivocalic.[168]

A "WHOLE MACHINERY OF CENSORSHIP AND CONTROL"[169]

This chapter has considered the evolution over nearly a hundred years of practices and institutions that participated in censorship. Focusing, as this chapter has, on the mechanisms of control may appear to suggest the kind of overwhelming systematization that Glynn Wickham and Frederick Siebert found in their studies of censorship. I would caution, however, against envisioning a linear pattern of accretion, accrual, or growth – or even of erosion or attrition. The practice – indeed practices – of censoring print during its first hundred years can be better understood in terms of the law itself – not the laws about censorship but the legal "system," which was not really a system at all. Statutes passed by the monarch and Parliament were law; so was the codified regulation of canon or church law. The common law, probably the most important form of law, was unwritten in the sense that it was uncodified, but countless manuscript reports recorded its pleas and decisions. Temporal jurisdiction included both prerogative courts and common law courts, and these coexisted with the ecclesiastical courts, though not always peacefully. "Civilian" lawyers trained at the universities in traditions of codified law practiced in the church courts; those called to the bar of the common law received their training in the Inns of Court, where they learned the vast (largely manuscript) literature of case law, attended moots and readings, and learned to prepare writs and pleadings.[170] While theoretical jurisdictional boundaries existed, litigants brought cases where they felt they could be best served. Cross-suiting – entertaining separate or counter-suits in the same or different courts – became such common practice in the sixteenth century that actions confined to a single suit in a single court were exceptions.[171]

One aspect of all of this that helps us understand the practice of the institutions of censorship presented in this chapter is the existence and use of precedents. Education in the common law was – and is – "a method, a cast of mind, rather than mere rules."[172] The readings at the sixteenth- and seventeenth-century Inns of Court were "not intended as a practical guide to current law, let alone an original account of a discrete legal topic, so much as a reiteration of inherited learning."[173] The record of the past provided the grounds in legal education for formal disputation, a practice that carried on into written and oral pleading in the courts. Given that statutory control of the press did not exist in England under the late Tudor and early Stuart monarchs (except very briefly during the reign of Henry VIII), regulating the printed word could come from a disarray of entities, interests, and occasions. At any given moment for any act of censorship there existed an amalgamation of inherited practices that, like court cases collected in reports, could or could not be brought to bear on the particular instance.

The interest of this chapter has been to provide an index of the kinds of agencies and practices that intervened in the first hundred years of print culture. It is a "reiteration" of those practices that were "inherited" not only by the government of Charles I, but also by the men and women who wrote and printed books, pamphlets, newpapers, and broadsides during his reign. During the reign of Charles I censorship became impressed upon the cultural imagination in a way that it had not been in the past – so much so, indeed, that after only fifteen years under Charles's rule, the Long Parliament pardoned men imprisoned for the books they wrote. A few years later Milton wrote his powerful objection to ecclesiastical licensing. It is difficult to imagine Milton writing *Areopagitica* in 1625 or before, not so much because to people in Tudor and Stuart England censorship seemed "a good idea," as Shuger proposes,[174] but because outside of the relatively small number of people who lost the fruits of their labors, their liberty, or their hands, censorship was rarely thought of at all. Pamphlets did not express indignation at John Stubbs losing his hand.[175] No one complained that John Hayward was imprisoned in the Tower of London. By 1629, however, the vagaries of the ecclesiastical licensing system were trumpeted in print. In 1630 the London printers objected to the decline in printing brought about by restraints on religious texts. Five years later Lincoln's Inn staged an elaborate, expensive, and well-attended masque to remove the taint of having William Prynne's *Histrio-mastix* dedicated to them. In 1637 a new Star Chamber decree on printing extended the licensing requirement to all new editions of old books.

The intention of this study is not to measure the relative degrees of state repression and authorial freedom, but rather to try to understand the cultural awareness of censorship that emerged between 1625 and 1640 and the local contexts in which texts were (or were not) censored. In response to growing discord in the Church between what writers at the time referred to as "Arminians" and "Puritans" (each side disparaging the other by these objectionable characterizations), Charles I issued a rare censorship proclamation that prohibited theological disputation within the Church of England. The proclamation and the events and books with which it was concerned are the subject of chapter 2, which shows that objections to licensing arose long before John Milton. Chapter 3 considers how the courts of Star Chamber and High Commission adopted and transformed the practices this chapter has described to become venues in which authors, as well as printers and publishers, were held accountable for printed texts. The two trials of Prynne – in 1634 and 1637 – as the opening of this chapter suggested, have dominated the discourses of Caroline press censorship. Chapter 4 seeks to place these extraordinary events within the context of the broader culture of religious writing in the 1630s, including the restraints that were imposed and the evasive strategies that were adopted. Chapter 5 focuses on conditions in the printing trade and the way these conditions interacted with trade regulation and censorship. The subject of the final chapter is censorship between 1640 and the beginning of the Protectorate. It begins with the role books and censorship played in relation to the "Scottish problem," and then turns to the actions taken by the Long Parliament, first, in response to the culture of censorship that had developed in the 1630s, and then in relation to the extraordinary transformation in print culture that accompanied the outbreak of the civil war.

CHAPTER 2

Print in the time of
Parliament: 1625–1629

In 1628 Henry Burton, the godly rector of St. Matthew's Church in Friday Street, London, noted a changing climate for preachers and religious writers that had begun, he said, seven years past:

Yea, what a Metamorphosis have wee seene already in these our daies? How unlike is the present time to the former which we have seene? For, as I told the L. Bp. of *London*, it was a pitifull thing to see the strange alteration of these times within this 7 yeares, from those former. For formerly, not a Popish, nor Arminian booke durst peepe out; but now, such onely are countenanced and published, & Orthodox bookes suppressed. It was not wont to be so, my Lord, quoth I. And ... [some] hath dared of late dayes to encroach even upon the liberty of Preaching itselfe, that [*sic*] in the most publicke place of the Kingdome. Preachers have been beene forced sometime before, to show their Sermons before they were preached, and some were not suffred to preach for their very texts sake ... Therefore you see the case is altered.[1]

As a conforming Calvinist, which he indeed was in 1628, Burton here expresses concern not only with the changing conditions of print culture that were occurring in the 1620s but also with the increasingly divisive climate within the Church of England as two rival factions struggled with what precisely it meant to be "Orthodox."[2] One group, aligned with Archbishop of Canterbury, George Abbot, adhered in varying degrees to Calvinist theology, identified strongly with Continental Protestants, enthusiastically embraced a preaching ministry, and strongly opposed the Church of Rome. The other, connected to Richard Neile, Bishop of Durham (and identified with his London residence as either Durham College or Durham House), objected to some Calvinist doctrines, favored ceremonialism over preaching, and generally took a far more irenic stance toward Rome. These factional differences might have been solely the material for church historians had both sides not only put forth their cases in print but engaged in campaigns to restrict their opponents' voice. Between 1625 and 1629 Durham House engaged in a strategy of silencing that invoked both licensing and royal proclamation, traditional tools of press control. English Calvinists called on the House of Commons, both by petition and print, to censure the "Arminians" and the man regarded as their principal spokesman, Richard Montagu. They also defied silencing efforts by speaking out in print against licensing practices, a strategy supported by printers in London and the universities, who not only printed unlicensed books but reprinted books formerly licensed that appealed to the godly. This chapter considers how books and their censorship participated in the "the strange alteration of these times" during the time of Charles I's first Parliaments – an alteration marked by an emerging perception of a "culture of censorship" for which the "Puritan" assault on licensing shared responsibility with the official system of restraints. In an effort to better understand press censorship between 1625 and 1629 – the years when Parliament kept Montagu and religious orthodoxy alive as an issue – this chapter considers the textual strategies of books on both sides of the controversy, the efforts of authors and publishers to disseminate their books, and the measures taken to control (or not to control) them.

In June of 1626 Charles I issued a royal proclamation with far-reaching implications for censoring the press by prohibiting "Writing, Preaching, Printing, Conferences, or otherwise" on "opinions concerning Religion" that differed from the doctrine and discipline of the Church of England.[3] This proclamation appeared in response to the recent rancor in press and Parliament that had been unleashed by Montagu's two books, *A new gagg for the new gospell? No: a new gagg for an old goose* (1624) and *Appello Caesarem* (1625). Montagu, who held the office of Canon of Windsor, was an experienced Church of England controversialist, and, like William Laud, a protégé of Richard Neile, Bishop of Durham. When *A new gagg* – which sought common ground between the Church of Rome and the Church of England's Articles of Religion and Book of Homilies – appeared in 1624, it so provoked long-time conforming Calvinists that they presented the House of Commons with a petition finding Montagu's book to be "full fraught with dangerous Opinions of Arminians quite contrary to the Articles established."[4] To defend himself against his accusers' claims that the views he expressed in *A new gagg* smacked of Arminianism and thus departed from the Church's published theological positions, Montagu wrote *Appello Caesarem*, which a Commons committee in Charles I's first Parliament judged "a factious and seditious Book, tending manifestly to the Dishonour of our late King, and to the Disturbance of our Church and State." Furthermore, the committee regarded Montagu's latest effort as having been composed in contempt of Parliament.[5] The second book, which argued fine theological points of predestination, justification, and free will at the same time that it attacked Montagu's opponents as unruly, seditious Puritans, proved even more provocative than the first and, as a result, provoked a flurry of replies, some radical and some from distinguished churchmen and MPs like George Carleton, Bishop of Carlisle; Daniel Featly; John Yates; and Francis Rous. Despite the intention of Charles's 1626 proclamation to quiet all this, between 1625 and 1629 both print and Parliament became concerned not only with defining religious orthodoxy in the Church of England, but also with assuring its continuity. While parliamentarians enjoyed a certain privilege to speak freely of these matters when Parliament was in session, the 1626 proclamation, which promised that the King would "proceed against all such offendors, and wilfull contemners of his gracious and Religious government," outlawed printed texts whose notions of orthodoxy differed from those of Charles and his chief ministers, many of whom were Church of England clerics associated with Durham House.[6] Even so, between 1626 and 1629, books with a Calvinist perspective continuously appeared from English presses. The preponderance of Calvinist writing in the wake of Charles's proclamation has prompted considerable debate among historians, not only about the nature, intent, and effectiveness of Caroline press control but also about the nature of theological orthodoxy.

THE ARMINIAN–CALVINIST DIVIDE

Nicholas Tyacke maintains that in the 1620s the rise of Arminian doctrine and the entrenchment of Arminian bishops at court and in the Church of England's hierarchy effectively destroyed a consensus among conformist and non-conformists that was held together by the "bond of Calvinist predestination."[7] From Tyacke's perspective Calvin's doctrine of predestination dominated the Church of England for nearly eighty years until at the beginning of Charles's reign the group of divines patronized by Richard Neile, Bishop of Durham, gained an ascendancy in ecclesiastical and court appointments that effectively isolated King Charles from widespread Calvinist belief and radicalized conforming Calvinists. Richard Montagu's books, according to Tyacke, represented a bold step forward by Durham House to oppose the Calvinist doctrine of predestination, to claim their views of free will and sacramentalism as those of the Church of England, and to cast those who disagreed with them as seditious Puritans. Peter White objects to Tyacke's conclusion on two grounds: first, that the principal source of evidence for a doctrinal "evolution" in the English Church comes largely from the latter part of the period, principally from William Prynne's 1629 book *Anti-Arminianisme*, a source White deems "by no means disinterested" from an author for whom the claim "that until 1640 ... [he] was a moderate should deceive no one."[8] White's second objection, which forms the substance of his *Predestination, Policy and Polemic*, is that the theological position of the Church of England, reflected in the Articles of Religion, the Book of Homilies, and the writings of the English delegation to the Synod of Dort, may partially accommodate but never fully embrace the position of either side – Calvin and Beza[9] on the one; Arminius, Vorstius, and Bertius on the other.[10] White regards Charles I's efforts to silence the dispute over predestination as such a "result of consensus" that, he concludes, "The religious tensions of 1640–2 had little to do with the doctrine of predestination."[11]

The legitimacy of both Tyacke's and White's positions has been widely contested. Kenneth Fincham, Peter Lake, and Patrick Collinson, among others, agree with Tyacke and readily view Durham House as the center of, if not Arminianism per se, at least of an agenda opposed to English Calvinism.[12] Like White, Julian Davies and Kevin Sharpe have been reluctant to acknowledge Durham House's views as anything other than orthodox Anglicanism.[13] Durham House's theology may be contested, but the fact of its existence is certain and its identity is clearer than Archbishop of Canterbury, George Abbot's constituency.[14] Among the clerics identifiable with Durham House, besides Neile and Montagu, were John Cosin (Neile's chaplain), Francis White (Dean of Carlisle), John Buckeridge (Bishop of Rochester), John Howson (Bishop of Oxford), William Laud, Augustine Lindsell, and Launcelot Andrewes (Bishop of Winchester) – though he was less active in court politics. Tyacke identifies a "Calvinist triumvirate" consisting of Archbishop Abbot and the Bishops of London and Winchester, John King and James Mountague respectively, as "counterweights to Neile."[15] Similarly Kenneth Fincham finds in John King, Miles Smith (Bishop of Gloucester) and Robert Abbot (Bishop of Salisbury) "a Calvinist counterpart to the more famous Durham House set."[16] While these men certainly constituted the center of Calvinist authority, they cannot be seen as a "party" by 1625. Abbot died in 1617, Mountague in 1618, and King in 1621. Although historians usually mention a Calvinist faction only in passing, Richard Montagu and his contemporaries certainly envisioned one. In letters to John Cosin about *Appello Caesarem*, Montagu repeatedly named the thorns in his side (those "Allobrogicall dormise") as Dr. John Prideaux, Archbishop Abbot, and

Abbot's chaplains, Thomas Goad and Daniel Featly.[17] The correspondence of Daniel Featly and Samuel Ward, Master of Sidney Sussex College, Cambridge, adds to this circle of Calvinist divines anxious over recent theological trends, Arthur Lake, Bishop of Bath and Wells, and Thomas Morton, Bishop of Chester.[18] Besides their attachment to Calvinist soteriology, these men shared Archbishop Abbot's evangelical vision of a church that enthusiastically embraced a preaching ministry and repudiated any taint of popery.[19]

BOOKS AGAINST MONTAGU

In addition to these clerics associated with Abbot, articulate laymen – William Prynne among them – launched an attack in print and in Parliament not only on the anti-predestinarian theology of Montagu's books but also on his conciliatory stance towards Rome. William Prynne's 1629 *Anti-Arminianisme. Or The Church of Englands old antithesis to new Arminianisme*, often seen as the central text against Montagu, actually followed more moderate voices, but voices which, nonetheless, prompted Charles I's efforts to quell controversy and protect Montagu. In 1626 Charles I issued the proclamation prohibiting religious controversy in the Church of England, and in 1628 he had the Articles of Religion published with a declaration that prohibited preaching or printing that interpreted the articles in any manner other than their "literall and Grammaticall sense."[20] It also forbade any disputation, printing, or preaching on the meaning of the articles in the universities, which traditionally had been the place for theological debate. Rather than reflecting the consensus White believed to have existed, Charles's proclamation and declaration (whose effectiveness will be assessed later) were directed at men of good will who were loyal to the Church of England, although they saw Calvinism as its theological status quo. In the past, religious censorship had been reserved for only the most outspoken opponents to the religious settlement, which, as their writings will show, these men were not.

Looking at a genuinely libelous book against Arminianism that was printed on the Continent reveals how moderate English books censored by the proclamation really were. In 1628 *The Spy discovering the danger of Arminian heresie and Spanish trecherie*, attributed to John Russell, appeared from the press of Giles Thorp in Amsterdam. According to a manuscript notation on one copy of *The Spy*, it was "Forbidden to be sold," and "He that fyrst solde this booke ... was fyned and an inquirie made amongst all ye booke sellers shoppes for it."[21] Although no further documentary evidence confirms this, the Secretary of State did hold up *The Spy* to the

London Stationers as the epitome of the kind of "schismaticall and heret-icall books" that they should not sell or "meddle with."[22] The book, clearly intended for the English market since it addresses Parliament, was printed abroad to avoid the ecclesiastical licensers, certainly necessary since it openly made scandalous claims about the Durham House clerics and libeled the Duke of Buckingham. In the prefatory materials the author, identifying himself as English, professes his sincere loyalty to his King and country and explains that this work – written to prevent his homeland from being "thrust blindfold upon the pikes of foreyne enemies, or the poyniards of domestick traitors" – should have "flutred abroad the last Parliament" except that "none durst adventure" to give it wings because of the "super-cilious lookes of over-awing greatnesse."[23] (That is, no printer would risk taking it before the ecclesiastical censors.)

According to David Colclough, *The Spy* participates in an ancient tradition of political counsel that embraces the rhetoric of free speech.[24] *The Spy* proposes to provide Parliament and the Crown with the knowledge requisite for good government. It begins with a prayer appealing to God,

that with the oracles of our Lawes, and the ornaments of our State, (especially with him that is the chiefe of both) they may worke the same effects, for the preventing of imminent danger . . . whose consultations that they may have free proceeding for the establishing such wholesome Lawes, as may tend to the advancement of Gods glory, his majesties honour, the Gospells Increase and the Kingdoms Welfare.[25]

The Spy's counsel takes the form of an extended poem in heroic couplets because, the author claims, it thereby can "scape the malice of the age" that befalls the "graver kind" of texts that "dare of speech be free / In truth's behalf."[26] In distinguishing itself from polemical works, the author frees himself (for better or worse) from the burden of proof and argument usually required.[27] So liberated, *The Spy* connects anti-Catholic, anti-Arminian, anti-Durham House, anti-Spanish, and anti-Buckingham senti-ments with a curious logic that Charles's government ascribed to even its most moderate critics.

Appropriate to its motives ("hate of Spanish treason, and true zeale / Unto the good of Church and Commonweale"[28]), the poem begins with nothing less than the cosmic battle between Christ and Satan for the true Church's soul. Rome's ecclesiastical hierarchy comprise Satan's legions and Protestant nations the true Church.

> We have the patients, you the agents bin
> In all massacres, treasons, persecutions,
> Close murthers, cruell bloudshed, and disruptions

> Of Cityes, kingdomes wofull devastations.
> Rebellions, powderplots, and wrong invasions
> Perform'd to force mens consciences, and make
> Inconstant soules, with error part to take.[29]

This devastation, the poem concludes, is not for religious conscience's sake but "to make / Entrance, for *Spanish* waspes" present in the "*English* hive" (the court), the wasp being the Spanish ambassador who captivated the judgment of "the wisest *Prince* on earth" (James I) to prevent him from fighting Austria on behalf of his daughter Elizabeth and her husband Frederick.[30] The pro-war propagandists who, like Archbishop Abbot, wanted James to go to war in support of the Protestant cause on the Continent originated the connection between James I's foreign policy and the combined interests of Rome and Spain.[31] Now it reappears as a plot newly hatched at the devil's council table between the Pope and the King of Spain, who, remembering the Spanish Armada and the dangers that attended open war, opt for a scheme of religious divisiveness directed at all Protestantism:

> His Holynes hath learn'd of *Machiavell*,
> (In whome all *Popes* have ever beene read well)
> T'advise his standardbearer, to devide
> Truths chiefest followers: that while they doe side
> In factions mongst themselves, he may with ease
> Destroy them all . . .[32]

"Got by *Pelagius*, and in *Rome* nurst up," Arminius foments division by representing Roman doctrine as Protestant, even though he outwardly denies it.

> Tell him the doctrine of the Pope is true
> Concerning merits, he will censure you
> For errour straight. Say that wee may attaine
> By nature, power salvation to gaine,
> By working it our selves: he will reply
> These doctrines are condemned for heresy:
> And yet (what positively he denyes)
> By necessary consequences implyes.[33]

This is not the sophisticated theology considered in Peter White's attentive analysis of Arminian doctrine. Instead, *The Spy* offers a popular version grounded in the central difference between Protestant and Roman soteriology articulated first by Luther – that salvation came by faith rather than works (merit) – and refined by John Calvin and Theodore Beza – that salvation was effected not by man's choice of faith but by God's will as part of his "everlasting and unchaungeable purpose … whereby he hath decreed from everlasting in him selfe, to choose certaine men for his owne purpose, To be saved in Christ."[34] *The Spy's* author is less concerned with theological disputation – which had it occurred in the schools, he says, would have defeated Arminius – than with the means by which the "dissembling" doctrine infected "silly soules, entangled by him"[35] and spread to England.

The Spy's real objection to the rise of English Arminianism is that its political divisiveness makes way for a Spanish conquest.

> No state, or Kingdome ever did sustaine
> Such fatall downfalls, gen'rall devastations,
> Final subversions, and depopulations,
> By open foes: (though ne'er so fiercely bent)
> As by intestine civill broyles …[36]

From this perspective, the English agents of Arminianism, dangerous though they may be on their own account, threaten England because their political ambitions unwittingly make them tools of the devil's agents – the Pope and Spain. That the Pope, the King of Spain, and the Arminians have succeeded in weakening England, the poem claims, is evidenced in the Duke of Buckingham's recent failed military campaign on the French Isle of Ré.

According to the legal principle of *Scandalum Magnatum*, making scandalous claims about important men of the realm was an act of seditious libel. This principle, which as we have seen originated in statute, was refined in a 1605 Star Chamber case against Lewis Pickering (who had attached a libel to Archbishop Whitgift's hearse). This case established that libeling a magistrate constituted scandal to the government because it implied criticism of the monarch who appointed him.[37] *The Spy* contains not only a thinly veiled attack on the court bishops, but an open assault on Buckingham, the King's favorite, as well. It accuses Bishops John Howson (Oxford), George Montaigne (London) and William Laud (Bath and Wells) of subordinating their pastoral duties to their political ambitions:

> Errour prevailes, and while they sheapheards sleepe
> Wolves in sheepes clothing, Worry all thy sheepe.
> Who, almost, cares which way religion bends,
> So they may compasse ther ambitious ends?
> *Howsone* doe those that should firme *Mountaines* be,
> For truth to buld on, *leane* to popery:

> Laude Romish lawes, and to disgrace endeavour,
> In truth's profession, such as would persever.
> So they may rise, they make their betters fall.[38]

The "betters" refers not only generally to Calvinist bishops, "such as would persever" (an allusion to the Calvinist doctrine of perseverance), but also particularly to Archbishop Abbot, who "violently (I know not why)'s throwne downe" by "proud Ambition."[39] (Abbot was sequestered in 1627 for refusing to license Robert Sibthorpe's sermon supporting the forced loan. The King appointed Bishops Montaigne, Neile, Buckeridge, Howson, and Laud to exercise the archbishop's jurisdiction.)[40] In their effort to seize power in the Church and State the ambitious churchmen employ a strategy of division which, like Montagu's books, denigrates the likes of Abbot:

> Nor doe these flattr'ing *Prelates* cease to bring
> Such men in hatred, dayly, with their *King*:
> And falsly, that th'are *Calvinists*, report
> Onely to make them odious in the court.[41]

These court bishops intend to climb via their Arminianism "to th' honour of a Cardinalls cap"[42] and thereby garner Spanish favor and enact treason just as Barnevelt had done in the Dutch Republic. This last passage reiterates *The Spy*'s obsession with Rome's political threat to England, a theme expanded in its characterization of Buckingham.

Remembering a time when government proceeded with the consent of Parliament ("When great ones did not scorne to be controll'd")[43] and kings were not subject to the whims of their favorites ("Such greene-wax councell"),[44] *The Spy* blames Buckingham for all of England's recent ailments:

> Thus is our land made weake, our treasure wasted,
> Our court corrupted, and our honour blasted,
> Our lawes are broke, our justice sold: and they
> That should reforme these mischiefes, glue their way.
> All symptoms of a Kingdome, that hath beene
> Declining long, may be in England seene:
> Our strength's decayd, the flowere of all the land
> Have perish'd under *Buckinghams* command.[45]

Blaming Buckingham in words such as these constituted an attack on the King unparalleled in the Calvinist response to Montagu.

The other men who penned responses to Montagu's books engaged in a measured response that eschewed the vituperation and gall apparent not only in *The Spy* but, to a lesser degree, in Montagu's *Appello Caesarem*. They did, however, share *The Spy's* conviction that the Church of England's orthodoxy embraced the doctrines of predestination and perseverance, and that name-calling was turning loyal churchmen into "Calvinists," "schismatics," and "Puritans." Written during the time of Parliament, like *The Spy*, these texts participated in traditions of political counsel. None of them, however, as we shall see, breached the bonds of decorum or engaged in libel, but all, like *The Spy*, were censored.

Montagu's opponents, all established clerics and laymen who held respected positions in Church and State and who can be described as conformable to the Church of England (in 1626, at least), shared the conviction that: "The decree of Election, or predestination unto salvation is the effectual will of God, by which according to his good pleasure, for demonstration of his mercy, he purposed the salvation of man being fallen; and prepared for him such means, by which he would effectually and unfallibly bring the Elect to the same end."[46] The means God prepared for the Elects' salvation was his Son's death on the cross "out of an especiall love and intention both of God the Father, and of Christ himselfe."[47] They also agreed that being in a fallen state with his will corrupted, man was incapable of turning to God without the assistance of God's grace, which was so tied to the absolute power of God that it could not be resisted. And finally, the Elect, called by God's grace to salvation, though they might stray into sin, could not totally fall from grace, nor through their fall, perish.[48] Montagu denied that beliefs such as these were the orthodox doctrine of the Church of England. He labeled them "Calvinian" and Puritanical and said that they were the private opinions of a radical party which gave the Church of England a bad name. Concern about Montagu's books, as even White acknowledges, was not limited to the theological issues. "The extensive publications of 1626 provoked by the *Appello Caesarem* confirm ... that for many Protestants the concern about Montagu far transcended the issue of predestination."[49] According to White, the other concerns individual authors addressed were the book's rapprochement with popery, its parallels with Pelagian heresy, its claim that King James supported the views of its author, and its repudiation of the Synod of Dort.[50] (This was a council with representatives of the reformed churches that met at Dort in 1618–19 to resolve and finally renounce the challenge to united Protestantism the Arminian party [the Remonstrants] posed in Holland.)

Given their civic and ecclesiastical stature, it is understandable that Montagu's opponents took affront at being labeled "Puritans" and at being accused of misrepresenting the doctrine of the Church of England by distorting the Articles of Religion. Bishop George Carleton best articulates this response in *An Examination of those Things wherein the Author of the Late Appeale Holdeth the Doctrines of the Pelagians and Arminians to be the Doctrine of the Church of England* (1626), when he says that

> the Author of the Appeale may consider what wrong he hath done to the Church of England, in obtruding, for Doctrines of our Church, the old rotten Heresies of Pelagious . . . to beare men in hand that these are the Doctrines of our Church; to scorne men that have been reverenced for their Learning. And will bee reverenced in the ages following; such as Arch-bishop Whitgift, Arch-bishop Hutton, Doctor Rainolds, Doctor Whittaker, and the other Bishops and Learned men, that joined with them, whom this man accounteth sometimes Calvinists and Puritaines . . . as if himselfe had that in Truth, which they did but seeme to have: Who being a Priest of the Church of England, accuseth Bishops, his superiours, to be Puritanes; as all must be to him, who yield not to his foolish and erroneous Doctrines.[51]

As Bishop of Chichester, Carleton was part of the ecclesiastical establishment that no one would think of as "Puritan." He had served as chaplain to Prince Charles and held the principal position in the British delegation to the Synod of Dort. Puritans, from Carleton's perspective, had historically troubled the Church of England because of their beliefs on ecclesiastical discipline.[52] Montagu, however, had accused Carleton and other members of the Dort delegation of turning their back on the Church of England on precisely this matter. Carleton joined with other members of the Dort delegation – Bishop John Davenant, Walter Balcanqual, Samuel Ward, and Thomas Goad – in challenging Montagu's accusation in *A Joynt attestation, avowing that the discipline of the Church of England was not impeached by the Synode of Dort* (1626), because they, "who have hereto subscribed our names, being interested in that Synode, and withal deeply in this crimination of Puritanisme, can doe no lesse then answere, and cleare in some publique manner this slander published against us."[53] In this they explain that their assent and subscription to the five articles approved at the Synod of Dort[54] was in matters of doctrine alone, and that in the process of deliberating the doctrinal issues among themselves, they decided that they ("who were assured in our consciences that their Presbyteriall Parity and Laicall Presbyterie was repugnant to the Discipline established by the Apostles, and retained in our Church"[55]) would verbally take exception in the Synod to the other churches' assent to presbyterian discipline, even though the Synod was not addressing articles on discipline. The distinction here between doctrine and discipline is significant, since none of the spokesmen for Calvinist orthodoxy who opposed Montagu in

1625–26 – however reform-minded they might have been – opposed the Church of England's episcopal discipline.

In 1626 Montagu's opponents reflected the diversity among church Calvinists (some of whom embraced *jure divino* episcopacy, others who were vehemently anti-papist, and others who might best be called godly) that Anthony Milton has documented so well in *Catholic and Reformed*.[56] Besides Carleton, Matthew Sutcliffe, Daniel Featly, and Thomas Goad participated in the ecclesiastical establishment. Matthew Sutcliffe, Dean of Exeter Cathedral and a prolific controversialist, embraced a strong anti-Puritan rhetoric against innovation in the Church of England in the 1590s,[57] but more often directed his pen against Rome. James I appointed Sutcliffe as the first provost of his pet project, Chelsea College, an institution created to wage a polemical battle against Rome. There Sutcliffe engaged such distinguished Roman controversialists as Cardinal Bellarmine and Francisco Suarez. Sutcliffe's *A brief censure upon an appeale to Caesar* shares *The Spy*'s concern that Montagu's writings are little more than a means of bringing to England the religion of Rome with its attendant political disorder.[58] Sutcliffe's principal objection to Montagu is his pretended moderation: "*Mountebanke* [Montagu] in this Church, and Arminius in the Low Countries, with their intempestive contentions, about grace, free will, predestination, and perseverance, & other points of refined popery have kindled such a flame, as I feare will not bee easily quenched ... his moderation is nothing but treason to religion, and his dislike of controversies a liking of Popery."[59] Like Sutcliffe, Daniel Featly, author of *Parallelismis* (1626), *Pelagius redivus* (1626), and *Second Parallel* (1626), and one of Montagu's *bêtes noires*,[60] was both a member of the episcopal establishment and a controversialist. Archbishop Abbot appointed him a household chaplain in 1617, and in this capacity he approved a majority of books authorized for print between 1617 and 1625, many of which shared his moderate Calvinist views. According to Arnold Hunt, in the late 1630s he became a royal chaplain, but when the Civil War broke out, he remained in London, "where his high reputation as a theologian led to his appointment as a member of the Westminster Assembly."[61] Featly's fellow chaplain, Thomas Goad, has been identified as one of Montagu's opponents, although the only printed texts associated with his name are A *Joynt attestation* and the three editions of *Suffragium Collegiale Theologorum Magnae Britanniae*, an account of the proceedings at Dort. Goad, like Featly, was instrumental in assuring that writings by Calvinists (and even some Puritans) received approval for the press, and he opposed Arminianism at Dort. Besides his appointment as Abbot's chaplain in 1615, he was Preceptor of St. Paul's Cathedral, and rector of an archiepiscopal living at Hadleigh.

Montagu's other opponents were more radical than Carleton, Sutcliff, Featly, and Goad. Although ordained in the Church of England and conformable to its discipline, Anthony Wotton, John Yates, and Henry Burton were among the godly. Anthony Wotton, once chaplain to the Earl of Essex and author of *A Dangerous Plot Discovered ... wherein is proved, that, Mr Richard Montagu ... laboureth to bring in the faith of Rome, and Arminius, under the name and pretence of the doctrine and faith of the Church of England*, was Professor of Divinity at Gresham College, London. A popular London preacher, Wotton defended the writings of the renowned Calvinist, William Perkins. John Yates and Henry Burton were the most radical of Montagu's clerical adversaries. Yates, an ordained minister, held a civic ministry at the Church of St. Andrew the Apostle at Saffron Walden in Essex. Yates wrote *Ibis ad Caesarem*, which – besides its dispute with Montagu about the nature of English orthodoxy in matters of predestination, irresistible grace, and perseverance – maintained that he had not informed against Montagu in Parliament and that he was absolutely loyal to the Church of England:

And before I conclude, seeing it is granted to every man to speake in the defence of his owne innocency publikely questioned, and wrongfully slandered; I solemnly protest before God, and this whole Kingdome, that as I have subscribed with my hand, so I subscribe with my hart, to the Doctrine and Discipline of the Church of England. I challenge Mr Montagu and all his Informers to make good against me that accusation that "I have been a Grandee of faction, as great and turbulent, as most be in the Diocesse of Norwich."[62]

Henry Burton, whose writings against the Laudian regime would earn him notoriety in the 1630s (by which time he could certainly be called a Puritan), was also an ordained minister. He had been Clerk of the Closet and chaplain to Prince Henry and in 1621 was appointed Rector of St. Matthew's in Friday Street, London. By the time he wrote *A Plea to an Appeale* in 1626 his opposition to Laud as being popishly affected had already marked him as an opponent to Durham House and earned him the temporary loss of his living at St. Matthew's, Friday Street.[63] That Burton in 1626 was not the kind of dangerous "schismatical," "Calvinian" Puritan Montagu reviled may be seen in *A Plea*'s discussion of Puritanism. Burton's book begins as a dialogue between Babylonious (a Roman Catholic) and Asotus (an English Protestant), with Babylonious commending *Appello Caesarem* because it "plagues the Puritans" and plots reconciliation between Rome and the Church of England.[64] Burton defines the character of contemporary Puritanism (and very likely of his own predilections) when Babylonious proposes consulting Asotus's minister about Montagu's writings but worries that the minister might be a Puritan. Asotus responds, "Surely, in one sence he is no Puritan, for he is conformable; none of the refractarles [*sic*], but doth both practice himselfe, and preach upon occasion, in the defense of Ecclesiasticall ceremonies, and that very earnestly." Asotus explains that formerly "Non-conformists onely, were accounted Puritans," but now, the term might appropriately be applied to conformists, if the word Puritan is used in a second way:

> to wit, for a Minister to be a diligent Preacher, and resident upon his charge; one that cannot away with non-residency, that will not take two Benefices, and makes conscience how he comes by one; that is of an honest conversation, and is a very sincere rebuker of Sinne; an urger of the more strict keeping of the Lords day as he usually calleth it ... and above all, a vehement inveigher against the Masse, and all the Idolatries, and Superstitions of the Church of Rome, as he termes them; and one, who I warrant you would never give his consent, that Jesuites and Masse-Priestes should bee in any way tolerated to live up and downe in our land.[65]

Asotus's minister (and Burton) may indeed be among the more radical clergy in the Church of England, but he is conformable, no enemy to ecclesiastical ceremony, and an opponent to Rome. If Wotton, Yates, and Burton are Puritans, as Anthony Milton has classified them, they are so only "in a second degree."[66] In the first degree, they regarded themselves loyal ministers of the Church of England.

The two other men who penned responses to Montagu in 1626 were both religiously committed and theologically informed laymen trained in the law, Francis Rous and William Prynne. Francis Rous, the author of *Testis Veritatis*, is described by Colin Burrow as a "religious writer of mystical leanings" and a politician.[67] Rous, who came from the Devon gentry, entered the Middle Temple in 1601, where he commenced the study of law "until a storme from heaven chased mee away to the studie of Eternite, wherein I have found so much comfort and assistance from above."[68] Rous's *Arte of Happiness* (1619), although its language might justify the description of "mystical," assures its reader that his joy comes from election, justification, regeneration, and perseverance. Anthony Wood says he was an ordained minister, but Colin Burrow says that was unlikely because of Rous's radical religious convictions, a questionable conclusion based on his writings before 1626.[69] Burrow's allegation of radicalism more properly belongs to Rous's later career in Parliament and the Commonwealth. Rous served in the early Caroline Parliaments, in 1626 as MP for Truro and in 1628–29 for Tregon. Given his conviction that popery was gaining ground, it is not surprising that with his step-brother, John Pym, he pressed the Commons to oppose what he regarded as the Arminian assault on the Church of England. When he wrote *Testis Veritatis* – his response to Montagu that compared passages from King James's writings, the Articles of Religion, the Book of Homilies, and the early Church Fathers on the topics of predestination, free will, justification, and perseverance – Rous identified strongly with the godly clergy. In referring to those in the Church of England who supported the doctrine of Arminius, he says, "I wish other Clergy-men had not also their Politicke endes, and did not seeke to get glory to themselves, by selling the glory of God . . . [which] . . . seemes to be a factious ground whereupon Politic men may worke their own ends."[70] Rous may not have had an ecclesiastical living, but like the godly ministers he likened himself to, he found danger in the means by which the likes of Montagu served themselves.

Like Rous, William Prynne was convinced that the doctrine of persever-ance provided assurance to the Elect, and that the Calvinist doctrines of predestination, justification, and sanctification represented Church of England orthodoxy. Prynne, however, pursued a career in law, having been admitted to Lincoln's Inn in 1621. Prynne was virtually unknown before publishing his response to Montagu, *The Perpetuitie of a Regenerate Mans Estate*, the "first fruites" of his studies.[71] Prynne's affront at seeing his Calvinist convictions labeled Puritan was not unreasonable. "Was Christ, his Prophets and Apostles," Prynne asks, "Puritans?" Indeed, "Were all the Fathers of the primitive Church Puritans? Are all the Protestant and reformed Churchs beyond the seas, and all their sound and orthodox writers Puritans? Are the Church of England, and all her chiefest worthies, Puritans? Or was King James a Puritan?"[72] In 1626 Prynne was no more a dangerous, seditious radical than Bishop Carleton, Daniel Featly, Thomas Goad, Henry Burton, Henry Wotton, Matthew Sutcliffe, John Yates, or Francis Rous.

Besides sharing their theology and their indignation at being called schismatic Puritans, Montagu's opponents all wrote in the spirit of polit-ical counsel, and spoke with a seriousness befitting this intent. Every book written against Montagu, with the exception of Prynne's, appealed to the King, Parliament, or Convocation to remedy the danger to Church and State posed by what they regarded as Montagu's distortions of orthodoxy. In doing so, they participated in a tradition of political counsel deeply engrained in both Renaissance humanism and Reformation Protestantism, which had been accepted by four generations of English monarchs. In *Freedom of Speech in Early Stuart England*, David Colclough establishes the degree to which the rhetorical figure of *parrhesia* (free, open, or direct speech, especially when advising a ruler) dominated the literature of counsel in both Reformation and Humanist writers. Calvinism especially adopted a tradition of plain-speaking based upon biblical traditions of *parrhesia*. According to Colclough, as long as religious debate had been decorous, James I had encouraged admonitory preaching that counseled the King.[73] Free speech in matters of counsel was both a civic duty and a Christian obligation necessary for the safety of the realm.[74] In the religious tradition, according to Colclough, "*parrhesia* as a Christian virtue was something to be exercised among friends or brethren and in relationship with God through prayer, but also defined the proper relationship of the individual Christian to those in power. This relationship should consist, Scripture made clear, in the bold and truthful witnessing of the word of God without fear, whatever the circumstances."[75] Since they came of age during the reign of James I, for Burton, Carleton, Rous, and Yates to address their books to King Charles was not particularly daring. Still within this tradition of political counsel, Wotton directs his book to Parliament and Featly his to Convocation. Prynne offers his book to Archbishop Abbot, who, "next to our gracious and Dread Soveraigne," had the most responsibility to "patronize the truth of God, and the established and resolved Doctrines of our English Church."[76] Every one of Montagu's respondents wrote with the clear conviction that it was his responsibility not only to speak freely and honestly to those ruling the land, but to uphold the word of God.

Upholding the word of God, for all of these writers, meant opposing Rome. The conviction that Arminianism was thinly veiled popery and that Roman Catholicism was making inroads in England filled their books. Only Prynne and Rous, however, subscribed to *The Spy*'s position that Arminianism represented a deliberate plot to undermine Protestantism in England, and only Rous shared *The Spy*'s view that Spain was implicated in the plot:

For there is not a Policy more advantageable to the Spaniard, then to bring in Division into a Land, by bringing in Arminianisme. This is not wordes but deedes, which I speake. For even this Division, had almost forfeited the Low-countreyes to the Spainiard. And whom the warres of so many yeares, did make still stronger, the peace of a few yeares with Arminianisme had almost brought to ruine. And it is well knowne to some that have traveled, that this very Counsell hath been given to the King of Spaine, by an excreable Author, for the destruction of England and the Low-countryes, even to bring in this doctrine, which now hath gotten the name of Arminiainisme.[77]

Although all the writers feared Rome, only Featly, Sutcliffe, and Wotton wrote against papal authority, or insisted that the Pope was indeed

Antichrist.[78] Similarly only Featly, Wotton, and Yates engaged the usual materials of anti-Catholic controversialists: opposition to images, the invocation of saints, papal infallibility, and transubstantiation, and to Rome's claim to be a true church that had been visible throughout history.

Even if these writers were not expressly concerned with the theological differences between Rome and the Church of England, they all agreed that the doctrine and discipline of the Church of England, as they understood it, was the true doctrine of ancient Christianity and thus of the Reformed churches. All but Prynne employed a careful analysis of the relevant Articles of Religion and of the writings of the early Church Fathers, especially St. Augustine, in disputing Montagu. Since such a strong historic sense marked these writings, it is not surprising that several writers addressed the Church of England's relatively short history in relationship to this past. Francis Rous, notable in this respect, draws careful parallels between James I's theological writings, the Church of England's "public" statements of belief, and the early Church Fathers. Burton, Featly, Wotton, and Sutcliffe refer to the writings and sermons of Elizabethan and Jacobean divines. Carleton, Rous, and Sutcliffe expressly consider the areas in which the consensus of the Continental churches that participated in the Synod of Dort agreed (or disagreed) with English church documents. The central issue being controverted by Montagu's adversaries was the character of the Church of England's history and her "public" documents in the theological matters at hand. Montagu, of course, claimed the public documents did not support "Calvinian" views, and his opponents said they did.[79] The Articles of Religion, themselves, belie claims made on either side since their allusive language encourages interpretation – perhaps purposely. Furthermore, for the most part, the historical choices that dictated that language – indeed the very choices of articles – had been largely forgotten by the 1620s.[80] While considering the books written in response to Montagu may not loosen the doctrinal knots in the controversy, these writings all testify to their authors' commitment to avoid the acerbic bitterness of Montagu's *Appello Caesarem*. They also warn against the long-term dangers religious faction posed to England.

CHARLES I'S 1626 PROCLAMATION "FOR THE ESTABLISHING OF THE PEACE AND QUIET OF THE CHURCH OF ENGLAND"

The danger religious faction posed to the peace of the Church was precisely the concern Charles I's 1626 proclamation addressed. The proclamation begins, "The Kings most Excellent Maiesty, in His most religious care, and

Princely consideration, of the Peace of this Church & Commonwealth of England," and then establishes itself as a response to the King's observation, "that in all ages great disturbances, both to Church and State, have ensued out of small beginning, when the seedes of Contention were not timely prevented."[81] This together with the next section, when read within the context of Montagu's opponents' writings considered above, seems to suggest that the proclamation shares their concerns. The proclamation identifies the problem as books on the tenets of "our religion":

which at first onely being meant against the Papists . . . have given much offence to the sober and well grounded Readers, and hearers of these late Bookes on both sides, which may justly be feared, will raise some hopes in the professed enemies of our Religion, the Romish Catholikes, that by degrees, the professours of our Religion may bee drawn first to Schisime, and after to Plaine Popery.[82]

As we have seen, all of Montagu's opponents feared that his books would lead England to popery, and they certainly regarded themselves as "sober and well grounded Readers." The proclamation goes on to declare to his subjects and the world the King's "bitter dislike of al those" who "move any new Opinions, not only contrary, but differing from the sound and Orthodoxall grounds of the true Religion, sincerely professed, and happily established in the Church of England" – again, precisely the objections of Montagu's opponents. To assure peace in the Church, the proclamation commands all the King's subjects, but especially the "Church men" who "by their Profession and places, ought to be Lights and Guides to others" that:

from henceforth they carry themselves so wisely, warily, and consciounable, that neither by Writing, Preaching, Printing, Conference, or other wise, they raise any doubts, or publish, or maintaine any new conventions or opinions concerning Religion, then such as are clearly grounded, and warranted by the Doctrine and Discipline of the Church of England, heretofore published, and happily established by authorities.[83]

To enact the prohibition, the proclamation commands "all his reverend Archbishops and Bishops in their severall Dioceses, speedily to reclaime and represse all such spirits, as shall in the least degree attempt to violate this bond of peace," and it promises offenders not only severity but "exemplary punishment of some few" so that "all others may be warned."[84] A masterpiece of equivocation, this proclamation can be seen as being directed at whoever opposes the orthodox opinions of the Church of England. Montagu and Laud (who is credited with assisting the King in drafting the proclamation), of course, regarded their views as orthodox.[85]

And, as we have seen, Carleton, Featly, Rous, Wotton, and Yates certainly did too. Either side could believe the King, caring deeply about the Church of England, favored its position.

Charles I's 1626 proclamation, while casting the King in a favorable light, differed from the censorship proclamations of his predecessors in three respects: its enactment, its penalties, and its target. While Elizabeth's and James's proclamations had depended largely on their subjects' good will, the 1626 proclamation places its administration in the hands of the episcopacy. A bishop or archbishop (or their factotums) thereby could bring anyone whose writing (or preaching) the cleric did not regard as "orthodox" before an ecclesiastical court. Church courts had long addressed matters of heresy, but with regard to the Montagu controversy, the definition of orthodox proved more slippery than definitions of heresy ever had. Should anyone be discovered publishing "unorthodox" views, he or she would be severely punished as an example to discourage other offenders. While Charles's forebears may well have shared a punitive philosophy such as this, the proclamation criminalizes theological disputation – a practice long established in the Church of England – and turns its practitioners into opponents of Church and State.[86] Never before had censorship been directed at writers, most of whom were ordained clergymen, who accepted the religious settlement, subscribed to – indeed celebrated – the Articles of Religion of the Church of England, and who engaged in well-mannered disputation that disparaged neither bishop nor ceremony. (And this may be said for both Montagu and his opponents!)

Scholars have differed in their assessment of the 1626 proclamation. Tyacke judged that it "opened the door to Arminianism" and by it "Calvinism was proscribed."[87] White criticizes Tyacke's assessment as an overreaction drawn from a single piece of evidence. A letter of Joseph Mead to Sir Martin Stuteville reported that once the proclamation was issued, the High Commissioners – including Archbishop Abbot, Dr. Balcanqual, and Thomas Goad – called in the Stationers, who had involved themselves in publishing the writings against Montagu and charged them "neither to print nor sell any of those 7 or 8 books which during the Parliament had been published."[88] White offers evidence of books published during Charles I's personal rule to illustrate that Calvinism was, indeed, not proscribed. In this, he follows the work of Sheila Lambert, who observes that "New books 'detailing the spiritual life with special attention to assurance, predestination and the order of salvation' continued to appear in abundance, while older works were endlessly reprinted."[89] Inclined to accept Montagu's version of circumstances surrounding the controversy, Lambert notes that "Montagu was a little impatient in complaining, at the end of June 1626, that only he was silenced by the proclamation while the other side continued to write with impunity: 'so little do they care for authority.'"[90] Indeed, observes Lambert, while the "most important" of Montagu's respondents' books (Prynne's) had appeared duly licensed before the proclamation, "new editions of this, of Bishop Carleton's *Examination* of Montagu's Appeal and of Francis Rous's *Testis Veritatis* were then published in defiance of the proclamation ..."[91] Faced with "outright defiance," Charles could not tolerate opposition. "All the evidence indicates that it was only those who were believed to have acted 'willfully' who were disciplined, and by the same token the Arminian case was likely to go by default."[92]

These accounts raise some interesting issues about the relationship of the proclamation generally to ecclesiastical and Stationers' Company licensing, printing, and sanctions, but before I consider these more fully, the problems they raise about the timing and "legality" of the anti-Montagu books need consideration. Mead's letter about the meeting of the High Commission, which Tyacke quotes but otherwise ignores, says the books to which the proclamation had been directed had appeared "during the Parliament." Outside of *The Spy*, the books we have been considering number eight, so presumably they were all published *before* the proclamation and, indeed, were its targets. Evidence from the texts themselves supports this. Following the "Writ of Error" that concludes his book, Featly asks Montagu to recant or face charges in "convocation now sitting."[93] Convocation was assembled on February 26, 1626 and dissolved in June 1626. Francis Rous said he "thought it a fit time" to publish his work as "evident Proofe and Testimonie, that his Maiestie, herein hath merited most glorious and incomparable Titles" because he had heard on February 7 that the King intended a decree opposing Arminianism.[94] Anthony Wotton addressed his book to the Parliament currently in session and dated his introduction June 1, 1626. None of these books was "illegal" because it flouted the 1626 proclamation. Most of them, however, were not printed with either ecclesiastical authorization or entrance in the Stationers' Registers.

Of the books opposing Montagu only Prynne's *Perpetuitie* was entered in the Stationers' Register. This means not only that we have no evidence of their receiving ecclesiastical scrutiny, but also that the books were probably not seen by the usual authorizers – chaplains to the Archbishop of Canterbury and the Bishop of London. Printing without authorization, while technically illegal given the 1586 Star Chamber decrees and the way James's 1624 proclamation interpreted them, was not without widespread precedent. Even so, that only one of these titles was entered in the Stationers' Registers supports contemporary allegations that obtaining ecclesiastical approval for a book against Montagu was virtually impossible. The first edition of Carleton's book was printed at Oxford, where, according to contemporary report, licensing was less rigorous than in London.[95] But even the London publishers do not appear to have been engaging in surreptitious or false publication. The printer or publisher's name and the location of his establishment appear on the title page of every book. Publishing so openly, often with the authors identifying themselves in the text, suggests that Montagu's critics expected that the governors of Church and State to whom they dedicated their books would take them seriously.

Ironically, although Prynne's *Perpetuitie of a Regenerate Mans Estate* was entered in the Stationers' Company Registers on April 7, 1626 with notice of authorization, this is the only book that refers to a censorship proclamation, and thus probably appeared subsequent to it. The third introductory epistle (in the first as well as later editions) addresses "all those of the Church of England who falsly and malitiously traduce, calumniate, and slaunder, the Patrons, of the total and final perseverance of the Saints in grace." Here Prynne writes,

To your third forgery and last accusation, That the Patrons of the totall and finall perseverance of the Saints, are such as doe contrary to the decrees of Caesar, and such as violate his Maiesties late and pious Proclamation. I answer, that you are much mistaken. For as most of their workes were published and printed, before the Proclamation was published or thought upon (and so are not within the compasse of it) so the onely end of his Maiesties pious Proclamation was to establish and settle the ancient settled, received and approved Doctrine of the Church of England in peace and quiet; and to keepe backe you and all other factious, scismaticall, novelizing, Arminianizing, and Romanizing spirits from opposing or disturbing it . . .[96]

This refers to Montagu's position that books on predestination were appearing contrary to a royal proclamation. (Prynne appears to be getting something wrong since he speaks about anti-Arminian books and the proclamation for peace in the Church, while Montagu's book had referred to James's 1624 proclamation against books by "Puritans.") It was not unusual for a title to be entered in the Stationers' Register prior to publication. Indeed, since the Stationers' Register identifies Featly as the ecclesiastical authorizer, a position from which he had been removed in 1625, the printer William Jones, who not infrequently bent rules, may have chosen to register the book before it was completed.[97] Given Jones's past – and Prynne's future – this is conceivable. Even if it was authorized and entered, Prynne's book was among the most provocative books against Montagu, especially in its objections to abuses in ecclesiastical licensing.

Prynne's dedication to Archbishop Abbot addresses those conditions in the world of London printing that Tyacke, White, and Lambert dispute. Prynne consecrates his "just ... defence of a principal ground of that Religion, which hath been long established and settled in our Church" until books by "factious and novelizing spirits ... were so bold and impudent of late to disturb it." Prynne complains that their books "are printed and reprinted, sold openly and dispersed publikely without control" while:

the pious, wholesome and Christian labours of all such as would confute them (by reason of those meanes which they have made) can either finde no license for the Presse: or if they chance to come unto the Presse by stealth or otherwise, they are eyther quelled or smothered in it before they come unto their birth, or else they are called in and quite suppressed, before they can bee published and dispersed, to clear and vindicate the truth ...[98]

Prynne is not alone among Montagu's adversaries in objecting to what he regards as contradictory practices in controlling books. Featly disapproves of the ecclesiastical licensers "who out of love to the Church, (as is pretended,) have had a jealous eye over the Presse, and have procured other Pamphlets to be called in, (though put forth by lawfull authority,) [but] have yet beene most forward to put forth this booke [*Appello Caesarem*]."[99] Of current practices among the ecclesiastical authorizers, Featly remarks, "Sure I am, that if a Puritan Gnat be caught by them in the Presse, they will straine it even unto death; but for many a Popish camel, they swallow it down readily."[100] Burton concurs. "Truth," he says, "complaines of hard usage, how shee is driven to seeke corner, sith shee cannot passe the Presse cum Privilegio, but must be silenced, ye Gagged, least ... she should by writing, cleare her Doctrines from the infamous terme of Puritanisme, and her selfe from being reproached for a Puritan."[101] According to Prynne, Featly, and Burton, even before the 1626 proclamation, obtaining permission from the official ecclesiastical authorizer to publish a book disputing Montagu – or indeed for any godly book – was becoming increasingly more difficult if not altogether impossible. Even so, books did "chance to come unto the Presse by stealth," and some of these, as well as books printed with allowance "by lawful authority," were suppressed. Virtually all the books written against Montagu agree with this picture of London print culture in 1626, which is both more repressive than White and Lambert admit and less effective in its controls than Tyacke suggests.

Judgments about the 1626 proclamation's intention to and effectiveness in "quieting" the voice of controversy were mixed. Montagu may have regarded himself as the proclamation's object, but Bishop John Davenant was concerned that Durham House would exploit the proclamation against its opponents.[102] Davenant's view seems justified since the recommendation that King Charles should issue a proclamation prohibiting further controversy on the issues Montagu's books raised came from Bishops Montaigne (London), Neile (Durham), Andrewes (Winchester), Laud (St. David's), and Buckeridge (Rochester) in a letter that commended Montagu to the King's "gratious favour & pardon."[103] The bishops conceived the ban to assure "the preservation of the truth, & the peace of the Church of England, together with the safetie of Mr. Montagu's person."[104] Looking at the allowance of books by godly authors supports Bishop Davenant's concern.[105] The ecclesiastical licensing establishment had been undergoing some upheaval since 1625, when Daniel Featly had been relieved of his responsibilities for authorizing books (although his name continued to appear in this capacity until 1629). In 1624 the names of Archbishop Abbot's chaplains, Featly and Goad, appeared as having approved 53 percent of the titles entered in the Stationers' Registers.[106] In 1626 Abbot appointed John Jeffray as his chaplain to replace Goad; even so Featly, Goad, and Jeffray's names appear for only 30 percent of the entries. In 1627 their names appear for only 12 percent of the titles entered. From this, it would appear that finding licensers for godly books – or books against Montagu – was as difficult as Calvinist writers claimed.

While changes in ecclesiastical licensing practices were not a direct consequence of the 1626 proclamation, they were related to it since the proclamation had charged bishops with its enforcement. Indirectly, then, bishops were capable of increasing restraints on preaching and writing. Many of the Durham House faction were bishops, and, as we know the Bishop of London, George Montaigne, along with the Archbishop of Canterbury, oversaw London publishing. Furthermore, we know that Durham House clerics were actively interested in restraining Calvinist writing. John Cosin, Neile's chaplain, was busily occupied in ferreting out publications against the proclamation.[107] Even so, books predisposed to Calvinism, indeed even some anti-Arminian books, continued to appear. (While I defer to White's position that Durham House was not technically Arminian, nor was the Abbot party technically Calvinist, since

"Arminian" and "Calvinist" are the labels each side gave to the other, in order to avoid complex circumlocutions I choose to employ these terms.)

The continued publication of Calvinist books has been taken as evidence that the 1626 proclamation was not intended to silence Calvinists. While there may be some merit in this argument, the question of "intention" poses problems. The proclamation probably did intend to silence Calvinists, but its failure to do so is less a matter of official intention than of the will and persistence of a few publishers who were willing to risk catering to a thriving market for godly publications. Calvinists were devoted to the printed word. The "Epistle to the Reader" of William Gouge's *Works* (1627) explains the grounds of this commitment.

Yet I doubt not but Gods people doe also receive much benefit in sundy [*sic*] Treatises in divers kinds published in print. For as Preaching is of power especially to worke upon the affections, so Printing may be one especiall meanes to inform the iudgment. For that which is Printed, lieth by a man, and may againe and againe be read, and throughly [*sic*] pondered, till a man come to conceive the very depth of that he readeth . . . If it be said, that there can nothing be written but what hath written before. I answer that though it should be true in regard of the summe and substance of matter, yet in regard of a more full opening, a more perspicuous delivering, a more evident proving, a more powerful urging and pressing of points, a more fit applying them to present occasions, more and more may be, and daily is added by sundry Authors, whereby the Church of God is much edified.[108]

Edification, "that process through which a true community of godly and properly self-conscious true believers were called together and sustained within the church,"[109] was the life-blood of church Calvinists. Gouge's convictions expressed here on the efficacy of printed treatises and sermons for edification explain both the market for books by godly authors and the willingness of Stationers to risk printing and publishing old or unlicensed books. While many members of the Stationers' Company worked to meet this demand, three in particular, William Jones, Michael Sparke, and Robert Milbourne, appear to have been motivated as much by conscience as by cash. Many of the books they provided for the London market can be classified as edifying, but even at their most edifying, these books, which were often vehemently anti-Catholic and anti-Arminian, found new ways to perpetuate controversy.

1627: BOOKS AFTER THE PROCLAMATION

Before looking more broadly at London publishing immediately following the 1626 proclamation, the publication history of a single edition of sermons shows how at odds the different religious parties were in relationship to the press. In September 1626 Launcelot Andrewes, Bishop of Winchester and scion of Durham House, died. By January Dorothy Jaggard, Isaac Jaggard's widow, was at work printing *Seven sermons on the wonderfull combate (for Gods glorie and mans salvation) between Christ and Sathan Delivered by the Reverend Father in God, Doct. Andrewes Bishop of Winchester, lately deceased* for Michael Sparke. On August 3, 1592, John Charlwood had entered the title "Wonderful Combat for God's Glory" in the Stationers' Register, which noted that the Bishop of London had approved the text, and *The wonderful combate (for Gods glorie and mans salvation) between Christ and Satan Opened in seven most excellent, learned and zealous sermons, upon the temptations of Christ, in the wilderness, &c.* appeared shortly thereafter with a title page imprint that read "Seene and allowed." By beginning the title of the 1627 edition with the words "Seven sermons" – instead of "the wonderful combate" which by pride of place was the title of the 1592 edition – Jaggard and Sparke would both draw attention to the popular genre of edification and deflect attention from the book's controversial potential. The seven Andrewes sermons that comprised both the 1592 *Wonderful combate* and the 1627 *Seven Sermons* expressed views sympathetic to Calvinist theology, which would make an important contribution to the Calvinist position that theirs was the established doctrine of the Church of England. Once the book was printed, however, the Bishop of London intervened to prevent its publication. Exactly why this happened depends on the source. According to Sparke, before "it could come out, the press was stayed for a while by command of the bishop of London, upon the information of some who labour to have the printing of the whole of the late bishop's works."[110]

The evidence that the books were stayed because they were being printed against the King's commandment "concerning the printing of the late Lord Bishop of Winchesters works" comes from Bishop Montaigne's letter to Secretary Conway.[111] The letter's purpose was to ask that the wardens of the Stationers' Company "and some others" be "brought to better obedience for they are exceedingly bold in their printings."[112] For the Bishop of London, who had considerable power over the London press, to appeal to the Privy Council to punish the wardens of the Stationers' Company for something that they did not do (print Andrewes's sermons) – especially since there is no mention of Sparke – raises doubts about the letter's intention. Montaigne also says in the letter that he had witnesses to confirm that he had "layd his Majesties command" upon the Stationers, and they "notwithstanding printed the book."[113] The King's commandment, which is curiously absent from the Stationers' records and state papers, looks more like the King's "strict charge"[114] Laud and John Buckeridge described in the dedication to *XCVI Sermons* (1629). The King told them, they said, to "overlooke the Papers (as well Sermons as other Tractates) of that Reverend and Worthy Prelate, and print all that we found perfect."[115] The most telling feature of Montaigne's letter appears in its insistence that he had not only conveyed the King's command but that he had "witnesses" to it. The assurance of witnesses suggests that Montaigne had somewhere been accused of dilatory behavior in the matter. Whether Montaine told the Stationers not to issue a license for Sparke's edition, or asked them to stop its printing, the timing of his remarks in relation to Sparke's publication is unclear. Also unclear is how Sparke understood his role in the matter. Referring to the intervention on behalf of someone wanting the printing of the whole suggests that Sparke is thinking in terms of rights rather than prohibitions, which explains why after nine weeks he proceeded to sell copies of *Seven Sermons*. According to Sparke, "Hearing no more of this business for nine weeks, and pressed to pay for the paper, and being in much want of money," he disposed of the books, an act for which the Privy Council performed the unusual act of committing him to the Fleet Prison.[116] Printers before Sparke had been sent to the Fleet for printing illegal works – either seditious books or books that lacked a license. *Seven Sermons* was illegal in neither respect.

Censoring Sparke's edition of the sermons looks like a simple matter of either sanctioning "bold" printing – punishing Sparke for going against the King – or assuring Laud and Buckeridge's proprietary interest in Andrewes's works. Which it is depends on the nature of the commandment that Montaigne conveyed. If Montaigne said the King forbade any printing of any of Andrewes's work, then Sparke was indeed bold, first for ignoring the commandment, later for selling the books. Even so, when the books involved in a matter like this were not seditious, the Privy Council customarily deferred to the authority of the master and wardens of the Stationers' Company. Such cases usually were heard in the Company's court of Assistants, which imposed sanctions. However bold Sparke may have been in selling the book, his imprisonment was unusual.

If, however, Montaigne told the Stationers' Company to expect that an edition of Andrewes's works would be printed by the King's "special Command" (as the Laud–Buckeridge edition's title page says it was), the matter would have been proprietary, and Sparke and the Company may not have considered that *Seven Sermons* was relevant to the "command." A royal commandment to print a book usually entailed a royal patent, which meant that allowing, printing, and publishing the work was entirely outside the Stationers' Company's purview. In matters of patent the master and wardens would have understood their responsibility rested in assuring that no Company member entered a competing claim (license) in the Company Registers. Sparke and his partners, however, would not have been obliged to make an entry for *Seven Sermons*. They already owned the copy and were thereby entitled to print it without further entry or allowance. An August 3, 1592 entry in the Stationers' Register established that the sermons were John Charlwood's copy, and since the entry testified to the Bishop of London's authorization, this license was undeniably legal. After Charlwood's death his right in the copy passed to James Roberts, who married Charlwood's widow. Subsequently, Roberts's titles and printing materials passed to William Jaggard, and on his death to his son Isaac, Dorothy Jaggard's husband. Dorothy, who inherited Isaac's titles, printed the 1627 edition of *Seven Sermons* for Sparke and Thomas Cotes, who had been an apprentice of William Jaggard and to whom Dorothy transferred her titles in June 1627. Had Laud and Buckeridge intended that the *Seven Sermons* would be included in their edition of Andrewes's sermons, they would have had to obtain permission from Cotes. Although Sparke may have been trying to score points for the Calvinist perspective by printing *Seven Sermons*, the book was not "illegal" from a proprietary perspective.

Not surprisingly, as it ended up, the sermons included in the 1627 Sparke–Cotes edition were omitted from the 1629 Laud–Buckeridge edition – almost certainly for ideological reasons. As Peter McCullough has persuasively demonstrated, the Laud–Buckeridge edition of Andrewes was conceived as "polemically aggressive, consciously constructed as a new authority and proof-text for the apologists who would defend the reconstruction of the church in the 1630s."[117] An enterprise such as this – one by which Laud defined Church of England orthodoxy – could neither include sermons that violated his definition of orthodox nor allow those sermons to appear in print outside the canonized text. Sparke's printing of *Seven Sermons* together with its suppression (in which Laud surely had a hand) exemplifies what McCullough has labeled "the chess game of Caroline bibliographical politics"[118] – a game at which both sides were becoming adept. This time they played with their knights, moving one square forward in ideology and two sideways in print protections and controls.

Not all the publishing games in 1627 were as dramatic as the efforts to publish and suppress Andrewes's sermons. Calvinist printing (authorized or not) flourished, and few publications met with efforts by Durham House to silence them. Sixty-three percent of the religious books printed in 1627 appeared from authors who can be described as godly, Calvinist, or even Puritan. On the other hand, as suggested by the brouhaha over Andrewes's sermons, Durham House was coming to recognize how valuable printing could be to advance their vision for the Church, especially when they turned from Montagu's intemperate controversial strategies to theological treatises and devotional writings, such as Thomas Jackson's *A treatise of the holy catholike faith and Church*. Thomas Jackson, chaplain to both Bishop Neile and the King, for some time had been writing a series of commentaries on the Apostles' Creed. His choice to publish his treatise on the Church in 1627 was, like the efforts of godly authors, ideologically adversarial without being actually controversial. Its cautious use of language assured that it did not violate the letter of the 1626 proclamation even with its strongly anti-Calvinist stance. This may be seen especially in the following passage that brackets predestination and election in its definition of the universal (catholic) Church:

some others define it to be *Coetus electorum*, the society or company of the elect. Against which definition or description, this exception may bee taken, that the Authors and Maintainers of it, have intangled this article or point of Believe, necessary to all that hope to be saved, with intricate and unnecessary questions concerning Predestination or Election, which I doe not meane to trouble the Reader in the explication of this Article.[119]

Jackson's position that no visible (national, including "Romish") church is the Holy Catholic Church was shared by most Protestants, but many Calvinists would find difficulty with Jackson's contention that any "visible" church that held to the unity of faith and doctrine expressed in the creed was a "true" visible church. Calvinists maintained that a visible church could be true only if the word was truly preached and the sacraments rightly administered, while the Roman Church maintained that the marks of the true Church were antiquity, universality, and continuity.[120] Jackson directed his argument to the terms of Rome's definition by arguing the antiquity and continuity of the Church of England and totally ignored the Calvinist criterion of preaching.

Durham House made its foray into strategically employing printing in its game of bibliographical politics more cautiously and slowly than Calvinists, who in the spirit of the Continental Reformation enthusiastically embraced printed controversy. It is no wonder, then, that although the 1626 proclamation called for silence on theological matters to assure peace in the Church, the Calvinist constituency responded by fulfilling the letter of the law rather than its intent. Writers refrained from engaging further in disputing with Montagu; they did not, however, refrain from taking swipes at what they regarded as Arminian inroads into the Church of England, or from arguing about matters besides predestination, or from ranting against Rome. While one might classify Calvinist writings as devotional or exegetical, many of the books printed in 1627 defy such categorization. With 63 percent of the books printed taking a godly bent, a comprehensive survey of their contents and strategies lies beyond the scope of this study. A few examples, however, can serve to illustrate how publishers and authors sympathetic to Calvinism promoted their anti-Catholic, anti-Arminian agenda. One strategy writers employed was to avoid London and have their books printed at one of the university presses. In 1626, upon visiting Oxford, Nicholas Pey wrote that he had an "ambitious vanity" to have a "thing" of his "composition" printed there "which would else in London run through much noise before hand, by reason of the licences that must be gotten."[121] George Carleton had published the first edition of his book against Montagu in Oxford. In 1627 nearly a third of the Calvinist books that were printed without entrance in the Stationers' Registers appeared from the presses at either Oxford or Cambridge. Another strategy to avoid the ecclesiastical authorizers in London was to reprint books that had formerly been licensed, as Sparke had done. In 1627 34 percent of books by Calvinist authors had either appeared in their first editions before 1625 or been printed before 1625 in multiple small editions. The edition of William Gouge's works, for example, could be printed without being entered in the Stationers' Register and resubmitted to the ecclesiastical authorizers because the individual sermons had been formerly printed and the printer/publisher thereby "owned" the copy. To bring out the works of so popular a preacher at this point, as its prefatory materials foreground, emphasizes the importance Calvinists placed on preaching. The sermons themselves underscore the differences between English Calvinists and Rome. The same things may be said of the decision to reprint Jacobean Calvinist Nicholas Byfield's *An Exposition upon the Epistle to the Colossians*, which seasons its conventionally Protestant rejection of the Catholic doctrine of works with a good dose of Calvinist perseverance. John Dod and Robert Cleaver's *Brief dialogue concerning preparation for the worthy receiving of the Lords Supper*, which appears to be solely an encouragement to private devotion, advances a characteristically Calvinist devotional agenda favoring attention to preaching, hearing, reading, meditation, conference, and the use of good books over observing holy days. They condemn any "Approbation of Idolatry by presence, speeche, gesture, silence," or "keeping of supersitious relickes."[122] Similar in purpose to Dod and Cleaver is William Bradshaw's *A preparation to the receiving of Christs body and Blood*, first printed in 1609, which refers to "that execrable Religion of the church of Rome" and calls its sacrament "Antichristian foppery." This little "devotional" work, thus, repudiates any efforts afoot to find common ground between England and Rome.[123] Anti-Arminian, as well as anti-Rome, John Carter's *A plaine and compendious exposition of Christs Sermon in the Mount*, printed for the first time in 1627 with Worrall's approbation, adds to its moderately Calvinist soteriology a vision of those excluded from the glory of Christ's redemption: "not the super-stitious rabble, in their traditions, will-worships, opus operatum, or bodily exercises; not the justitiatie, parisaicall, or papisticall, in their legal right-eousnesse, or merit of workes; nor the Pelagian, Papist, or Arminian, in their freewill: but hee that glorieth, let him glorie in the Lord Jesus Christ."[124]

Previously printed, printed at the universities, unauthorized or allowed, besides the books that hid their anti-Arminianim in the guise of edifica-tion, several books appeared in print that openly attacked the Church of Rome in a manner that had become conventional during the reigns of Elizabeth and James. Typical of this is Fredrich van Hulsius's *The character of a Christian: As Hee is distinguished from all Hypocrites and Hereticks. With the freedome of the faithful: As they are proposed by our Saviour in the words of the Gospel*, which was approved by Abbot's chaplain Jeffray but published anonymously.[125] This book begins by looking for common ground with Rome but soon expresses a concern that the faithful thereby may be led astray by false prophets ("wolves"). False prophets arise when the doctrine of the New Testament is not duly preached, and in this Rome fails – but so do the Arminians:

And in what better estate must they needs bee, who, most contrary to the Word, (as I shewed above) teach new doctrines of election, not of grace, but according to forseene faith, repentance, charities, &c.? And so in other the Arminian errours about redemption, conversion and perseverance of the Saints: wherein they receive not the love of the Truth: for yee see it manifested, that they cannot be said to receive the love of the Truth, that obstinately resist the Word in any things.[126]

Van Hulsius's style, more diatribe than argument, serves well his end of linking the errors in the Church of Rome with an attack on Arminianism. Given the tenor of this work – and the fact that it violated the intentions of the 1626 proclamation more than other Calvinist books – it is surprising that it fell below the government line of sight when another anti-Catholic book did not: Henry Burton's *The Bayting of the Pope's Bull, or An unmaking of the iniquity, folded up in a most pernitious Breeve or Bull, sent from the Pope lately into England, to cawse a Rent therein, for his Reentry.*

Burton's book, which reproduced a 1626 papal bull advising English Catholics that it would be better to suffer martyrdom than to take an oath of allegiance to King Charles, responded point by point to the bull and made the rather unexceptional point that English law punished Catholics only for crimes against the state and not for their religion. (Lord Burghley had made the same case in *The Execution of Justice in England* in 1583.) *The Bayting of the Pope's Bull* begins with a dedication to Charles that tells of the author's experience of having a Jesuit attempt his assassination and warns the King that he may be placed in similar peril by the papal bull since "Such Breeves never come, but they betoken some notable mischiefe not farre off."[127] (One, he says, had appeared before the Spanish Invasion in 1588.) The dedication praises Charles, asks the King to call for a public fast to counter the Pope's prayers for English Catholics, and apologizes for the author's liberty. A second dedication, this to Buckingham, admonishes the Duke to protect the King: "Doth not the safety of the Kings Person and Crowne, of this Church and State, of three goodly Kingdoms, yea of the Gospell of Christ, and of true religion at home and abroad, even over Christendome & throughout the world, depend in a maner upon this trust, committed to your Grace?"[128] The danger, Burton cautions Buckingham, comes from flattering Jesuits in "the Court itselfe, especially your Graces house."[129] Borrowing words from the Old Testament, Burton warns, "Thinke not with thy selfe, that thou shalt escape in the Kings howse: for yf thou altogether holdest thy peace at this time, then shall inlargements and deliverance arise to Gods people from another place: but thou and they fathers howse shall be destroyed."[130] Bishop Montaigne ordered Burton's book suppressed shortly after it was printed. In both of the book's dedications – which contemporaries took to be the cause of the book's suppression since its authorizer, Dr. Jeffray, when questioned, said he had not seen them – Burton expresses anxiety about giving frank counsel.

By invoking and calling attention to the frankness of his counsel, Burton virtually asks for the book to be suppressed. Indeed, it is almost as though he stages its suppression to prove that men around Buckingham and the King are little more than Jesuits in disguise. Part of the dedication to Buckingham suggests this.

But you want not those, that are able to performe the office of good Chapleins. Yet if any, in stead thereof, shall not onely bee silent; & negligent, but on the other side, bee too officious to sow pillows under your Elbowes, to applaud and approve you in all your doings, yea to perswade and counsel you, wherein perhaps theyr conscience tells them, it ought not to be so: woe be unto them. But wee hope better things. But if any shall goe about to find a knot in a bulrush, by picking some quarrel with this booke, where hee hath no just cawse (bee his pretence never so faire guilded over, or seem his reasons never so farre fetcht, yea from his abstruse speculations in state-pollicy) & shall by hooke or crooke labour the suppressing of it, or hinder your Grace from reading of it, though so necessarie to imploy your saddest thought in it, it so neerely concerning the safety of your gratious Master our Dread Soveraine ... no doubt but your Grace will take that man for no other, but a pestilent Traitor, & if hee be not a Jesuite, yet certainly possessed with a Jesuitical spirit, as seeking to smoother such an important Overture as this.[131]

Burton here concedes that Buckingham has about him men who can be good spiritual advisors ("Chapleins"), yet there also may be some, "silent" or flattering, who are "on the other side" – who by picking a quarrel with this book and "by hooke or crooke labour the suppressing of it," reveal their "Jesuitical spirit." The choice of the word "chaplain" is telling. Being at court, Buckingham had about him many chaplains. John Cosin and Thomas Jackson were Bishop Neile's chaplains; as Laud had been previously. Richard Montagu was a royal chaplain. All these chaplains, like Buckingham's own, Thomas Lucy, were "on the other side." The point Burton makes here is that those who are interested in seeing this book suppressed, those on the other side, are traitors – an accusation that evidently was not taken lightly since the book was so readily censored. The dedication is not really warning Buckingham about Jesuits; it is calling upon him to be wary of the Arminians. Burton's complaints about Arminianism are no stronger than van Hulsius's, but he manages to draw attention to himself and to the potential for censorship his book faces. In doing so, he calls attention to a political dimension in the practice of censorship – a dimension to which he and other anti-Arminian writers would return frequently in the future.

The most interesting feature of press controls in 1627 is that the books the government sought to suppress were not the kind of books that had been prohibited by the 1626 proclamation. In addition to the two occasions described above – Sparke's edition of *Seven Sermons* and Burton's *Bayting* – Bishop Montaigne was sufficiently concerned about Robert Cotton's anonymously published *A View of the Long Life and Reign of Henry III King of England* that he forwarded the book to the King along with examinations of all who were found "guilty of the selling of it," and reported that he would bring them all before the High Commission. Montaigne had questioned Cotton and accepted the author's assurance that the book was published "without his knowledge or hand in the printing of it."[132] Apparently the book's London sales were stayed, but most of the copies had been sent to the countryside, one with a letter that said the book was printed in Dort.[133] The title page had no publisher's name or place of publication, so clearly the publishers recognized the book's potentially inflammatory contents. The history, whose title page says it was "Presented to King JAMES," concerns itself far less with recounting the events of Henry III's reign than with making observations about politics. The threats to his authority a monarch might face included "Commons greedy of liberty, and the Nobility of Rule" (a2v), an immoderate and powerful favorite, "factious Bishops" who "use their bitter pens and speeches"(c2v), judges "sent in Circuits under pretext of Justice to fleece the people" (c4), and Parliaments where "more malignant humors beganne to raigne in them, then well composed tempers" (d1). Charles I had recently dissolved the 1626 Parliament because it had been more interested in impeaching Buckingham than in meeting his demand for supply; he then turned to his judges and other officials to levy a forced loan. The history's publishers surely recognized the parallels between Cotton's history and the current times, since at least one of them tried to pass the book off as having been printed in Dort. Although Montaigne said he intended to proceed against them in the High Commission for printing without license, official sanction was not really the issue, and it is not clear that he actually pursued prosecution. Despite the parallels to the times, the book, like Burton's, places its confidence in the wise and good king who rules well in difficult times. Kevin Sharpe, skeptical of Cotton's claim that he had written the book twelve years before, suggests that even if it had been written earlier, the book came out in 1627 as an instrument of royal counsel.[134]

RELIGION AND PARLIAMENT FROM 1626 TO 1628

With the exception of Sparke's edition of *Seven Sermons*, all of the books that were the focus of censorship in 1626 and 1627 – including Montagu's *Appello Caesarem* – were politically engaged. As literature of counsel they addressed the King or Parliament (or both). The books against Montagu, as we have seen, were written before Charles dismissed Parliament in 1626. They participated in the effort of conforming Calvinists not simply to silence Montagu but to move Parliament to repudiate Arminian doctrine. Parliament had taken up the issue in 1625 and returned to it again in 1626. Lambert's position that the Arminian question concerned only a few radical MPs, I think, misses the point that becomes clear in most of the anti-Montagu pamphlets and in Parliamentary proceedings.[135] The Arminian question was part of a general anxiety about the Roman church – an anxiety that, as Peter White points out, also motivated Montagu. (From White's perspective Montagu wrote out of a pastoral concern for the need "to win over church papists, and perhaps even more importantly to arrest the trickle of converts to Rome."[136]) Montagu was not alone in his perception that things were amiss. In 1625 Parliament petitioned the King to make a public declaration that he would enforce the recusancy laws at the same time that the King was receiving pressure from France as part of the marriage treaty to increase toleration for English Catholics.[137] For Parliament, anti-Catholic sentiment, anxieties about war with Spain and France, and concern for the health of the Church of England became intimately linked.[138] According to Conrad Russell,

In the atmosphere of a popery scare, the charge of Arminianism was far more dangerous than it had been in the comparatively calm and secular atmosphere of 1624, for it was precisely on the "fundamental points" which had hitherto been the common bond of English Protestantism, the points of justification and predestination, that the Arminians were on what their Protestant contemporaries regarded as the wrong side.[139]

The "wrong side" here is, of course, Rome, but in the contemporary political climate, it was also Spain and France, the focus of England's military efforts (and failures) in the late 1620s.

The question of Montagu and encroaching Arminianism became a parliamentary issue in the 1620s that was intimately bound up with war with Spain and France. Paradoxically, as Russell observes, one of the difficulties for Charles "was that if he supported Arminians and war with Spain together, those who were his natural supporters in foreign affairs were his natural opponents in religion."[140] Given this, it is understandable why the ideal situation would have been to put an end to the issue altogether by silencing the dispute. When the 1625 Parliament sought to bring Montagu before them to answer charges of dividing the Church and tolerating popery, Charles attempted to diffuse the issue by intervening on Montagu's behalf. As the King's servant, Montagu was not required to appear before Parliament. Charles also refused until the very end of the session to address parliamentary grievances on religion, and when he did, it was solely on the matter of recusancy.[141] When Parliament met again in 1626 the issue of Montagu's books persisted, but Charles dissolved Parliament before a scheduled conference between the Lords and Commons could determine the matter. The 1626 session had been

particularly contentious, not because of religion, but because of impeachment proceedings against Buckingham, which took precedence over supply. Even so, the barrage of books against Montagu that had appeared
during the parliamentary session sufficiently intensified the sense of strife.

By the time Parliament was summoned in 1628 circumstances had
changed. Russell refers to this period as "The crisis of 1626–28," which
derived, he says from" England's administrative inability to fight a war."[142]
In October 1626 in the face of Spanish threats of war, Charles called for his
subjects to loan him money, not as a precedent but until Parliament could
conveniently be called.[143] When the loan met with resistance, Laud directed the clergy to preach on the necessity of obeying the King. In February
1627 Robert Sibthorpe preached a sermon at the Northampton assizes that
assured damnation to "Puritan" rebels who in resisting the King resisted
"the power and ordinance of God."[144] In July 1627 the royal chaplain Roger
Maynwaring preached two sermons that likewise affirmed the King's
divine right and equated disobedience to the King with disobedience to
God. Laud shepherded both men's sermons into print (despite Archbishop
Abbot's refusal to license Sibthorpe's), and they were printed by the King's
command. Despite such propaganda efforts, the loan met with continuing
resistance, which led Charles to arbitrarily imprison refusers. Furthermore,
the forced billeting of soldiers in people's homes intensified discontent.
When Parliament convened in 1628 the question of subjects' rights was
foremost, and according to Russell, "there was a remarkable degree of
unanimity in concentrating on the four which ultimately found their
way in to the Petition of Right: the Forced Loan, arbitrary imprisonment,
billeting of soldiers, and the use of martial law."[145] In addition to this,
several MPs felt that the rise of Arminianism constituted an equal threat to
the liberty of the subject.[146] The Committee on Religion added the
sermons of Sibthorpe and Maynwaring to their agenda against Montagu.

It must have been quite perplexing to be a publisher or an author during
this time of "crisis," especially since so many contradictory impulses
affected print culture. The 1626 proclamation had prohibited writing
that differed from the established doctrine of the Church of England,
but the question of orthodoxy was contested and books on both sides
appeared in print. The ecclesiastical licensing establishment was perceived
as becoming more restrictive, but books on both sides were approved for
print. Despite the paradoxical condition of simultaneous liberty and
anxiety, few books were actually suppressed, and those that were differed
little from those that were not. It is no wonder then that in 1628 printers
and authors took greater liberties – and ecclesiastical licensing became

more restrictive. The percentage of books that received official authorization declined from 74 percent to 47 percent. This suggests that the
ecclesiastical licensers were becoming more rigorous – or at least were
perceived as being so. Even though the total number of religious books
increased from 89 to 105 in 1628, the number of books printed for the first
time declined. In 1627 70 percent of the religious books printed were first
editions; this declined to 54 percent in 1628. The number of religious books
that can be identified with Calvinists – conforming and otherwise –
increased only slightly, from 63 to 68 percent. The number of these
books that were authorized, however, declined from two thirds in 1627 to
just over 40 percent. The kinds of religious books that appeared in print in
1628 changed little from 1627, except for one thing – open controversy,
which in 1627 had subsided (with the exception of Calvinist jabs at their
opponents buried in devotional or anti-Catholic writing), once again
erupted. This time, however, the issue was not predestination, but ceremonialism and the nature of the Church.

John Cosin's *A Collection of Private Devotions*, which appeared in 1627,
provoked two responses, both in 1628: Henry Burton's *A tryall of Private
Devotions or A Diall for the Houres of Prayer*, and William Prynne's
A Briefe Survay and Censure of Mr Cozens his Couzening Devotions.
Cosin's book of devotion displays continuity between Rome and the
Church of England that is apparent in the book's full title imprint:
"*A Collection of Private Devotions in the Practice of the Ancient Church,
Called the Houres of Prayer. As they were much after this maner published by
Authoritie of Q. Eliz, 1560*." From the time of the "primitive" Church
particular prayers had been designated for certain hours, and a book that
contained these prayers was called a "book of hours." The first known book
of hours was one associated with the Rule of St. Benedict in the eighth
century. Primers (as books of hours were called in England) continued to
be published after the Reformation, although 1560 appears to be the latest
date of publication – perhaps because the market for them diminished.
Cosin's decision to title his devotional book "Houres of Prayer" hearkens
back to the pre-Reformation Church, an idea that is reinforced by
referring to the "Practice of the Ancient Church." Cosin's publication
strategy is thus every bit as ideologically motivated as Sparke's titular
"Seven Sermons" had been. That Cosin expected this book to be provocative may be seen in the unusual imprimatur printed on the back of the title
page: "The Approbation, FEB XXII, 1626 I have read over this Book, which
for the encrease of private Devotions, I think may well be printed; and
therefore doe give Licence for the same. GEO:London." While Laud would

require that the ecclesiastical imprimatur be printed inside of books once he became Archbishop of Canterbury, prior to that a printed imprimatur was not only unusual but totally unnecessary. Not serving an obligatory function, this imprint seems to be performing other kinds of work – both ideological and bibliographical. It both foregrounds the importance of ecclesiastical licensing and advances the book's ideological agenda, and, perhaps inadvertently, in linking the two underscores the ideological end of religious licensing. Despite positioning itself as authoritative and authorized, according to one contemporary report, the book was called in because of objections to a prayer for the soul of the deceased, an error which was blamed on the printer. (Prayers for the souls of the dead were associated with the Roman Catholic doctrine of purgatory, which had been repudiated by the Articles of Religion.) Although the corrections were made, the first impression containing the prayer continued to be sold "almost in every shop in London," suggesting that both versions continued to be printed.[147]

Clearly ceremonialist in its approach, Cosin's book opened with a calendar of saints' days and a table of moveable feasts. In addition to a form of worship for each of the liturgical hours, the book contained seven penitential psalms, a litany, collects for Sundays and Holy Days – liturgical days and years – prayers before and after Eucharist, a form for confession, prayers for the King and Queen, prayers for ember days, prayers for the sick, prayers at the hour of death, and the prayer for the soul mentioned above. An address from the printer to the reader anticipated and sought to contain whatever "reproachfull imputation of waymaking to Popish Devotion and apish imitation of Romish superstition" the book might elicit by defending the book's "Collector . . . & others that were therewith acquainted" as being "as ready to engage their credits, and lives, in defence of the Faith of the present Church of England, by Law established, and in opposition of Popery, and Romish superstitions as any others."[148] Cosin rightly anticipated the kind of objections his book would provoke.

Burton's epistle dedicatory, "To the Most Blessed and Beloved Spouse of Jesus Christ, the Church of England, my deare Mother," offers *Of private Devotions* as proof of the errant ways of one of her sons who "goeth about to reduce you to an union with the church of *Rome*, as your only Mother, & to entertaine againe a conformitie and communion with her in her superstitious Rites and Ceremonies."[149] Burton objects that other sons, besides Cosin, "have already dared to add to the *Communion* booke; as the whole forme of the consecration of Archbishops, Bishops, Priests, & Deacons," and if it please you but to make search, you shall find in the great printing house at *London* a Communion Booke, wherin the Author of the booke of *private Devotions* (and I saw it with mine eyes) hath in sundry place noted with his owne hand (as they say) how he would have the Communion booke altered; as in the *Rubrick* or *Calendar* he tells where and how he would have such a Saints day called, and where he would have red letters, put for the blacke, and so to canonize more Holidayes for you to observe. Also throughout the Booke, where he finds the word *Minister*, he would have *Priest* put in stead thereof; such an enemy is he to the very name of *Minister*, as if he would have the world believe, he had rather be a popish Priest, then a Minister of the better Testament.[150]

While ostensibly addressing the Church, Burton's book directly appeals to the King and Parliament "now assembled" "that an Act of ratification may be decreed for the Religion hitherto maintained; and an Act of Prohibition for the suppressing of all Popish & Arminian bookes henceforth."[151]

Burton frames his objections to Cosin in a dialogue between two court ladies, Curia, who has given the book as a gift, and Charis, who received it. Charis expresses wonder that the book is so well received at court, and Curia responds that Protestants at court "are in a great strait" faced with "on the one side ... importune impossibilities" and on the other "Romane Catholicke Ladyes ... with their exemplary practice of pietie and devotion." Charis replies, "Madam, all such Romish practice of devotion is not worth Godamercie, or that it should stand in the least competition, or comparison with true devotion."[152] Lady Curia then reads "the Writing of M. Iohannes here set downe; concerning the Booke intituled, *A Collection of Private Devotions*: or, *The Howres of Prayer*." Besides the usual remarks about saints, seven sacraments, and so forth, Burton's principal objections are Cosin's abusive use of the precedent of devotional works printed during the reign of Elizabeth and his slight to those who in observing the sabbath "offend under a pretence of serving God more strictly then others (especially for hearing and meditating of Sermons) doe up their Fasts, and certain Judaizing observations condemne the joyfull festivitie of this high Holy day, which the Church allowes as well for the necessarie recreation of the body in due time, as for the Spirituall exercises of the Soule."[153] Given the centrality to Calvinists of the word truly preached, Cosin could not have expected such a remark to go unnoticed.

Cosin, however, must have been surprised by Burton's exercise in textual scholarship. Burton objected to Cosin's marginal comment that his book was from "The Horary set forth with the Queenes authority, 1560. and renewed 1573. imprinted with priviledge at London, by William Seers."[154]

Burton turns to "copies of those Moth eaten bookes" to discover a 1564 edition which he compares with the 1560 and 1573 editions to find

the last very different from the first, not onely in their forme and matter, but in their Title. For the first, in 1560 is intiluled [*sic*], *Horarium*: but the two succeeding, the one 1564 and the other in 1573. are intituled *Preces privata* &c. The *Horarium* indeed setteth downe the houres of prayer; but the latter bookes recommend onely Morning and Evening prayer, with their matter and forme, together with a short forme of prayer at rising, and going to bed; but without prescribing at what houres.[155]

By saying that his Book of Devotions essentially had the imprimatur of Elizabethan Protestantism, Cosin was advancing the position of Durham House that their views reflected the Church of England orthodoxy. The case Burton makes here is that Elizabethan orthodoxy looked considerably different from the version of it Cosin was advancing.

Even more directly than Burton's *Tryall of Private Devotions*, Prynne's *A Briefe Survay and Censure of Mr Cozens his Couzening Devotions* addresses the Parliament "now assembled" in its dedication and commends them for their "pious zeale, and zealous pietie, in questioning some Popish and Arminian Bookes, which have been lately published ... inexpiable blemish of our orthodox and Apostolicall Religion."[156] He writes both to animate them further and to assist them in identifying "virulent and popish poison, which is couched in the veines, and cloaked under the Coule, and Saint-like habit of those new Devotions, which now expect, nay neede, your doome and censure."[157]

Prynne's objections, including misappropriating the Elizabethan prayer book, agree with Burton's, except that at the book's end he sets up parallel columns, one with Cosin's prayers, the other with prayers taken from a Roman devotional book entitled, according to Prynne, "Our Ladyes Prier." Besides calling on the current Parliament to add Cosin's book to those that already had warranted their censure, Prynne remarks on the lamentable publishing conditions in London for "orthodox writers." The "swaying, great, and zealous Prelates" are patronizing "popish" books, and instead of supporting "Answering, and inhibiting them" as they should, "not onely deny to licence, but likewise diligently suppresse and intercept all Answers and Replies unto them, as the intercepting Mr. Burtons Answer at the Presse, and the detaining of the Copie of this my present Censure in the Licensers hands, who will neither licence nor deliver it."[158]

In April Cosin complained to Laud about the "two barking libellors" whose "licentioius [*sic*] libels" had been "lately printed without license." He says he will not answer them, but (as he is "bound") will leave their "chastisement" to Laud, whose "government & authoritie as they have so notoriously & improvidently also abused." With regard to the accusations of altering the prayer book, he says that he has, indeed, marginally noted directions to the printers "to be of helpe to them in amending of such faults & omissions in their several volumes for which they had been a little before schooled by your lordship." Cosin appeals to Laud for his continuing protection and that of His Majesty.[159] By labeling the books against him as unlicensed "libels," Cosin calls for action against Prynne and Burton on two accounts. As noted earlier, libels – attacks on persons – were actionable at law, and Prynne's naming of Cosin might technically be construed as libel – even if his accusations would not have come within libel's most common definitions (which receive further consideration in the next chapter). Printing without ecclesiastical license, however, was becoming increasingly prevalent, as we have seen. Cosin's letter also points to Laud's interest in printing. Laud had directed the King's Printers in amending the Book of Common Prayer; and Cosin regards him as possessing some authority over printing. In April Laud had been sworn as a Privy Councillor, and on July 1 Charles submitted the *congé d'élire* to the Dean and Chapter of London, requesting Laud's election as Bishop of London. As Bishop of London, Laud would assume principal authority for authorizing books and controlling the press. In the past this authority had been shared with the Archbishop of Canterbury, but in June of 1628, Archbishop Abbot was still suffering the eclipse of his prestige at court, a consequence of having refused license to Sibthorpe's sermon. From Prynne's account, Laud responded promptly to Cosin's interest in seeing the offenses against him "revenged." The sales of both his and Burton's books were stayed.

It would appear from the circumstances in which Prynne's and Burton's books were suppressed – as "revenge" for their offenses – that something unusual was happening. While this act of censorship may be regarded simply as an effort to control controversy, especially important in this time of Parliament, other unlicensed and unauthorized books, many with claims of growing Arminianism, did not meet with similar restraints. Even though their principal focus was challenging Cosin's Arminianism, both Prynne and Burton called upon the 1628 Parliament to direct its attention to resolving the religious problem. They were not alone. One of the godly set such store in the 1628 Parliament remedying the growth of Arminianism that he warned his errant son (who had gotten into some trouble at school): "If this Parliament have not a happy conclusion, the sin is yours."[160] Facing war with Spain and a country troubled by the forced loan, when Charles summoned Parliament in 1628, he also called for a public fast to obtain God's blessing on its proceedings. 1628 saw the publication of several sermons preached at the fast, mostly admonishing repentance and godly living. Jeremiah Dyke's fast sermon preached to the Commons was, however, different. He warned that the cause of God's displeasure with England – a displeasure that could be seen in the successes of her enemies – came from "the growth of Popery and Idolatry" and "the departure of our old Truth in the increase of Arminianism."[161] He admonished Parliament to pray, to make warlike provision and preparation, and to fast. "Yet," he said, "if Reformation be neglected, there is vanity in all these."[162] He asked Parliament to "Keepe our old God, and our old truth,"[163] to purge God's house, to provide "an able preaching Ministery," and to rid the land of the "Romish Locusts" that "goe about to draw away men from obedience both to God and the King."[164] Dyke's sermon, which subsequently appeared in print and was entered in the Stationers' Registers but not authorized, raised no objections. While Burton's and Prynne's appeal to Parliament to act on encroaching Arminianism may have struck a common chord among Calvinists in Parliament, the King had not summoned Parliament to discuss religion. Burton's and Prynne's books were fueling a fire that Charles and his ministers wanted put out so they could proceed to the important question of supply. The cross purposes of Charles and the 1628 Parliament could not have been made more clear than when, as one of its first actions, the Commons censured Maynwaring for his printed sermons, and sought to proceed further against Montagu.

While the King met parliamentary demands to suppress Maynwaring's book (he did so by proclamation on June 24, 1628), he refused to concede to their interest in seeing Montagu punished, and, instead, on July 4, 1628, rewarded him with the bishopric of Chichester. On July 18 he presented Maynwaring to the rectory of Stanford Rivers, which Montagu's elevation left vacant. In 1628 the King commanded that the Articles of Religion, approved by the 1562 Convocation, be reprinted along with his declaration, "That the Articles of the Church of England (which have been allowed and authorized theretofore, and which Our Clergie generally have subscribed unto) doe containe the true doctrine of the Church of England." The King's declaration allows that there have been some differences, though "ill raised," but takes the clergy's subscription as evidence that they "all agree in the true usuall literall meaning of the sayd articles." Even so, the declaration charges "that no man hereafter shall either print or preach, to draw the Article aside any way, but shall submit to it in the plaine and full meaning thereof: And shall not put his owne sense or Comment to bee the meaning of the Article, but shall take it in the literall and Grammaticall sense." The consequence of violating this was "censure in our Commission Ecclesiasticall."[165] Charles's effort once again to silence disputation responded to more than the continuing controversy on fine points of predestination.

BOOKS ON THE TRUE CHURCH

While Prynne and Burton had not actually disputed fine points of theology in their responses to Cosin, further theological controversy – still in part in response to Montagu – emerged in 1628. A debate on whether or not Rome was a true church, and on the continuity of the true Church within the Church of England, as we have seen, had long been an important question – and it was one in which objection was taken to Montagu's position. In the 1625 Parliament in a report from a subcommittee on religion, the recorder had objected that Montagu's writings had claimed that the Church of Rome was a true church: "The whole frame of the book was to encourage Popery; in maintaining the Papists to be the true church, and that they differ not from us in any fundamental point."[166] In 1627 in an effort to reconcile the differences brought on by Montagu's books, *The Olde Religion*, written by Bishop of Exeter Joseph Hall, appeared from the press. Hall was not just any Calvinist; Montagu saw him as one of his principal opponents, who had accused him of doctrinal error to Parliament.[167] The occasion of Hall's book was his appointment in a diocese that had for some time been vacant. In the dedicatory epistle, Hall told his new cure that he has been assured that "false Teachers, catching the Fore-locke of occasion, have been busie in scattering the tares of errours amongst you." To prevent their success and to "winne Soules" not "gall them," Hall has written this book, "bending my stile against Popish Doctrine, with such Christian moderation, as may argue zeale without malice."[168]

The "olde religion," Hall argued, could be found in the Church of England's Articles; the practices in the Church of Rome that differed from those Articles were new. Among Rome's innovations were justification by inherent righteousness (the doctrine of merit, transubstantiation) "halfe-communion," "Missal Sacrifice," indulgences and purgatory, divine service in an unknown tongue, sacramental confession, absolution before satisfaction, invocation of saints, seven sacraments, and the Bishop of Rome's claims for universal headship, infallibility, superiority, and papal dispensation. As part of his moderate approach, Hall allowed that

under the Papacie is true Christianitie, yea the very kernel of Christianities ...
under the Papacy may be as much good as it selfe is evill; Neyther doe we censure
that Church for what it hath not, but for what it hath: Fundamental truth is like
that Maronaean wine, which if it bee mixed with twenty times so much water
holds his strength ... No more doth the Romane, loose the claime of a true visible
Church, by her manifold and deplorable corruptions; her unfoundness is not lesse
apparent, then her being; If she were once the Spouse of Christ, and her adulteries
are knowne, yet the divorse is not ...[169]

Hall's generosity towards Rome did not go unnoticed by Henry Burton,
even though both were Calvinists.

Burton's *Seven Vials*, while not properly an "answer" to Hall, disputes
Hall's nod to Rome as "a true visible Church." Burton's book is a commentary on the prophecy in Revelation 15 and 16 in which the contents of
seven vials are poured out in preparation for a time when "God shalbe
present with his Church, in a more conspicuous manner."[170] In the pour-
ing out of the seven vials, which in Burton's account occupies the period of
time from Luther to the near future, the errors of Rome (the marks of the
Beast) become more and more visible, and the dominion of the true
Church gets closer and closer. Requisite for Burton's prophecy, however,
is that Rome be the false Church, the domain of Antichrist. According to
Burton,

if we yield the Church of Rome to be a true, or truly visible Church, we may as well
call it a true Church. For how can wee call that a true Church, which is not truly
visible? And if a Church be truly visible, what letts, that it should not be a true
Church of God, or at least in mans judgement?[171]

If Rome lacks the marks of the true Church, as defined by the Church of
England's homilies as *"Pure and sound Doctrine*: the Sacraments ministred
according to Christs holy Institution and the right use of Ecclesiastical
Discipline," then it cannot be a true church. Burton rejects Hall's metaphor of the Maroneaen wine by saying Rome's innovations have poisoned
the wine, and calls for the "Reverend author" to give a "humble and
ingenious Retraction."[172]

When the second edition of *Olde Religion* appeared, Hall added an
"Advertisement" to clarify his position, and shortly thereafter published
The Reconciler. Hall's *Reconciler* very cautiously and carefully explains that
what he had meant to say was that the Roman Church was "True in
existence, but false in Beleefe"; then, using the criteria formulated by the
German theologian, Girolamo Zanchi, he describes a true church.[173]
Feeding the controversy further, Robert Butterfield's *Maschil* (1629) and
The State of the now-Roman church (1629) by Bishop Hall's chaplain, Hugh

Cholmely, defend Hall from Burton's criticisms, but because these books are far more conciliatory to Rome than the *Olde Religion*, they prompted responses. Thomas Spencer replied to Butterfield in *Maschil Unmasked* (1629), and Burton replied to both Butterfield and Cholmely in *Babel No Bethel* (1629), although he indicated in a dedicatory epistle to Bishop Hall that he accepted the position set forth in *The Reconciler*.[174] Cholmely, however, according to Burton, "in stead of vindicating" Hall, "who denieth the church of Rome to be an Orthodox or true believing Church," forgets himself and Hall too "to vindicate the Church of Rome, and to prove it to be an Orthodox Church."[175] Among all these, only Hall's and Cholmely's books were authorized, although Burton objected that Butterfield's was as well.[176] It would be an overstatement to say that the essence of these books lies in splitting hairs about the definitions of Greek, Latin, and English words. Although controversial in tenor, this is not an Arminian/Calvinist controversy. This debate must be placed within the context of a nation anxious about Roman Catholicism. Burton's epistle dedicatory to Parliament even suggests that England's recent military defeats may be a consequence of insufficient care for the Church. Spencer calls on Parliament to punish offenders who oppose the Articles of Religion. The rationale for his demand also reveals anxiety about the times: "If Opposers in matters of faith bee not reckned offendours, then Opposers in matters of State must be held innocent, seeing the first is of more dangerous conse-quence then the second. If we may oppose the State, who will obey? seeing liberty is better fancied then subjection, If wee are freed from obedience, then farewell government."[177] Spencer and Burton address Parliament, again in session in 1629, because the question of religion still has not been resolved, and both appeal to Parliament to, in Burton's words, administer a cure because the circumstances require "present remedy": "This your wisdoms observing you happily began with the Symptome; and now remaines the maine disease to bee cured, which is, the State of Religion."[178]

One aspect of the controversy that followed Hall's *Olde Religion* was that even though this was not properly a Calvinist/Arminian debate, Calvinism and Arminianism were very much in play. Burton identified the views of Cholmely and Butterfield with Arminianism, and Hall engaged in self-justification in order to remove any taint of Arminianism. For under-standing licensing and censorship, however, few examples are more val-uable than those surrounding Bishop Hall's *The Reconciler*. On April 20, 1629 articles were objected in the High Commission against several London Stationers for "unlicensed printing," including Nathaniel Butter

for his involvement with *The Reconciler*, which had been entered in the
Stationers' Register on January 12, 1629. The entry named Hall as the
authorizer. While the next chapter will consider printing cases in High
Commission and Star Chamber, the articles against Butter are relevant here
because they reveal contemporary thinking on controlling Arminian/
Calvinist writing. According to the articles, Butter had given *The
Reconciler* to William Stansby to print with his assurance that "it was all
lawfully Licensed." The articles remind Butter that

within these three yeares last past you for your part as in like manner all others that
are free of the Company of Stationers of the Citty of London have bene often
advised & admonished & especially once within this half yeare last past by or from
some in authority not to print or cause to be printed ... any unlawfull or
unlicensed [unauthorized] book.

Butter's real offense in this case had been that he caused to be printed a
passage in *The Reconciler* "which the licenser did not allow of nor approve
and which the author of the said booke had formerly obliterated and put
out with his owne hand."[179] At some time, then, after January 12, Laud's
chaplain, Thomas Turner, perused the book, apparently judging Hall's
license to be insufficient, or, perhaps, at Hall's request. (Prior to this time,
it had not been unusual for prominent clergymen to be identified as the
authorizer of their own works.) Since *The Reconciler* was printed in both its
censored and uncensored versions, we can see Laud's chaplain's intentions.
Nearly one hundred pages, which Hall had certainly intended to have printed
since they vindicated him of the taint of Arminianism, were cut from
the original book. Hall had sent a manuscript of his intended publication –
an address to the Earl of Norwich discussing Zanchi's marks of the
true Church – to four prominent Calvinist ministers: Bishop Morton of
Coventry and Lichfield, Bishop Davenant of Salisbury, Dr. Prideaux of
Oxford, and Dr. Primerose, Minister of the French Church in London.
Each had written a responsive opinion of Hall's orthodoxy intended
for print. Laud's chaplain had not only struck these out, but he prohibited
the epistle dedicatory to the "Christian Reader" in which Hall expressed
chagrin that even after all his efforts to quell dispute and restore peace in
the Church he is "not a little troubled to see the peace of the church yet
disquieted with personall, and unkinde dissertations."[180] Hall also had
maintained in the epistle that his view of the Church was entirely consistent
with the Articles of the Church of England, and used the letters between
himself and the Calvinist theologians to prove it. Without actually violating the 1626 Proclamation, the complete *Reconciler* made the case that

Hall's Calvinist views were, indeed, the orthodox views of the Church of England, and his letters and the distinguished theologians' testimonials confirmed that these views were more widely accepted than might be suggested by radicals like Prynne and Burton. While Butter's reprinting of "passages" struck out by Turner was certainly an egregious violation, the nature of the censored material points to the chaplain's interest in suppressing writing that suggested that the Church of England opposed Arminianism.[181]

Another publisher the High Commission singled out for unlicensed (unauthorized) printing on this occasion was Michael Sparke. Like Butter, Sparke published books that were anti-Arminian, as well as unauthorized. One part of Sparke's answer to the articles (all of which the next chapter considers more fully) shows something of how the London printers were being monitored. One of the articles against him had charged that he had "heard a letter read openly in the Stationers hall sent from the Secretary of State concerning the *Spy* and . . . other schismaticall and hereticall books" which he had been warned not to sell or "meddle with."[182] Compared to *The Spy*, which was genuinely objectionable for its criticism of the government of Church and State, the books Sparke printed, as he maintained, were not "contrary to the established doctrine and discipline of the Church of England."[183] Besides upholding ecclesiastical licensing and illustrating the nature of books that should not be printed, the High Commission started watching authors more closely. Burton mentions having been called before the Bishop of London on at least three occasions, once regarding *The Bayting of the Popes Bull*, and twice regarding *Israel's Fast*,[184] but in October 1628 he was summoned before the High Commission for his writing. Prynne met the same fate, he claimed, after the end of the 1629 Parliament. Such proceedings against printers and authors in 1628 and 1629 indicate that in late 1628 and early 1629 the government was intensifying its surveillance of the press. These actions were accompanied by small changes in ecclesiastical licensing brought about by Laud's translation to the London see. Despite the initial changes that came with Laud's appointment, once Abbot's chaplain, John Jeffray, began vetting books in 1629, publishers found it easier to obtain licenses for books by godly authors.

The effect of Laud's appointment to London, the King's declaration on the Articles of Religion, and increased government surveillance of printing can be seen in the kinds and numbers of books printed and authorized in 1629. In 1629 a group of London printers petitioned Parliament, complaining that the restraints the late proclamations put on printing together with

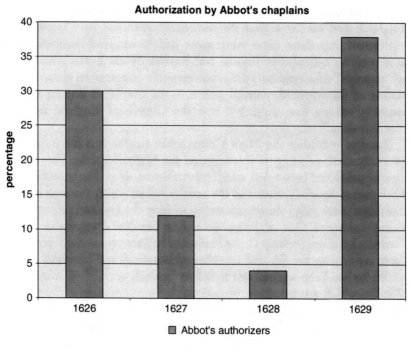

Figure 2

current ecclesiastical licensing practices placed them in dire economic straits.[185] The printers must have perceived greater restraint on printing than actually existed since in 1629 more religious books were printed than in either 1627 or 1628. Indeed, religious printing increased 15 percent each year after the 1626 proclamation. In 1629 the number of these that were authorized increased 9 percent over the previous year. In 1629 65 percent of the books printed were by Calvinist authors. (In 1627 it had been 63 percent and in 1628 68 percent.) The kind of Calvinist books differed little from what had appeared in the previous two years. Besides the controversial books we have been considering, the publication of the Church of Ireland's Calvinistic religious articles lent weight to the Calvinist case for orthodoxy. Dyke's fast sermon appeared in print along with his book *Good Conscience*. Authorization for these books, more frequent than in the previous year, rose from 42 to 65 percent. This would look like greater compliance with demands that books be seen by the ecclesiastical licensers, except that just over half of these books were seen by the current ecclesiastical licensing

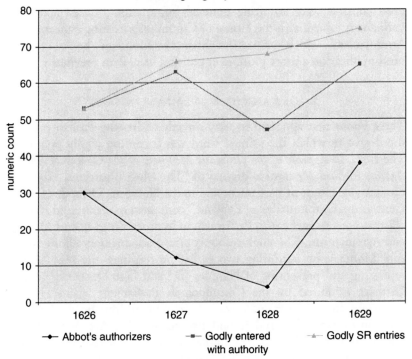

Figure 3

establishment. In 1629 two thirds of the godly books printed had their initial publication before 1625. The proceedings at Dort were reprinted. Biblical exegesis and treatises by Ezekial Culverwell and James Ussher joined devotional works by Arthur Dent, William Pemble, and Thomas Taylor to edify the elect. It would seem, then, that claims by the likes of Prynne and Burton that books on their side could not be printed overstated the case, though obtaining authorization for them was not particularly easy. Likewise, their claims that the presses overflowed with Arminian books were overstated, even if books like Cosin's *Devotions* (1628), Thomas Jackson's *Treatise of the Divine Essence* (1629), and the 1629 Laud/Buckeridge edition of Andrewes's sermons were so visible and of such importance that they seemed to overwhelm the publishing world. What statistics on publishing and licensing and my survey of books printed in 1629 do not reveal, however, is that by 1629 questions of printing and press controls were acquiring political importance. Printed appeals to Parliament joined with the House of Commons's existing concern about Arminianism – which had been heightened by Montagu's books – to make press publication a more prominent political issue than previously.

BOOKS AND THE 1629 PARLIAMENT

Three books that appeared in 1629 directly addressing Parliament show the degree to which the printed word was becoming highly politicized. The first, *An Appeale of the Orthodox Ministers of the Church of England Against Richard Montagu* addressed to "The Most Illustrious, High, and Honourable Court of Parliament and to the Nobilitie, Orthodox Clergie, Gentry, and Communaltie of England," contains a moderate and reasoned effort to encourage the 1629 Parliament in its proceedings against Montagu and Arminianism. The book recounts prior parliamentary efforts to censure Montagu by reprinting two earlier proceedings: the 1625 "Act for repressing and preventing of Haresies [*sic*] and false Doctrines" and the "Articles exhibited by the Commons in Parliament against Richard Montagu" from March 1626, with the comment "But by the fatall dissolution of those first and second Parlaments, that Act, and that your Charge in those Articles, slept." Similar efforts in the 1628 Parliament were unsuccessful "by reason of other matters of high consequence, and the suddaine Prorogation of that Parliament."[186] The next document that *An Appeale* prints is a set of objections drawn up by "a Doctour of the Arches" protesting the election of Montagu to Chichester. In the court proceedings, according to *An Appeale*, the objections were set aside because they were not "in due forme of Law."[187] That the book's presentation of these objections and Montagu's confirmation proceedings are its real focus becomes clear in the words of the appeal:

> Wee most humbly supplicate that this new made Byshop Montagu, who though hee now raungeth him selfe amongst Spirituall Lords and temporall Peeres in the Upper HOUSE of this high Assemblie of Parlament, may yet bee taken into consideration ... And that hee having deserved (as we conceive) rather Fire and faggot than futher Preferment, may come maturely to be censured and degraded ... and his pernicious Bookes to be at length called-in and burned.[188]

An Appeale concludes with a letter to Montagu requesting him to recant and a "Briefe Supplication of the Ministers of the Church of Scotland" concurring with the terms of *An Appeale*. The publisher's postscript envisions a plaque affixed to the House reading "Sacred to Memories and to

Posteritie, the (Long Expected) Happie Parliament" to celebrate the united hearts of King and Parliament that in unanimous agreement reformed "matters now much amisse in Church and Common-wealth."[189] This book reveals not only how hopeful conforming ministers were that the political process would remedy conditions they found objectionable, but also how confident they were that the printed word could effect political action. The publishers understood, however, that counseling Parliament in print might warrant sanctions; although printed in London, the book bore the false imprint "Edenburgh."

The second book which called upon the 1629 Parliament to act on the religious question was William Prynne's *Anti-Arminianisme: The Church of Englands Old Antithesis to the New Arminianism*. Its title page bore the imprint "London" and the year but did not name printer or publisher, although Prynne signed the epistle dedicatory. The book's purpose was to provide an "anti-Arminian index" that relied on the ancient documents of the Church of England (the Articles of Religion, the homilies, the Book of Common Prayer, etc.) as a guide, he tells Parliament, "to further your religious and happy Proceedings, in the discovery and suppression of those Hereticall and Grace-destroying Arminian novelties."[190] The book is similar to those that Yates, Featly, and Carleton had written in 1626 with much the same decorous tone. This, however, is very much a lawyer's book, since the material is presented as preparation for a trial. In his dedicatory epistle to "the High and Honourable Court of Parliament," Prynne reminds them that "the onely infallible way to determine, to find out the ancient, the undoubted Doctrines of our Church, is to compare them with the Rules at Triall."[191] Prynne is not here totally without rancor – he calls on Parliament to discover the protectors of "our Arminian mungrell rabble"[192] – but he attempts to defend himself from accusations that his is an attack on the Church hierarchy by a second epistle dedicatory to the bishops, which in a deferential voice asks them to uphold the Articles "to perpetuate the dignity, the respect of your Episcopal Jurisdiction, which hath grown distasteful unto many through the defaults of some."[193] Prynne's book, which was one of the books for which he was summoned by the High Commission following the 1629 Parliament, expresses a confidence not only in Parliamentary jurisdiction in religious matters (he provides precedents to prove it) but in Parliament's will to resist Arminian innovations.

Prynne's *Anti-Arminianisme* was probably the last book written against Arminianism that was neither libelous nor treasonous. The last of the three books directed at the 1629 Parliament possessed none of this moderation. Alexander Leighton's *An Appeal to the Parliament; or Sions Plea aginst the*

Prelacie played a far more dangerous game than either Prynne or the orthodox ministers. During the time that Leighton was seeing his book through the press in Utrecht, he was preparing to be ordained in the English separatist church there. Letters to his son and wife indicate that he set considerable store in his book appearing while Parliament was in session, though he understood the inherent dangers in the project.[194] Leighton promised Parliament that England's current woes resulted from "the fire of Gods wrath" that "will never cease till it hath consumed us from being a nation" if "our domineering nationall sinne be not removed."[195] That sin, according to Leighton, was the Church hierarchy: "If the Hierarchye be not removed, and the scepter of Christ's government, namely Discipline, advanced to its place, there can be no healing of our sore, no taking up of our controversie with God."[196] Leighton applied the arguments of important Reformation theologians against the Roman hierarchy to the English bishops because as "Mountigue [*sic*] proclaimeth" they follow "Arminianisme or blanched Popery."[197] He then proposed six means by which England may be rid of the "prelacie." Most likely Leighton's zeal would have led him to write such a book even if Montagu's books had not started a controversy. Leighton really was the "schismatical Puritan" that Montagu had accused the conforming Calvinists of being.

Leighton's book, which was intended to appear in England in March near the end of the 1629 parliament, had no impact on parliamentary proceedings since it appeared after Parliament was dissolved. It may, however, have heightened government anxieties about the dangers of print, especially given the tumultuous end of the 1629 Parliament where the leaders of the House of Commons were imprisoned for refusing the King's dismissal.[198] The sixth and last means Leighton proposed for removing the prelacy from England was "the continuance of a Parliament, till the tenets of the Hierarchie be tried":

The Kings royall word; the confirmation of the lawes, and giving of subsidies, imply a necessity of redresse of grievances; which cannot stand with the dissolveing of a Parliament, till reformation be effected ... Your Honours know, that everie dissolution of a Parliament, without real reformation, is against right, reason, & record ... this Court should continue sitting so long, as there were any matters belonging to this high Court to be determined.[199]

While the parallel between this and the concluding events of the 1629 Parliament looks today like historical irony, to Charles or his chief ministers who read Leighton's book, the parallel must have underscored the disturbingly disruptive power of the printed word. It is probably not a coincidence that following the 1629 Parliament the government turned increasingly to the courts to enforce licensing – as chapter 3 will show – and to punish errant writers like Leighton, who in 1630 was tried in the court of Star Chamber for seditious libel and condemned to the pillory and ten years in prison.

THE RHETORIC OF CENSORSHIP

This chapter began with Burton's complaint about the "the strange alter-ation of these times." What we have seen is that to some degree Burton was right – Calvinist and godly writers found it more difficult between 1625 and 1629 to obtain ecclesiastical licenses, and surveillance of printing seems to have increased. Censorship was not directed, as Lambert suggests, only at books that posed serious danger to the Church and State. Writings by bishops and chaplains to the Archbishop of Canterbury met with censor-ship. On the other hand, books by Calvinist and other godly writers – even some by non-conformists – accounted for most of the product of England's printing presses. That could not have happened if the kind of rigorous censorship Burton alleged actually existed. The really extraordinary "strange alteration of these times" was the degree to which printed texts and their control became a matter of interest. While Charles's predecessors had all engaged in censorship, the topic of ecclesiastical licensing and press control had never before become part of a broader political discussion. In the late 1620s the Commons exercised itself about condemning books, the court exercised itself about condemning books, and books, especially by Calvinists, exercised themselves about condemning books – everyone, it seems, was interested in whether or not books were being printed and authorized. During the seven-year period to which Burton referred there emerged in England a culture of censorship for which anti-Arminians like Burton were as responsible as the official system of restraints.

To many of the anti-Arminian books this chapter has considered are appended extensive preliminaries – addresses to Parliament, to the King, to "mother Church," to the Christian reader – that recount in considerable detail the Arminian campaign against those writers who only a few years before had been a part of the mainstream Church of England. The quotation from Henry Burton with which I began this chapter makes the case against the ecclesiastical licensing establishment repeated so often in these preliminaries – "formerly, not a Popish, nor Arminian booke durst peepe out; but now, such onely are countenanced and published, & Orthodox bookes suppressed." The Arminians' principal tool of abuse, according to the Calvinists, was the misuse of the King's proclamation intended "to establish and settle the ancient settled, received and approved Doctrine of the Church of England in peace and quiet."[200] The abusers were the ecclesiastical licensers. The objection is not to licensing per se, but to using licensing (silencing) as a means of establishing legitimate doctrine by fiat rather than by reasoned debate. In the second edition of *The Perpetuitie of a Regenerate Mans Estate*, Prynne questioned his opponent's claims that theirs was the ancient and settled doctrine of the Church by asking:

And if it bee the doctrine of our Church, why doe you not joyne issue on it, and put it to the triall? Why do you not answer and refute, but only labour to suppresse, the workes of those who doe oppose it, and challenge it as unsound? Indeed the truth is this: yo[u] know your cause is bad: you know that this your doctrine is but false and counterfeit, and quite repugnant to the doctrine of our Church: wherefore you dare not put it to the tryall, for feare it should bee proved to bee false.[201]

The language used here to question the Arminians reveals two entirely different epistemological systems that are in opposition: Calvinist epistemology espoused the word and debating the word; and the anti-Calvinists (Arminians) embraced silence.

Calvinist enthusiasm for the printed word dates from the early days of the Reformation. The printing press had provided the Reformers with both an effective medium for edifying the emerging Church of Christ and an efficient disciplinary tool for admonishing and correcting "severely" the existing Church of England. The Reformers' language relied on scriptural metaphor. From a historical perspective Christ and the Apostles had left the Church a healthy body sustained by scripture. The Popes of Rome in usurping authority from the biblical Church had poisoned the body's health. Those vestiges of Papacy that remained in the English Church – its "daungerous and desperate deseases" – had to be purged by the "wholesome hearbes" of scripture that could restore the biblical Church. The metaphor of the Church as a flock of lambs taken from Matthew 7:15, 16 ("Beware of false Prophets which come to you in Sheepes clothing, but inwardly they are ravening Wolves: Ye shall know them by their fruits") was used to condemn clerical practices in the English Church and served as an effective means to characterize the Church's vulnerability to ravenous predators – the Pope was the wolf ever outside the door, but hypocritical deceivers worked their ways inside the fold. In 1570 looking back to the

Marian martyrs, the Reformers could claim "by Gods power we have fought with the Wolfes of these & such like Popishe chaffe, & God hath given the victorie, we have nowe to do with the Foxes, let us not feare."[202] In 1628, looking at Arminian licensing practices, Burton said, "Here we come more plainly to discerne the Wolfe in Sheepes skinne, or in the Sheepherds cloke. For here he breakes down a gap, and whistles out the Sheepe, that straying, hee may devoure them."[203] In a 1629 prefatory letter to the bishops, Prynne reminds them, "You are the chiefe Pastors, and Shepheards of our Church; to guard, to rescue her from those wolves, those theeves, and robbers which seek for to devoure her."[204] While the Elizabethan Reformers had proposed herbs and purgatives to cleanse the Church of popery's relics, following another scripture, Calvinist writers in the late 1620s proposed eliminating licensing and the Arminians who employed it, using the language of Matthew 15:13, "Every plant which my heavenly Father hath not planted, shall be rooted out." Here Prynne appeals to Parliament to

Proceede, therefore as you . . . have already done: to inquire out the Heads, the Nurseries, rootes, and grand Protectors of our Popish, our Arminian mungrell rabble . . . and when you have once discovered them . . . it will be worth your labour to hew them downe with speede, both root and branch, at once . . . Strike therefore at the roots, as well as at the branches of these prevailing Factions.[205]

(The language of "root and branch" should not escape students of the Long Parliament.)

Part of the Calvinist opposition to Arminian silencing derived from a long tradition of printed controversy. From the earliest days of the English Reformation, Reformers wrote to the end that they might be answered *in print*. From the beginning, title page after title page carried the legend from Luke, "I told you, if those should holde their peace, the stones would cry" (19:40). Clearly Burton identified with this tradition when in 1628 in a preface opposing Arminian licensing he said, "I am the least, and unworthiest of all Gods Prophets. And some must speake, least the crying of the senselesse Stones should convince us of unfaithful cowardice . . ."[206] Luke's crying stones are especially relevant in a culture of censorship since the image represents religious truth's dependence on overcoming silence. In all the controversies during the reign of Elizabeth, even when books were censored, they were answered. The idea of suppressing legitimate religious disputation ran counter to the tradition of English Protestantism. No wonder Prynne could ask: "And if it bee the doctrine of our church, why doe you not joyn issue on it . . .?"

This attack in the late 1620s on ecclesiastical licensing is important to our understanding of early modern culture because its use of tropes, which had long been part of a Protestant imaginary, provides a language of radical change that politics appropriates in the 1640s. The great irony, of course, is that the attacks on licensing that characterized how impossible publishing Calvinist writings had become were appended to books extolling Calvinist doctrine. Clearly, the claims of suppression were exaggerated. Even though Laud's program for ecclesiastical licensing may have been more "thorough," more to the letter of the law, as we have seen, it was still ineffective in suppressing all undesirable books. Prynne, Burton, and Featly, to name but a few, flouted the Laudian licensing establishment. Featly veiled his attack in *Cygnea Cantio* by praising King James and showing how considerate James was in scrutinizing religious texts. In remembering the burning of a book by the Calvinist William Elton, however, Featly likened its censor to a "Popish shaveling Priest."[207] Prynne and Burton wrote to the King and Parliament as the protectors of the true Church. They wrote to expose a "faction," a malicious minority some of whom were prelates, but they did not write against episcopacy generally – at least until the mid 1630s. Although these Calvinists have been characterized by Stephen Foster as a Caroline underground, they regarded themselves as a disenfranchised majority who were victimized by a minority of popish bishops, and, in the 1620s at least, they were not underground. This persistence of Calvinist writers and the language used in their campaign against licensing helps to explain why the Star Chamber "show trials" in the 1630s failed to achieve their intended ends. Instead of impressing on the public the dangers of illegal printing and seditious writing, according to David Cressy, the Star Chamber trials, especially the 1637 trial of Burton, Bastwick, and Prynne, only vilified the Caroline regime.[208] The victims of censorship would become the martyrs of the English Civil War. Considerable contention exists regarding the relationship between political events in the 1620s, especially the Caroline Parliaments, and the political upheaval of the 1640s. Whether or not the events of the 1640s have their "roots" in the politics of the 1620s, what I have argued here is that continuity exists in the imaginative implications of censorship and the language of religious controversy. Free theological debate and a religious press free from an inequitable system of ecclesiastical licensing were as important to Church Calvinists in the 1620s as they would be to John Milton in the 1640s when he wrote *Areopagitica*.

CHAPTER 3

Transformational literalism: the reactionary redefinition of the courts of High Commission and Star Chamber

In *The Original and Growth of Printing* (1664) Richard Atkyns looked with considerable nostalgia to an earlier era – before the collapse of the court of Star Chamber – when an ordered kingdom derived from a controlled press. "Printing," he says, "is like a good Dish of Meat, which moderately eaten of, turns to the Nourishment and health of the Body; but immoderately, to Surfeits and Sicknesses: As the Use is very Necessary, the Abuse is very dangerous."[1] Atkyns had a ready means to control un unruly press – punishment. "How were the abuses [of printing] taken away in Queen Elizabeth, King James, and the beginning of King Charles his time, when few or no Scandals or Libels were stirring? Was it not by Fining, Imprisonment, Seizing the Books, and breaking the Presses of the Transgressors, by Order of Councel-Board?"[2] Despite Atkyns's nostalgia, in 1641 England was rife with criticism of both the Star Chamber and High Commission. Addressing Parliament, Charles Howard, Earl of Berkshire's remarks reflect the spirit of the times:

> Your Lordships well know, there was a statute framed, *tertio H7.* authorizing ... the Kings Councell to receive complaints upon Bill, or Information; and cite such parties to appear, as stand accused of any misdemeanour: And this was the Infancy of the Starre-Chamber ... from whence being altogether unlimited, it is growne a monster, and will hourely produce worse effects ...[3]

Berkshire's contemporaries in Parliament required little persuasion about what they regarded as the abuses in this court, and in the court of High Commission as well. On the third day of the Long Parliament's opening session amidst a debate about these courts, Mr. Grimston had remarked: "The Judges have overthrown the laws, and the Bishops the gospel."[4] Within a month the Commons established a committee to consider the jurisdiction and abuses of these courts.[5] The Long Parliament's decision ultimately to eliminate the courts of both Star Chamber and High Commission has indelibly colored the historical knowledge of these courts' procedures – especially their role in enforcing press censorship – largely because documentary evidence of their cases and procedures went the way of the courts.

The most prevalent view of the role of these courts in controlling the press is perhaps best summarized by Harold Weber. According to Weber, prior to 1641, when Parliament assumed the power to regulate the press, the monarchy had controlled the press: "the royal proclamation and order of the Star Chamber – which began as the king's Privy Council sitting in a judicial capacity – constituted the primary weapons in the campaign against unlicensed and unlawful printing."[6] In the hands of different historians, this account has met with refinements – and been put to multiple uses,[7] but its central features remain consistent: pre-print approval of printed works by government appointed censors (licensing), restraints on printing through decrees of the monarch's Privy Council (Star Chamber decrees), and prosecutions in the prerogative courts of Star Chamber and High Commission for seditious writing – or for violations of licensing, as Philip Hamburger has it[8] – and a certainty that between 1558 and 1640 these mechanisms operated with remarkable regularity and consistency. According to Hamburger, "the efficacy of the licensing laws was closely tied to the enforcement powers of the prerogative courts. Both Star Chamber and the Court of High Commission had jurisdiction over offences against the licensing laws, and their freedom from the restraints of common law procedures and the excessive bias of the judges ... made acquittals rare."[9]

As persistent and influential as this view of the relationship between censorship and the prerogative courts has been, it also has had its detractors – among them Sheila Lambert. Lambert says that while the "prerogative" courts of High Commission and Star Chamber may in part have been used to control radically dissident texts against the government, the "vast majority" of cases in these courts – even for libel – "were not brought by the Crown but by private individuals."[10] Star Chamber, according to Lambert, only took actions to shore up Elizabeth's 1559 licensing Injunction, and the High Commission was the principal instrument of government that heard disputes related to the press. Star Chamber had virtually nothing to do with monitoring the printed word except to issue decrees to regulate the trade.[11]

The contrary views in the debate on press control and the mechanisms of Tudor–Stuart Star Chamber and High Commission have not changed much over the three centuries since Berkshire and Atkyns – this because scholars tend to look at the mechanisms of press control in Tudor and early Stuart England as being a piece of whole cloth. Censorship, rather than being motivated by a pervasive government desire to control a new and unruly technology, was local and ad hoc. The mechanisms employed – with the exception of statutes that remained in force unless repealed – differed in kind and in time, especially in courts. In English jurisprudence each case brought before a court depends on the precedents of other cases for such things as jurisdiction, causes, pleadings, and so forth, and, in turn, any case creates new precedents for subsequent cases. While ostensibly the government of Charles I may be seen to have been entirely consistent in its control of the press with its predecessors – whether repressively or bene-volently – small refinements in pleadings, an extension of jurisdiction, and the denial of a prohibition all could change the law. Historian of Star Chamber Thomas Barnes gives a good explanation of how such a system worked.

Although the individual try-on does not have much future, a system of litigation that permits, indeed encourages, a constant refining of pleading by a process of mutation and variation on a theme raises the try-on from the plane of forensic tactics to the realm of judicial strategy. Add to such procedural openness, vitality, and suppleness a considerable inchoateness in substantive law and the try-on becomes the vehicle for legal change. In the early decades of the seventeenth century, the English legal system of litigation was a system in which the try-on was an accepted and wholly acceptable device.[12]

Although Charles I and his Archbishop of Canterbury, William Laud, maintained their orthodoxy and conservatism in all things religious and legal, the transformational literalism they employed in their legal "try-ons" created subtle alterations in the way the English legal system controlled the press during the reign of Charles I. This transformational literalism pro-duced change that operated so entirely within the system that scholars have overlooked it. Indeed, some have been misled to believe that Charles's principal ministers Stafford and Laud were simply "thorough."

Charles I and his closest advisors repudiated innovation in religion and state and repeatedly affirmed the King's conscientious adherence to the laws of the realm. In 1628, responding to objections to the King's imprison-ment of the men who refused to pay the forced loan, Lord Keeper Thomas Coventry, at the King's command, assured both Houses of Parliament that the King would govern by the laws and statutes of the realm and that his subjects could find "as much security in his royal word as in any law."[13] This speech also made it very clear that the King would permit no interpretation of law. Although Charles and Laud repeatedly insisted that nothing they did in Church or State constituted innovation, they read legal precedents so literally that their conservatism effectively produced extraordinary transformation. We can see how consciously this process worked on one occasion in 1629 when Laud, at that time Bishop of London, and the King had been discussing church matters, and the proposition of revising Elizabeth's 1559 Injunctions arose. Afterwards Laud wrote to Secretary of State Viscount Dorchester (Dudley Carleton) asking him to remind the King of this prospect. A few days later Laud wrote again to Dorchester voicing his opinion on the injunctions: while some pertained to particular conditions at the beginning of Elizabeth's reign, they were effectively regarded by lawyers during the reign of James "as ecclesiastical laws in force, though the Queen were dead," although, Laud added, he had no knowledge of how the lawyers would regard them now.[14] Nearly a month later Laud reported to Dorchester that he was less certain about using these injunctions since "there are divers other Canons & Constitutions made in the Queens tyme beside the Injunctions, all which must be taken into Consideration, or else the busines wil be very imperfit & . . . some things will fall out soe cross that the busines will be badly related . . ."[15] In these communications Laud definitely envisions some change or alteration transpiring, but one that will attend carefully to the interpretation of precedents from the reign of Elizabeth I. In the 1630s, when Laud was strengthening ritual in the Church of England's liturgy by calling for such things as bowing at the name of Jesus and kneeling at newly installed rails around altars for Communion, he would appeal to Elizabethan canon law to justify liturgical changes. Although we lack the intimate picture of the King conspiring with Laud and the chief secretary to "legally" alter the courts as they would the Church, we can find in this the same kind of transformational literalism. Through appeals to legal precedents taken from the reigns of Elizabeth and James that were cunningly reapplied, legal "try-ons" effected changes in both the courts of High Commission and Star Chamber.

THE COURT OF HIGH COMMISSION

In his measured study, *The Rise and Fall of the High Commission*, Roland Usher calls into question the claims of the Commission's opponents that it was oppressive and tyrannical by demonstrating not only that both Archbishops George Abbot and William Laud intended to assure the regularity of its procedure but also that 95 percent of the court's cases were brought by individuals rather than the commissioners.[16] Even so, Usher identifies changes in the High Commission's composition, the increase in both its membership and quorum, and the renewal of its visitorial authority in Charles's 1625 letters patent as evidence of Charles's and Laud's intention to increase the High Commission's power and authority. Certainly we know that Laud saw the High Commission as an essential tool of authority. In a 1624 letter to the Duke of Buckingham, Laud, who had been excluded by Archbishop Abbot from the High Commission, called the High Commission "a place of great Experience for anye man that is governour in the Church." For this reason he requested Buckingham's assistance in gaining a seat on the High Commission. In his appeal to the Duke to help him obtain what he regarded as his rightful place, Laud wrote, "I would be loath to be excluded from that which might give me experience & soe enable me to performe my dutye."[17] Buckingham saw to Laud's appointment, and the influence of Laud and his fellow clerics from Durham House came to be felt on the High Commission, even under George Abbot's leadership.

The Commission's new strategy appeared as soon as Charles I came to the throne, as evidenced by the new letters patent he issued. The 1625 document incorporated a clause used in Elizabethan patents that had been absent in James I's 1611 letters patent for the Commission. According to this clause the High Commission received "full power and authority . . . to visit, reform, redress, order, correct and amend in all places within this our realm of England all such errors, heresies, crimes, abuses, offences, contempts and enormities spiritual and ecclesiastical wheresoever."[18] According to Usher, this clause, which followed "the older and more indefinite Elizabethan model" rather than what had appeared in James's patent, "imparted to the Commission during its later years an aspect of newness, of innovation upon former precedents."[19] Although Usher does not expand upon this character of the Caroline High Commission, it was in its effort to control the press that this innovation upon former precedents (its transformational literalism) became a fundamental strategy for silencing religious controversy.

The necessity of strengthening the tools of press control did not become fully apparent to Charles until his religious and political policies produced the flood of oppositional writings in 1627–28, even though the 1626 proclamation to establish peace in the Church had sought to put an end to religious faction. In its effort to quell controversy, Charles I's proclamation had prohibited "publishing or maintaining any new inventions or opinions concerning Religion than such as were clearly grounded and warranted by the Doctrine and Discipline of the Church of England."[20] While this proclamation ostensibly sought to silence both sides, as we have seen, church Calvinists found it increasingly more difficult to obtain ecclesiastical licenses for their publications, while books from the Durham

House coterie were readily allowed for print. By persisting in publishing unauthorized books attacking both Arminian theology and the licensing establishment, church Calvinists provoked Charles's government to employ the High Commission to enforce ecclesiastical licensing in a way that, while consistent with its written patents, departed from over forty years of practice. It proceeded against authors and printers of Calvinist writing by appealing to a variety of legal precedents taken from the reigns of Elizabeth I and James I. While the precedents in and of themselves were legitimate, their application to current circumstances constituted a radical redefinition of High Commission practice. The first instance of this appeared in 1628, in a case against Henry Burton.

On October 29, 1628 an article was objected by the High Commission against the author of several anti-Arminian pamphlets and minister of St. Matthew's Church. It stated,

We article and object that notwithstanding you have since 20th December 1623, without license or warrant, caused sundry books of your own making to be imprinted and published before they were viewed or licensed, and that you have given or sold and disposed of 1,000, 500, 100, 50, 30, 20, or at least ten several copies contrary to the decree of Star Chamber, and expressly against these proclamations as, viz., a book entitled *Israel's Fast, The trial of Private Devotions, A Plea to an Appeal, The baiting of the Pope's Bull, The Seven Vials,* and sundry other books of the like titles, which you ought not to have caused to be printed and published without first being perused and licensed.[21]

In its accusation against Henry Burton, the information made an extraordinary appeal to a series of precedents relating to licensing, Star Chamber and the High Commission. It stated first,

That by the injunctions made in the reign of Queen Elizabeth, and confirmed by a decree in Star Chamber 28 Elizabeth, now in force, it is ordained that all persons uttering, causing to be imprinted or sold, any book which has not been first viewed or allowed by the Archbishop of Canterbury, the Bishop of London, or some person authorized by them, shall be proceeded against and punished according to that decree, and we do object that you do know or have been informed of its contents.[22]

It then referred to James I's 1624 proclamation, "dated at Hampton Court, 25th September," which it said, "did make known his great dislike against printing and publishing of books without license, not only ratifying the said degree of Star Chamber, but by proclamation signifying that either by the Court of Star Chamber or High Commission respectively, the penalties therein mentioned should be inflicted upon the offenders . . ."[23]

Ecclesiastical licensing, as we have seen, was instituted by Elizabeth's 1559 Injunctions and until late in the reign of James I, had been concerned principally with controlling books against the religious settlement. (Statutes proscribed writing against the State.) This concept of official authorization was upheld by the 1586 decree in Star Chamber for order in printing, which stated that all books should be "allowed" by the Archbishop of Canterbury or the Bishop of London "according to her Majesties Injunctions." For the printer who failed to comply with this, "all such presses, letters, and instruments as in or about the printings of any such bookes or copyes shalbe employed or used, to be defaced and made unserviceable for ymprintinge forever." Additionally, the printer was subject to six months' imprisonment "without Bayle or Maynprise."[24] Publishers, booksellers, and binders were subject to three months' imprisonment. The 1586 decree neither made provision for, nor envisioned, punishment for the writers of unauthorized books. In the years immediately following the decrees (1586–1602), the Stationers' Court Book B records twelve searches in which presses were seized, all for printing illegally by violating royal patents or the Stationers' Company's license.[25] The Elizabethan High Commission proceeded five times against printers who operated illegal presses: once against Robert Waldegrave, a Stationer, for printing *Diotrephes* (an unauthorized and unlicensed book), twice against Catholic presses (illegal, non-Company, presses printing unauthorized and unlicensed books), and twice against non-Stationer Roger Ward for printing books that belonged to another man by virtue of royal patent on an "illegal" press. During the reign of James the Stationers' court of Assistants ordered only two presses destroyed for printing seditious books, but on three other occasions "illegal" presses were ordered by the High Commission to be defaced: one for being above the number of presses the Stationers' Company allowed, one for printing another Stationer's copy; one for being a non-Stationer printing a Stationer's copy. From the time of Queen Elizabeth the court of High Commission adjudicated cases involving violations of the Star Chamber decree – but only when the Stationers' Company's court of Assistants held no jurisdiction (that is, when violators were not members of the Stationers' Company) or when matters could not be resolved within the Company.

One of the difficulties in looking to Elizabeth's 1559 Injunctions and the 1586 Star Chamber Decree as definitive in matters of "illegal" printing lies in the ambiguous language these documents employed. "Illegal" could mean printing works against the intentions of the laws of the realm, including statutes and proclamations, but it could also mean printing by a non-Company member, or printing a book registered to a Company member, or printing without license (the Company's as well as the Archbishop's). Neither of these documents contained language as explicit as James's 1623 proclamation referred to in the information against Burton, which states that anyone who imports, sews, stitches, binds, sells or puts to sale, or disperses "any seditious, schismaticall, or other scandalous Bookes, or Pamphlets whatsoever" is subject not only to the "paines, punishments and imprisonments" dictated in the 1586 Star Chamber decree, but also to "such further censures, as by Our Court of Star-chamber, and high Commission respectively, shall be thought meet to be inflicted on them."[26]

The High Commission's case against Burton, as an author, was unusual. Burton as a clergyman was already subject to the High Commission's disciplinary jurisdiction, but that was not the grounds upon which it proceeded in this case. Had it done so, the information and any subsequent trial would have engaged the theological issues of Arminianism and Calvinism present in Burton's books – something which the ecclesiastical establishment was assiduously avoiding in order to uphold the King's proclamation for peace (and quiet!) in the Church. By bringing an action related to licensing, the content of Burton's books became moot, and the High Commission was free from being a site of theological controversy. Precedents for a High Commission case on the unlicensed printing of a transgressive book did exist – but not for action against an author. In 1624 the High Commission had imprisoned the printer of *Votivae Angliae*, a diatribe against James I critical of his foreign policy in the 1620s.[27] Applying the precedents of the 1624 proclamation and of the 1586 Star Chamber decree against Burton as the author of unlicensed books was sheer innovation. First, he was charged with crimes of which printers and publishers were usually accused – the publication, "causing to be printed or sold," of unlicensed books. (Stationers, after all, by virtue of entry in the Company's register book did "own" the titles they published or printed.) Second, the relationship between licensing and punishment received a subtle redefinition. By referring to James's proclamations, the charge against Burton implied that he was justifiably subject to any punishment the High Commission might administer because of the punishments indicated by the 1586 Star Chamber decree for printing without license. The precedent to which Burton's charges referred – of being "punished by the decree" – were likewise innovative. Burton was not a publisher, printer, binder, or bookseller. The accusation that he "caused sundry books" of his "own making to be imprinted and published before they were viewed or licensed" effectively redefines the notion of "publisher" as it was employed in the 1586 decree and understood in the printing trade.[28] (Publishers – as the word was commonly understood – were understood to be members of the printing trade and as such members of the Stationers' Company.) Perhaps even more innovative in the charge against Burton was the statement that Charles, upon his succession, "ratified" these former "acts" – that is, Charles affirmed the legality of the 1586 Star Chamber Decree and adopted James's 1623 and 1624 proclamations linking the decree to punishments in High Commission and Star Chamber. How precisely this "ratification" proceeded is not at all clear in the charges against Burton. Historically, a law court's decree carried the same weight as any other legal precedent; it could be introduced in subsequent legal arguments – but it was also subject to a later court's interpretation and, thus, to change. The legal authority of a King's proclamation, however, died with him. The "ratification" to which Burton's information alluded possibly may have derived from the proclamation issued by Charles on March 20, 1625, by which he confirmed the officers of his father's Privy Council as his own and indicated:

That all orders and directions made, or given by the Lords of the Privie Counsell of the late King, in his life time, shall bee obeyed and performed by all . . . and every thing, and things to be done thereupon, shall procede as fully and amply, as the same should have been obeyed or done, in the life of the said King.[29]

In all the Privy Council acts, royal proclamations, and state papers from the reign of Charles I nothing appears any more explicit than this that might represent a "ratification" of either the 1586 decrees in Star Chamber for order in printing or the proclamations of James I[30] – indeed, the entire notion of "ratification" employed here constitutes yet another creative application of legal precedents.

Given the unusual use of precedents in the charges against Burton, brought home by the High Commission's insistence to him that "we do object that you do know or have been informed of" the Star Chamber decree and its contents, Burton's reply that the "proclamation and injunction alluded to concern bookseller and printers, not authors" was far less disingenuous than has often been suggested. Furthermore, Burton's confidence that there was nothing in his books "repugnant to the doctrine or discipline of the Church of England" points to an understanding of ecclesiastical licensing attuned to both Elizabeth's Injunctions and the 1586 Star Chamber decree.[31] The High Commission, however, did not concur – and in taking this course created a new principle by which it could proceed against authors and printers alike.

Throughout the 1630s the High Commission brought repeated actions against authors and printers, always for books the government deemed politically or religiously objectionable, rarely merely on the grounds of not having been seen and allowed. Initially, the High Commission proceeded cautiously by charging that objectionable books violated government licensing provisions as they had in the case against Burton. On April 29, 1629, in an action more conventionally brought against printers, the High Commission filed informations against London Stationers William Jones, Augustine Matthews, Nathaniel Butter, and Michael Sparke for printing books without license, "according to the Decree in the Star Chamber of the 28th year of Queen Elizabeth," – that is, for printing unauthorized books.[32] This, however, was no mere instance of "unlicensed" printing; the books, *The Reconciler, Babel no Bethel* by Henry Burton, Thomas Spencer's *Maschil Unmasked*, and William Prynne's *Anti-arminianisme* all opposed Arminianism. When the charges were preferred in the High Commission, Michael Sparke had already spent eighteen days as a "safe prisoner" in Fleet Prison "for printing and publishing offensive books without licence or warrant."[33] In the 1580s, at the height of government efforts to eradicate the Elizabethan Puritan movement, one of the Puritans' principal criticisms of the Elizabethan High Commission had been that non-conforming clergy had languished in prison without trials. At the end of Elizabeth's reign and for most of James's, however loudly the High Commission's foes complained, their objections addressed matters of the court's jurisdiction and its use of the oath *ex officio mero* (which was administered to the accused before charges and indictments were read) rather than abusive imprisonment practices.

Michael Sparke's May 5, 1629 answer to the articles against him, while a flagrant and legally questionable denial of the High Commission's right to prosecute him (especially for printing unauthorized books), raises some interesting issues. Sparke pleaded the "hereditary" liberty of the subject, Magna Carta, and the Petition of Right against the binding authority of the 1586 decree in Star Chamber. He proceeded to argue that he printed the books "to the glory of God, the honour of the King, the good of the Church and the welfare of the doctrine of the Church of England and the religion established." While it is not surprising that such an argument would fall on deaf ears, Sparke essentially makes the case that the books he printed were not engaged in practices that Charles's patent for the High Commission described as its purview. Sparke makes it clear that the books he printed did not engage in "errors" or "heresies," nor were they against the "doctrine of religion, the Book of Common Prayer, or

[the] ecclesiastical state."[34] His defense points to the innovative manner in which the High Commission was employing its jurisdiction. Sparke, of course, engages in a legal "try-on" of his own in questioning the "binding" authority of the Star Chamber decree because it denied the subject's "hereditary liberty" contrary to Magna Carta and the Petition of Right – arguments which, while invoking recent events in Parliament, were making little headway in England's law courts. Sparke's remarks, however, may be seen as a kind of foundational moment in the rhetoric of freedom. He links the freedom of the press to the rights of the subject! Juxtaposing Sparke's answer – that the content of the works did not oppose the established Church – to Burton's claim that the Star Chamber decree did not concern authors, brings into high relief the High Commission's creative redefinition of older precedents and practices. The Elizabethan High Commission had primarily focused on writing against the Church of England as it was established by the 1559 Act of Uniformity – in practice it silenced separatist Protestants and Catholic controversialists. And while the Star Chamber decree had addressed unlicensed printing (illegal presses and unauthorized texts), it had only served as the grounds upon which to proceed against printers and publishers, most frequently in matters of illegal presses, or printing that violated royal patents and Company licenses. Regardless of Burton's and Sparke's objections, the High Commission continued to pursue both printers and authors of texts the Commissioners deemed objectionable.

Shortly after the information had been filed against Sparke and the other Stationers, the High Commission again objected articles against Henry Burton – this time for committing scandal against Dr. Joseph Hall by writing *The Seven Vials* and *Babel no Bethel*, the first of which had been part of the former charges for unlicensed printing. Burton was charged with "perverting" Dr. Hall's words "as if he intended to maintain that the Church of Rome is a true orthodox Church of Christ."[35] This time the principal charge does not relate to Burton's involvement with an unauthorized text, although a secondary charge accuses Burton of procuring "the said book" to be imprinted by Michael Sparke and of distributing 200 copies. The accusation of "perverting" the Bishop's words is most peculiar. There is no question that, according to its letters patent, the High Commission had the authority to "enquire and search for all heretical, schismatical and seditious books."[36] The charges here against Burton, however, do not mention heresy, schism, or sedition, and while the connection may have been in the Commissioners' minds, the novel accusation of "perverting" replaces language that might more properly belong to the Commission's jurisdiction. Burton, as a cleric in the Church of England, was certainly answerable to the authority of a bishop and the High Commission, and in this case could have been held accountable for a slur upon a bishop, but the case against Burton was not one of clerical discipline. Burton's answer to the articles shows that the content of his writing was the issue. He denied that he had perverted Dr. Hall's words and maintained, instead, that the book was written in response to tracts by Hugh Cholmely and Robert Butterfield that argued that the Church of Rome was a true visible church, a position Burton regarded as inconsistent with principal theological writings of the Church of England.[37]

In 1630 another book provoked the High Commission into action, *Christ's confession and complaint*,[38] but this time the Stationers questioned were far more cautious – and compliant. Their responses suggest that the Stationers had quickly learned – and learned how to deflect from themselves – the new strategies the High Commissioners employed. This time Sparke raised no questions about the Commission's authority when he was asked about the book in question; instead he replied that while he was in the country,

41 of the books articulate were left with his servants, and were sent to divers of his chapmen in Oxford and Salisbury, and other parts. On his return [he] received a note to place *Christ's Confession and Complaint* foremost, whereupon, perusing the book, he found it dangerous, and, as he believed, unlicensed, and thereupon brought the residue of the same into the Registry of this Court.[39]

Sparke's initiative in taking the books to the High Commission's registry stands in stark contrast to his earlier claims that the 1586 Star Chamber Decree violated the liberty of the subject! The High Commission's articles had also sought to discover the book's author and printer, but Sparke maintained his ignorance of these, as did Nicholas Bourne and Henry Overton, the other London Stationers against whom the High Commission likewise had filed articles regarding the book in question. Both maintained that packets of the books had been left for them anonymously.[40] Bourne's reply indicates that the High Commission also wanted to know the names of people who purchased the book, and although Bourne had sold all but three of the thirty he had received, he maintained he did not know the names of the purchasers. Overton's reply – that two months before, because of former troubles with illegal books, he had refused two men in sailors' dress that had come to his shop demanding to be paid for the books – seeks to strengthen the Stationers' claims of ignorance by suggesting that the books were printed abroad.[41]

The High Commission campaign against objectionable books did not go unnoticed, nor was the court alone the object of criticism. In late February of 1630, Laud, then Bishop of London and a High Commissioner, received an anonymous letter that began with the statement that a "bishop is almost become a terror to a faithful soul."[42] While this letter contains what by this time had become a conventional accusation that Laud and Neile and their adherents were executing "stratagems" for "the bringing in of Popery by Arminianism," the principal means this letter identifies for pursuing this agenda is the bishops' assault on preaching and writing: "If one Salisbury, Coventry, or such like as Leighton, do but cross their way, by a sermon or book, they send for him, and give him or them a pill, and stop his passage . . ."[43] While this letter is certainly not without bias – indeed, it participates in the kind of politicized assault on ecclesiastical licensing considered in the last chapter – it serves as a reminder that *all* unauthorized books were not the High Commission's concern. Indeed, many printed books that had not been seen and allowed failed to attract any attention from the court. Instead, "unlicensed" became a charge that could be made against objectionable books that may not really have been filled with heresy, error, or sedition as they were defined by law. Rather than proceed in a heresy or sedition trial, it was far more expedient for the High Commission to object articles against Stationers for printing scandalous books on the grounds that they violated the "Late Queenes Injunctions" and "sundry other orders and decrees." (The articles listed every possible kind of licensing provision to add teeth to their articles.)[44] Among the books for which they objected articles were: *Rome's Ruine*, the prophecies of Eleanor Davies printed in Amsterdam, *A Treatise of the Separation of the Church of England* printed in Amsterdam, *A Defense of the most ancient and sacred Ordinance of God, the Saboath Day*, and Geneva Bibles. Once sedition received definition in the courts, however, High Commission articles had only to indicate that a book separated the King from his people or the people from the Church and then require the printer's or author's admission that he or she, indeed, had written or printed the specified book.[45] In one such case in 1636, William Jones was fined by the Commission for printing "seditious" books that were charged with being "much derogatory to the church of England."[46] By the mid 1630s the High Commission called for considerably less than the evidence of a "seditious" or an unlicensed printed book to place someone in jeopardy. The High Commission, acting merely on what it deemed "credible evidence" of sectaries, authorized John Wragg, the messenger of the chamber, to take with him a constable "and such other assistance as he shall think meet" and enter into any suspicious house to search for sectaries "as also for unlawful and unlicensed books and papers; and such persons, papers, and books so found, to bring forthwith" before the Commission "to be dealt with as shall be thought fit."[47] By reinterpreting legal precedents' "literal" language and by creatively extending their application, the government of Charles I gradually transformed the manner in which the court of High Commission controlled the press.

The expansion of the High Commission's authority over seditious writing by such transformational literalism in legal interpretation has escaped the recognition of some of the most scrupulous political and legal historians, which has, in turn, contributed to misunderstandings about Caroline press control. On the one hand, because the High Commission had been in existence in some form from the beginning of Elizabeth's reign and because it had been associated with some form of press licensing and control, its apparent continuity has often eclipsed the very subtle yet real changes in notions of legality, in court jurisdiction and procedure over time, and in objectionable writing that concerned the court. Some historians, reading backwards from the Long Parliament's dissolution of the High Commission for its abuses, have understandably generalized the Commission's abusive nature across the life of the Commission. On the other hand, the rhetorical emphasis of Charles and Laud on the rule of law and on legal precedents and procedure – combined with their insistence that they did not engage in novelty or innovation – has disguised a particularly focused assault on one particular kind of controversial literature as an upright effort to rout out scofflaws in the printing trade. Because the court's interests were rather narrowly focused, the claims that historians like Sheila Lambert and Kevin Sharpe have made that the government of Charles I was largely uninterested in controlling the press beyond matters of trade and dire assaults on the State appear equally justifiable.[48] With regard to the High Commission's control of the press, as we have seen, both sides are mistaken. The Caroline High Commission differed in important ways from its predecessors in how it defined its own authority over printing, in how it defined "illegal" and "unlicensed" printing, and in how it extended printing agency from printers and publishers to authors. In doing so it contributed to the culture of censorship that defined the era of Charles's personal rule. Had the High Commission alone been engaged in creating this culture, the Long Parliament's judgment upon it might not have been so dire. (The High Commission, after all, though it charged devastating punitive fines in an effort to deter certain kinds of behavior, usually mitigated those fines in later sessions.) The perceived abuses of the High Commission combined with those of the court of Star Chamber – as well as its highly visible "show trials" of outspoken critics of the Laudian Church – to provoke the Long Parliament to act against them. The place of the court of Star Chamber in histories of the period has been as colored by the Long Parliament's actions as the High Commission's has been. It is not surprising, then, that subtle changes in the Star Chamber's role in press control should have passed unnoticed – especially during the reign of Charles I. During the 1630s the court of Star Chamber engaged in prosecutions of authors for seditious writing, which, though few, were notorious. Its jurisdiction in such matters looked to precedents in slander and libel law, but, like the High Commission, by engaging in transformational literalism, it expanded these principles to provide new grounds for prosecution.

THE COURT OF STAR CHAMBER

The court of Star Chamber's jurisdiction over the printed word derived from three principles – the court's jurisdiction in clarifying decisions of other courts, the court's authority to enforce royal proclamations and patents, and its historic jurisdiction in cases of slander and libel. In its first capacity, as we saw in chapter 1, it issued decisions like its 1586 decree for order in printing, but this was not the grounds upon which it proceeded in cases against seditious writing during the reign of Charles I. Its notorious prosecutions of Alexander Leighton, William Prynne, Henry Burton, and John Bastwick drew upon on a body of case law in matters of slander and libel – but law that was as subtly redefined by government attorneys as the High Commission's practices were. Legal definitions that addressed writing and speaking first appeared in the English legal system as prohibitions on slander and libel, terms often used synonymously in practice but which came to be distinguished as spoken (slanderous) or written (libelous) assault on a person's character.[49] By the thirteenth century the content of a slander or libel was clearly defined as a malicious and false allegation of a criminal act published to a third party. In a private argument between two parties anything might be said. Telling a neighbor that another man was a scoundrel or a rake could not lead to prosecution in the courts, but declaring him an adulterer, murderer, or a thief could. Slander and libel were initially actionable only in the ecclesiastical courts, where clearing the injured party's name or excommunication were the only available remedies. Later, when injured parties sought damages, cases were heard in the common law courts. While defendants frequently claimed the truth of an allegation as a defense, neither ecclesiastical nor common law recognized this as a valid defense. Furthermore, the common law demanded that for a case of slander or libel to proceed, the plaintiff must have suffered some form of material damage as a consequence of the words. By the end of the sixteenth century the common law also recognized allegations of malfeasance in a trade or profession as grounds for an action of slander or libel.

Two special forms of slander and libel received statutory definition – words written or spoken against either the monarch or powerful aristocrats. In the first instance, the first treason statute, which appeared during the reign of Edward III (25 Edw. III, stat.5, ca. 2) and was designed to protect the safety of the state, made it treason to "compass" or imagine the King's death. Words expressed against the King were later interpreted as an overt act which evidenced an intention to kill the King. During Elizabeth I's reign, when the printed word had become commonplace, Parliament passed eleven statutes addressing treason and sedition that included within their definitions some form of the phrase "by Wryting Pryntinge Preachinge Speache expresse Wordes or Sayinges." The statutory ground for prosecution was clear: speaking, writing, or printing anything denying the monarch's political or ecclesiastical authority, advocating the right of anyone else to that authority (including writing on the succession), advocating rebellion, and "compassing" bodily harm to or slandering the monarch came within the compass of treason. Even these statutes, however, required interpretation, and in the seventeenth century Edward Coke maintained in the *Institutes* that scandalous words against the monarch, unless they were words that disabled his title, were not an overt act from which a "compassing" of his death could be inferred – "it is commonly said that bare words may make a heretick, but not a traytor without an overt act."[50]

In the second instance, a statute passed during the reign of Edward I (3 Edw. I, ca. 34) commanded that "none tell or publish false news or tales whereby discord may grow" since devisers of tales led to "discord between the King and People or Great men." The principle of this statute, which has been referred to as the statute of *Scandalum Magnatum*, as we saw in chapter 1, was further refined during the reign of Richard II (2 Ric. II, ca. 5) by defining great men as prelates, earls, barons, other nobles, the King's ministers, and officers of the courts. All of the early treatises on the court of Star Chamber recognize the court's jurisdiction in cases of *Scandalum Magnatum*, although cases were also brought in King's Bench.[51] Until the late sixteenth and early seventeenth centuries, the principles set forth in the ancient *Scandalum Magnatum* statutes served as the only grounds upon which an individual could be prosecuted for seditious libel – or libel against the State. In 1578 in a King's Bench's decision on pleadings in Cromwell's case, the court held that "scandaling prelates, nobles and great officers" constituted "scandaling" the King himself and hence the government. It also affirmed the principle that had long been upheld in case law that "sedition cannot be committed by words but by publick and violent action."[52] These principles were refined in 1605 by the Star Chamber judges' decision in Pickering's Case, in which a poem attacking the deceased Archbishop of Canterbury was attached to his hearse. The court concluded that slander and libel – "written or by work, by pictures or by sign" – of both individuals and magistrates constituted a breach of the peace and was hence seditious (although the slander of magistrates was more serious). Further, the slander's truth or falsity was dismissed as a defense: "for in a settled state of government the party grieved ought to complain for every injury done to him in ordinary course of Law." This decision, along with others, brought together the principles that earlier had made slander and libel against individuals distinct from scandal and libel against the government.[53] Sir William Holdsworth sees Pickering's Case as the legal foundation for Star Chamber cases in matters of seditious libel, and F. S. Siebert extends the principle to the press.[54] According to Siebert, the implication of Pickering's Case was that "to publish libelous or seditious material was just as criminal as to invent it."[55]

In his study of the development of the law of seditious libel in the eighteenth century, Philip Hamburger maintains, correctly, that Holdsworth and Siebert, among others, have misinterpreted several decisions and events to justify the link between seditious libel and seventeenth-century prosecutions for seditious printing.[56] The evidence of cases filed in Star Chamber for seditious books during the reigns of Elizabeth and James I supports Hamburger's contention that prosecutions for seditious books rarely proceeded in Star Chamber. During the reign of Elizabeth the only Star Chamber case in such matters was against two men and a woman who at one point harbored a secret press that printed some of the Martin Marprelate pamphlets. During the reign of James I an information was filed against William Jones for printing a book that objected to the High Commission, *The Argument of master Nicholas Fuller, in the Case of Thomas Lad, and Richard Maunsell, his Clients*, but the case was not prosecuted.[57] While Hamburger properly discredits Star Chamber as an agent of press control, he errs in his confidence in the efficacy of state licensing as a tool of press control under Elizabeth and James. He maintains that the government of Elizabeth sought out the 1586 Star Chamber decree on printing with its provisions to enforce state licensing because "English governments had experimented with a number of laws for restricting the printed press, most of which were unsatisfactory," and that press prosecutions in the sixteenth and early seventeenth were nearly always for what he refers to as "licensing laws."[58] As we have seen, under Charles, the High Commission extended the scope of prosecutions for publishing insufficiently licensed books to books that were otherwise objectionable. Star Chamber's prosecutions in the 1630s for seditious writing proceeded from a similar extension of legal principles, rather than the lapse of confidence in "licensing laws" that Hamburger alleges.[59]

The kind of transformational literalism that strengthened the High Commission's control of printing during the time of Charles I's personal rule may likewise be found in the use that Charles I's government made of the court of Star Chamber to prosecute authors for writing books the government deemed "seditious." Although Star Chamber had had some jurisdiction in cases of slander and libel, the precedents that are relevant to the Caroline transformation of Star Chamber practice came not from cases of seditious libel, but from legal actions taken by Charles against members of the House of Commons, whose words and actions at the close of the 1629 Parliament so offended the King that he had them imprisoned. As chapter 2 demonstrated, the meetings of the Commons in all of the Parliaments in the 1620s were contentious. Instead of, or as a condition for, granting the King's repeated requests for supply to support his war efforts, the Commons insisted on pursuing its own concerns, including parliamentary privilege, the growth of Arminianism, the censure of the Duke of Buckingham, and what they perceived as the King's abuse of Magna Carta in billeting soldiers in homes of private citizens and in imprisoning men who refused to pay the forced loan. All this contentiousness climaxed in 1629 when Charles adjourned Parliament.

On February 25, 1629, only a month after another contentious session of Parliament convened, the Speaker of the House, John Finch, delivered to the Commons the King's commandment for adjournment that met with several members' objections on the grounds that the Commons should decide adjournment. Sir John Eliot then presented Finch with a remonstrance on the subject of tonnage and poundage, and when Finch refused to read it, Eliot did. When Finch rose to adjourn the debate, Denzil Holles, aided by Benjamin Valentine, forced Finch back into his chair and holding him there, proclaimed, "God's wounds he should sit still till it pleased them to rise." On March 2 the King issued a proclamation dissolving Parliament because of the "disobedient and seditious carriage of certain ill-affected persons of the House of Commons"[60] and subsequently issued warrants to nine members of the House of Commons, including Eliot,

Holles, Valentine, William Stroud, Walter Long, and John Selden, request-ing them to appeal. They refused to answer "out of Parliament" for what was said and done in Parliament, and the King had them committed close prisoners. Shortly thereafter legal maneuvering on both sides began.

According to Conrad Russell, Charles was determined that the prisoners would not gain a release without a submission, and the Star Chamber seemed the likely court in which to proceed.[61] On April 25 the King summoned the judges to Serjeants-Inn to confer on the charges. The King wanted an opinion on whether the members of Commons enjoyed the privilege of free speech on matters debated in Parliament, whether a refusal to be examined was "not a high contempt in him, punishable in the Star Chamber, as an offence against the general justice and government of the kingdom," and whether "if a parliament man raise slanders and rumours against the council and judges, not in a parliamentary way, but to blast them," it would not be "punishable in Star Chamber after Parliament."[62] On another day the Attorney General asked the judges if a Parliament man being called before the court of Star Chamber *ore tenus* did not submit to examination "for such things as did concern the king and the government of the state," he might not be be proceeded against *pro confesso*.[63] (*Ore tenus* proceedings allowed the judges to question the offender orally and without a written bill of complaint. Proceeding *pro confesso* could occur when the offender confessed; then the court could proceed to summary judgment. What was being proposed here was to take the offender's refusal to be questioned without a formal written complaint as an admission of guilt.) The judges advised that *ore tenus* was not "the justest way" for the King to proceed according to the rules of Star Chamber, and that "it would not be for the honour of the king, nor the safety of the subject, to proceed in that manner."[64] On May 7 Attorney General Robert Heath filed charges in the Star Chamber in the hope of resolving the matter of privilege, but the charges were dropped by the end of summer when it became clear that the judges inclined towards the defendants' claims for privilege.[65]

While the King's lawyers were pursuing the case in Star Chamber, the defendants sued for writs of *habeas corpus* on the grounds that they were unjustly committed to prison without cause – the same issue that had prompted the Petition of Right passed in the 1629 Parliament. The King's return to the writ maintained that they had been imprisoned "for notable contempt committed by them against ourself and our government, and for stirring up sedition against us." All of the attorneys on behalf of the imprisoned MPs contended that "sedition" did not appear as a chargeable offense in the law books, and that "sedition" was rather the general quality of an offense. According to Mr. Mason, the counsel for MP Walter Long, "sedition is nothing but division."[66] According to Edward Littleton, the attorney for John Selden, "For sedition, and the general notion of it, we have not either in the division or explication of offences that occur in our books an express definition, description or declaration of it, though it occurs sometimes as mingled with some other offences ... Nor hath there been yet found any indictment or proceeding upon the crime of Sedition."[67] If sedition appeared at all, it was in conjunction with some other crime, as in "seditious words" or "seditious libel," which if the crimes "seditious" described were not capital crimes, release on bail was warranted. The defendants, therefore, should either be bailed or released on the grounds that the charge was insufficient, that is that it was not a crime specified by law, or that if it were to be interpreted as a crime like seditious words or seditious libel, the offense warranted bail.

The King's attorneys argued on the King's behalf that the King could imprison at will when a case was outside the issues in the Petition of Right, and, furthermore, that the words of the return were not general, as the defendants claimed, but specific. In explaining precisely how they were specific, the King's sergeants, Robert Berkeley and Humphrey Davenport, provided a definition of sedition that represented an interpretation of former legal principles. Berkeley argued that, according to Glanville, "to do anything in sedition of the kingdom, or of the army is high-treason" but "sedition tendeth to the disinheritance of the king ... And in this sense sedition is no stranger in our law; and such sedition which severs the people from the king, is treason."[68] Davenport argued that he found the word sedition in the law "and the consequent of it likewise, which is *seduction populi.*" Sedition, he maintained never appeared in a good sense, but "is always ranked and coupled with treason, rebellion, insurrection, or such like as it appears by all those statutes which have been remembered on the other sides."[69] According to Russell, when Charles learned that the judges in King's Bench were inclined to bail the prisoners, he moved them from the custody of the marshal of the King's Bench and had them confined to the Tower by his own warrant, placing them outside the jurisdiction of the court. In October 1629 the King offered the prisoners bail in exchange for their submission to his authority. Most refused and were remanded to prison. In 1630 Eliot, Holles, and Valentine were tried in the King's Bench and found guilty of sedition.

Although the court never made a decision on the writ of *habeas corpus* for the MPs, the definitions of sedition that both sides employed in their arguments proved invaluable in causes the government brought against its enemies in the 1630s. In 1630 the information exhibited in Star Chamber against Alexander Leighton, "a Scotsman born, and a Doctor of Divinity" and author of *An Appeal to the Parliament, or Sions Plea against the Prelacie*, charged him with "framing, publishing, and dispersing a Scandalous Book against King, Peers, and Prelates, wherein amongst other things he sets forth ... false and seditious Assertions and Positions."[70] In his answer Leighton confessed to writing the books but maintained he had no ill intention. At the hearing the parts of the book the government deemed seditious were read aloud, and since Leighton had confessed to writing the book, the court proceeded to its sentence: "That it evidently appeared upon Proof, that the Defendant had printed five or six hundred of the said Books, and that in their opinions he had committed a most odious and heinous Offence, deserving the severest punishment the Court could inflict, for framing and publishing a Book so full of most pestilent, devilish and dangerous Assertions, to the scandal of the King, Queen and Peers, especially the Bishops."[71] Leighton never had the opportunity to argue whether or not his writing constituted "sedition," but the court's judgment established a precedent that books written to the scandal of the King, Queen, peers, and bishops engaged in sedition.

In May of 1630 proceedings were initiated in Star Chamber against the Earl of Bedford, the Earl of Clare, the Earl of Somerset, Sir Robert Cotton, John Selden, and Oliver St. John for publishing a seditious and scandalous writing by some unknown person. The information stated "some malicious persons who are as yet unknowne to your said Attorney, being ill affected to your ma'ty, and to your happy gov'nment, and intending to raise false scandals, and seditious rumours against your ma'ty, and your gracious governme't, have of late wickedly and seditiously framed, contrived, and written, a false, seditious, and pestilent discourse ..."[72] The pestilent discourse began "The proposition for your majesty's service, containeth two parts: the one to secure your State, and to bridle the Impertinency of Parliaments: the other, to increase your majesty's Revenue" and is supposed to have been written by Robert Dudley at Florence in 1613.[73] A case against the named defendants, all distinguished parliamentarians, could not be established and the proceedings were dropped, but the language of the information shows the way in which the government was drawing upon principles employed in recent cases to develop cases for seditious writing. It maintains unspecified rumors against the King – an offense that comes within statutory definitions of scandal – and it alleges, albeit implicitly, an attack on the King's government.

A few years later, William Prynne was tried in Star Chamber for writing *Histrio-mastix*. The information, as it is described in *State Trials*, accused him of compiling and putting into print "a libelous volume" against plays, maypoles, people, and kingdom. To assure his conviction, the information cautiously spelled out how this book, granted approval by an ecclesiastical licenser, engaged in sedition: "he hath therin written divers incitement, to stir up the People to discontent, as if there were just cause to lay violent hand on their prince."[74] In barely four years "sedition" by words went from an act that English law had not deemed a crime (or a word whose adjective form defined a specific crime like slander or libel) to the crime of "stir[ring] up the People to discontent." When the MPs' attorneys in 1629 had referred to sedition in the old statutes, they had maintained that sedition, though not itself a crime, was often associated with the crime of treason when it led to actions intended to unseat the King. In the court of Star Chamber in 1634 it was sufficient merely to evoke the possibility of provoking to treason: "*as if* [emphasis mine] there were just cause to lay violent hand on their prince" and compound it with stirring up the people for the crime to be "sedition." In 1578 in Cromwell's case, the judges had maintained that "sedition cannot be committed by words but by publick and violent action."[75] In only four years, by appealing to the literal language in arguments on both sides of a single case, the government of Charles I abandoned an ancient principle of English law and created a crime by which it could proceed against the authors of books whether or not the books were licensed by the ecclesiastical authorities. The principle of sedition, as we shall see in chapter 4, became an essential tool by which Charles's government proceeded "legally" not merely against genuine agents of rebellion, but against opponents of liturgical changes in the Church of England – changes that in the reign of James I and Elizabeth probably would have been regarded as matters indifferent to salvation.

In her essay "State Control of the Press," as we have seen, Sheila Lambert said that the government of Charles I only engaged in censorship in egregious cases which jeopardized public order or the integrity of his foreign policy, or that libeled the King.[76] Frederick Siebert suggested that censorship actually declined during the reign of Charles I from the onerous system that had been put in place during the reign of Elizabeth I.[77] The evidence presented here suggests that both Lambert and Siebert were mistaken. Rather than enacting censorship against books that were clearly against the law, Charles transformed the law to make many more books illegal. Instead of using the High Commission and Star Chamber to adjudicate licensing and patent problems among the London Stationers,

Charles used the courts to prosecute authors who "stirred up" the people. In the name of resisting innovation, Charles's attorneys scanned the law for principles that could be asserted as adhering to the literal law, while employing his courts to expand that law to effectively create transformation. The rhetoric of injustice that has been employed in attacks on Star Chamber – language that has seen Star Chamber as a "despotic prerogative court . . . incompatible with the common law's protection of the rights of Englishmen" – has attacked too broadly the court and its practices.[78] The changes Charles's Star Chamber attorneys introduced were far more subtle and, indeed, outwardly appear to support the view of Thomas G. Barnes that Star Chamber was an ordinary court that upheld English law and employed traditional procedures: "The law which Star Chamber implemented was the common and statute law of England" and its proceedings "scrupulously" employed "the pleadings (pleas, demurrer, replication, rejoinder) sacred to the common law on its civil side."[79] Through entirely legal means and procedures consistent with the common law, the court of Star Chamber extended the principle of sedition to include printed books that the State could predefine as intending to separate the King and his people, and in so doing used Star Chamber as a tool of press censorship in a novel manner. Regardless of how "legal" the actions of Star Chamber and the High Commission were, it is important to remember that censorship became highly visible during the reign of Charles I – but it also became more common. While James I had engaged in censorship twice as often as Elizabeth I, Charles imposed censorship five times more often than his father – and only Charles regularly resorted to the courts of High Commission and Star Chamber to practice censorship.[80]

In certain respects, then, with regard to the courts of High Commission and Star Chamber, both Whig and Revisionist historians have been right – and wrong. The Whigs were correct in their view that these courts participated in press censorship under Charles I. And the Revisionists have been technically correct in the position that Charles's government did not engage in "innovation" – that it did not create official licensing, the High Commission, or the court of Star Chamber. The Whigs, however, have erred in their teleology: there was no march towards freedom from the repressive Tudor dark ages. And Revisionists have erred by accepting at face value the claims of Charles and Laud that they honored the law. The question, however, remains whether, as Christopher Hill would have it, the government of Charles engaged in political and religious censorship to "prevent the circulation of dangerous ideas among the masses of the population," or whether, as Sheila Lambert maintains, it censored books merely to maintain the integrity of its foreign policy and preserve domestic order.[81] While this chapter has considered the manner in which the government of Charles I adapted the High Commission and Star Chamber to serve its ends in controlling the press, the rigor of the cases mentioned here cannot truly be assessed without examining more fully the books involved and the contexts in which they were written. The next chapter considers the politics of provocation both on the side of those writers who by the 1630s were identified as "Puritans," and on the side of the government, which in the 1630s engaged in what David Cressy has shown to be theatrical show trials.[82]

CHAPTER 4

Censorship and the Puritan press

In 1654, Thomas Gataker, a conforming clergyman in the Church of England whose prolific pen reflected decidedly godly sympathies, remembered the 1630s as "those fore-passed troublesome times under the Prelates."[1] During these times, he said that he "maintained a good correspondence, and some inward familiaritie with the moderater sort on either side: as well with some few of the Prelatical partie." Those prelates with whom he associated, while "stiff for the Ceremonies legally established" came to "mislike those innovations that in the latter times began to creep in." Furthermore, they disapproved "the carriage of businesse with that rigor and extremitie against such as refused conformitie."[2] Gataker's remarks point to three aspects of the conditions of godly religious life during the 1630s. First, clergy – even bishops – who had in prior years zealously upheld such ceremonies as wearing the surplice, signing the cross at baptism, and using rings in the wedding ceremony saw such Laudian ceremonies as bowing at the name of Jesus and kneeling for Communion as "innovations." Secondly, he reminds us that he perceived that the measures taken to secure ceremonial conformity were not merely rigorous but extreme. Finally, his own stance of "good correspondence" with moderates on both sides when taken alongside his harsh judgment of the times suggests that conformity was distinctly different from approbation. That the ten-year hiatus in Gataker's writing career corresponded to the height of the Laudian reforms has been taken as evidence that "Gataker was forced, or else chose, to maintain a low profile and to observe as an impotent, muzzled bystander Charles I sliding to disaster."[3] Whether Gataker feared the rigors of Caroline licensing or simply chose not to enter the fray, he is far from the character of the "schismatic Puritan" that Laud's biographer, Peter Heylyn, found in any of the "Calvinians" who objected to the Laudian impulse towards order in the Church of England.

In his biography of Laud, Peter Heylyn, like Gataker, remembers the 1630s as a polarized time – although he blames the "Faction." Laud himself, however, remembers the years of his prominence in the Church as a time of consensus and order. Defending himself before the Long Parliament in 1643, Laud maintained,

> Ever since I came in place, I have laboured nothing more, than that the External Publick Worship of God (so much slighted in divers parts of this Kingdom) might be preserved; and that with as much Decency and Conformity as might be. For I evidently saw, That the publick neglect of Gods Service in the outward face of it, and the nasty lying of many Places dedicated to that Service, had almost cast a damp upon the true and inward worship of God, which while we live in the body needs externall helps, and all little enough to keep it in any vigour. And this I did to the utmost of my knowledge, according both to Law and Canon, and with the consent and liking of the People.[4]

Laud's interest in conformity and bodily worship had not been lost on Gataker, but it was on the matter of "consent and liking of the People" that their memories of the times diverged so radically. Where Laud saw approbation, Gataker remembered trouble.

The divergence that marks these contemporaries' memories of the 1630s continues in historical accounts of the period, especially with regard to censorship. This impasse, Debora Shuger contends, results from the persistence among scholars of thinking about censorship from the perspective of our own categories and not from those of early modern England. We privilege a free press that "stands on the side of liberty, tolerance, republicanism, truth, and literature," and we equate censorship with "hegemonic state power; with the repression of criticism, dissent, and 'dangerous ideas'; with punishing 'attempts to deliver the truth'; with orthodoxy, authoritarianism, vested interests, and class privilege."[5] When we look at the "early modern position," we wrongly invert our own values and envision them as "preferring dogmatism over tolerance, hierarchy over transgression, orthodoxy over inquiry, containment over subversion, state over individual."[6] While Shuger affords us a useful warning to shed our post-Enlightenment perspectives, her own argument that early modern censorship represented a system of formal and informal controls that enforced culturally accepted norms of "truth, charity, respect, and order" whose end should be seen "not as silencing a theological position but as suppressing hate speech,"[7] stands firmly on Laud's side and in doing so perpetuates a divided (and divisive) image of the 1630s.[8]

Perhaps more than our post-Enlightenment blinders, the problem that dogs our understanding of censorship is one of evidence – not so much the lost pieces of the puzzle, as Shuger suggests,[9] but rather its genre. If one looks, as Christopher Hill did, to the "many mouths" opened by Star

Chamber's abolition in 1641,[10] censorship's dress looks quite different from what one finds in Laud's speeches in such venues as the courts of Star Chamber and Parliament – especially in printed accounts of them. Confidently linking government licensing to the Stationers' proprietary interests and focusing on the Stationers, as Adrian Johns and (to a degree) Joseph Loewenstein do, will yield a distinctively different picture from the one constructed out of State papers and Privy Council acts. This is not to say that one form of evidence should be privileged over another but that we need to approach all evidence with a measure of skepticism that attends to the rhetorical implications of its production. Certainly, for example, it was in the Stationers' Company's best interest to assure that certain kinds of texts printed by Company members were duly authorized by the ecclesiastical authorities, but doing so did not necessarily mean complicity with the government, nor did their disregard make them scofflaws. We must, I think, concede, that evidence of censorship will always be partial, for as Arnold Hunt reminds us, "Effective censorship is invisible ... the best-documented cases of censorship may be the ones that are least representative."[11] Hence this chapter takes as its focus both the regular practices of book production and licensing and the extraordinary Star Chamber "show trials" in order to assess whether for godly writers the 1630s were "troublesome times" or times of willing conformity and good order during which the only end of censorship was to ban hate speech.

In the prefatory remarks to his authoritative essay on Stuart licensing practices (to which I shall later return), Anthony Milton reminds us of some of the most difficult problems that arise in discussing Caroline religious censorship. One is a problem of language. "Obedience" and "order" did not mean the same thing to everyone, thus,

What constitutes a threat of political disorder is very much in the eye of the beholder, and Charles I and Archbishop Laud are notorious for having discerned the threat of puritan populism in a whole range of political and religious beliefs and patterns of behaviour where other contemporaries would have seen nothing of the kind. Moreover, polemical literature in this period sought at every point to discredit the opponent's belief by claiming that it potentially threatened the social and political order. The point at which criticism constituted a threat of disorder was therefore itself the battleground in the seventeenth century ...[12]

The other problem is that because of the complex nature of religious affairs, "The question of precisely what was a threat depended on exactly what one thought was there to be threatened, and here opinions varied as to what was the precise doctrinal position of the Church of England."[13] It is because the nature of order and orthodoxy were themselves contested that censorship cannot be deemed a "simple" confrontation between government hegemony and oppositional writers.

Religious censorship in the 1620s, as we saw in chapter 2, was focused on the question of predestination and the theological differences between the "Arminian" party ascendant at court and the conforming Calvinists who perceived their "orthodox" views as being endangered by the altering religious climate. In the 1630s, while the divisiveness persisted, the issues changed when Laud began to remedy "the publick neglect of Gods Service." Peter Lake has given us the useful term of "Laudianism" to provide "handy shorthand for the policies and religious temper of the Personal Rule." He does so, he says, "not to imply anything about the role of Laud in either originating or disseminating the views" he associates with the Laudian style.[14] "Laudianism," according to Lake, existed "as a coherent, distinctive and polemically aggressive vision of the Church, the divine presence in the world and the appropriate ritual response to that presence."[15] From this perspective, the physical edifice of a church, a site of worship, was quite literally the house of God. "God's presence in the church suffused the whole structure and all the physical impedimenta used in his worship with an aura of holiness," thus any object employed in the divine service became a holy object.[16] God's presence in the church demanded not only outward reverence, but regular attendance at divine service, where "outward, physical acts of reverence and piety, choreographed by the liturgy and performed at the promptings of the priest, served both to express and inculcate various spiritual qualities or habits of mind."[17] Laudianism envisioned a uniform public worship where decency was represented by members of the congregation "kneeling, rising, standing, bowing, praising, praying altogether."[18] The sacrament of the Lord's Supper became the central focus of the liturgy, while sermons were seen merely as a means to call people to prayer in preparation for the sacrament. This led to one of the "central features" of the Laudian program, "to have moveable communion tables converted into altars, railed in at the east end of the church."[19] From a Laudian perspective the sacrament conferred grace, and grace was dispensed through the priest as an intermediary. Such an attitude enhanced the prestige and authority of the church and the clergy, and, according to Lake, a natural consequence of this was an emphasis on the Church's authority to establish holy times and days, an attitude that placed Laudianism in direct opposition to the Puritans' rigid sabbatarianism.[20]

Lake's caution in characterizing Laudianism responds to the position taken by many historians that Laud did not really institute changes in the

Church but merely enforced canons and injunctions that had been neglected. This is certainly the position Laud articulated at his own trial and at the 1637 Star Chamber trials of Henry Burton, John Bastwick, and William Prynne. His 1637 Star Chamber speech was subsequently printed, Laud asserts, at the King's request. The work of Kenneth Fincham poses a convincing challenge to Laud's claims that there was no innovation. According to Fincham, "by the mid-1630s, at the latest, Charles I and Laud had created a new agenda for clerical conformity, amounting to a wholesale rejection of Jacobean evangelism and the accommodation of moderate Calvinists."[21] According to Fincham, the altar policy, kneeling at Communion, and enforcing the Book of Sports were all new, and requiring the clergy to enforce them created a "new conformity" that joined with the "old" conformist matters of clerical dress, employing the Book of Common Prayer, and signing the cross at baptism. Fincham demonstrates that these changes were indeed innovations by looking at the full texts of the historical canons Laud employed as evidence that there was nothing new in his reforms. "Laud," Fincham reminds us "defended the new position of the communion table with reference to the Elizabethan Injunctions of 1559," but he ignored the second clause, "permitting it to be moved elsewhere in the chancel at the time of communion."[22] According to Fincham,

Neither the Injunctions of 1559 nor the canons of 1604 envisaged rails or the reception of communion there. Canon 7 of 1640 gave retrospective warranty for the altar policy, although some latitude was permitted about reception at the rails. It also recommended bowing towards the east end on entering and leaving Church, a ceremony urged by Laud and several other bishops in the 1630s at a time when it had no canonical basis.[23]

Episcopal visitations became a tool Laud employed to assure conformity, and these, Fincham demonstrates, explicitly articulated Laudian reforms. The instructions for visitations between 1634 and 1637 in twenty dioceses clearly express the regime's priorities:

Ministers were to read divine service in its entirety with no omissions and hold services on Wednesdays and Fridays as the Prayer Book stipulated. Proper clerical attire was essential: this meant "constantly" wearing the surplice during services, and outside Church "never" failing to use a canonical cloak ... A premium was placed on reverent conduct during services: parishioners should bow at the name of Jesus and stand at the creed and gospels, as canon 18 stated. Most significant of all, the communion table was ordered to be "set at the upper end of the chancel north and south and a rail before it or round about it". Reception of communion at the rails was to be encouraged. Secondly, preaching was to be carefully monitored. Official concern at ill-regulated sermons and lectureships had already been voiced in the royal Instructions of 1629, which stated that catechizing must replace Sunday afternoon sermons in parishes, that only "grave and orthodox" ministers be permitted to join combination lecturers, and that lecturers be persuaded to accept benefices. Brent reminded preachers of these instructions ...[24]

Fincham notes the difference between Jacobean and Caroline visitation articles as a measure of the difference between the old conformity and the new. Equally important, from my perspective, is the difference that can be seen between the reports on visitations Archbishops Laud and Abbot made to King Charles. In 1633 Abbot reported to the King, "There is not in the Church of England left any unconformable minister"; still, he noted, "the lord bishop of London [Laud] and Lincoln [Williams] have been forced to deprive two or three ..."[25] Laud scrutinized the visitation reports and remarked every instance of traditional and ceremonial non-conformity, and his letters to the King carefully noted the dioceses where infractions occurred and named the bishops who should be encouraged to enforce more vigorous adherence to the ceremonies and compliance with the altar policy.[26]

As problematic as, quite literally, coming to terms with "Laudianism" and Laudian innovation has proven, "Puritanism" presents a greater challenge – in part because it has a longer history through which it underwent mediation and accommodation, in part because the word "Puritan" has been so often used in a pejorative sense. In *The Boxmaker's Revenge*, Peter Lake establishes the intricate workings during the early 1620s of the London "Puritan" community's "underground" religious culture. While Lake demonstrates the shifting doctrinal emphases that took place among "Puritans" between the early years of James's monarchy and the 1640s, it is possible to distill from Lake's study common ground shared by the "godly" – a term which Tom Webster prefers to "Puritan" because "'the godly' referred to themselves as such."[27] According to Lake, the Calvinist doctrine of predestination was a premise shared by the godly, and it was through election that the community of the godly was formed. The godly then shared convictions in the primacy of preaching, the importance of the sacraments, and a strict observance of the Sabbath. For the godly, preaching conferred grace: "In order for the ordinary Christian to experience an effectual calling, God had to add power to the outward calling of the word. While the initiating cause in this process was God himself, his usual instrument was the word preached ... the sacraments merely sealed and confirmed the grace already conferred by election and justification."[28] For the godly, hearing the word preached and receiving the sacraments was not simply a public act of worship, but also the occasion for private devotion. The right receiving of the Lord's Supper required introspection, which, with reading and studying the word of God, formed an essential individual and personal dimension. According to Lake, "the Sabbath joined the word preached and the sacraments as one of the three uniquely scriptural ordinances around which the both the public life of the national church and the private devotions of the godly community could be arranged."[29] Lake refers to the London Puritan community as an "underground," but in some respects, I'm not sure that is quite the right word. The cohesiveness and persistence that Lake demonstrates suggest instead a shadow church. Many of the godly leaders were ordained ministers in the Church of England, and their afternoon sermons joined the Sunday worship in shaping godly identity. There existed, as Lake demonstrates, a "recognizably puritan or perfect protestant intellectual and pastoral tradition" that included "the book of homilies, through John Foxe and William Perkins to Thomas Rogers, Paul Baynes and Bishops Morton and Francis White (the latter in his reformed rather than his Arminian phase)."[30] This was a tradition, I might add, whose books were regularly authorized and authorized for print.

While Montagu's books had created a point of contention in the 1620s between the godly community and the ascendant clerics of Durham House, conformity had not been an issue. Archbishop Abbot tended to overlook what he regarded as minor infractions; the cleric who did not always wear a surplice, or who abandoned clerical cloaks outside the church was rarely vulnerable to sanctions.[31] The churches in which the conforming godly found themselves in the 1630s – beautified, sanctified, and deemed living sermons – where preaching could not take its necessary precedence, were alien places. On the other hand, for the Laudians, who emphasized uniformity and order in public worship as the essence of the Church, a shadow church that privileged the preaching of the word and believed that the Lord's Supper confirmed rather than conveyed grace was justifiably demonstrating "the public neglect of Gods service." We can best understand the impasse between the godly and the Laudians, and between the two historical interpretations that tend to privilege either the Laudian interest in ceremonial order and the beauty of holiness or the experience of the godly during the "troublesome times under the Prelates" by recognizing that each side was equally zealous about the rightness of its own very important view of the means by which a Christian received grace – through the word preached or the sacraments properly celebrated. The essence of

Laudianism was the unseen and invisible – the silent spiritual center. The godly defined their very existence in "the word." "Preaching the word truly" was the center of Calvinism. Every treatise, sermon, and ceremony was tested against scripture; that which failed the test was answered, usually in print. Disputation and controversy were the Calvinist way, silence and order the Laudian.

The godly response to Laudian measures taken to assure order and uniformity were threefold: repudiation, resistance, and outward compliance. The story of repudiation is the familiar one of the Puritans whose dissent led them to the United Provinces and to America. Some of them – men like John Davenport, John Cotton, and Thomas Hooker, for whom conformity in the Jacobean Church and under Archbishop Abbot had been possible – were either deprived by the church courts or, finding the new ceremonial conformity unconscionable, fled England.[32] Others stayed within the Church of England but took the risks of outspoken criticism, men like Henry Burton and John Williams, Bishop of Lincoln, to whom, with Prynne, this chapter will return. Others, like Gataker, continued in the shadow church that sought to edify the community of the Elect through preaching and publishing. Webster makes the distinction that such men did not "conform," but rather were "conformable."[33] During the 1630s the writings of each group appeared in print in England. Publishers in Amsterdam and Leiden printed not only radical anti-Episcopal tracts by Separatists like Alexander Leighton, but also provided a voice for more moderate Calvinist theological writing. In the early 1630s books critical of the ceremonies were printed in England – a few even received licenses, though most were technically "illegal." Legal books by godly authors filled the bookstalls throughout the 1630s.

It is the presence of these legal books that has led historians to conclude that the Laudians did not seek to silence godly writing. Peter Heylyn, however, remembered it differently. He recalled two kinds of writing that Laud saw fit to suppress: anti-Catholic and Calvinist books. The anti-Catholic books, which were "full of bitternesse and revilings against the Church of Rome itself and all the Divine Offices, Ceremonies, and Performances of it," he said, had come from the time of Queen Elizabeth who "beheld the Pope as her greatest Enemy." Calvinist books came from a similar distant past:

There was a time also when the Calvinian Doctrines were embraced by many for the Genuine Doctrines of this Church, to the great countenancing of the Genevian Discipline and Forms of Administration: and not a few of the Books then Printed, and such as after were Licensed in Abbot's Time, aimed principally at the Maintenance of those Opinions, which the latter Times found inconsistent with the Churches Doctrines.[34]

Heylyn's remarks, while offered to explain Laud's interest in the censorship provisions of the 1637 Star Chamber Decree, are salient here not only because they attest to the persistence during the 1630s of both anti-Catholic and Calvinist books, but also because they indicate that Laud objected to anti-Catholic books and books that regarded Calvinist doctrines to be consistent with those of the Church of England. (They also suggest if not Laud's, then certainly Heylyn's irenic attitude toward Rome, another matter of contention between the godly and the Laudians.) Heylyn's assessment of the motivations for Laudian censorship is entirely consistent with the findings of Anthony Milton.

In "Licensing, Censorship, and Religious Orthodoxy in Early Stuart England," Milton investigates how both the godly and the Laudians manipulated printing controls to advance their own ideas of orthodoxy. The "linchpin," for Milton, was the licensing system and the licenser. (Here, of course, Milton refers to ecclesiastical licensing and licensers.) Milton recounts several pieces of evidence to demonstrate that during the 1620s Daniel Featly, Archbishop Abbot's chaplain and a prominent licenser, required authors on the one side to soften radical anti-Puritanism, and, on the other, to make Puritan texts more palatable by removing "overtly Presbyterian or anti-ceremonialist material."[35] In the 1630s, when Laudian licensers were active, many godly authors found their books being subject to suppression or revision.

[C]atechisms and pietistical works were generally not targeted by licensers, even when they dealt with predestination or ceremonial issues in some detail. Rather, licensers seem to have targeted the sort of works that prompted the unrest in the first place, that is, systematic works of controversial divinity and polemic (hence stopping of treatises by Davenant and by Bishop Downham, and also the extra-ordinary lack of published works on the issue of antichrist after 1633, or replies to controversial pamphlets regarding the Sabbath, the altar, and so on). Nevertheless, some sermons and bible commentaries were stopped at the press . . .[36]

(When Milton says "stopped at the press," he refers to the practice of licensers refusing their approval for printing until objectionable material was purged.) Among the kinds of passages that were systematically purged were those that included anti-popery, and those that addressed ceremonies, preaching, ministry, the visible Church, and the nature of the sacraments.

The significant aspect of this censorship, according to Milton, was that "this was not a purging of puritan opinions, but of positions argued by moderate Calvinist bishops such as John Davenant, and represents a censoring of more fundamental positions regarding the visible church which might have been interpreted as placing an unwelcome inhibition on the strident ceremonialism being advocated by Laud and his colleagues." According to Milton, moderate Calvinists like Davenant were regarded as a far more serious threat than Puritan radicals because their writing kept alive a rival version of doctrinal orthodoxy. Rather than prevent the Calvinist moderates' books from being printed altogether, the licensers "massaged" them "to enable them to speak with a Laudian accent." Among the "more sophisticated" means taken to recast the work of opposition writers was to reprint a work in inappropriate circumstances, to print a Calvinist work with a Laudian foreword, or even to force a godly divine to license a Laudian book.[37]

Milton also considers as evidence of Laudian censorship the number of godly books that appeared in 1641 that had been circulating in manuscript. Milton takes as an example books on the Sabbath:

whereas no replies to Laudian pamphlets were published in printed form in the 1630s (except for Burton's solitary clandestine publication) no less than eight were published in 1641, all in response to Laudian tracts that were published over the period 1634–7. There seems little reason to doubt Henry Burton's claim that, if there had been freedom to publish, Francis White's works on the Sabbath would soon have had too many confutations to handle.[38]

Besides works that were written against the Laudians' position on the Sabbath for which he cites evidence of manuscript circulation, Milton also finds books written against the altar policy and on predestination that were circulated in the 1630s and then printed in 1641.[39]

Milton demonstrates that the Laudian licensers paid very close attention to both the doctrinal differences and anti-Catholicism that Heylyn saw in Laudian censorship. One might, as Shuger does, dismiss Milton's conclusions by contending that Laudian censorship used as its criteria the orthodox doctrine of the Church of England as it was expressed by the Thirty-nine Articles. This, I think, ignores the principal purpose of Milton's argument – to set aside the dualistic view of censorship as a discourse of control and opposition in favor of a more complex analysis that recognizes that printing controls were themselves a battleground for competing religious groups – indeed "a crucial area in which the battle for religious orthodoxy was fought."[40] Printing controls could be variously employed. There is, of course, "benign" censorship such as Milton finds in Featly's practices. Peter Lake has expanded on this in *The Boxmaker's Revenge* to suggest that the censorship practices of Featly and fellow chaplain, Henry Mason, actually served as "an extension, even a welcome beefing up, of the internal self-regulating mechanisms and impulses of the godly themselves." In this capacity, "Their role in regulating access to the public medium of officially sanctioned print resembled more that of unofficial referees or umpires in the doctrinal squabbles and discussions of the godly than that of spokesmen for an authoritarian and univocal 'orthodoxy'."[41] We should not, however, confuse the ecclesiastical licensing practices of Featly and Mason with Laudian licensers in the 1630s, as Arnold Hunt has effectively demonstrated.

Hunt sees in Milton's account of ecclesiastical licensing "very little difference between censorship in the 1620s and censorship in the 1630s: the mechanism of the licensing system remained the same; all that had changed was the clerical faction in control of the system, and the type of orthodoxy being promoted."[42] Hunt does not actually dispute Milton but instead refines his evidence by considering more fully two books, Daniel Featly's *Clavis Mystica* (1636) and Richard Clerke's *Sermons* (1637), both of which Milton mentions when he considers evidence presented at William Laud's trial. Hunt explains that while Featly's book of sermons was in the press, Laud summoned Featly to Lambeth Palace and, rejecting Featly's assertion that the sermons had been formerly allowed, "commanded" him to submit the book to his chaplain, William Bray. While the evidence from Laud's trial contended that Bray removed anti-Catholic polemic, Hunt shows that the book's anti-Catholic sentiments remained, but "in a slightly more moderate and persuasive way, consistent with Laud's expressed wish to appeal to the 'understanding Papist' who might be deterred by gratuitous abuse."[43] Elsewhere, Bray revised what had been Featly's objections to church art and images as idolatrous, to suggest that religious images might be tolerated.[44] Through Featly's case, Hunt shows both that Laud directed licensing and that its end was to uphold Laud's religious agenda and not to merely moderate extremism.[45] Moreover, since vetting was done against Featly's serious objections, it can hardly be seen as a benign exercise in "editing." In the case of Clerke, Laudian licensers heavily censored the text without consulting the author, who had died in 1634. These cases, according to Hunt, represented a departure from the ecclesiastical licensing practices of the 1620s, where a license indicated that there was nothing in the book that prevented its publication (*nihil obstat*), the effect of which was to legitimate diverse doctrinal positions that were, "by the standards of the Church of England, neither unquestionably orthodox nor positively erroneous but merely indifferent." In the 1630s, however, for the first time, the licence started to be used as an imprimatur rather than a *nihil obstat* – in other words, a positive recommendation of a book's orthodoxy, printed with the book and often declaring that its publication will be to the public benefit, "cum utilitate publica". This "positive" rather than "negative" interpretation of licensing permitted the licensers to intervene far more radically to alter the meaning of texts.[46]

The "imprimatur" printed in the book to which Hunt refers was itself a Laudian innovation. On January 11, 1632 the minutes of the Stationers' Company court of Assistants records that at Laud's direction no books should be printed without the license being printed in the book.[47]

One of the remarkable things that both Milton and Hunt reveal in their outstanding contributions to our knowledge of ecclesiastical licensing practices is the abundant evidence they find for the 1630s. Milton is quite right in his assessment that we have for the period "an unparalleled collection of religious material allegedly stopped at the press."[48] Similar evidence for the reigns of Elizabeth and James, in contrast, is largely absent. The mere quantitative difference in evidence lends support to the qualitative difference Hunt finds between the 1620s and 1630s. I have argued elsewhere[49] that, besides preventing treasonous publications, the principal end of pre-print censorship as it was instituted by Elizabeth was to assure that books against the religious settlement did not appear. This effectively allowed books on a surprisingly wide range of Protestant doctrine, including books by Luther, Melanchthon, Calvin, and Beza. While most Roman Catholic writing could not be published in England, the practice of printing the other side's position before answering it in controversial works meant that readers had access to a range of theological opinions. Even if the sting of Laudian censorship was not universally felt by godly writers, their perception that the regime had become more rigorous – that toleration for a diversity of opinions that had formerly been allowed no longer existed – surely fed anxieties about censorship.

Despite the very convincing case that Milton and Hunt make about the intention and practice of Laudian licensers, the evidence that Peter White and Sheila Lambert have provided on the large number of Calvinist works that appeared between 1626 and 1637 (some of which I have considered in chapter 2) requires some attention. White identifies twenty-one Calvinist publications.[50] Besides Carleton's *A Thankfull Remembrance of God's Mercy* (1630) and Humphrey Sydenham's *Five Sermons* (1637), and the multiple editions of John Ball's *A Treatise of Faith*, Lambert takes sermons by John Preston and Richard Sibbes, the works of William Perkins, and multiple Calvinist catechisms as evidence that there was little censorship of Calvinist writing. While Milton and Hunt dispute White and Lambert by showing the mechanisms of ecclesiastical licensing, and by opening up the question beyond the subject of predestination, they do not adequately consider the presence of Calvinist books in the marketplace. Indeed, we get no real sense of the scope of religious printing during the 1630s. Looking at the kinds of books that were available in print, together with the larger questions of licensing conformity and practice, can account for and explain the divergent accounts of censorship during these years. Doing so will establish that while Laudians used ecclesiastical licensing to silence the godly, godly writing still dominated religious publication during the 1630s. As effective as the Laudian licensers were at devising means to silence the godly, the rhetoric of silence espoused by the outspoken critics of Laudianism effectively concealed an extraordinarily effective publication program that united and edified the godly – a program that, for the most part, simultaneously conformed to and eluded licensing requirements.

RELIGIOUS PUBLICATION IN THE 1630S

One reason contradictory explanations for Caroline censorship have persisted has derived from misunderstanding the ecclesiastical licensing expectations and compliance with them. First of all, licensing was not as universal as Shuger, Milton, White, and even Lambert have implied. Franklin Williams has claimed that one-third of the books published were not entered in the Stationers' Register and only 30 percent of books bore an official imprimatur,[51] but he takes this as a measure of the failure of Laudian licensing policies. Milton allows the discrepancy between the theoretical prescription that all works should be seen by the ecclesiastical licensers and the number that were by conceding Lambert's observation that the ecclesiastical licensers were under "potentially crippling pressure of work, and could not be expected to read a good deal of what was put in front of them with anything more than a cursory glance."[52] Shuger, of course, maintains that no one really objected to licensing. White and Tyacke, although on opposite sides, assume that most books were seen by the ecclesiastical licensers and use the presence/absence of Calvinist works as evidence of their intentions. To be able to assess the validity of the arguments about ecclesiastical licensing, a better understanding of licensing compliance is necessary.

Since Williams's 1960 statistical study of Laudian licensing, Maureen Bell and John Barnard have provided a quantitative annual analysis of publications listed in the Short Title Catalogue.[53] They demonstrate a

London licensing conformity 1630–39

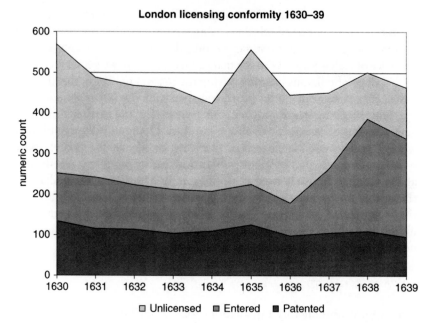

Figure 4

steady increase in the number of texts printed between 1475 and 1700. The 1620s showed a 15 percent increase over the period 1610–19, which showed an 18 percent increase over the previous ten years. The 1630s, however, show only a 4 percent increase. While this alone is certainly not evidence of increasingly rigorous press controls – a matter to which the next chapter attends – it does lend some support to Hunt's view of quantitative changes resulting from licensing's qualitative changes. More germane to under-standing the impact of Laudian licensing on print output is the fact that that during the 1630s slightly less than 30 percent of the books printed in London were entered in the Stationers' Registers.[54] Actually, before the 1637 Star Chamber Decree, between 1630 and 1636, the average rate of entry was 19 percent. Among the books printed but not entered – and thus presumably that were not seen by the ecclesiastical licensing establishment – were all official books printed by the King's Printers, which included not only proclamations and books for which they held special patents, like Bibles, but also any official Church of England publications like the Book of Common Prayer, special liturgies, and visitation articles. Almanacs and metrical psalms, also printed under special patents and not entered,

License and authority 1630–39

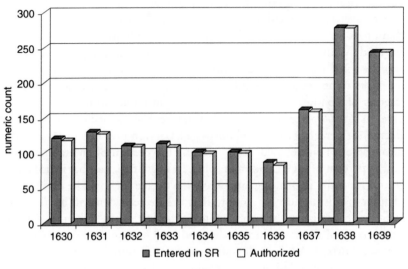

Figure 5

appeared in large numbers. The output of such patented texts, on the average, accounts for 23 percent of the total number of titles printed in London in the 1630s. This meant that prior to the 1637 Star Chamber Decree the current ecclesiastical authorizers scrutinized only 40 to 50 percent of printed texts.

More important as a measure of compliance than Register entry, however, is the number of entries that attest to official approbation – more than 97 percent of the titles entered during the 1630s indicate official authorization.[55] This shows a very high rate of compliance with the official understanding that the condition for books being entered in the Stationers' Register was licensing by a church or government official. By comparison, during the reigns of Elizabeth and James evidence of licensing ranged from a low of 44 percent in the 1590s to 84 percent in the 1620s.

As far as compliance went with official demands that books be seen and allowed, then, I think it is reasonable to conclude that members of the Stationers' Company took seriously the kinds of warnings against unauthorized printing represented by the cases in High Commission and Star Chamber considered in the last chapter.

Another measure of the attention printers were paying to demands for ecclesiastical licensing compliance may be seen in the years 1634 and 1638. As we have seen, it was in 1633 that Laud, as Bishop of London, ordered the Stationers to print the imprimatur of his chaplains in the books they licensed. While this may be seen as a way of guaranteeing that the book was doctrinally acceptable, as Hunt has suggested, it may also be taken as an effort to assure accountability; for it was in 1633 that establishing the licenser of Prynne's *Histrio-mastix* became important to the prosecution's case. In 1633 96 percent of the 101 Registers' entries carried notice of official license (21 percent of the total output of London presses); in 1634 all but two of the 101 entries evidenced licensing (98 percent of entered titles but still 23 percent of total London output). In 1637 Star Chamber issued a new decree for order in printing, and while the decree itself will be discussed in chapter 5, it is useful here to note that the decree's demand for licensing increased compliance both in entry and authorization. In 1638 only 4 percent of the entered titles were not authorized, and in 1639 all the entered titles were authorized. Additionally, after the Star Chamber decree was passed, for the first time ecclesiastical oversight of ballads was understood as being requisite for entry. Indeed, the apparent increase in the number of titles entered in 1638 and 1639 derives from the license and authorization of ballads.

Arnold Hunt says we should not be surprised by what appears to be a relatively low level of compliance with licensing regulations. This, he says, has little to do with the official will and more to do with how licensing requirements were interpreted. Since the interest of licensing was in controlling heretical and seditious texts, according to Hunt, the vast majority of material printed would not be objectionable (an assessment with which I agree for print trade practices between 1558 and 1629). The real interest in licensing as late as 1636, Hunt says, was still religious writing, as it had been in the sixteenth century.[56] During the 1630s, however, for titles entered in the Stationers' Register the high rate of authorization I have found applies equally to religious and non-religious texts. This, however, is misleading since an unusually high number of godly texts that were entered in the register were not printed – something that will be considered more fully below. Furthermore, between 1631 and 1639 an average of only 23 percent of the religious books that were printed were approved for print by Laud's licensing establishment. The lowest percentage of religious books seen by Laud's chaplains came in 1636, the year before the 1637 Star Chamber Decree; the highest in 1638, the year after the decree – and this does not include texts by the King's Printers or other patent holders.

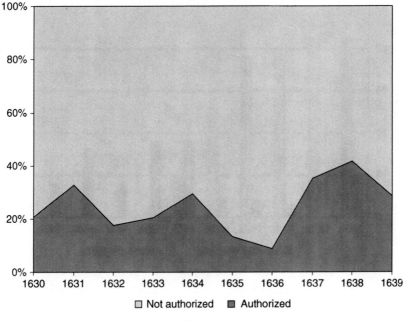

Figure 6

Before turning to the enormous number of religious books that in the 1630s were not seen by the ecclesiastical licensers, we need to look more closely at those licensers and how they may have influenced the author-ization of books for print. Until Archbishop Abbot died in 1633 his chaplains, Robert Austen, John Jeffray, and Thomas Buckner, served as ecclesiastical licensers, and even once they had ceased to review books for print, entries appeared in the Stationers' Registers that continued to identify them as authorizers. Three entries for Austen appeared as late as 1639. Entries also appear for Thomas Goad and Daniel Featly, who had stepped down as Abbot's chaplains in 1625, when Featly was called before King James for allowing books by the Puritan authors Edward Elton and William Crompton. (Thomas Gataker, who had been imprisoned for adding a preface to Elton's book, recalled that in this "business others far greater than myselfe, even the Archbishop himself, were aimed at."[57]) Abbot's chaplains approved 115 books between 1631 and 1639, or 53 percent. Charges by the likes of Prynne and Burton that godly writers were unable to get their books licensed were not entirely the case.

Ecclesiastical authorizers 1630–39

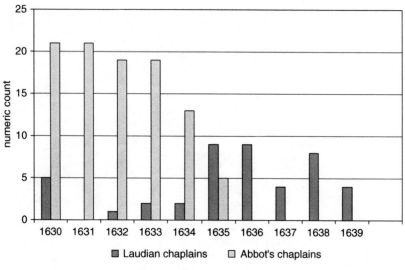

Figure 7

As Milton and Hunt have demonstrated, Laud's chaplains undoubtedly had a clear agenda for the books they authorized, but besides the occasions for which Milton and Hunt have provided fine accounts – occasions when men like Featly suffered severe "gelding" at the hands of Laud's chaplains – godly books were able to be approved as long as sympathetic licensers were available. This was the case throughout the 1630s, even after Abbot's chaplains stopped licensing, since from 1635 onward Thomas Wykes served as one of the principal licensers of books. Wykes was chaplain to the Bishop of London, William Juxon, who though he had long ties with the Laudian party, tended towards moderation and pragmatism. Not only was Juxon notoriously lax in his visitation reports, but his absence on the day when Laud's rigorous 1640 canons were signed protected him from impeachment.[58] It is unlikely that Juxon rigorously monitored Wykes's ecclesiastical licensing activities, and since Wykes continued to license books during the Long Parliament, his moderation may be allowed. Even if one is reluctant to do so, Wykes looks like one of Lambert's overtaxed licensers: 536 titles between 1634 and the end of 1639 (48 percent of all authorized titles). If we add to the 115 godly titles licensed by Abbot's chaplains, Wykes's 67, it means 85 percent of the godly books that were licensed for print in London were seen by sympathetic licensers. This seriously complicates a version of licensing like Lambert's, which finds censorship uninterested in anything but the most dire attacks on the government. The search for sympathetic licensers suggests that something more was at stake. It also challenges Shuger's view that Laudian licensing was merely interested in upholding civility, truth, and good doctrine. Laud's chaplains approved only twenty-eight godly books for print, but the names of such prominent godly authors as Thomas Gataker, William Gouge, Thomas Morton, Richard Sibbes, joined those whose works Hunt and Milton take into account in their studies of ecclesiastical licensing. It might appear that ecclesiastical licensers sympathetic to godly writers were meant to be part of the scheme except for two things: the memory of Laud's biographer, and the peculiar anomaly of books by godly authors that were licensed but not printed. Heylyn says that the books licensed in "Abbot's Time" were by "the latter Times found inconsistent with the Churches Doctrines" and that Laud sought to hinder "any thing which might disturb the Churches Peace, or corrupt her Doctrine."[59]

During the 1630s more than 40 percent of the titles with godly authors identified in the Stationers' Registers entries were not printed. Numerically 253 titles were entered and not printed, and 369 were entered and printed. Some of these, of course, may have been printed and lost. Estimates of survival rates from the period vary, and we know, for example, Bibles and Books of Common Prayer were virtually used up. If these lost titles were devotional works or catechisms we might assume they were printed and shared a similar fate, but that was not the case. Most of the unprinted titles are sermons and treatises by prominent Puritans and godly ministers, including Paul Baynes, William Gouge, Richard Sibbes, and William Pemble. One might conclude that printers chose not to print the books because of the costs of paper and labor, but this is unlikely since works by these authors sold very well. A more probable cause was that printing titles that strongly resonated with Calvinist interests and had been approved by Abbot's chaplains may have been seen as risky because of recent events.

Abbot's chaplains, Austen and Buckner, approved one third of the titles that were licensed and not printed, and most of these were entered in the Stationers' Registers between 1632 and 1634. I think the Stationers involved may simply have decided to be very cautious. Printers were being prosecuted in Star Chamber for printing unauthorized books. Puritan authors were complaining about the hostility of Laud's chaplains to their writing. Furthermore, ecclesiastical changes were underway. Half of the unprinted titles that Austen approved showed up in the Registers in 1632 and 1633,

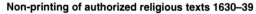

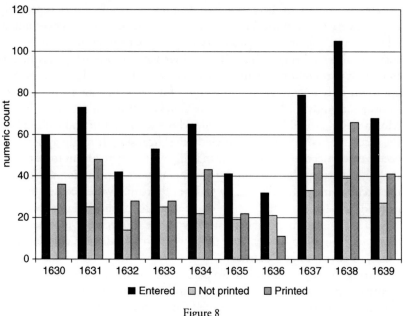

Figure 8

close to the time that Laud became Archbishop of Canterbury. If printing had not yet commenced, printers may have decided to wait and see what changes would take place. Similar concerns also may have related to titles Buckner approved, but he had another problem as well. In 1633 Buckner was investigated for approving Prynne's *Histrio-mastix*, and early in 1634 he was prosecuted in Star Chamber for allowing an unacceptable book to be printed. While Stationers might risk printing godly books, they would not have wanted the scrutiny that might attend to Buckner's license. All the titles Buckner and Austen found acceptable that were not printed point to Calvinist theological interests and to the kind of attacks on Rome that had been legion among Jacobean Calvinists: "Apology against the slander of Puritanism," "Three questions of free justification," "Internal and externall workes whereby a Christian may be assured of Salvacion," "Beza's larger note on the New Testament," "Sabbath Sanctification," "Tractatus de provedentia Dei," "Demonstracen of Antichrist," "Popery and the very picture of pagan Idolatrie," and "Celestial Publican, the vitious Courtier, The Jesuite and the Divelle." Also among the books not printed were titles by William Crompton and Edward Elton, the godly authors the approving of whose books had caused Featly problems. Another third of the books not printed were allowed by Wykes. Here, I suspect, it was less the contents of the books than timing. The unprinted titles that Wykes approved were entered in the Registers in 1638 and 1639 and might well have been printed but were instead set aside by printers in favor of more topical texts in the political uproar of 1640–41.

Laudian licensers also approved unprinted titles, about 30 percent of them. Laud intervened to cancel the license for one of these, a tract on antinomianism approved by Haywood. Nearly half of the unprinted titles Laud's chaplains approved were by authors whose other books, as Milton and Hunt have demonstrated, were "edited" to be more consistent with Laudian interests. Printers with godly sympathies may have chosen not to print books that gave to godly and Puritan leaders, John Prideaux, Featly, Sibbes, and Thomas Hooker, if not a Laudian voice then a Laudian accent. Or possibly, the authors persuaded printers to hold back such books. But this is mere speculation. While it is reasonable to associate Abbot's chaplains' unprinted books with the facts of their changing circumstances, to guess Laud's chaplains' licensing practices led to books not being printed participates in the kind of paranoia that is rife in *Canterburies Doome*. We may, I think, more safely say that, as for the titles Austen and Buckner approved, printers were exercising considerable caution about what they printed.

Before turning to the larger question of the books that were printed that were not seen by current ecclesiastical licensers, it is important to note that employing sympathetic licensers was not a practice employed only for godly authors. Sixty-three percent of Laudian books were seen by Laud or his chaplains, while Abbot's chaplains saw only 17 percent. (Wykes issued 14 percent of the licenses.) Even for Laudian books that were duly authorized some irregularities existed. Twice books were printed with imprimaturs but they were not entered in the Stationers' Registers, and twice authors "licensed" their own books. The Stationers' Registers, for example, identify Francis White as having approved his *Treatise of the Sabbath*. Since Laud took such interest in the principle of ecclesiastical licensing, it is rather surprising that 20 percent of the books sympathetic to Laudianism do not appear to have passed through the ecclesiastical licensing establishment, or, at least, they did not appear in the Stationers' Registers, a matter I consider below. Even so, an 80 percent compliance rate for Laudian authors is historically high.

Godly licensing compliance, on the other hand, would appear to be historically low. Although there was considerable yearly variation, during

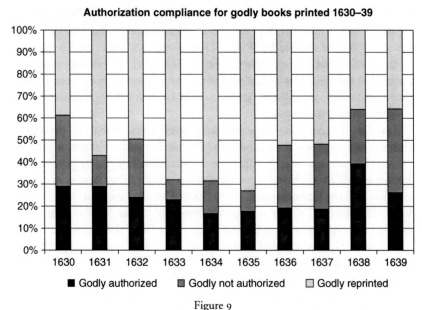

Figure 9

the 1630s three quarters of the godly books that were published did not pass through the current ecclesiastical licensing regimes. This discrepancy is, I believe, one of the main causes we have misunderstood Caroline censorship. On the one hand, we have considerable evidence for careful licensing, as Milton and Hunt have shown us. We also know that sanctions were imposed on "unlicensed" printing; printers and authors, as we saw in the last chapter, were brought before the High Commission or Star Chamber. On the other hand, texts by godly authors, even by Puritans and separatists, regularly appeared in print. London publishers were able to print these books "legally" because during the 1630s they were printing second and third, even twenty-third, editions of titles that had been previously printed. Indeed, over half of the books by godly authors that were printed in London between 1630 and 1639 had been formerly printed. The printers and publishers printed books for which they held the equivalent of copyright because they had entered their titles in the Stationers' Registers, the "copies" had been assigned to them, or the Stationer was recognized as the legitimate owner of a "copy" because he had previously printed the book. Once a copy was entered in the Stationers' Register, that title became the entrant's legal copy; it was property that could be transferred or, on rare occasions, sold. The entry in the Register book, which usually contained

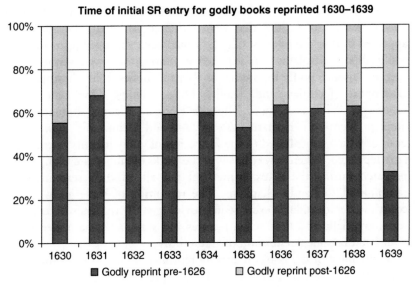

Figure 10

the notice of official authorization, could only be changed through a court action. This meant that all aspects of the license (company license and entry and official approbation) were durable. Before the 1637 Star Chamber Decree, no requirement existed that a new Company license be issued or entered for subsequent editions of a title. Similarly, there was no requirement that subsequent editions had to receive further ecclesiastical approbation. (Even after 1637, as Sheila Lambert observes, the Stationers found the new edition-based licensing requirement so unworkable that they appealed to Laud to repeal it.[60])

In the 1630s, then, London publishers were printing books written by Jacobean and Elizabethan Calvinists that had been reviewed, for the most part, by ecclesiastical licensers appointed by Archbishop Abbot. Sixty percent of the books that were reprinted during the 1630s were first printed before Charles I came to the throne. Included among these were most of the works of the Calvinist, William Perkins, and theological treatises by Calvin, Beza, and Pareus – even though James I had ordered the burning of books by Pareus, a Heidelberg theologian. Also included were sermons and biblical treatises by such popular godly preachers as Paul Baynes, Henry Smith, Thomas Gataker, Arthur Dent, Edward Dering, William Beadle, William Bradshaw, John Dod, and Robert Cleaver. John Ball's *Catechism* and *Treatise of Faith* with their fluid titles were reprinted almost on an annual basis. Other titles that were reprinted, although they had first appeared during the reign of Charles I, had been approved prior to 1630, while Abbot's chaplains were very active. Among these were sermons and treatises by such godly luminaries as Richard Sibbes, John Preston, John Davenport, Jeremiah and Daniel Dyke, George Downame, John Goodwin, William Gouge, Thomas Hooker, Richard Bernard, and Stephen Dennison. Bernard's *Isle of Man* and Dennison's *White Wolf*, both of which contributed to the formation of godly identity, were regularly reprinted. When new editions of the works of Sibbes and Gouge were prepared during the 1630s, some, but not all, of their sermons were resubmitted to Laud's chaplains. The reprinting of these godly books constituted a formidable exercise in providing godly readers with edifying texts, especially at a time when lectures and sermons came under attack after Laud became Archbishop of Canterbury.

While most of the books that were reprinted served to edify the godly community, a few of them allowed the expression of godly opinion in matters that during the Laudian regime came to be controversial. Books on Christian duty reinforced a godly view of the Sabbath. Treatises on preparation for receiving the Lord's Supper – and there were usually three or four printed each year – perpetuated a view of the sacrament that was very different from the sacerdotal sacramentalism that was the grounds of Laudian altar policy. In essence the books that were reprinted during the 1630s worked in much the same way that they had in the 1620s, as Lake's *Boxmaker's Rebellion* establishes, to define Puritan orthodoxy and to spiritually nourish the godly community. London publishing in the 1630s, by entirely legitimate means, was thus effectively sustaining the Caroline "shadow church" at precisely the same time that Laud, through rigorous episcopal visitation, was attempting to bring decency and conformity to the public worship of the Church of England. While the shadow church may have had to become more of an underground church as the 1630s progressed, the godly community of the Elect continued to hear the word truly preached, although in print, on a scale that has not been understood fully. We can get some sense of the scale if we see the degree to which godly books dominated the London market place. Laudian authors may have had an easier time obtaining ecclesiastical licenses, but only two Laudian books were reprinted often: Cosin's book of devotions and Andrewes's sermons. Outside of books in disputes on ceremonialism, altars, and the Sabbath, most of the books that can be identified with a Laudian perspective were visitation sermons preached by little-known

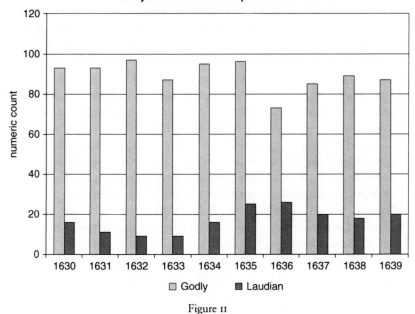

Figure 11

clergymen who praised the beauty of holiness – none of which was reprinted. If reprinting is a measure of market, then we can conclude that the demand for godly books far exceeded that for Laudian ones, a conclusion that an analysis of the number of books printed supports In only two years, 1635 and 1636, were more than twenty Laudian books printed. In only one year (1636) did the number of books by godly authors fall below eighty. While information on print runs is scarce, we can get some idea of the sense of scale by looking at one occasion on which we know the size of an edition. The publisher Robert Milbourne said that he lost 900 books when Edward Elton's catechism was burned in 1625.[61] Elton was a popular preacher in the godly community, and this was the first time the book was printed, so he would have been uncertain of demand. If we assign 900 as an admittedly arbitrary number for a print run, this would mean that approximately 75,000 godly books appeared in the London market place each year (compared to approximately 15,000 Laudian books). An estimate based on print runs of 900 is very conservative, since we know that in 1631 the Oxford printer, William Turner, printed 3,000 copies of Arthur Dent's sermons on repentance and 2,000 copies of five sermons by

John Preston,[62] print runs that far exceeded what is generally regarded as the limit set by the Stationers' Company at 1,200.

The scale of godly publication, then, reflects neither the fatigue of Laud's licensing regime nor a failure of its will, especially given the high degree of ecclesiastical licensing conformity in the 1630s as indicated by the Stationers' Registers. Instead, the large numbers of books by godly authors in the market place, especially since so many of them were reprinted frequently, speaks to the economics of supply and demand. A vital godly community, many of whom were willing to (or forced to) conform in ceremonial matters, sustained their identity though books and created a strong demand. Laudian licensing probably did prevent the publication of new books that it saw as unsympathetic to its goals, but its effect on the overall production of books by godly authors was nowhere as significant as its critics claimed. Keenly aware of the market, the Stationers turned to titles they already owned, which ironically fed the very religious beliefs and practices Laudianism sought to eliminate or change. A genuinely repressive censorship would have raided the bookshops and shut down presses, but that was neither Laud's nor Charles's way. That the changes in Star Chamber and High Commission practices, as well as in the ceremonial innovations in the Church, were accomplished according both to law and canon were matters in which the Caroline regime took considerable pride. Laud must have understood the scale of this godly publishing industry, but the opportunity to bring it into line did not present itself until he could call for a change in the entire licensing program (Stationers and State) as part of an effort to remedy a host of other problems in the London print trade. Whether or not it was ultimately implemented or enforced, the 1637 Star Chamber Decree contained the provision that any new edition or issue of a book required licensing.

Despite high ecclesiastical licensing compliance for new books and the legal printing of old ones, an average of 25 percent of godly books and 20 percent of Laudian books still did not pass through the London licensing regime. Some were secretly printed in London with nothing more than the year on their imprint – or with a false imprint. Others were printed at either Oxford or Cambridge. Even though the licensers at the university presses were believed to be more lenient than those in London, the number of religious books printed at university presses is fairly constant – and fairly low – and titles published there are nearly equal for Laudian and godly authors. (Both, however, employed the university presses for controversial books.) Rather than resort to the university presses where some form of licensing existed, godly authors turned to presses in Scotland and the

Locations for religious publishing 1630–39

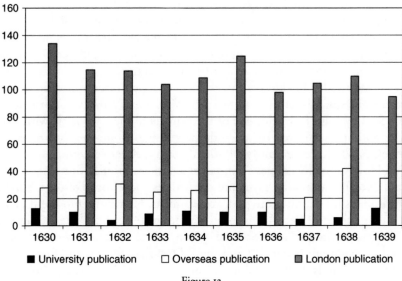

Figure 12

Netherlands. Overseas publication has been seen as an index of repressiveness of censorship on the assumption that overseas publication was significant. Actually, relatively few books for the English market were printed abroad in the 1630s. This, however, was the chosen option for writing by separatist authors like William Ames and by writers like Prynne and Burton, once their books grew radical.

RELIGIOUS CONTROVERSY IN THE 1630S

Laudianism may have embraced dignity, order, and peace in the Church, but that did not mean that a traditional area of religious writing – controversy – disappeared altogether. During the 1630s three religious controversies produced books on both sides that provoked open censure and censorship. In 1630 six books appeared on bowing at the name of Jesus. On the question of the nature of the Sabbath at least seven books appeared between 1632 and 1637. In 1636 and 1637 several books appeared on the Laudian altar policy. Ecclesiastical historians have studied the theological issues involved, but here the conditions of their publication, the character of their prose, and the means of their censorship provide a telling index to the Caroline religious climate. Both Charles and Laud disliked controversy, as Sharpe has shown. Indeed, Charles's 1626 proclamation and 1628 declaration have been seen as measures of this distaste and of his genuine interest in promoting ecclesiastical peace and good will. If, indeed, the interest of Caroline censorship was in merely silencing controversy, rather than silencing godly opinion, the production and censorship of books on ceremonialism takes a rather unusual turn.

In 1630 Giles Widdowes threw down the gauntlet on bowing at the name of Jesus. His sermon entitled *The schysmaticall puritan* was printed at Oxford by John Lichfield, one of the printers to the university, with "for the author" imprinted on the title page. Like Montagu's controversial books, Widdowes employs "Puritan" as a pejorative term. Although Widdowes initially defines a Puritan as a non-conformist, one who rejects the Book of Common Prayer and the Articles and Canons of the Church, he extends his definition to godly conformists. He says that to presume to be predestined to election "is to sin without feare or wit."[63] He attacks the "factious Sermonist" as one whose "pureness is to serve God with sermons, and extemporary praiers,"[64] and the Sabbatarian, for whom "Preaching" and not "Gods holy worship" is made "to be the keeping holy the Sabbath."[65] These Puritans, for Widdowes, are no different than Separatists, Anabaptists, and Familists. The book's conclusion calls for all "Puritans" to bow down on their knees and ask God's forgiveness.

Widdowes's book prompted a surprisingly mild response from William Prynne in an "Appendix on Bowing," added in 1630 to the second edition of *Anti-Arminianisme*. According to Prynne:

> The bowing of the head or knee at the name of Jesus, if it be any thing, must either be, *a duty of the Text*, as the Sorbonists, Rhemists, Bp. Andrewes, and Mr. Adams phrase it: or else *an indifferent, innocent, harmelesse Ceremony* (which *no man*, writes *Mr. Hooker, is constrained to use*, though some now presse it as a duty) as Zanchius, Mr. Hooker, Dr. Boyes, and Mr. Widdowes stile it. But neither of these two is it, as I shall make it evident.[66]

Prynne maintains that the bowing is not literally "corporial" but is instead a spiritual humbling.[67] He admits it is a ceremony, but not a harmless one, since "Papists" and "ignorant Protestants" use it to adore "Images, Altars, Hoasts, Crosses & Crucifixes; which we count Idolatry."[68] Prynne's argument, which culls evidence from the early Church Fathers, refrains from insult and invective and barely mentions Widdowes at all.

Widdowes took considerable offense at the small consideration Prynne afforded him, and in the preface to *A Lawlesse kneelesse schismatical Puritan*, he leveled the perfect insult to draw Prynne into combat. He addressed

Prynne by name as "Mr Ignormamus," and dismissed him as "a young scholler, a stranger to Metaphysicall Divinities."[69] Widdowes's pamphlet, which argues point by point against Prynne's "Appendix," is so precise that it almost looks like a parody of scholastic method worthy of *As You Like It*'s clown, Touchstone. After a laborious argument that bowing at the name of Jesus is every Christian's duty, Widdowes once again insults Prynne's intelligence and then accuses Prynne of opposing Christ and the King:

And now you may know evidently that Jesus is the name at which every knee must bow: whether they be knees of the regenerate or the glorified. And let Master Prinne be ashamed of his fighting against Jesus, and his Church. This is his folly: he hath dishonored Jesus, and so the King, the Vice-Gerent of the Lord Jesus . . . the writing violence of a Schismatique is impudent, and endless. It is certaine that you are more will than intellect, therefore your submission to Jesus, to his Vice-Gerent the King, and to the church may become you well. If you dare not dispute, and will not conforme, then write not more for shame.[70]

The "dare not dispute" attacks Prynne's failure to follow the rules of formal disputation; "will not conforme" assaults Prynne's image of himself as obedient to the orthodox doctrine of the Church of England. These are very palpable hits that, for Prynne, shame him into writing more.

Prynne's full title for his reply to *A Lawlesse kneelesse schismatical Puritan* clearly articulates its contents:

Lame Giles His Haultings, Or A Briefe Survey of Giles Widdowes His Confutation of an Appendix, concerning Bowing at the name of Jesus. Together with a short Relation of the Popish Originall and Progresse of this groundlesse novell Ceremony: Wherein Mr. Widdowes his manifold Forgeries, Oversights, and Absurdities are in part detected; and the point Of bowing at the name of Jesus, together with that of Cringing to Altars and Communion-tables, is now more largely discussed.

The title page's scriptural legend from Proverbs 26:3, 5 – "A whip for the horse, a bridel for the Asse, and a rod for the Fooles backe. Answer a Foole according to his folly, lest he be wise in his owne conceit" – captures the essence of Prynne's spirited response. The book contains a series of letters that introduce a comparatively brief dissertation on ceremonies. The first letter, addressed as a dedication to his alma mater Oxford University, seeks to acquaint her with the "notorious Errours . . . come forth in print of late under your Authority" from a "Sonne of yours, which I meane. Is one Giles Widdowes, a Poore halting widow in truth for braines and learning, of which he never had two mites."[71] The second letter, purportedly a copy of one he had written to the university chancellor, provides a survey of the mistakes he has seen in a manuscript of Widdowes's book (Prynne claims that at the press he saw the copy corrected by Mr. Page) and asks that the book be stayed at the press.

[B]ut my desire is to conceale his knowne weaknesse, (if not the Universities and your owne Oversight) by a timely discovery of his authorized grosse mistakes; which if they should take printed wings, and fly about, (as they are almost ready to forsake their nest) I shall be forced in my own defence, to pass a publike Censure on them.[72]

Prynne also sends along a copy of a letter addressed to Widdowes, cataloging his pamphlet's errors. In all these materials the object of Prynne's scorn is Widdowes's scholarly pretension as well as his theological errors. Representing himself as would-be censor-cum-protector of both Widdowes and his alma mater, Prynne assumes the character of the reluctant controversialist concerned about peace in the Church. He also manages a critique of pre-print licensing at the university by suggesting that the press licensers had "so mangled, so interlined and razed"[73] the book that he expected no error in Widdowes's printed text, which was not the case. That errors persisted, then, justifies his own critique. The essence of *Lame Giles His Haultings'* argument appears in the section entitled "A short Relation of the true beginning, and progresse of bowing at the name of Jesus; necessary for the determination of the present Controversie,"[74] which begins with the statement from the respected parliamentarian Edwin Sandys's *Europae Speculum* (1629) that the Pope grants twenty years of indulgence for every bow – a good enough reason for any good Protestant to dislike the practice.

William Page jumped to Widdowes's aid with his 1631 *Treatise on Justification*, which, like both of Widdowes's books, Lichfield printed at Oxford. Like Prynne, Page addresses his dedication to Oxford, his alma mater, but he complains of her other son's youthful folly and error in failing to recognize that she has already approved the propriety of bowing at Jesus' name. Page objects that Prynne is creating a controversy where there is none, all the learned divines (i.e., Andrewes, Richard Hooker) having claimed the antiquity and integrity of the practice. Page replies point-by-point to Prynne's "Appendix" rather than to *Lame Giles*. Following this appears a second treatise entitled "A further Justification of Bowing at the Name of Jesus" prefaced by a new title page and letter to the reader. Since the signature continues unbroken from the first part, the entire book appears to be the product of a single printing. Page informs the reader that he "neither mangled nor interlined nor altered one word" of Widdowes's book and announces that "what fault soever escaped uncrossed, was not by my approbation."[75] In this continuation Page addresses Prynne's use of the Church Fathers.

The arguments in this controversy, as my analysis should suggest, distinctly articulate the positions on both sides. Widdowes's attack on the dearly held principles of godly conformists – the sermon, the Sabbath, and predestination – using "Puritan" as a pejorative label, provokes a reasoned response to ceremonialism. Widdowes and Page argue the ceremonies' antiquity and necessity. The direction the arguments on each side takes depends on the authorities the author produces. Both sides engage in name-calling, and both sides warn the other of dire consequences for his position. On one side, to deny bowing is to deny God is to deny the King. On the other, to bow is to commit popish idolatry; to unrepentantly worship idols is to be damned. If the sure sign of Laudian censorship was its interest in quieting controversy and assuring civility, then this is an example of its total failure. Both sides overstep the bounds. Page readily admits to licensing Widdowes's second book for the press, so we learn both that books at Oxford were licensed and that the licensers there, or one of them at least, were sympathetic to Laudianism. Prynne's *Anti-Arminianisme*, which contained the "Appendix," was printed in London without license. *Lame Giles*, probably also printed in London, implies that Oxford is its place of printing by its imprint, "Imprinted for Giles Widdowes, MDCXXX." Given this, that the printer Michael Sparke, who had been sanctioned for printing the first edition of *Anti-Arminianisme*, should once again be under scrutiny is not surprising.

In April 1631 articles were objected in High Commission against Michael Sparke; the Oxford printer, William Turner; and two London booksellers, James Bowler and Solomon Turner, for printing, binding, selling and distributing to Cambridge University *Anti-Arminianisme* and *Lame Giles His Haultings*, both unlicensed. They were also charged with having books printed at Oxford "without authority," including sermons by Arthur Dent and John Preston, "The Book of Promises" (Antony Fawkner's *The Saints Legacies; or a collection of certain promises out of the word of God*), and something called Markham's Methods.[76] In their answers both Sparke and Turner denied any knowledge of *Lame Giles*, and Sparke pointed out that he had already been sanctioned for Prynne's *Anti-Arminianisme*. Additionally, Turner denied any partnership with Sparke, though he says he printed Dent's and Sibbes's sermons believing that they were Sparke's copy.[77] Although this case reflected some interest in books belonging to London Stationers being printed at Oxford, the "unauthorized" printing that most concerned the High Commission was of controversial books and books by godly authors.[78]

The controversial writings on bowing elicited another measure of censorship besides the High Commission's. William Baker wrote to William Page on Archbishop Abbot's behalf requesting Page not to publish his treatise on bowing at the name of Jesus, something of which "Mr. Widdowes foolishly and Mr. Prinn scurrilously have already to the scandal and dignitie of the Church" written. Baker expressed the Archbishop's "dislike of them both," especially in a time when great "distemper . . . will draw on new replies (for Prinne will not sitt downe as an idle spectator) and beget bitterness . . . amongst ourselves." Baker directed Page not to proceed in publishing his work, or "if your treatise be at the press to give it a stopp" and "by no meanes to suffer the same to be divulged."[79] If notwithstanding Baker's admonition, Page should choose to publish it, he would "repent" it. Baker's letter shows Abbot's anxiety about the currently contentious religious climate and shows him anxious to calm the waters – theoretically an anxiety shared with both Laud and King Charles. That Page's treatise, contrary to Abbot's order, was printed "by command" – especially at a time when measures were being taken to suppress Prynne's books against ceremonies – points to Laud's distinctive interest in intervening on behalf of writing that supported his plans to bring order to the Church, whether or not it contributed to the distempers of the times.

A measure of the danger ceremonial opponents perceived in the current climate appears in Henry Burton's decision to publish his response to Widdowes and Page in Amsterdam, where it bore the imprint, "Printed at Hambourgh, 1632. Reprinted Anno 1634." Burton's *The Opinion, Judgement, and Determination of two reverent, learned and conformable Divines of the Church of England, concerning bowing at the name, or naming of Jesus* is dedicated to Archbishop Abbot "& to the rest of the orthodox bishops of the Church of England." The pamphlet consists of two small treatises, purportedly by two different divines, followed by two letters from the publishers to the reader and a portrait of "An Arminian or mere Mountaguist" in the currently popular fashion of literary characters. The pamphlet's positions, outside of the character, are moderate. Relying on the Church Fathers, as well as on Continental Protestants, it argues against both the antiquity of and scriptural authority for bowing. Learned in its approach, it locates the grounds of Contention in problems of scriptural translation and context. It speaks to respect for both episcopal and royal authority and refrains from invective. It objects to Widdowes and Page on the grounds of their approach – "the one a Rayler, and the other a

Sophister" – but employs no more fulsome epithets than these.[80] Burton's choice to publish in Amsterdam is less a measure of the volatility of his text than of an ecclesiastical licensing culture that was radically transformed when Austen and Buckner stopped perusing books for the press. Burton shortly before had published two books that Buckner licensed: one, *The Christians bulvvarke, against Satans battery* (1631), a treatise on justification; the other, *The law and the Gospell reconciled* (1632), on the moral law, which included a short treatise on the Sabbath. Having been in trouble in 1629 and 1630 for writing books that were not "licensed," Burton's compliance with ecclesiastical licensing in the early 1630s, together with a more moderate voice than he had had in the late 1620s, correspond with the *Opinion, Judgement, and Determination*'s title page's characterization of its authors as "two reverend, learned, and conformable Divines of the Church of England." Burton saw himself as a conformist with a conscience. The decision to publish this work abroad, which was not unlike those Buckner had approved, indicates that the few avenues that had existed for publishing "legal" new books by conforming Calvinist and godly authors diminished when Laud's new chaplains took the place of Abbot's in 1633.

Laud's program for assuring decency and conformity in the Church of England contained another program that proved to be as provocative as bowing at the name of Jesus: moving the communion table to the east wall of the church "altarwise," elevating it, and surrounding it with rails where the communicants were to kneel to receive the Lord's Supper. Laud advanced the altar policy in the name of decency, warning that if altars were not railed in the chancel, "churchwardens will keep their accounts at the Lord's table, parishioners will sit round it and talk of parish business ... schoolmasters will teach their boys to write upon this table, and boys will lay their hats, satchels and books upon it ... and dogs will defile the Lord's table."[81] It was not really the question of decency, however, that provoked controversy. As David Cressy has shown, altars came to represent larger questions of discipline, theology, and liturgy.[82] In 1633 Charles declared that in the question of altar placement, parish churches should follow their cathedral church. In 1634 Laud issued orders that within his province of Canterbury church officials should require that all churches comply with the practice of Canterbury cathedral, which moved and railed its communion table. Archbishop Neile sought similar compliance in the northern province. John Williams, Bishop of Lincoln, objected to the rigid enforcement of the altar policy, and expressed his views in a letter that was circulated in manuscript beginning in 1633.[83] In 1636 Peter Heylyn wrote a book "acceptable to higher persons" that, by misrepresenting the circulating manuscript, sought to discredit Williams.[84]

Heylyn's *A coale from the altar. Or An ansvver to a letter not long since written to the Vicar of Gr. against the placing of the Communion table at the east end of the chancell; and now of late dispersed abroade* was entered in the Stationers' Register as having been written by the vicar of Grantham and licensed by Baker. The letter in question was purported to have been written by John Williams, rebuking a vicar in his diocese for carrying out the altar policy.[85] Heylyn ridicules cryptic selections from Williams's alleged letter to the vicar of Grantham, including Williams's supposed remark that "the Countrey people would suppose them, Dressers."[86] Heylyn's book concludes with a copy of the King's 1633 resolution on altars, passed in the Privy Council. While Williams would subsequently respond to Heylyn's misrepresentation of his letter, other writers joined Heylyn in praising the altar policy. Heylyn's foray into the altar controversy, however, was not without critics, even among those without godly or Puritan sympathies. One observer, Jasper Fisher, told of an archdeacon (unnamed) who at his Visitation remarked that "knowing the Author," he "yet had most despitefully & irreligiously abused the Bishop, as the Jesuites dealt with King James his books where they pretended not to know in the Answer; and had shewed himselfe the greatest puritane that could be in so abusing a prelate."[87] Fisher concluded that Heylyn's book posed a danger to Laudianism: "But now we . . . shall rather give offense to the bretheren & advantage to the adversary. For it hath made many more backward to all Church-order, and increased puritans generally, so that they are more resolute & stubborn than heretofore."[88]

Heylyn was not alone in intensifying the divisiveness surrounding the altar policy. Among the writers who argued the case for altars were Robert Shelford, *Five pious and learned discourses* (1635); Edmund Reeve, *The communion booke catechisme expounded, according to Gods holy Word, and the established doctrine of the Church . . . Wherein also are explained sundry of the highest points in divinity, and matter greatly considerable in these present times. In speciall there is demonstrated, that his most excellent Majesties declaration to his subjects, concerning lawfull sports to be used, doth tend unto a very great encrease of true godlinesse throughout [sic] the whole kingdome* (1635, authorized by Wykes); and John Pocklington, *Altare Christianum* (1636, authorized by Bray). By the time that the controversy about altars emerged, Laudian licensing was securely in place, so it is not unusual that no authorized books on altars appeared from the presses either in London or the universities. William Prynne, however, was able to have his book responding to Heylyn, Reeve, and Pocklington, printed in Amsterdam. *A Quench-coale*, which Prynne wrote while imprisoned for *Histrio-mastix*, appeared in 1637 from the Richt Right press. The book, which is characteristic Prynne in its lengthy (358 pages), heavily documented, and tedious argument, is dedicated to King Charles, and takes as its secondary intention, proving to the King that his "good Subjects" are "abused by a packe of lewde companions, and the High Commission made the Instrument, not only of oppressing his Majesties best subjects, but of patronizing knaves and offenders in their open contempts against his Majesties Lawes and Declaration ... "[89] Prynne objects that Laud's licensers would approve such "popish trash," and he hopes for a "time of reckoning ... to ease our Church of such viperous Apostates."[90] Although not among the books specifically named for which Prynne, Henry Burton, and John Bastwick were tried in the court of Star Chamber in 1637, Prynne's book on the altar policy engaged in the kind of activity named in the information: publishing "various libelous books with intent to move the people to discontent against the King's ecclesiastical government."[91]

In 1637 John Williams's *Holy Table, Name and Thing*, a direct reply to Heylyn, appeared anonymously in six editions. The title page said that it was printed for the diocese of Lincoln, and, in addition to the title, declares that it was "Written long ago by a Minister in Lincolnshire, in answer to D. Coal, a judicious Divine in Q Mairies dayes." That the stated provenance is a pretense becomes clear from the beginning when, without naming Heylyn specifically, the book proceeds to object to the pretended letter to the vicar of Grantham. It becomes clear that Williams, indeed, had written to the vicar, but his letter differed from Heylyn's representation. He says the "poor fellow" (Heylyn) "makes himself an Adversary, not out of the Letter, but out of his owne phantasie; and driving him before him (as he in Aristotle did his shadow) from one end of the Book to the other shoots all his Arrows at this man of his own rearing, and yet with all this advantage never stirs him."[92] The book objects to Heylyn for misrepresenting the issue about moving the Communion table. Williams explains that the actual letter had been written when a "controversy had arisen in the church between the vicar and the aldermen with some violence," and the bishop said to do nothing until he visited.

The Bishop entering into a discourse of the indifference of this circumstance in its own nature, the Vicar came suddenly into the Hall, pale and staring in his looks, and either with his journey, or some other affrights much disordered ... The Vicar brake out into a passion and scares, and said they threatned to set his house on fire.[93]

Williams then includes the actual letter, which contains his proposed solution for the parish, "that your Communion-Table, when it is not used, should stand in the upper end of the Chancell, not Altar-wise, but Table-wise" and be brought forward for the Lord's Supper. The rest of the pamphlet contains a treatise that represents itself as having been written much earlier and that relies on examples and evidence from the time of Elizabeth relating to the table's placement and to the role of the monarchy in directing ceremonies.

Williams was summoned before the High Commission and questioned about his involvement with *Holy Table, Name and Thing*.[94] Williams's response consists of a host of denials, many of which are highly suspect. On the one hand he said that he *believed* that he did not license the book, that it was printed without license, and that he did not direct the words "Printed for the Diocese of Lincoln" to be "added in the foot of the title." On the other, obviously responding to articles questioning his understanding of ecclesiastical licensing policy, he said he *believed*, based on Elizabeth's Injunctions and the "old Decree of the Star-Chamber," that "every Bishop in England hath power by Law and prescription to license any Divinity book, especially written by himself or any other in his own Diocese."[95] Williams had been in and out of the court of Star Chamber in suits and counter-suits that had begun over a remark he made in 1627, which indicated that King James favored being liberal with Puritans for political reasons. In 1629 a bill of information was brought in Star Chamber that remarked Williams's leniency towards Puritans and charged him with "publishing divers false Tales and News to the scandal of his majesty's Government" and "revealing some things contrary to the duty of his place and oath as a Privy Councillor."[96] Once the case began to proceed in earnest in 1633, questions arose about perjury and suborning witnesses. On June 16, 1637 additional charges were brought in Star Chamber, and Williams's trial occurred in July. Given the serious nature of the causes already in place against Williams, his responses in Star Chamber, equivocal as they are – he did not "believe" that he authorized the book – are understandable. In August 1637, following his Star Chamber censure for those matters before it, Williams was questioned in the Tower on the matter of *Holy Table, Name and Thing*. In his submission to the King, he admits having approved, "made," and caused to be printed the said book. Because the book was the cause "of many factious persons to disobey and disaffect divers Laudable Rites and ceremonies of the Church, and the endeavour of the Reverent Bishops and others to settle a decent order," Williams says that he "uttlerly disclaims it as erroneous and faultie."[97]

Williams was not alone in being in trouble for this book. On July 3, 1637, the Stationers' Company's court of Assistants took action against four of its members for "the undue printing of my Lord of Lincolnes Booke called the holy Table name & thing, by mr Bourne without the wardens hands & orderly Entrance, & fyned him at 5li for his offence." The printers were also fined "at 3 li a peece."[98] On the outside, this appears to be simply a matter of unauthorized printing, but clearly, as Williams's submission reveals, this was another instance where the state of licensing afforded a means to warn Stationers to be wary of the kinds of books they printed.

The final area of controversy that led to some books being censored and others being protected was on the question of the nature and origin of the Sabbath or the Lord's Day. Debate about the manner in which the Sabbath should be observed dated back to the reign of Elizabeth. The Caroline publication that rekindled the debate purported to have been written during the reign of James. In 1630 Edward Brerewood's *A Learned Treatise of the Sabaoth* appeared from Lichfield's press at Oxford. The treatise was directed to the godly minister Nicholas Byfield and bears the date, "MAY 16, 1611 AT Gresham House." The treatise accused Byfield of causing a crisis of conscience in Brerewood's ward, John Brerewood, who, having heard Byfield preach, was overcome with guilt for doing his master's bidding on the Lord's Day. Brerewood, who maintains that the laws of the Jewish Sabbath were only ceremonial and thus non-binding for Christians, argues that a servant's obedience requires that he do whatever his master requires. If there is any sin at all in not keeping the Sabbath, it is the master's. Brerewood challenges Byfield to enter into a disputation to justify his doctrine of the Sabbath. Apparently, Byfield responded in a letter refusing to debate and suggesting that John Brerewood may have misrepresented the events. The second part of Brerewood's *Treatise* responds at length to very short passages of Byfield's letter, and tells him that his refusal to dispute the matter fully "is a blemish to your reputation, and prejudice to your doctrine."[99] Brerewood's *Treatise* was reprinted in 1631, and in 1632 *A Second Treatise of the Sabbath* appeared from Lichfield's press at Oxford.

Before Brerewood's second treatise appeared, Nicholas Byfield's brother, Richard Byfield (also a godly minister), wrote a reply to the first treatise that answers him point by point in the conventional controversial style that prints extended passages of the offending text followed by a detailed answer, which in this case is very learned. Byfield's response, published by Meredith and Stephens in London in 1631, was approved for the press by Robert Austen, Abbot's chaplain. Byfield was spurred to respond by "the base language of the reply in the end of that Treatise" as well as "the very novelties and dangerous vilenesse of the Doctrine, without any reference to things personall." Byfield objects to Brerewood because he sees in his arguments "the whole right of the Law for the time of Gods worship alleviated."[100] Byfield argues from scripture and the Church Fathers that the sanctification of the Sabbath is part of the moral law because it is expressed in the fourth commandment, and that while the Church changed the Sabbath to the Lord's Day, the moral law was not abrogated. Byfield concludes his response by objecting that while the author may not have intended to destroy the peace of the Church, the publishers did:

It is no new thing to heare Christian Doctrine charged for seditious, and disturbing both Church and state; but it is much audaciousnesse and perversenesse to charge this docrine so, which having beene taught, and printed, and found in the hands of the whole kingdome, it never bred the least disturbance in any familie . . . You would exasperate authoritie against painefull and conscionable Ministers, you would suggest hard things against the quiet of the land, you would cast Jealousies causelesse.[101]

Byfield was probably correct on two counts – both that by printing Brerewood's treatise the publishers had intended to provoke a controversy (Brerewood had called on Nicholas Byfield to participate in one) and that this was an old dog that should have been left sleeping in the interest of peace in the Church and State.

In 1631 Henry Burton's *Law and the Gospell Reconciled*, which spoke to the relationship of the Sabbath to the moral law, argued that Sabbath sanctification was, indeed, part of the moral law, therefore Christians were bound to sanctify the Sabbath. Christ's resurrection on the first day, however, made that the Lord's Day. Christians, then, were bound to observe the Lord's Day as the sanctified Sabbath. The principal focus of this book, however, is the implicit antinomianism upon which arguments like Brerewood's appeared to be based. Burton's book, published by Michael Sparke, was authorized by Thomas Buckner, Abbot's chaplain. This was the last godly book on the Sabbath question that was authorized for print in London. John Sprint's *Propositions, tending to proove the necessary use of the christian sabbath, or Lords day*, however, was published by John Grismond in 1635, but this printing was based on the 1607 license.

The next book that appeared in the controversy so bristled at Brerewood's antinomian tendencies that its overreaction spurred the authorities to drastic measures. In 1632 Theophilus Brabourne's *A defence of that most ancient and sacred ordinance of Gods, the Sabbath day* was printed in Amsterdam. Brabourne, a London minister, had also published an earlier version of the work, *A discourse upon the Sabbath Day*, in London in 1628 without allowance, which at that time went unnoticed by the authorities. This time, Brabourne was arrested and imprisoned in the Gate House, and charged by the High Commission not only for violating the Star Chamber decree by publishing the *Defence* illegally abroad and the *Discourse* illegally in London, but also for having opinions that "broached" on being "heretical and judaical." In 1634 the High Commission judged him to be "A Jew, a heretic and schismatic." Brabourne was deprived of his livings, excommunicated, fined £1000, and returned to prison.[102] Brabourne's position, that the Church should practice the Jewish Sabbath on the seventh day, was certainly a position so extreme that the High Commission's intervention may be seen to be within its ecclesiastical jurisdiction. I do, however, find it interesting that Brabourne took the position that were the Church not ready to accept his proposition, it could at the very least observe the Lord's Day as an authentic day of Sabbath sanctification – a far more modest proposal. He also defers to the King and the bishops of the Church as having full authority in the matter.

Following the High Commission's judgment upon Brabourne, no other godly treatises on the Sabbath were authorized for print in England. Writing against sabbatarianism, however, continued among the Laudians, in part because in October 1633 Charles I reissued the Book of Sports, which approved Sunday recreations. The first of these works to appear employed a devious tactic which, like other efforts Hunt and Milton found among the Laudian licensers, ventriloquized prominent Calvinists. Following Brerewood's Oxford publishers' strategy of resurrecting an old text, Peter Heylyn translated and had published *The Doctrine of the Sabbath* (1634), written by John Prideaux, Regius Professor of Divinity at Oxford and a prominent Calvinist leader. The treatise, first printed in Latin in 1626, had appeared in a collection of lectures entitled *Orationes novem inaugurals*. Preceding his translation of Prideaux's treatise, Heylyn provides a substantive preface that, according to Milton, "scandalously misrepresents the regius professor's words on the issue."[103] Prideaux's treatise itself was an analysis of the divergent views on the Sabbath among both ancient and modern theologians, which cautions against extremism. According to Prideaux, the observation of the Sabbath "is founded on the fourth Commandement ... there is in the fourth Commandement something Morall, and some things Ceremoniall; the circumstances Ceremoniall, but the substance Moral."[104] In Heylyn's hands, however, Prideaux seems to favor many Sabbath recreations and oppose the godly position that the moral law commands a sanctified Sabbath. Milton sees Heylyn's scheme as achieving some success in bewildering the Puritans, but he also observes that others appear to have regarded Prideaux as having been set up.[105]

In the next few years several more books appeared that subscribed to the anti-Sabbatarian views expressed by Brerewood and Heylyn-via-Prideaux, including one printed at Laud's command without entry in the Stationers' Registers, Francis White's *A Treatise of the Sabbath Day* (1635). Among them, besides White's, were: Peter Heylyn's *History of the Sabbath* (1634), authorized by Haywood; Christopher Dow's *A discourse of the Sabbath and the Lords Day* (1636), authorized by Bray; David Primerose's *A treatise of the Sabbath and the Lords-day* (1636); *A soveraigne antidote against sabbatarian errours. Or, A decision of the chiefe doubts and difficulties touching the Sabbath* (1636), identified on its title page as being written by a "Reverend, religious, and judicious divine" and said in its preface to have been "approved to be printed for the publicke edification of the Church";[106] and John Pocklington's *Sunday not Sabbath* (1636), authorized by Bray and entered in 1637 in the Stationers' Registers. Both Primerose and the "Reverend, religious, and judicious divine" seem to suggest that their authors have been won over by the merits of the Laudian position, especially Primerose, since the work seeks to capitalize on him being a Protestant brother from the Continent. That from the perspective of English publication this controversy appears to be entirely one-sided testifies to the success of Laudian licensing policies, which, while they may have silenced the English presses, were not entirely successful in stilling all controversy.

Henry Burton entered the fray through the auspices of the Stam press at Amsterdam. His anonymously printed *A brief answer to a late Treatise of the Sabbath day* (1635), which responds to White's *A Treatise of the Sabbath Day*, consists of a dialogue between two "divines." The central position is that White's is a dangerous book because it "overthrows the doctrine of the Church of England."[107] The argument proceeds by quoting sections from White's book and comparing them to statements in the Articles and Homilies, and to early Protestant theologians in England and on the Continent. Gentle in both its tone and its argument, this does not participate in the kind of immoderate Puritanism with which Burton's writings are so often charged. The same may be said of the second edition of *A brief answer: The Lords day, the Sabbath Day*, which expands the argument of the first through extensive reference to the Church Fathers. While the approach of these books is learned and moderate, the first contains a seed of the kind of criticism that would lead to Burton's censure by the Star Chamber in 1637; he criticizes the prelates directly and Francis White by innuendo. One of his two "divines" says, "Now tell me Brother, what thinke you of this, that those Prelates and Clergy of England in the very first duskish downing of the morning should be so cleare, orthodox, and zealous in the point of the Sabbath, and now ... so many, with their eyes closed up, doe with both hands fight against this truth?"[108] (Earlier in his career, White had been more sympathetic to Calvinist theology.) Burton's *Brief answer* received ready condemnation as a "lawlesse pamphlet."

In *An examination and confutation of a lawlesse pamphlet, intituled, A briefe answer to a late treatise of the Sabbath-day: digested dialogue-wise betweene two divines* (1637), a book entered in the Stationers' Registers under his own authorization, White commences with an *ad hominem* attack that calls the pamphlet's author a "clamorous and audacious Scripturient, a Person of a very weak judgement" who is "notorious for his ignorance, envy, and presumption."[109] Not only is Burton a "violent Man," but he is "so far transported with bitter Zeale, that whatsoever proceeds from him, is litigious, clamorous, scandalous, and abusive: and his Pamphlets are fraughted with such Materials, as are apt to poison Christian people with contempt and hatred of Ecclesiastical Government, and present Religion established in our Church."[110] While Burton had certainly disagreed with White's position, White's characterization of him is as clamorous and abusive as he claims Burton's book to be. The timing of White's book suggests that it may be more than Burton's *A brief answer* and *The Lords day* that provoked him.

In 1636 another book by Burton on the Sabbath appeared secretly from Stam's press: *A Divine Tragedie Lately Acted, or A collection of sundry memorable examples of Gods judgements upon Sabbath-breakers, and other like libertines, in their unlawfull sports, happening within the realme of England, in the compass only of two yeares last past, since the booke was published worthy to be knowne and considered of all men, especially such, who are guilty of the sinne or arch-patrons thereof.* Expressly against the Book of Sports, Burton rehearsed fifty-five examples of occasions where God visited punishments on people who broke the Sabbath. A man who engaged in sport lost an eye, another who fetched a maypole went lame. Boys who went swimming drowned. It concludes with an epilogue that calls upon parish priests to admonish their people to keep the Sabbath, and upon magistrates to "take care" that solemn days should be "piously celebrated." Following the epilogue a final example of God's judgment appears, this time inflicted on the Attorney General, William Noy, who for prosecuting William Prynne in the matter of *Histrio-mastix* fell ill and died of a disease in which he "voyded" blood.[111] In January 1637 Burton was questioned about this book, which he admitted having written although he denied writing the section on Noy. It was for this book that Burton was suspended from his lectureship and deprived of the profits of his living.[112] Whether or not Burton wrote the passage on Noy, this book was among those that led to Burton's 1637 trial in Star Chamber along with William Prynne and John Bastwick. The Star Chamber censorship trials, which will be considered next, while they should not be taken as illustrative of the general practice of Caroline censorship, should be regarded as participating in the climate of escalating controversy about Laud's measures to ensure "decency" and "conformity" in the Church of England.

One of the problems that have arisen in understanding Caroline censorship of religious writing has been that, for the most part, the several aspects of censorship – ecclesiastical licensing, efforts to restrain religious controversy, and what David Cressy has called the "show trials" of the Puritan martyrs, William Prynne, Henry Burton, and John Bastwick – have not been regarded as intimately interconnected. With alterations in ecclesiastical licensing practices and in the licensing establishment between 1631 and 1634, conforming Calvinist writers increasingly turned to Continental printers. In doing so, they became more and more outspoken. Relatively restrained objections to ceremonial innovations turned to personal attack first on writers who advanced ceremonial policies and then on the prelacy itself. The persistence of written opposition to ceremonialism undermined the efforts of the Laudian licensers to ventriloquize conforming Calvinist leaders and claim them as proponents of a ceremonialist middle ground.[113] Admittedly, as we saw with Widdowes, proponents of Laudianism worked very hard to cast their opponents as seditious schismatics. This strategy might have succeeded except for the vast readership of godly authors who were sustained and edified by a legal "Puritan" press. Laud, of course, could have taken measures to restrain the publication of Elizabethan and Jacobean Puritans – as he indeed tried to do in the 1637 Star Chamber Decree – but his conscientious effort to assure that his program to "preserve" "decency and conformity" came within the scope of the law meant that he had to move cautiously.

PURITAN "SHOW TRIALS"

The appearance of Prynne's *Histrio-mastix* at the end of 1632 afforded Laud an opportunity to harness the power of the legal system to teach a lesson to licensers, printers, and authors that the line between godly and seditious writing, even when it was officially authorized, was a fine one. Even though *Histrio-mastix* did not technically come within the compass of Charles's 1626 proclamation against writings that contained religious innovations, the spirit in which Prynne was punished reflected not only the proclamation's promise that offenders would meet with severity but also that there would be "exemplary punishment of some few" so that "all others may be warned."[114] Prynne, as we know, had authored *Anti-Arminianisme*, along with several books in the controversies about Laudian ceremonialism whose suppression ostensibly was sought because they were unauthorized and not because they opposed the doctrine of the Church of England. Using "licensing" as a grounds for summoning printers and writers to appear before the court of High Commission was proving an ineffective tool for silencing opponents of ceremonialism – especially when legally printed books nursed the theological positions upon which this opposition was founded. For Charles's government, proving in the court of Star Chamber that an authorized book with a conventionally godly position (that playhouses were the devil's workshop and unrepentant players and playgoers alike risked damnation) would provide a useful link between Puritans and sedition.

Whether or not prosecuting Prynne, along with *Histrio-mastix*'s publisher, printers, and licenser, served the legitimate end of protecting the Caroline Church and State, the intermediate need of bolstering the Caroline licensing establishment, or, more cynically, Laud's interest in silencing a querulous and persistent critic of his personal agenda, has been the bone of historical contention for generations. I can certainly see some merit in the positions of all the historical camps. Laud had cause to dislike a man who was never shy about criticizing any shift in the Church of England away from the moderate Calvinism that had prevailed during most of James's reign and who showed little respect for the institution of ecclesiastical press licensing. Furthermore, Prynne's book did quite a bit more than advance a conventional godly position about stage plays. It objected to instrumental music in the liturgy, to bowing at the name of Jesus, and to such folk traditions as New Year's gifts, Christmas feasts, maypoles and morris dances. It was often vitriolic. It promised God's severest judgments on playgoers and Sabbath breakers alike. It condemned the fashions of the times, and it called on magistrates not only to set an example by spurning theatrical performances but also to restrain playing altogether. The King's attorneys made a compelling case during the course of the trial that the book personally attacked the King and Queen and that it approved killing monarchs. On the other hand, some procedural irregularities do seem to have occurred. Having been denied bail, Prynne languished in prison for over a year before he was tried. His appeals to the King and Queen for clemency, which seem to have met with a favorable response, were ignored.[115] Furthermore, in the court of Star Chamber, Prynne's case was judged by Privy Councilors, who, as Charles's valued advisors, had vested interests.

The Prynne problem – that is, the extraordinary degree of difference that appears in historical assessments of Prynne's 1634 trial – has often been regarded as one of historical perspective. Rather than being a matter of interpretation, the real problem we have with making sense of Prynne comes from inconsistencies in the documentary record. Since most of the records of proceedings in the court of Star Chamber during the reign of Charles I disappeared during the Civil War, it is not surprising that for this case we lack the Attorney General's bill of information to the King that sets out in detail the grounds for proceeding in Star Chamber. We know that Prynne made his formal reply sometime during the late summer of 1633 since he mentions it in his letter of submission to the King, but this answer is not extant (though we do have the authorizer, Thomas Buckner's). We do, however, have Prynne's answer to an initial examination before the Attorney General, but this would have been part of the preliminary investigation to prepare for the formal information. There are no copies of interrogatories directed at either principals or witnesses in the matter of Prynne, though, again, some exist for Buckner. All this might suggest that the problem with Prynne's trial, then, is an absence of information. This, however, is not the case. Three accounts of the trial are in print: one in T. B. Howell, *State Trials* (1816), another in John Rushworth's *Historical Collections* (1690), the third in S. R. Gardiner's *Documents Relating to the Proceeding Against William Prynne* (1877). In addition, there exist in manuscript at least four accounts (besides the one printed in Gardiner) and several fragmentary notes, usually in contemporary news letters. We have, thus, a wealth of documentary evidence, but unfortunately, one that introduces inconsistencies.

None of the accounts of the trial appears to be the official witness to the entire proceedings. Gardiner reprints a seventeenth-century law report that is part of a manuscript collection. As such, it frequently summarizes lengthy material or even omits perceived irrelevancies. *State Trials* reprints Rushworth's account (which, by Rushworth's own admission, is not disinterested), but introduces an error in the year. Rushworth correctly assigns Prynne's trial to February 1633/34. Howell apparently "corrects" what he regards as Rushworth's misuse of new dating, taking February 1633 to actually be February 1632/33. Both Rushworth and Howell give February 7 as the beginning day of the trial. Gardiner gives February 14,[116] which coincides with the manuscript versions that begin on the second day of the trial – February 15. Rushworth assembled his collections for the period of the personal rule, so that the reader might know the arts and methods of government "in such a long suspension of the Exercise of the Supream Legislative Power."[117] One reason he assembled these documents, he says, is that "The Reader may with ease, by Reflections made upon these annals, inform himself . . . What unusual Powers of Judicatory were assumed and exercised in the ménage of the Government during that time . . . "[118] The provenance for the account of the trial in *Historical Collections* is not given, but that it would be an official account of the trial seems unlikely since it is both inaccurate in its representation of the number of days on which the proceedings occurred (it reports four and accounts only for three) and incomplete, as we shall see. Of his report of a proceeding in another court, Rushworth says, "The Author took with his pen verbatim (as near as he could) . . . "[119] Whether or not this was the case here, Prynne's trial is presented with all the writerly attention to narrativity, stylistic eloquence, and grammatical consistency that marks the *Historical Collections*.

The four manuscript accounts of the trial in the collections of the Bodleian, British, Houghton, and Huntington libraries agree with each other.[120] Indeed, they seem to be scribal copies of a common source, since they use carat inserts for dropped words but in different places. The similarities between the Houghton and Huntington manuscripts extend to very close pagination, with some evidence (dropped catchwords, compressed letters) that even in pagination the scribes are attempting to stay close to a common source. With one exception, the variants in the four manuscripts result from such scribal idiosyncrasies as spelling and capitalization. For example, the Houghton scribe uses "thiere" and the Huntington uses "their." The one significant difference appears in a comment made by Archbishop Laud during the testimony of Mr. Herbert on behalf of Thomas Buckner, *Histrio-mastix*'s authorizer. In his defense of Buckner's licensing on Huntington f. 14, Herbert says that "Mr Buckner sett his hand to noe part; but was approved by both the Universities."[121] In response to this remark, Laud interjects

Doctor Reiynolde & doctor Whitgift were at both the Universities, I Remember that as doctor Reiynolde disputed against them in the divinitie Scholles; Doctor Gentilis at the same time defended them in the Lawe Schooles, and [they] that were of the younger sort thought that Doctor Gentilis had as good Reasons in the defense of playes as Doctor Reiynolde had against them.[122]

In the Houghton manuscript Laud's remarks are on f. 13, and appear to be totally out of context. The Stowe manuscript agrees with the Huntington, but none of the printed copies contain this passage or identify Herbert as Buckner's counsel – a difference to which, with others, I will subsequently return. None of these manuscript accounts are transcripts of court pro-ceedings. British Library and Bodleian are bound with other historical tracts. Huntington and Houghton appear separately bound in a quarto format with lined paper, and appear to be the work of professional scribes writing with impeccable though distinctive secretary hands. The Houghton and Huntington manuscripts are both bound in brown pol-ished calfskin decorated with ribbon ties and gold stamping. The existence of these four manuscripts points to a lively interest in the Prynne affair, especially since they focus on the defense's arguments and the court's censures. All four begin "In Camera Stellata 15 die February 1633," report two days of proceedings, with the last day being Monday, February 17. They omit the government's case against Prynne that occupies the first day of the trial in the printed copies, though they contain a summary of Attorney General Noy's response to the defense's arguments that does not appear in the printed versions.

The presence of three divergent trial accounts, while interesting in and of itself, serves as a reminder of the principal problems we have in assessing any evidence from Prynne's trial. First, as for any trial, the arguments on both sides need to be regarded as rhetorical exercises designed to persuade the court. Second, this trial took place in the very public venue of the court of Star Chamber. Even if an official account of the trial existed – which does not appear to be the case – all of the proceedings should be evaluated for the impact they would have on a public audience and not just for the impression they would make on the judges. Finally, whatever speeches are more fully and carefully reported will alter the way the trial is represented. For example, all of the accounts of the trial attend carefully to one or another of the speeches rendered in judgment of Prynne – but not equally to all of them. Lord Cottington's speech comes first in all accounts, and many of the other court members simply refer to and concur with it. This speech is most fully represented in Rushworth and Howell, least in the four manuscripts. The substance is the same, but the details differ, except for the penalty of imprisonment for Prynne. All versions condemn Prynne to perpetual imprisonment, but the four manuscripts say "imprisonment

perpetuall; or at the Kings pleasure."[123] That the accounts also vary significantly in the number of speeches they include likewise colors the
perspective. Hence the absence of Archbishop Laud's speech in both
Rushworth and Howell turns their account into something quite different
from those in Gardiner and the manuscripts. Laud's accusation that
Prynne committed high treason – a charge totally unwarranted by any
reading of statutory treason laws – heightens the sense of Prynne's peril.
Archbishop Neile's speech, which appears only in the manuscript versions,
reveals a factional interest in using the proceedings to quell even the most
modest godly sentiments: "But you come to speake of your own Sort, You
style them holie, Religious Saintes, good Christians. Thus much I can tell
you, that your Sort has growne soe stiff, that it was fayne to be styfled at
Tyborne and Chepside with a halter."[124] Neile's remarks veer away from
Laud's pronounced efforts to characterize Prynne as a traitor in order to
prevent him from becoming a religious martyr.

Before considering more fully what these divergent accounts reveal, a
timeline for the production and condemnation of *Histrio-mastix* should
prove useful.[125]

October 16, 1630	Stationers' Register entry to Michael Sparke, authorized by Thomas Buckner
Before December 28, 1632	Printing completed, imprint reads "1633"[126]
January 1633	Prynne presented Attorney General Noy with a copy of the book[127]
January 9, 1633	Queen's Pastoral acted at Denmark House[128]
Before January 24, 1633	Prynne examined "before one of the Secretaries"[129]
Before January 31, 1633	Prynne brought into the High Commission and Star Chamber for "publishing a booke (a little before the Queenes acting of her play) of the unlawfulness of plaies"[130]
January 31, 1633	Prynne examined before Attorney General, William Noy
February 1, 1633	Prynne imprisoned in the Tower of London
June 21, 1633	Information exhibited against Prynne in Star Chamber
July 3, 1633	Contempt order against Prynne for failing to answer the information
July 5, 1633	Prynne's motion to Star Chamber to have counsel assigned[131]

August 10, 1633	Star Chamber ordered Prynne's imprisonment in the Tower until he prepared his answer to the Bill of Complaint and to the prosecution's interrogatories
September 1633	Prynne filed his answer to the Bill of Complaint[132]
September 1633	Prynne submitted to the King and petitioned for pardon or bail
February 14, 1634	Star Chamber trial of Prynne, Sparke, Buckner and printers, the government's case
February 15, 1634	Star Chamber trial of Prynne, Sparke, Buckner and printers, the defense's case
February 17, 1634	Judgments rendered. Prynne imprisoned in the Fleet
Late February, 1634	Prynne petitioned Privy Council for mitigation of sentence[133]
May 7, 1634	Pynne pilloried at Westminster and his ear cut off
May 10, 1634	Pynne pilloried at Cheapside[134]
June 11, 1634	Prynne's letter to Laud responding to his censure during the trial

According to contemporary accounts, the principal cause against Prynne – in January 1633 at least – was the perceived offence to the Queen. On January 31, 1633 in a letter to Sir Thomas Puckering, George Gresley reported that Prynne was in trouble for

publishing a booke (a little before the Queenes acting of her play) of the unlawfulness of plaies wherein the Table of his booke & his briefe additions thereunto he hath these words; woemen acters notorious whores; and that St. Paul prohibited woemen to speake publiquely in the church; & does then sayth he any Christian woman be so more then whorishely impudent as to act to speake publiquelie on a stage (perchance in mans apparel & cutt haire) in the presence of sundrie men & woeman, which wordes is thought by some will cost him his eares, or heavely punished & deeplie fined.[135]

A year later, according to the printed accounts, Prynne was tried for "writing and publishing a scandalous and libelous book against the state, the Kinge, and all his people." Prynne was accused of writing a book which, by casting "aspersions" on the King and Queen and "countenancing violence against princes who favor plays, moves the people to discontent and sedition."[136] Some part of the information apparently accused him of commending Dr. Alexander Leighton and the Jesuit, Juan de Mariana, both of whose books had received public condemnation. Additionally, based on the manuscript accounts, Prynne was charged with equivocation and perjury (the most common cause of actions in Star Chamber) for responses to interrogatories that contradicted evidence of other witnesses. Doctors Harris and Goad claimed to have refused to authorize Prynne's book on plays; Prynne said the only ecclesiastical licenser who saw *Histrio-mastix* was Buckner. During the trial Prynne's attorney explained that Prynne had taken a book on plays to Harris and Goad, but it was a different book.[137]

As this instance of the difference in the charges indicates, discrepancies among the various trial accounts can have serious implications. While the question of the differences warrants a full investigation – a substantive project in and of itself – for our purposes here of assessing the place of the trial in Caroline press censorship, I will briefly characterize the various accounts. Rushworth/Howell gives the clearest sense of the general course of the proceedings. On the first day the government's case is presented through reading of the information, the defendants' answers, and the witnesses' depositions, and then the government's case is presented with arguments from the text of *Histrio-mastix*. It places at the end of the first day the beginning of Prynne's defense, which all other accounts place on the second day. The second day contains the defense's arguments and the third the censures by the court. Rushworth/Howell contains the greatest detail in reporting the information and the answers. When it comes to the government's case, it mentions twice that passages from *Histrio-mastix* were read but does not report them nor does it mention page numbers – although it does contain an exact transcription of the book's dedication to the "Masters of the Bench of the honourable flourishing Law-Society of Lincoln's Inn," the accuracy of which suggests a transcription from a printed source rather than an aural reporting.[138] For the second day of the trial Rushworth/Howell gives only the arguments of Prynne's attorneys, and not those for Sparke or Buckner. It indicates that Prynne's attorneys submitted passages out of the book in Prynne's defense but says, "Which Passages were opened by the Counsel, but not read."[139] One significant difference between this account and the others is that the others contain as part of the proceedings a request on behalf of Prynne to have more time to prepare a response to the government's case, which was denied. Although not a part of the proceedings in Rushworth/Howell, Atkins, Prynne's counsel, refers to this request: "The weight of this Cause, and the aggravations upon it by the king's Counsel, made me the last day (without desire of my client) to crave farther time, for we durst not then give any Answer." Lacking this desired time, Atkins then says, that "all" he can "now say" is that Prynne's oath (his sworn answer to the information) will have to serve as his defense: "His oath is admitted as proof against him, in the acknowledgement of his Book; and shall it not be admitted by him, to clear the integrity of his heart?"[140] There is no reporting for the third day (which was a Sunday, so the court would not have met), but the censures occupy the fourth. Rushworth/Howell reports by far the fewest censure speeches, although the ones that do appear are the most fully reported and stylistically polished. It includes speeches by Francis Lord Cottington; Chief Justice of the King's Bench, John Richardson; Secretary of State, John Coke; and the Earl of Dorset; but omits those by Lord Heath, Secretary Francis Windebank, Sir Thomas Jermyn, Sir Henry Vane, Sir Thomas Edmonds, Chancellor of the Exchequer, Lord Barrett of Newburghe, the Bishop of London (John Juxon), the assents of the Earls of Suffolk, Pembroke, and Arundel to Cottington's speech; and the speeches of Lord Chancellor James Hamilton, the Lord Privy Seal (Henry Montague), Archbishop Neile, and Archbishop Laud, and the Lord Treasurer (Richard Weston, Earl of Portland). It does, however, contain the very interesting procedural note that the censures began with Cottington,

whose turn was first to speak, as being in the lowest degree of quality by his place. And commonly he that beginneth, as he openeth the matter at large, so he inclineth thereby many lords to forbear making of speeches, and only to declare themselves to concur in Sentence with him that began first, or with some other lord that spake before them, as their judgments lead them.[141]

Rushworth/Howell also indicates a process of selection in the censure speeches because they "in effect comprehend all that was said by the others."[142]

    The trial account printed in Gardiner, while less thorough in its representation of the course of the procedures or the contents of documents read at the trial (examinations, answers, depositions), contains a remarkably detailed account of the government's case based on Prynne's book. While Rushworth/Howell mentions twice that the Attorney General requested that passages be read, Gardiner has four requests. Mr. Mason reported the passages that tended to the "censuring of all the people in general, actors and spectators of maskes and playes, and of Magistrates to indure it." Mr. Recorder read the passages that "traduce the government of the kingdom." Mr. Solicitor read the "Scandalles and Aspertions, layde upon the Kinges howse and Courte,"[143] and Sir John Finch reported the passages that reflected badly on the Queen and that suggested the legitimacy of killing rulers who attended stage plays. The trial account in Gardiner contains page references to Prynne's book and quotes passages as evidence, although all passages paraphrase the text. With this detailed reference to the book, the prosecution's case is quite long. The comparative brevity with which Prynne's defense proceeds in both Gardiner's and Rushworth/ Howell's accounts, suggests that, indeed, Prynne's attorneys lacked the time to prepare "agaynste the heareing," even though Attorney General Noy, at the beginning of the proceedings as reported in Gardiner, told the court that "which affadavitt being not to be believed in respecte of the tyme hee hath already had" should be "taken off the ffyle and cancelled."[144] For the final day, the roster of censures in Gardiner is nearly complete, lacking only the Lord Chamberlain's, the Lord Privy Seal's, and Archbishop Neile's.

The account of the trial that appears in the four manuscripts reports only the second and third days. The second day's report is more extensive than those in the printed texts, and includes both evidence from *Histrio-mastix* and some interesting asides, like the one mentioned above where Laud comments on the debate on plays in the universities. On the second day, according to the manuscripts, attorneys for Buckner and Sparke, as well as Prynne, made their arguments. Although Buckner denied having authorized the entire book, Prynne's attorney provided depositions that indicated that Sparke did not release the printed book until he received Buckner's approval. He also argued "the dislike was de facto after the Booke was licensed." To which the prosecution remarked, "whither it were authorized or not authorized, in regard that it was scandalous the case was not materiall."[145] The question of the preparedness of Prynne's attorneys does arise in the manuscripts, but occurs on the third day rather than the first – which makes little sense since the defense's case had been presented on the second day. As for Prynne's defense, while it is certainly not as full as it might have been, Mr. Holborne argues directly against the charges and offers textual support for his arguments. The manuscripts contain Attorney General Noy's reply to Prynne's case in which he basically says he does not believe the arguments and concludes "when a man hath done ill, he is not to be believed."[146] The third day's censures, although generally not as fully reported for the individual speeches as they are in Rushworth/Howell, are present for all but one of the judges, the Lord Treasurer. Both Archbishops Neile's and Laud's speeches appear to be fairly carefully reported.

The most significant issues that emerge from the discrepancies among the trial accounts are the way in which the government constructed its case from the text of *Histrio-mastix* and the possibility that Prynne's counsel for some reason was ill prepared. The manner in which the State prepared its case against Prynne is only clear in the account in Gardiner, which has page numbers. These page numbers are significant because they correspond to those that are in a document among the state papers that is calendared as "Passages extracted from Prynne's work entitled 'HistrioMastrix'." According to the calendar account,

The passages are grouped under the seven following headings; 1st Words of unchristian censure and general offence, wherein all ranks and sorts of people are included. 2nd Particular passages tending to the dishonour of the present State and the magistrates therein. 3rd Such scandalous passages as aim at the discredit of the King's Court, and the customs of it. 4th Odious and undutiful speeches, tending unto the scandal and dishonour of the King's person. 5th Scandalous and offensive speeches reflecting personally on the Queen's highness. 6th Dangerous and disloyal passages which may be used to the distruction of His Majesty's most sacred person. 7th Titles of honour bestowed by Mr. Prynne upon the Puritans, their innocency, loyalty, and piety.[147]

These headings correspond to the sections of the book assigned to be read in the course of the trial to Mr. Mason, Mr. Solicitor, Mr. Recorder, and Mr. John Finch. The manuscript of the calendared document provides a lengthy and careful analysis of Prynne's text that appears to have been made in preparation for the trial – as when, for example, it remarks "Fifty dangerous and disloyal Passages which may be used to the destruction of his Majesties most sacred person."[148] Under each of the above-mentioned headings appear paraphrases of several passages in the text, with the page number given for each passage. Marginal notes containing a brief remark on the potential offense appear to the left of the paraphrases. At the end of each category is a summary stating what "inferences" might be drawn from Prynne's text.

A few examples illustrate the document's method. One paraphrase reads "that all the devils chappells (for soe the fathers called all play houses) being five in number are not sufficient to conteyn all the plays in London: whereas in vitious Neros tyme there were but three standing ... though far more spatious then our present London." The note in the margin reads "The King more vitious than Nero." The inference is drawn that current times are worse than pagan times.[149] Shortly after this passage comes one with the marginal note, "Layton & Mariana much used by Prynne." This glosses the following assessment (though not actually a paraphrase) of Prynne's text: "he makes much use of Marianas book De Regis Institutiones wherein that Jesuite lays down the Lawfulness of killing kings for an holesome doctrine. For note the booke was burnt at Paris. Both boke and man much extolled and magnified by Prynne."[150] From the passages on Nero, Leighton, and Mariana, the author remarks, "the

inference to be shown that the occasion is as just for any Christian subject
to kill their king if either they frequent or behold stage plays."[151] It then
concludes that since Prynne "so often cites" Leighton and Mariana, he
must agree with them, then adds, for evidence that the whole doctrine of
the "Puritan faction" is to overthrow princes, "let Pareus testifie."[152]

As we have seen, shortly after Prynne was first examined about *Histrio-
mastix* in 1632/33 a contemporary believed that the book's condemnation
of women actors would be the cause of Prynne's censure. The ways in
which the "Passages extracted" used his book in this regard is particularly
interesting. For the marginal gloss "women notorious whores," the paraphrase mentions that on page 414 of Prynne's book a marginal note speaks
of "a play intended to be acted" by women in August 1629, an event
Prynne judged to be "impudent . . . unwomanish if not more than whor-
ish." Furthermore, "St Paul (saith hee) forbideth women to speak in
Church."[153] Following this, in the section on inferences, the text turns to
the remark in the index "woemen actors, notorious whores," noting "there
is no such matter in the judgment as is here layd down" and none "extant in
the printed" book; therefore, the compiler of the "Passages extracted"
concludes, "that it was forced in of purpose att the conclusion of the
Booke to scandalize the Queen and her intendments then on foote."[154]
Given the prosecution's arguments in Prynne's trial, the compiler of the
"Passages extracted" from *Histrio-mastix* finds surprisingly few passages
that commit scandal to Queen Henrietta Maria – and those that he does
find are largely inferential.

In all the accounts of Prynne's defense, long or short, Prynne's attorneys
argue that Prynne did not "intend" to offend King Charles or his Queen
and that his meanings were misconstrued. This is perhaps most eloquently
stated in Rushworth/Howell:

He confesseth himself to be justly brought before your lordships for his ill
expressions which may prove an occasion of scandal by misconstruction, and so
some dangerous principle may be infused into the subjects. And he beggeth your
lordships to consider of them, according to the intentions of his heart, which were
fair and honest, though harsh in expression, that he may receive a favourable
construction, for that he citeth his Authors, and their words, and not his own.[155]

Prynne's attorney in this account goes on to argue that the book was duly
authorized and openly printed, that he presented the Attorney General
with a copy of the book, and that Prynne had not acted like a guilty person.
He is so far from disloyalty that he commends the King and the State: "and
all the charges that lie upon him for his foul intentions are but inferences

upon his Book, and consequences, and such for them only that be strained, and not of necessity."[156] With the caveat that this is an argument in court intended to persuade, this defense corresponds both with the "Extracted Passages" method and with the manner in which Prynne's text is employed in the Gardiner account.

Besides the inferential nature of the government's case against Prynne's book, another matter on which there is some disagreement concerns procedure. As we have seen already in this study of Caroline censorship, trials in the court of Star Chamber unjustifiably have often been regarded as inherently abusive. The court of Star Chamber, as Thomas G. Barnes has shown, was mired in procedural concerns. As the timeline above shows, it took a long time for this case to move from Prynne's initial examination to formal information in the court, to answer, to trial. On the one hand, Prynne appears to have been fairly effective in buying time; on the other, he was operating from the Tower, having been denied bail. We have three contemporary complaints about the procedures, and while all certainly reflect Prynne's interests, they need to be taken into account. The first was Prynne's own notorious letter to Laud following his public punishments; the second was a very brief mention of the proceedings appended to Henry Burton's *A Divine Tragedie Lately Acted*; and the third was a relatively short relation that appears in Prynne's 1641 pamphlet on his 1637 Star Chamber trial with John Bastwick and Henry Burton.

Prynne's letter to Laud, if seen outside of the context of the manuscript accounts of the trial, looks more like a diatribe than it actually is. (Cressy calls the letter "a remarkable performance."[157]) The decision to compose such a letter certainly speaks to Prynne's disrespect for Laud's position – but it also reflects Prynne's frustration over the trial proceedings. The letter essentially answers the terms of Laud's censure that appears in the four manuscripts – that Prynne committed treason and that in all Prynne's arguments "there is not one true Syllogisme in all his Booke, either the proposition is false, or if he chance to make a sure conclusion, then its false by Accidents."[158] Prynne also took offense at a remark Laud evidently made in the course of the trial that went unrecorded in all accounts – that Prynne could not have composed this book alone because of the enormous volume of reading it reflected and Prynne's youth. Prynne's letter accuses Laud of committing scandal for the aspersions cast on his scholarship and his loyalty to the King. It also painstakingly takes Laud to task for incorrectly representing Prynne's syllogisms and misconstruing them. As to the matter of treason, ever the lawyer, Prynne rehearses the relationship between the treason statutes and his alleged crimes. On the whole the letter is more tedious than it is inflammatory – except that Laud apparently could brook no more of Prynne, even in a private venue. Laud sent a copy of the letter to the Attorney General, who then took the letter to Prynne and ask him if it was in his hand. At this point Prynne took the letter and tore it up. For this once again he was called into the Star Chamber.[159]

The other objections to the proceedings are more general. Burton's *Divine Tragedie*, which as we have seen gave forty-two examples of God's judgment against Sabbath breakers, concluded with a passage on Attorney General Noy. According to this Noy has incurred God's judgment for his conduct at Prynne's trial:

> he eagerly persecuted this wel-deserving Gentleman of his owne profession and Society, (to whom he was formerly a friend in appearance, but in inveterate enimie in truth) for his *Histrio-mastix*, compiled onely out of the words and sentence of other approved Authors of all sorts, against the use and exercise of S[t]age-playes, Enterludes, Morisdances, Maygames, May-poles, Wakes, lascivious mixt Dauncing, and other Ethnick pastimes, condemned in all ages, without any thought or suspitioun of giving the least offence, either to the Kings most excellent Majesty, the Queene, or State, as he averred in his Answer upon Oath.[160]

The objection against Noy expressed here is that he suppressed "the Gentlemans exhibits and defence" and that he wrested the book's words and meanings but refused "to discover the particulars of the booke on which he would insist, though ordered so to doe by the Court." As a consequence the "gentleman: could not instruct his Counsell how to reply or "make any justification or defence to cleare his innocencie."[161] While this account might be readily dismissed since it is supposedly by Prynne's kindred spirit, Burton, all the trial accounts taken together show Prynne's counsel seeking additional time in order to reply to the State's arguments as presented in the trial. They also depict a poorly ordered defense strategy. Finally, in *A New Discoverie of the Prelates Tyranny*, Prynne says that following the information against him he was not allowed bail "nor yet so much as to repaire to his Counsell, with his keeper," claims that appear to have been true.[162]

While the court of Star Chamber was not in itself an abusive court, nor was it necessarily a tool to excoriate political enemies of the State, by conflating accounts of Prynne's trial and comparing them with outside evidence, it appears that Prynne's defense may not have had sufficient access to the prosecution's evidence to prepare the kind of detailed point by point response that appears in Prynne's letter to Laud. Furthermore, from all the trial accounts, as well as Prynne's submission to the King, it looks as though Prynne invoked the customary Star Chamber procedure of submitting in order to receive the King's pardon but was denied this option. Moreover, some evidence suggests that the Queen's willingness to mitigate Prynne's sentence was ignored. Had Prynne been tried and convicted for his actual crime of scandal – indeed *Scandalum Magnatum* – or even of seditiously libeling the King and Queen, his trial would have occupied far less space in the annals of history. Having been censured for sedition (separating the King from his people) and for justifying the murder of kings for attending stage plays (essentially treason), especially when "inference" was so apparent in the State's case, Prynne saw as unjust. Before February 1634 Prynne's criticism of the Church and State had been carefully measured, after that, his objections shifted from Laud's zealous ceremonial agenda and society's moral failings to his enemies and the institutions that protected them. (Indeed, with all its marginal notations, I suspect it was Prynne, and not Burton, who condemned Noy in the epilogue to *A Divine Tragedie*.)

Shortly after Prynne suffered the loss of his ears and began his sentence of perpetual imprisonment, the authorities intensified their scrutiny of other "Puritan" writers. Prynne's trial established for all the world to know that this was not merely a matter of theological contentiousness. Prynne and his like – Puritans – threatened the State. In November 1634 a search of John Bastwick's study produced three parliamentary diaries and books by Prynne and Burton. How exactly Bastwick came to the attention of the authorities is unclear, except that Bastwick appears to have had some personal enemies. In 1635 he was brought before the High Commission, where he was charged both for privately expressing dislike of bishops and ceremonies and for writing two books (*Elenchus Papisticae Religionis* and *Flagellum Pontificis*), printed without license in Amsterdam, that corrupted the King's subjects and caused schism. *Elenchus Papisticae*, first printed in 1627 with both license and allowance in England and written in Latin, disputed the tenets of Roman Catholic teaching, including the Pope's primacy and the authority of the Roman Catholic bishops. *Flagellum* was another edition of *Elenchus*. While the High Commission might justly prosecute "unlicensed" printing, and had frequently done so in recent years (especially for books printed in Amsterdam), condemning a scholarly treatise written in Latin was unusual – particularly since the charge specified that the book was corrupting the King's subjects. Bastwick's real crime in the eyes of the High Commission seems to have been his association with Alexander Leighton, and his praise for the contents of *Zion's Plea*. Given that praise for Leighton (and Mariana) was one of the charges brought against Prynne in his trial, it appears that one's position in relation to Leighton had now become a litmus test for sedition. Having "proved" that Bastwick had written the books, the High Commission excommunicated Bastwick, suspended him from his medical practice, fined him and condemned him to prison. The books were condemned to be burned.[163] Bastwick's experience in the court of High Commission radicalized him, and in the next few years he turned from writing against the Pope and the Church of Rome's ecclesiastical hierarchy to writing against the ecclesiastical hierarchy of the Church of England and its court of High Commission. His *Apologeticus: ad praesules Anglicanos, The Letany of John Bastwick, The Answer of John Bastwick, A More Full Answer of John Bastwick* brought him before the Star Chamber in 1637.

On November 5, 1636 Henry Burton preached two sermons objecting to innovations in church ceremonies and doctrine. On November 17, 1636 articles were objected against Burton in the High Commission for uttering "scandalous and offensive speeches."[164] Burton did not answer the articles; instead he appeared and entered his appeal to the King. In early December, Burton was called before a private commission, which, though he did not appear, suspended him. Burton meanwhile procured the printing of the sermons with the title, *An Apology of an Appeale*, and dedicated it to the King in an effort to justify his earlier appeal.[165] By January, as noted above, Burton's authorship of *A Divine Tragedie Lately Acted* also came into question. In early February, Burton was taken into custody, his study searched, and his books and papers seized. On February 2 he was imprisoned in the Fleet.[166] A few months later, with Bastwick and Prynne, he was tried for his seditious writing. His books specifically named in the trial were the *Divine Tragedie* and *An Apology of an Appeale*.

On March 10, 1637 an information was exhibited in Star Chamber against John Bastwick, Henry Burton, and William Prynne for making and divulging "divers scandalous bookes & libels, against the whole clergie of the kingdome, & against the Government of the Church of England." According to the information, Bastwick, Burton, and Prynne had for a long time "maligned" the King's "happie Government" and "good discipline of the Church." They had "laid scandalous and fraudulent imputations" on the proceedings of the courts of High Commission and Star Chamber, and attempted to stir the people to disobedience against the ecclesiastical government.[167] Besides Bastwick's and Burton's books mentioned above, Prynne's *Newes from Ipswich* was named in the information. Though unnamed, other provocative books Prynne had written in recent months included *A Breviate of the Prelates Intollerable Usurpations, The Unbishoping of Timothy and Titus*, and *Briefe Instructions for Churchwardens*.

Few historians have referred to these publications as anything other than "recklessly hostile," "inflammatory," and "vituperative."[168] They strenuously objected to all the ceremonial innovations, to abusive proceedings in the courts of High Commission and Star Chamber, and to the "lordly prelates" whom they deemed responsible for everything that had gone awry in the Church and State. Latter-day accounts of the proceedings that followed have described them as a travesty of justice, but even Prynne's own account in *A New Discoverie of the Prelats Tyranny* reveals that the court attended carefully to its usual procedure, appointing counsel, requiring answers, proceeding *pro confesso* when answers did not appear signed by counsel. The defendants took every means available to them to try to obfuscate the proceedings – they countersued, objected, petitioned, and, insisting on the legitimacy in other courts of self-representation, filed long, handwritten answers.[169] Cressy's characterization of Bastwick, Burton, and Prynne as martyrs may justly be assigned to the trial itself as well as to their conviction. (All were fined and condemned to the pillory and to lose their ears.) By all accounts, they wanted to level the same kind of attack on their adversaries in the courtroom that they had in their writings.

Something of the spirit with which Bastwick, Burton, and Prynne faced their accusers can be found in one of the sermons Burton included in *An Apology of an Appeale*. Burton preached on the duty and fear a subject owed the King, but he placed the fear of God above the fear of men. A Christian, Burton proclaimed, need not fear the consequences of placing his loyalty to God above his fear of the civil consequences he might suffer for not complying with the innovations of men:

A man may by his discretion, or Christian Prudence (as they call it) so carry the matter, as to secure himselfe from fear of the world; for he can give way, and conforme himselfe quietly to all humaine imposition, and can command his conscience to beare with them ... Thereby he shall preserve his Ministry, and his credit too ... Alas poore soule! Whats this Ministry worth when thou hath abused it, and inthralled it to the impious inventions and impositions of men.[170]

Implicit in this is Burton's denial of the bishops' divine authority; in objecting to the ceremonies, he is objecting to the bishops – the Laudian bishops – who instituted them.

In the eight years from the close of the 1629 Parliament, Prynne and Burton went from learnedly disputing doctrine (a long-accepted practice in the Church of England) to challenging the authority of the bishops and their courts. The Durham House strategy (begun by Montagu) of marginalizing church Calvinists by calling them "schismatic" Puritans, combined with a propaganda campaign advancing ceremonies and a censorship campaign silencing objections to them, ended up actually creating schismatic Puritans. It failed, however, to successfully marginalize their voices, as the 1637 Star Chamber trial and punishments demonstrate.[171] According to Cressy, while "the state showed its power by imposing pain and disfigurement," Bastwick, Burton, and Prynne turned their punishments "into a triumph of propaganda."[172] Crowds attended them at the pillories. The common people threw herbs and flowers in their paths. Supporters and critics alike remarked their fortitude and dignity.[173] When Bastwick, Burton, and Prynne departed London for distant prisons, crowds gathered to wish them well, and along their way, they met with expressions of goodwill and sympathy. It appears that Burton and Prynne's insistence that popish innovations were creeping into the Church resonated with a fairly wide audience – one whose Calvinist and godly sympathies most likely received nourishment from the thousands of "legal" printed books that kept alive the teachings of Elizabethan and Jacobean Calvinists.

Studies of Caroline censorship cannot escape confronting the phenomenon of Prynne and Burton – and to a lesser degree Bastwick – as evidence alternatively of either the abusiveness or the political necessity of Caroline press censorship. I would propose, instead, that the two "show trials," as Cressy has aptly called them, represent anomalous and desperate efforts to contain religious opposition. As such, they are a measure not of the success of Caroline press censorship but of its failure. Beginning with the writings of Montagu, the Durham House constituency had tried to make the case that Calvinist doctrine was contrary to the established doctrine of the Church of England and that those who espoused it were therefore "schismatics." By commanding an end to theological disputation on the subject of predestination, the 1626 Proclamation for peace in the Church effectively forced the conversation "underground." However, by failing to eradicate Calvinist doctrine as it persisted in sermons and treatises written by Elizabethan and Jacobean church Calvinists, as well as in hundreds of Puritan lectureships, Calvinism persisted not only among those "Puritans" who could be marginalized but among godly conformists as well.[174] As long as Abbot was Archbishop of Canterbury some toleration existed for godly ministers, and some new books received licenses. Prynne's trial for *Histrio-mastix* tried to make two points, first that godly moral views (Puritanism) were not only schismatic but seditious; second, that even an ecclesiastical license could not protect a Puritan writer or printer from being prosecuted. By the time Prynne was actually tried in 1634, of course, Laud had become Archbishop of Canterbury and his chaplains replaced Abbot's as licensers. Unfortunately, greater rigor in ecclesiastical licensing and its enforcement came at the same time that Laudian propagandists put their pens to work to defend altars, bowing, and the Book of Sports, subject on which Puritans could not keep silent. Sparke's punishment for printing Prynne's book may have cautioned London printers but printers outside England were not subject to the same controls. The greater liberty overseas printing offered led writers to take far greater risks. Even if the likes of Bastwick, Burton, and Prynne could be marginalized – as certainly diverse efforts even before the 1637 Star Chamber trial sought to do – godly sentiment was too deeply planted and richly nourished to allow an enthusiastic reception in the Caroline Church of Laud's efforts to instill the beauty of holiness. The 1637 Star Chamber trial, especially given that the punishment included transporting the censured men to distant places of imprisonment where they were deprived of paper and pen, looks like a desperate effort to hold off flood waters with the proverbial thumb in the dike. Throughout the 1630s, Prynne's and Burton's concern for what up until 1625 had been the "orthodox" teaching of the Church of England and their opposition to what now was being advanced as the "orthodox" teaching of the Church of England resonated with even the most moderate of the godly brethren. The condemnation of bishops appeared very late, and clearly as a last resort when their "adversaries," as Burton called them, ignored all protestations of loyalty to King and Church. Opposition to ceremonies across the English Church did not necessarily mean opposition to episcopacy; it would take more than Bastwick, Burton, and Prynne's objections to what they perceived as their persecutors to turn the country against their King.

AFTERWORD: ONE CENSORED CATHOLIC BOOK

One of the better-known cases of censorship in Caroline England did not involve a Puritan book but rather a Catholic one, the 1637 edition of Francis de Sales's *An Introduction to a Devout Life*, published first in French on the Continent in 1609. The first English edition, translated by John Yakesley, was printed in 1613 at Douai. In 1616 Nicholas Okes printed an edition based on Yakesley's translation but with significant alterations to make it acceptable to the Protestant licensers.[175] A second London edition appeared in 1637, probably printed by Nicholas Okes's son, John,[176] but, though based on a Yakesley translation, it did not reprint the 1616 edition.

On May 14, 1637 King Charles issued a proclamation calling in the book and ordering that it be "publikely burnt." According to the proclamation the book had been brought before the Archbishop of Canterbury's chaplain (William Haywood) "for Licence and Allowance" and was "expunged and purged of divers passages therein tending to Popery," nevertheless, the book was published with the "same Popish and unsound passages" reinserted. The King issued the proclamation "out of His pious and constant care, to uphold and maintain the Religion professed in the Church of England."[177] Copies of the book had actually been burned on April 20, 1637. In his footnote to the proclamation, Larkin suggests that the account of the events presented in the proclamation is doubtful. The report of one contemporary observer suggests why this may be so. According to George Con, the Scottish agent from the court of Rome, Puritans were denouncing Laud and his chaplain for allowing the book to be printed. Such complaints were echoed by William Prynne, now the prosecuting attorney, at Archbishop Laud's 1644 trial. When he accused Laud of being responsible for the publication of books of popery, *An Introduction to a Devout Life* was among them.[178] N. W. Bawcutt observes that two alternative contemporary versions of the book's publication exist: Haywood's supporters, including Laud,

asserted that Haywood did his best to censor the book, but was tricked by Catholics who managed to re-insert the greater part of the deleted material. Their opponents ... argued that Laud and Haywood colluded to have the original Yakesley version reprinted as part of their campaign to restore Catholicism in England, and when exposed tried to put the blame on other people.[179]

It appears that both sides, as is so often the case in disputes between "Puritans" and Laudians, are right. Christopher Barrows, a Catholic, representing himself as the book's translator, took the book to Haywood, who ordered revisions and purgations. Before the book was printed, Barrows apparently restored the Catholic language and doctrine. In the course of the book's printing, someone in the printing house observed that the book was still "popish," and went to Haywood to have the printing stopped. From all accounts, Haywood did nothing. Haywood's enemies took this as proof that all along he intended to assure the publication of a popish book; his defenders maintained that the passages shown to Haywood were trivial and that he merely exercised good judgment.[180]

Bawcutt's assessment that the circumstances surrounding the 1637 publication of *A Devout Life* "were so unusual that the event remains anomalous and untypical" is, I think, appropriate.[181] The evidence he presents demonstrates that the book's publication was neither party to a Laudian plan to reintroduce popery nor a scheme to embarrass Laud and his chaplain. I would add to this that this occasion of censorship should not be seen as evidence that Caroline censorship was interested in suppressing positions favorable to Catholicism and Puritanism equally – as the proclamation seems to imply. Neither should the proclamation be regarded as a gesture taken to moderate Puritan outcry against the book's publication. With a Catholic Queen on the throne of England and an irenic stance towards France and Spain, Caroline policy took interest in admitting some virtues in the Catholic Church. As both Hunt and Milton have shown, Laud's censors massaged the writings of leading godly writers to make them appear more tolerant towards whatever virtues Rome might be shown to possess – a strategy taken less as a gesture towards Rome than as a measure to marginalize the staunchly anti-papal wing of English Protestantism. I suspect Haywood's revisions sought to soften de Sales's book on precisely those points that proved so provocative to the godly. When the book appeared decked out in all the plumage of Rome at a time when strict measures were being taken to assure that all books were to be authorized (the 1637 Star Chamber Decree would be published a few months after), censoring the book doubly served Laud's ends. It would draw a distinct line between those aspects of the Roman Church that might be respected in England and those practices from which Laudianism sought to disassociate itself. Furthermore, it would demonstrate that the government would not tolerate disregard for its program of licensing, which, as the next chapter will show, the upcoming Star Chamber Decree greatly enhanced.

Before turning in the next chapter to Caroline censorship from the perspective of the London Stationers' Company, I want to return to the divergent views about the 1630s expressed by Laud and Gataker with which this chapter began. The 1630s were indeed, as Gataker remarked, "troublesome times" – but not just for the godly. In some ways the godly suffered less than some historians would have it. At the same time that episcopal visitations sought outward conformity to ceremonial reforms, a steady stream of printed treatises and sermons nurtured the godly community and strengthened their spiritual resolve. Opposition to the ceremonies did not go unspoken. A gauge of how effective were the measures taken to edify the godly shadow Church can be found in Laudianism's pains to marginalize ceremonialism's most outspoken critics and ventriloquize the most prominent members of the godly community. The times were troublesome not because a repressive regime rigorously controlled what people could think and read, or because the regime's critics suffered the punishments of Burton, Bastwick, and Prynne. Nor were the times troublesome because "the faction" waged a war of paper bullets to bring down the Church and State. It was not in these extremes where what was most troublesome can be found The times were troublesome because moderate men like Gataker could not be persuaded that the ceremonies enforced "according both to Law and Canon" were not "innovations," as Laud insisted. While the transformational literalism on which these innovations were based may have persuaded many within the Church of England that ceremonialism was nothing new, in looking back at the 1630s Laud overestimated the "consent and liking of the People" for the measures he took to assure "as much Decency and Conformity as might be" in public worship. The times were troublesome on both sides.

CHAPTER 5

The printers and press control in the 1630s

In 1637 the court of Star Chamber issued a decree "touching the regulating of Printers and Founders of letters." The preamble to the decree acknowledges that in the twenty-eighth year of Queen Elizabeth's reign "and before" "divers" decrees and ordinances had been made for "the better government and regulating of Printing and Printers"; experience, however, had shown these decrees to be defective in some respects. Furthermore, according to the preamble, new abuses had arisen since then.[1] The 1637 Star Chamber Decree serves as an important benchmark in any discussion of Caroline press controls, although the nature of its inception and intention are contested. Before turning to the decree and the dispute that surrounds it, understanding the conditions in London print culture during the reign of Charles I can help us to better understand both how new abuses could arise and how earlier decrees may have proven defective. The Elizabethan decrees had responded to external challenges to the authority both of the Stationers' Company's monopoly and of royal patents, as well as to complaints from the journeymen printers about insufficient work. In the seventeenth century, although economic problems persisted, circumstances differed. Outside challenges to the Stationers' monopoly posed less of a problem than structural changes within the company – both economic and regulatory. The seventeenth century also saw an important generic change that required increased government oversight – the emergence of news publications ("corantos"). When these are taken together with the circumstances considered in the last three chapters – inhibitions on theological disputation, structural transformations in the courts of High Commission and Star Chamber, and a persistent Puritan press (both legal and illegal) – we can better understand how the former Star Chamber decree may have seemed defective.

THE STATIONERS' COMPANY IN CAROLINE ENGLAND

Because the London Company of Stationers came into existence by virtue of a royal charter, the characterization of the relationship between the

Stationers and the Crown as a "lasting romance, its partners clasped in an economic and ideological 'embrace',"[2] persistently dominates discussions of the Company. Ian Gadd helps us to understand the Company's identity in terms of its relationship not to the Crown but to other London companies as a corporate London entity.[3] He explains that for anyone to be a freeman of the city of London, he needed to belong to one of dozens of guilds, "who represented and regulated various trades and crafts in the city."[4] Like other London companies, in the mid sixteenth century, the Stationers were

a privileged body (recognised by both the city and the crown) whose membership was drawn primarily from a particular sector of the urban economy (the book trade). Through a combination of powers vested in it by external authorities, it had been granted jurisdiction over much of the economic and social life of its members as both regulatory body and welfare provider. Structurally divided into a larger essentially non-privileged body of freemen and a smaller privileged group of liverymen, it was governed by a senior elite of liverymen – the court of Assistants – from whose ranks the important annual offices of master and wardens were drawn. It owned a hall in London for its own internal bureaucratic and social purposes; and it kept records of its membership and their economic activities.[5]

This description draws our attention to three aspects of the company that can help us understand some of the changes that took place between the sixteenth and the seventeenth centuries: first, that the membership consisted of a privileged group of liverymen and a non-privileged body of freemen and, second, that through its court of Assistants, it regulated the economic and social lives of its members. Even though the company's membership was bipartite, according to Gadd, the company possessed a corporate identity, the third important quality for explaining alterations in the seventeenth century. On one hand, the corporate identity gave the Stationers a solidarity by which outsiders might be defined; on the other, it conferred a legal status that made the body subject to regulation and prosecution.

One of the most significant changes that took place in the Stationers' Company between the mid sixteenth and the early seventeenth century was in its regulatory capacity. The single most important function that the Company's regulatory capacity exercised was protecting the product "crafted" by its members. While other companies might do this by imposing standards of craftsmanship – making sure all products were comparable – the Stationers needed to assure that all products were unique. It did so by issuing the company "license" that recognized a member's unique proprietary interest in a title, and, for most of the reign of Elizabeth I, the word "license" referred to that interest. Members who printed a book either without license or in violation of another member's license were brought before the court of Assistants, which imposed sanctions. Requirements that books be so "licensed" issued from inside the corporation and were intended to the good of the membership.

Another aspect of the Stationers' Company's corporate identity that concerned regulation was its monopoly. Only members of the Stationers' Company could print, bind, and, later, sell books. When outsiders presumed to print, however, the Company's self-regulatory mechanisms were insufficient. When in the late 1570s and early 1580s outsiders challenged both the Company monopoly and royal printing privileges (most of which were held by senior members of the Company), the court of Star Chamber heard the cases and, subsequently, issued its decrees. Although the 1586 decrees neither claimed Star Chamber jurisdiction for future cases challenging the Company's monopoly nor specifically deferred that jurisdiction to the court of High Commission, sometime after 1586 the High Commission became the venue for external challenges to the Company's monopoly. The cases the High Commission subsequently heard for "illegal" printing were, for the most part, cases where non-Stationers set up "illegal" presses which were printing "unlicensed" books (books not entered in the Stationers' Registers) or books legally "licensed" to Company members. Since cases for illegal "unlicensed" and "licensed" printing became part of the High Commission's jurisdiction, that it would likewise become the venue for hearing cases where "legal" presses likewise printed books without "license" is not surprising. During the reign of Charles I, as we have seen, the court of High Commission assumed jurisdiction in some "licensing" cases, although it did not conveniently discriminate between the Company license and the ecclesiastical license (authorization). An example of this appears in 1631 when the High Commission investigated Michael Sparke and William Turner for printing "unlicensed" books at Oxford – those by Prynne had been unauthorized, but books by Arthur Dent, John Preston, and Antony Fawkner had Company licenses but to other Stationers. What was truly remarkable about the cases that chapters 3 and 4 considered was that members of the Stationers' Company were prosecuted in these external courts rather than in the court of Assistants as they would have been during the reigns of Elizabeth and James.

Becoming increasingly subject to outside regulation was one of the significant features that, according to Gadd, distinguished the Stationers from other London companies. While all London companies regulated their members' social and economic activities and were, to a degree, subject to regulation by the city and the Crown, for the Stationers' Company:

what does seem to have been notable was the extent to which these alternative regulatory authorities encroached upon aspects of the trade that, in other companies, were part of the corporate prerogative. In fact, the experience of the book trade in the century and a half after incorporation was increasingly more dictated by the actions and decisions of other institutions and officials than by the Company itself.[6]

Even though the Stationers' Company's self-regulatory capacity changed over time, neither the corporation nor the outside regulators clearly defined the scope and limits of the various parties' roles – not, at least, until the 1637 Star Chamber Decree.

Besides its changing regulatory role, the Company experienced internal structural changes: first, in its composition, and second in its corporate activities. One of the problems that the 1586 Star Chamber decrees had addressed was the growth in Company membership at all levels. Based on the findings of a commission that had been appointed to investigate the complaints filed by journeymen printers, there was insufficient work to keep all of the presses in all the London printing houses busy. The Company had permitted too many master printers to establish printing houses; some of the houses had too many presses; and some of the master printers took on too many apprentices, whose labor displaced the journeymen. Additionally, many of the masters held lucrative government printing patents that kept their presses busy, while unprivileged printers begged for work. To address the problem of the Company's poor printers, in 1584 (probably in preparation for the 1586 decrees) some of the patents for popular books were transferred from individual printers to the corporation, with the expectation that privileged books were to be printed by the Company's poor. The 1586 decrees further addressed these issues by requiring that all existing master printers register their printing establishments and the number of presses with the Archbishop of Canterbury. The court of Assistants was directed to admit no new presses until the numbers had subsided, and then, only with approval by the Archbishop of Canterbury. Furthermore, the decrees placed strict limits on the number of apprentices.

While the 1586 decrees had provided reasonable means to remedy the problems at that time, subsequent growth in the trade, taken together with the regulations, changed the corporate spirit. According to Gadd, membership in the court of Assistants remained fairly constant at around twenty members between 1586 and 1637. Furthermore, there were twenty-five master printers in 1586 and the same in 1637. (Since the 1586 decrees had sought a reduction in the number of master printers, this might be seen as a regulatory failure.) The major change that took place, however, was in the number of freemen, which nearly tripled during this time.[7] The biggest problem that accompanied this shifting demographic was that Company members saw themselves less as part of the corporation than as individuals with special interests. Gadd points to a 1628 agreement among the master printers to limit themselves to two presses each as evidence that the interests of one group of Stationers were not identical with the interests of the Company as a whole.[8] I think that the same might be said of the printers and publishers whose commitment to the enterprise of reprinting godly books, as well as of the few who risked printing and selling unlicensed books, increased surveillance of the Company's activities and diminished its internal regulatory role. Ironically, however, it was probably the print-ers' and publishers' reprinting of the Elizabethan and Jacobean godly authors that kept many journeymen from penury. They opened up a printing venue that could, to some degree, compensate for the hardship the journeymen printers claimed to have suffered as a result of King Charles's 1626 Proclamation.[9] In addition, during the 1630s new abuses arose – for example, books were printed in large impressions and forms were left standing – which prompted the journeymen to appeal to the government for reformation.[10] In the 1630s, then, the cohesion forged among the journeymen joined with the self-interest of the masters to diminish corporate solidarity within the Stationers' Company.

One thing that surely contributed to the sense of divided interests in the Stationers' Company was the English Stock. In 1603 when James I rescinded Elizabethan monopolies, he granted the Stationers' Company corporate privilege in several best-selling titles and gave the court of Assistants authority to administer and enforce the grant. The court of Assistants subsequently established the English Stock, a stock company which published not only the patented titles the King had conferred, but also those titles that in 1584 had been given to the Company for the benefit of the poor. Any member of the Stationers was entitled to purchase shares in the English Stock, from which they drew dividends, but the number of shares were restricted by the member's position in the Company. While the English Stock was a distinct entity, since the court of Assistants both administered it and regulated the Company, the Stock became a company within the Company. Since the larger printing houses and syndicates derived the most benefit from the Stock, the Company's corporate identity was further diminished, and abuses arose on both sides. Unemployed printers resorted to piracy of the Stock Company's best-selling titles, and stockholders resorted to printing stock titles overseas.

Abuses were not confined within the Stationers' Company. The King's Printer for Scotland, Robert Young, printed Bibles for the English market in his Edinburgh printing house, depriving London Stationers of work.[11] London booksellers accused monopolists (English Stock and King's Printers) of artificially elevating book prices by locking existing stock in warehouses.[12] On the other side, London booksellers imported Geneva Bibles printed in Amsterdam with title pages and formats that represented themselves as a 1599 edition from the King's Printing House, as well as copies of Old and New Testaments, Books of Common Prayer, and liturgies printed abroad. These foreign-printed English books were sold across the countryside as well as in London.[13] In the 1580s men outside of the sacred circle of Stationers led the assault on privileged printing and monopolies; the 1630s saw internecine warfare among the printers and booksellers. Conditions in the English book trade were in such disarray that a government officer even tried to exploit them.

In 1634 a customs official by the name of John Egerton received intelligence that a consignment of Bibles and prayer books printed abroad was going to arrive in the Essex river port of Maldon and would be conveyed to a London inn. Egerton seized the books at a customs inspection and then proceeded to sell them to a Lothbury bookseller named William Lee and his man, Thomas Cowper. Afterwards, Egerton apparently approached other booksellers and proposed that, for a fee, he would assure that they would receive the illegal imports regularly. If they failed to pay him, however, their supply would be cut off. Egerton was tried in the court of High Commission, and at some point during the procedures proposed to the court that his source of information was such that, for a price, he could altogether stem the tide of such illegal imports.[14] The High Commission deprived Egerton of his position as a government searcher, fined him £200, and committed him to the Gatehouse. Egerton's case suggests that a sufficient market existed to make trading in English books printed on the Continent worth the risk.

NEWS: "A DISPENSIBLE COMMODITY"?[15]

The English taste for foreign news, which had appeared fitfully during the reign of Elizabeth, burgeoned with the outbreak of the Thirty Years War. News, according to Fritz Levy, "was part of the market-place of fashion."[16] What began as essentially a domestic interest in the fate of James I's daughter, Elizabeth, and her husband, the King of Bohemia, gave way to curiosity about political events across the Continent. The earliest reports about the progress of what would come to be called the Thirty Years War appeared from continental presses, but London Stationers quickly seized the market. Nicholas Bourne, Nathaniel Butter, William Stansby, Thomas Archer, and Edward Allde all published news about the war with such regularity that their news book publications took up the name of similar Dutch publications: "corantos" or currents of news. The seventeenth-century phenomena of both coranto printing and English news interests have met with considerable scholarly interest, although scholars differ in their interpretations of how rigorously the government controlled their publication and dissemination.[17] Even historians who see a degree of laxity in foreign news, however, recognize the potential of such news to impact foreign diplomacy. It is no wonder, then, that news should warrant scrutiny. In 1621 George Cottington was appointed to authorize foreign news, and he served in this capacity until 1624.[18] No new government licenser was designated to oversee news books until 1627, when England's war with France revived the trade in news books. In a letter to the Stationers' Company, Secretary Edward Conway complained that of late news books were appearing from the London presses that were "false and sometimes scandalous to the proceedings of his Maiestie and his Allyes," and to remedy this, demanded that nothing "of that kind" should be printed without the "approbation of my servaunt Weckherlin."[19]

Georg Weckherlin, a native of Stuttgart, had represented the Palatinate in England in the 1620s, and from November 1625 served on Secretary Conway's staff. His facility in German, French, and Latin suited him to translation and diplomatic correspondence. Because of the nature of his responsibilities, including imprinting the Privy Seal, Weckherlin enjoyed an informal relationship with the King that made him part of the King's entourage. According to Anthony Thompson, Conway's appointment of Weckherlin as official licenser for news did not signal a change of direction for Charles's government but rather presented a solution to a recurring problem.[20] Conway had previously written to the Stationers to express "his majesties dislike of the liberty taken in printing of weekeley Courantoes and Pamphletts of newes without anie rule or warrant."[21] In 1627, however, England was engaged in a particularly sensitive international enterprise: relieving the Huguenot colony at La Rochelle, and news accounts soared – and offended. Nathaniel Butter was imprisoned in the Gatehouse on August 2, 1627 for illegally publishing news about the campaign. Weckherlin's task was to assure that the printed news reflected favorably on the English enterprise. The success of Weckherlin's licensing strategy, however, ultimately posed a problem for the Caroline regime. Butter and Bourne's news had intensified popular expectations of success. When Buckingham failed to achieve the ends anticipated, news books faced the difficult task of explaining away the failure – and pleasing the King. According to Thompson, "After the Ré fiasco, Charles and these counselors came to see news, no matter how closely it was supervised, as a dispensible commodity."[22]

After Ré, the market for international news dwindled, but Charles's government reiterated its interest in overseeing potentially dangerous political writing. Dudley Carleton, Viscount Dorchester, replaced Conway as secretary of state. (Conway was promoted to Lord President of the Council.) In 1629 Dorchester wrote to the Stationers once again stating that it was the King's "expresse will and pleasure" that "any matters of newes relations histories or other things in prose or in verse that have reference to matters and affaires of State" should not be printed "without the view, approbation and license" of Weckherlin," who was to inform the King of any "cause."[23] To me, this represents a significant shift in Weckherlin's role: he was no longer responsible only for sanitizing international news accounts; now he must attend to "any matters" that refer to the affairs of state. This should not be taken as evidence of the kind of draconian censorship found by Hill and other scholars who subscribe to seeing the Caroline regime as intensely repressive, but neither does it attest to Lambert's certainty that Caroline censorship was interested in suppressing only dangerous criticism of the Church and State. We see here King Charles's interest in knowing precisely what is being said about affairs of state so that he might, if necessary, prevent publication. This interest appears to have become more intense since in 1631 the King himself sent a letter to the Stationers' Company remarking the "promiscuous publishing which is dayly practised" and noting that "the former boldnesse and disorder hath been continewed."[24] According to Thompson, "Charles went on to mention Weckherlin twice as the proper authority for licensing, promised to 'take strict accompt' of individuals who transgressed, and added ecclesiastical works to the proscribed list."[25]

One particular incident involving two manuscripts reveals both the concerns of Weckherlin and King Charles as well as Weckherlin's readiness to inform the King when he saw just cause. Weckherlin sent a memo to the King which summarized for him the contents of the two books. The first by Sir Robert Filmer, presumably his *Patriarcha*, was written "of Governement and in praise of Royalties and the supreme authority thereof"; the second compared the King of Sweden to the French King,

Henry IV. In both cases, Weckherlin sought the King's wisdom "whether such a subject at this time is fitter to bee made publick or kept in."[26] That Charles approved neither manuscript Thompson sees as evidence of the good understanding King and licenser had of each other. He also concludes from this that "Charles construed 'matter of state' very broadly and was serious in his belief that almost any discussion of politics or international news led to 'scandall of government and disadvantage of our service'."[27]

Despite understanding the King's interests well, Weckherlin's government licensing efforts were apparently insufficient to control a new proliferation of news pamphlets that occurred in 1631, when Gustavus Adolphus of Sweden began to win victories on the Protestant side in the Thirty Years War. On October 17, 1632 the Privy Council ordered weekly news books to cease publication. According to Lambert, the ban was issued in response to the insistence of Spanish agents: "they were banned for inadvertently printing a translation reporting that the duke of Olivares had been dismissed for peculation."[28] Nathaniel Butter, who printed the report, appealed to Secretary Coke, who assured him the ban would be lifted shortly. It was, however, the "Spanish" secretary, Francis Windebank, who had conveyed the ban, so Butter's appeals did not reach the proper person, and the restraint on international news remained in place until 1638.

THE 1637 STAR CHAMBER DECREE

On July 10, 1637 John Bankes, the Attorney General, "produced in Court" a decree that was "drawn and penned by the advice" of the Lord Keeper, Archbishop Laud, Bishop Juxon, the Lord Treasurer, the Chief Justices, and the Lord Chief Baron.[29] The preamble's attention to the "libelous, seditious, and mutinous bookes" that had been "unduly printed, and other bookes and papers without licence, to the disturbance of the peace of the Church and State" has led to the common judgment that the decree reflected a distinctive political style: "the 1637 decree made censorship a political instrument of despotic government."[30] It was, from Siebert's perspective, "the most complete and detailed regulation of the early seventeenth century."[31] At his trial Laud readily admitted that the decree was produced by his agency. According to Laud's biographer, Heylyn, Laud sought the decree to provide "both at home and abroad, That neither the Patience of the State should be exercised (as in former times) with continual Libels; nor the Church troubled by unwarrantable and Out-landish Doctrines."[32] "The Archbishop," according to Heylyn, was "intent upon all Advantages of keeping down the Genevian Party, and hindring them from Printing and Publishing any thing which might disturb the Churches Peace, or corrupt her Doctrine."[33] Furthermore, Heylyn said that Laud was also concerned about anti-Catholic and Calvinist books that had been previously licensed, and it was "With equal diligence he endeavoured by this Decree to hinder the Reprinting of the one and the other, that so the Church might rest in quiet, without any trouble or molestation in her self, or giving offence to any other."[34]

Despite Heylyn's claims, Lambert maintains unequivocally that the 1637 decree "was sought for by the Company and met their require-ments."[35] In this Lambert is following the work of Cyprian Blagden, although her argument relies on archival materials on the Stationers' Company unknown to Blagden.[36] While much of the documentary resour-ces on the Stationers and the decree had been available for some time, the more recently discovered Tanner manuscripts which Lambert uses contain communications – letters and petitions – between the Company members and Laud as well as information on the numbers of printing houses, presses, and apprentices. By bringing these resources to bear upon previ-ously known conditions in the printing trade, Lambert documents the relationship between the Star Chamber Decree and appeals to Laud from both master printers and journeymen. For example, documents in the Stationers' Company's court book, which Blagden had used, indicate that the master printers came to an agreement in 1615 specifying the desired number of printers and restricting the number of presses in any printing house to two. According to Lambert, further archival evidence indicates that the masters continued to control the number of presses, even though they experienced some problems with enforcement.[37] Similarly, she points to the government's legitimate concerns about the book trade that have come to light: the price of books, complaints about the English Stock, poor workmanship in the King's Printing House, patronage practices in admit-ting master printers, and the practice of English printing partnerships looking to foreign presses for the production of legitimate titles. Many of the documents relating to the trade in the 1630s have generally been regarded as part of the government's preparation for the 1637 Decree, but Lambert points to several problems, including dating, which indicate that the documents are more properly placed closer to 1633 and 1634 and thus probably did not participate in a government plan to obtain a decree in Star Chamber. Indeed, the investigation of the print trade that is the subject of many of these documents, Lambert contends, was probably initiated by the master printers.[38] However, based on petitions from individual printers and from the Stationers' Company objecting to regularizing the presses of Robert Raworth, John Norton, Richard Hodgkinson, and Richard Badger, Lambert concludes that the Stationers were pressing the government to extend and enforce the agreements master printers had reached privately in 1628. Lambert also concludes from a document in Privy Council records relating to Company searches, that the "Company moved the Privy Council to grant them a new search warrant" that would allow them to look for English books printed abroad that were protected by royal privileges and patents or by the Company's license.[39]

At the same time that the master printers were pressing for assistance in controlling imported books and for restrictions on presses, the journeymen were petitioning Laud to remedy the masters' breaches of the 1586 decree, particularly in the matter of employment of apprentices. According to Lambert, Laud had initially turned the matter over to the Bishop of London, but when he did nothing, six journeymen and six members of the court of Assistants produced a twenty-article agreement, which was incorrectly entered in the Court Book. The journeymen again petitioned Laud, who said the articles would be "registered" in the High Commission. Subsequently the journeymen provided details of irregular employments in the printing houses, still leading to no remedy.

Lambert's work on the Star Chamber Decree presents a persuasive argument that the 1637 decree was much more than "a political instrument of despotic government," as it has so often been represented. Of the decree's thirty-three items, eighteen of them sought to remedy the central problem Lambert has found in London print culture in the seventeenth century: a limited market for printed materials and a relatively young trade whose membership had grown too quickly.[40] In the face of this, master printers sought to restrict the number of both printing houses and presses; journeymen printers sought employment guarantees and restrictions on the number of apprentices any master could take. Furthermore, it was in the interest of all members of the Stationers' Company to prevent non-Stationers from engaging in any trade practice: printing, binding, selling, or importing books. It was also in everyone's interest to prevent competition from presses at Oxford and Cambridge and from foreign printers.

The 1586 decrees in Star Chamber for order in printing had addressed most of these issues, and, indeed, had proposed similar solutions. In many respects the trade measures added in the 1637 decree are slight. First and foremost, both decrees upheld the Stationers' Company's monopoly on printing by prohibiting non-Stationers from printing and any printer from printing titles protected by the Company's license or royal patent (items 7, 13). Additionally, the 1637 decree requires booksellers to be members of the Stationers' Company (item 10) and brings print founders, four named specifically, within the sphere of privilege and regulation (items 27–30). Both decrees vest Company officials in the right of search and seizure to enforce the Company's monopoly, although the 1637 provision allows the master and wardens "to take unto themselves such assistance as they shall think needful" (item 25).[41] The 1586 decrees had proposed a moratorium on printing houses and prohibited admitting any new master printers (printing house operators) until the numbers diminished, and, then, only with permission of the Archbishop of Canterbury upon the recommendation of the Stationers' Company court of Assistants. It also had required printers to register the number of their presses with the Stationers' Company. The 1637 decree likewise restricts the number of printing houses and calls for registering presses (items 15 and 16), but specifies the names of the twenty current master printers (item 15). With the exception of former Company masters and upper wardens, it also limits all master printers to two presses (item 16). The 1637 decree proposes a further measure to assure adherence to these restrictions: it prohibits anyone from erecting a printing house or building a press without the knowledge of Stationers' Company officials (items 13 and 14).

To address journeymen's complaints the 1586 decrees had restricted concurrent apprenticeships to three for present and past Company masters and senior wardens, two for present and past junior wardens, and one for Company yeomen. The 1637 decree allows the same for masters and senior wardens and yeomen, but permits two apprentices to all members of the Company's livery (item 19). The 1637 decree seeks further protections for the journeymen: first, by requiring the master and wardens of the Company to accompany any journeyman printer seeking work and requiring master printers to employ at least one journeyman so accompanied; second, by imposing sanctions for masters and wardens who "refuse or neglect to go along with any honest and sufficient Journey-man Printer, so desiring their assistance" (items 20 and 21).[42] It also prohibits master printers from employing anyone who is not a Stationers' Company freeman or apprentice (item 23).

Given the terms of the 1637 decree's provisions for improving conditions in the trade – which, indeed, are Lambert's focus – why a new Star Chamber decree would have been necessary is not altogether clear. From all appearances, outside of requiring the Stationers' Company officials to aid the journeymen obtain employment, little changed from the remedies provided by the 1586 decrees. Two differences, however, did exist – one that Lambert does consider (measures relating to importing books) and one that she does not (enforcement). The 1586 decrees had ignored the question of importing "illegal" books, presumably because the 1566 ordinances to which the 1586 decrees appealed had already addressed this and provided a sufficient precedent by which to proceed. Probably, too, in 1586 illegally imported books were not posing much threat to the Stationers. Lambert observes that in the 1630s one of the trade concerns was that London printing syndicates were turning to foreign presses to print their titles for the first time. One of the provisions of the 1637 decree prohibits printing any English book over the seas (item 11) and another (item 9) prohibits printing a book with the imprint of another printer. These provisions do not simply reflect journeymen concerns about syndicates printing overseas; they also address the interests of the King's Printing House, which had complained to the Privy Council about imported books. As we have seen, London booksellers were importing Geneva Bibles dated 1599 with the imprint of the King's Printing House, as well as liturgies and other books that infringed on the King's Printers' patent. Although Lambert does not mention it, another provision about importing responded to another contemporary complaint. Between 1633 and 1637 David van Hooganhuison of Amsterdam was importing books from Holland, both Dutch books for the English market and Latin books that were also printed in England.[43] On a few occasions London booksellers complained to the Privy Council about the competition. Item 12 of the decree prevents foreign agents from marketing books in England unless they are working with a member of the London Stationers' Company. While the 1586 decrees could have been used to take action against the booksellers who violated the King's Printers' privilege, it really had no provision for restraining foreign agents importing and selling books in London. The provisions against imported books were given extra teeth, as were so many aspects of the 1637 decree, by providing explicit means for their enforcement. Item 5 of the new decrees required booksellers to register their intention to import books; item 6 required that all packages of imported books be opened before both Stationers' Company officials and the Archbishop of Canterbury or one of his chaplains; item 32 confined importing to the port of London.

In more general terms of enforcement, the 1586 decrees had conferred a general oversight of London printing on the Archbishop of Canterbury and the Bishop of London, but the enforcement of its specific provisions were left to the court of Assistants. (Indeed, the court of Assistants even proposed the candidates for master printers to the Archbishop.) Court books from the 1590s and early seventeenth century confirm that the court of Assistants exercised jurisdiction over infractions of the 1586 decrees, especially when the issue involved an illegal press or printing another member's copy. As we have seen previously, the court of High Commission became involved in printing disputes only when matters could not be resolved by the Stationers' Company court. On a few occasions trade disputes, like the one in the 1590s when the Stationers sought to prevent members of the Drapers' Company from selling books, were brought before the court of Star Chamber. (On this occasion the court decided in favor of the Stationers, thus extending their monopoly to bookselling.)[44] The most significant feature of the 1637 Star Chamber decree is that it places *all* oversight of the trade in the hands of the Archbishop of Canterbury and the Bishop of London and all enforcement in the hands of the courts of High Commission and Star Chamber. Understanding the implications of this may be found in one particular example (though consideration of others will follow): the provision for Company searches (item 25).

The Stationers' Company's authority to search for anything printed against its monopoly or against its members' rights in copy had been clearly set out in the Company's 1557 charter. This was upheld in 1566 and again in 1586 by the court of Star Chamber. The new provision continued to allow jurisdiction over searches to the Company's master and wardens, but also specified that the Archbishop of Canterbury or the Bishop of London could also independently appoint "any two licensed Master-Printers" as searchers. Where before seized goods and refractory printers had been subject to discipline by the Company, item 25 specifies that searchers will "seize upon so much as is printed, together with the severall offenders" and "bring them before the Lord Arch-Bishop of CANTERBURY, or the Bishop of London … that they or either of them may take such further order therein as shall appertaine to Justice."[45] Such a provision bypasses entirely the Stationers' Company's regulatory oversight.

It is not only in the matter of searches that the 1637 decree altered enforcement. Anyone who printed or imported patented books or books protected by the Stationers' Company was subject to "such Fine, or other punishment" deemed fit by the Star Chamber or the High Commission (item 7). Anyone found erecting a printing house was subject to "paine of imprisonment, and such other punishment" as the Star Chamber or High Commission saw fit.[46] These courts were to punish those who built presses, who violated provisions for keeping apprentices, who failed to assist or hire journeymen seeking employment, who imported books without registering them with the Archbishop of Canterbury or the Bishop of London, who used a false imprint, or who hired non-Stationers. Furthermore, all presses were to be registered with the High Commission and either the Archbishop of Canterbury or the Bishop of London. These entities likewise appointed new master printers and punished printers who kept too many presses.

Besides shifting regulatory authority from the Stationers' Company's court of Assistants to the courts of Star Chamber and High Commission, the 1637 decree introduced one other means of enforcement beyond the 1586 decrees. According to the 1586 decrees a printer who violated them risked losing his letters and having his press broken. The 1637 decree specified that, by "Order" of the court of Star Chamber, anyone "upon Complaint or proofe" of setting up an illegal press or doing any work in an illegal printing house "shall from time to time ... bee set in the Pillorie, and Whipt through the Citie of London" (item 24).[47] This punishment registers a significant change in how printing is perceived. Throughout the life of English trade guilds their crafts were deemed their "mysteries" or their *métiers*, something that belonged exclusively to guild members.[48] Such exemplary punishments as the pillory and being whipped through the city's streets, especially when exercised only "from time to time," proclaims not only that the products of the printing house but that printing itself belong to the public domain. As such, the government will impress upon its subjects a clear sense of what punishment they might endure for transgressive conduct. While I certainly am not prepared to align my view of Caroline censorship with those who frame the discourse between the competing poles of authorial freedom and state repression, this single item of the 1637 decree's provisions for enforcement – though it should not be taken as proof of the rigors of Caroline press censorship – reveals the government's will to drive the regulation of printing from what Adrian Johns has described as Stationers' Hall's secret recesses[49] into the London streets. Practices in the world of print culture now possessed public significance – a phenomenon to which the 1637 decree's preamble also attests: this decree was recorded in the Star Chamber "to the end the same may be publique."[50]

That pillory and whip, the usual penalties incurred by slanderers and seditious libelers, seem strangely inappropriate in a document procured by the Stationers only to remedy abuses in the printing trade, calls for looking more closely at Lambert's strategy in her study of the decree. Lambert places her analysis of trade conditions within the context of the debates of seventeenth-century historiography. She opens "The Printers and the Government, 1604–1637" with the statement, "The title may lead to the expectation that this paper will be concerned with the regulation of the press, for the belief that the only relationship there could be between the government and printers was one of repression is proving very hard to get rid of."[51] Her essay intends, if not to "get rid of" the meddlesome notion of repression, then at least to restore a sense of balance. In order to accomplish this, she refuses to be seduced by the conventional language of repression – "seditious," "scandalous," "schismatic," "pillory" – choosing instead to explain all documentary evidence from the perspective of trade regulation. For the most part, such a strategy is justified, since a word like "illegal" in sources on the Stationers' Company almost always refers to presses and printing that violate the Company's monopoly. (Similarly, "lewd" in Tudor and early Stuart letters and state documents simply means objectionable and never "obscene.") The issue of "seditious," "scandalous," and "schismatic," however, is different. By 1637 these had become virtual code words in legal proceedings. As we saw in chapter 3, the concept of "sedition" as an act dividing the King from his people had emerged as a legal principle. After Richard Montagu, church Calvinists and godly ministers, as well as conforming Puritans, all became "schismatics," whether or not they were in fact so. "Scandal" increasingly became less a matter of private defamation actionable in both the ecclesiastical and common law, than an offense to the Crown and Church of England. Given this, Lambert's analysis may be missing useful evidence. This is certainly so in the case of one occasion where she identifies Company lobbying for the 1637 decree.

As noted above, Lambert concludes that the "Company moved the Privy Council to grant them a new search warrant" that would allow them to look for English books printed abroad that were protected by royal privileges and patents or by the Company's license on the basis of a Privy Council order.[52] The document in question, which does indeed relate to searches, is a warrant that "commands" unstated officials to assist the Stationers' Company's master and wardens, or their deputies, "as well within the city as without" to search for "persons who are probably suspected to imprint, import or put to sale any schismatical and scandalous books as also all books printed contrary to the said [1586 Star Chamber] decree." The preamble indicates that the Privy Council had "ordained" in an "information from the Companie of Stationers of the Cittie of London that divers ill disposed persons as well within this kingdom of England as in partes beyond the seas doe print, binde, imprint and putt to sale seditious, schismatick and scandalous bookes" as well as "other bookes" such as Bibles, psalters and almanacs "though lawful in themselves yet printed and vented contrary to the decree in the Star Chamber."[53] Given the date, September 15, 1634, this looks considerably less like a "new search warrant" – important because it gives authority over persons as well as merchandise and is a part of a program of Company pressure towards a new decree from the Star Chamber – than a special warrant directed to a particular infraction. "As well within the city as without" represents a geographical extension to the Stationers' authority, and in 1634 the High Commission was investigating Thomas Cowper and William Lee in the matter of John Egerton's customs fraud. Egerton served in the customs house at the river port of Maldon in Essex. Cowper and Lee were booksellers in Lothbury, just outside of London. Some of the illegal books in question were indeed the "other books" that violated the 1586 decrees, but others were illegal in the first sense. In September 1633 a letter from the English Ambassador at The Hague notified Secretary Coke that illegal books were being smuggled into England as blank paper. Among the books in question were not only illegal Bibles but also a book against the ceremonies of the Church of England by William Ames (most likely *Fresh Suit against Human Ceremonies in God's Worship*). In addition Henry Burton's *The opinion, judgement, and determination of two reverend, learned, and conformable divines of the Church of England, concerning bowing at the name, or naming of Jesus* was printed in Amsterdam in 1634.[54] It seems that the Privy Council's stated concern about books that were "schismatic" and "seditious," along with books "though lawful in themselves yet printed and vented contrary to the decree in the Star Chamber," should not be dismissed altogether.

Admitting that government concern about books' contents may have provided some impetus to publishing a new Star Chamber decree helps to explain thirteen provisions in the decree only peripherally related to economic issues in the book trade. Perhaps the most important of these is the first item that prohibits presuming "to print, or cause to be printed, either in the parts beyond the Seas, or in this Realme, or other his Maiesties Dominions," importing, selling, binding, stitching or sewing "any seditious, schismaticall, or offensive Bookes or Pamphlets, to the scandall of Religion, or the Church, or the Government, or Governours of the Church or State, or Commonwealth, or any Corporation, or particular person or persons whatsoever." Given that the alternative definition of illegal – for which "the said Company of Stationers, or any other person or persons have, or shall by any Letters Patents, Order, or Entraunce in their Register book, or otherwise, have the right, priviledge, authority or allowance soly to print"[55] – does not appear until item 7, the 1637 Star Chamber decree may fairly be acknowledged to express the government's intent to control a fairly particular kind of illegal content. This concern is likewise expressed with regard to imported books in item 6, which specifies that one of the Archbishop of Canterbury's chaplains must be present when any package of imported books is opened so that "if there happens to be found any seditious, schismaticall or offensive booke or bookes, they shall forthwith be brought unto the said Lord Arch-bishop" or to the Bishop of London or the High Commission, so that the offender would be punished by the Star Chamber or the High Commission.[56] Article 26 calls upon Stationers' Company searchers to look out for books "contrary to the doctrine and discipline of the Church of England, or against the State and Government";[57] this is in addition to the article that confirmed the Stationers' rights of search and seizure. As we have seen, by 1637 the "Puritan" press had become so radicalized that this concern may be seen as legitimate. While the government of Charles I may not have been interested in silencing all criticism, efforts to quell religious controversy had turned theological disputation into the kind of criticism that item 1 of the new decree defined as illegal. (Of course, as we have seen, notions of orthodoxy and schism were far less stable than the decree might suggest.)

Another item that testifies to Caroline interest in controlling the content of printed texts appears in the items addressed to licensing – and this is to official oversight of printed texts and not to the Stationers' Company "licence" and "entrance" that approximated "copyright." While the 1586 decree had required that all books and pamphlets be licensed according the Elizabethan Injunctions, item 2 of the new decree required oversight of "every the Titles, Epistles, Prefaces, Proems, Preambles, Introductions, Tables, Dedications, and other matters and things whatsoever thereunto annexed."[58] This acknowledges the ability of paratextual materials to alter a text's original intention – ironically something that occurred in the case of Heylyn's translator's preface to John Prideaux's *The Doctrine of the Sabbath* (1634). Unlike the 1586 decree, which had simply given the Archbishop of Canterbury licensing oversight, the new decree sets out clearly defined parameters for licensing. Item 3 assigned oversight of common law books to the Lords Chief Justices and the Lord Chief Baron; state histories and books on the "present times" and affairs of State were to be seen by one of the principal secretaries of State; and books on heraldry, arms, and titles of honor were placed in the Earl Marshall's purview. Everything else, "whether Divinities, Phisicke, Philosophie, Poetry, or whatsoever,"[59] was to be seen by the Archbishop of Canterbury, the Bishop of London or one of the vice chancellors of either of the universities, although the university licensers could license books only for the university presses.

Item 4 instituted a measure to assure that the books actually printed conformed to the copy licensed: two "written copies" were to be presented for licensing one of which would be kept in the registry of the Archbishop of Canterbury; the other in a secure place by the licenser. This item reiterates the interest in controlling content in its statement that the licenser shall:

> testifie under his or their hand or hands, that there is nothing in the Booke or Books contained, that is contrary to Christian faith, and the Doctrine and Discipline of the Church of England, nor against the State or Government, nor contrary to good life, or good manners, or otherwise, as the nature and subject of the work shall require . . .[60]

This testimony was to be printed in the book with the licenser's name. While this statement appears to represent a rather moderate standard for press control, the degree of moderation is less important than the fact that, for the first time, a standard is specified, and, by having their names imprinted in the book, licensers would be held accountable to the standard. When he first became Archbishop of Canterbury, Laud had attempted to institute such accountability by requiring the Stationers to include the imprimaturs of his chaplains in the printed books. That so few books actually carried this imprimatur must have made Laud acutely aware of the discrepancy between the numbers of books officially licensed and those printed, a problem that the 1637 decree also sought to resolve.

In item 18 the 1637 decree sought to end the practice that dominated religious printing in the 1630s and that flooded the market with books by conforming Calvinists and godly writers active when a Calvinist consensus had existed in the Church of England. Item 8 prohibited printing or causing "to be reprinted, any booke or bookes whatsoever (though Formerly printed with licence) without being reviewed, and a new Licence obtained."[61] Lambert observes that this is the only article in the decree that prompted objections from the Stationers. Regardless of whether or not this was withdrawn, or simply not enforced, is less important than its inclusion in the decree. From Heylyn's perspective, as we have seen, the reprinting of books that were either "Calvinian" or anti-Catholic motivated Laud to procure the decree. These books, though they were not seditious, scandalous, or schismatic, nonetheless prevented the "peace in the Church" Laud and the King so desired. After the 1637 decree was recorded in the Star Chamber and published, Laud had to face much greater matters than outdated sermons and theological treatises. Charles's government was facing outright opposition in Scotland to its religious regime. At home, Laud's energies were taken up with drafting new canons that would establish that the ceremonies were not simply adiaphorous.

The 1637 Star Chamber Decree, then, sought to remedy the defective features of the 1586 decrees by providing a means to assist journeymen in finding employment, by defining "illegal" writing more clearly, by articulating a clear government licensing procedure, by transferring enforcement from the Stationers' court of Assistants to the courts of High Commission and Star Chamber, and by specifying sanctions. None of these provisions, outside of the provisions for journeymen, represented innovation. Just like the limits the master printers imposed on their own numbers, most of these practices were already in place, largely through practices of legal precedence. Beginning in 1629 the High Commission had assumed jurisdiction over prosecuting printers (and some authors) of unlicensed books – although I think it needs to be restated here that there were many unlicensed books not on the subject of religion whose authors and printers went unsanctioned. The court of Star Chamber tried the printers and authors of books it deemed schismatic, seditious, and scandalous to the Church and State, most notably in the cases of Leighton, Prynne, Burton, and Bastwick. With regard to government licensing, like his father's, Charles I's regime had always understood that all books should be so licensed, and although an imprinted imprimatur looks innovative, it had already been required in some cases. Similarly, the designation of official licensers for law books, heraldry, and political texts may appear to alter licensing, except that from the time of Elizabeth, the Stationers' Registers record the names of licensers whose approbation depended upon their expertise. Weckherlin, an employee of Secretary of State Conway, already had been appointed to license news and other political writing. With respect to the 1586 decrees' defective features, then, the 1637 Star Chamber Decree did little more than integrate into a single document stipulations for practices that already had legal precedence. It should not then be surprising that its impact would not have been monumental.

The 1637 decree's other intent had been to address new abuses that had arisen since 1586. These abuses, most of which related in one way or another to imported books, were surprisingly local and particular. A false English printer's imprint – the King's Printer – appeared on Geneva Bibles printed by one publishing house. The practice was not widespread, although the number of books significantly impacted the English market. One corrupt customs official outside of London called attention to the dangers of books coming into other ports. London booksellers complained about one Dutch book importer. By drafting specific provisions to address singular local events, it seems as though the 1637 decree's architects were trying to envision every possible kind of problem that might ever conceivably arise in the world of print. This also explains, again, why the decree produced few changes in practice.

One feature in the new decree that addresses neither an old inadequacy nor a new abuse was probably its most consequential change: its denigration of the Stationers' Company's court of Assistants by placing oversight of and sanctions for all forms of "illegal" printing, importing, and bookselling in the hands of the courts of High Commission and Star Chamber. After 1637 the principal business of the Stationers' court involved deciding disputes among Company members over copy ownership. Formerly, it had done this, but it also had jurisdiction over illegal presses and presses printing illegal books, the 1586 decrees having called upon the master and wardens to impose the sanctions for illegal printing the decrees had specified. In the larger world of London's print culture between 1637 and 1640, the shift in court jurisdictions might appear to be an insignificant change, especially since a rigorous system of oversight was still in place. The abolition of the courts of Star Chamber and High Commission in 1641, however, would find the Stationers' Company much more economically vulnerable than it would have been had the 1637 Star Chamber Decree never been passed. Not only did the Stationers' Company lose the means to enforce its trade monopoly, but individual members found it difficult to protect their rights in copy, as the next chapter will show.

From all available indicators, besides the matter of the court of Assistants, the 1637 decree had little effect on London publishing. The one instance where changes in the regulations may have affected the way in which a detractor was sanctioned occurred in December 1637. John Lilburn was summoned into Star Chamber offices to answer for dealing illegally in imported books, an infraction that had not received precise articulation prior to the new decree. The authorities' real concern, however, was not that Lilburn was trading in imported books, but that he had procured the overseas printing of some of the books that had led to the Star Chamber trial earlier that year of Burton, Bastwick, and Prynne.[62] Lilburn denied the charge and refused to sign the examination containing an informer's evidence that he had caused some ten to twelve thousand

books to be printed in Holland and brought to England. In February
he was brought before Star Chamber, where he both persisted in his
denial and refused to take any oath. He was sentenced to a £500 fine. A
few month later he was whipped through the streets from the Fleet Prison
to Westminster, where he was confined to the pillory. The new Star
Chamber Decree probably made it easier for Lilburn to be charged in
Star Chamber for having "seditious" books printed abroad, and it certainly
prescribed his punishment. Had the new Star Chamber decree not been in
place, Lilburn might possibly have been prosecuted for unlicensed printing, but given the trial of Burton, Bastwick, and Prynne and Lilburn's
alleged publishing of books in this case, this seems unlikely.[63]

The new decree may have brought small changes to the manner in which
the government apprehended, prosecuted, and punished the publishers of
seditious libels, but it apparently did very little to remedy problems within
the Stationers' Company. In 1638, as Lambert has observed, the journeymen complained further to Laud that the masters were acting in violation
of the decree's provisions for improving the journeymen's lot. The new
decree, however, did effect one significant change: licensing compliance
increased. From 1625 to 1636 an average of 76 percent of entries in the
Stationers' Register showed evidence of ecclesiastical authorization. In 1638
and 1639 99 percent of the titles entered were licensed and in 1640 all
of them were – although in 1640 entry declined significantly. Additionally,
a higher percentage of the books printed were entered in the Registers.
In addition, a very slight decline in the number of books printed in
England occurred, but a decrease of thirteen titles does not really represent
a significant number. The number of religious titles entered in the
Stationers' Register actually increased from 79 in 1637 to 105 in 1638, but
it returned to 68 in 1639. Given the radically changing political conditions
after 1638, it is virtually impossible to say anything more about the impact
of the decree on London printing.

Beginning in 1638 the books that most offended Charles I and the
church officials did not come from London; they came from Scotland
and some were reprinted in Amsterdam. Carried in knapsacks and on
horseback and disseminated through informal distribution networks in the
countryside, the Covenanter pamphlets, which justified Scottish refusal of
an English service book, proved to be the real "paper bullets" that deeply
wounded the Caroline regime. As the next chapter will show, the Scottish
propaganda campaign fired the shot whose reverberations forced the Long
Parliament, an action that drastically altered the ways in which print was
employed and controlled.

CHAPTER 6

The end of censorship

In *England on Edge*, David Cressy reminds us that between the time the Long Parliament convened in 1640 and civil war broke out in 1642 print culture in England underwent radical changes that transformed its political and social circumstances.[1] One of the English Revolution's "most revolutionary features," according to Cressy, was "the explosion of print" in the opening years of the Long Parliament.

> There were more items published in 1641, than in any year in the previous history of English printing (2,177 in the English Short Title Catalogue, of which the bookseller George Thomason collected 721). More appeared in 1642 than at any time again before the eighteenth century (4,188 in ESTC, including 2,134 in Thomason). If anyone doubts there was revolution in mid-Stuart England they have only to look at these peaks.[2]

For most historians, the sharp rise in printed titles resulted from the end of Caroline censorship.[3] According to Fredrick Siebert, "the printers of the realm found themselves free for the first time to print what they pleased" when the "controls of King, council, Star Chamber, and High Commission" weakened or disappeared.[4] Bibliographical historians, including D. F. McKenzie and Sheila Lambert, however, have challenged the claims made for the impact of the "lapse of licensing."[5] When the historical understanding of Caroline press censorship is itself as vexed as this study has found it to be, that historiographical interpretations differ on censorship in the closing years of Charles's reign should be expected. This chapter considers the role books and their control played at the end of the reign of Charles I.

THE SCOTTISH PROBLEM

On February 27, 1639 Charles I issued a proclamation expressing his will and command to his "loving Subjects" that "they receive no more ... seditious Pamphlets sent from Scotland, or any other place ... And that such of Our Subjects here, as have already received any of these Rebellious Pamphlets, do presently deliver them to the next Justice of Peace."[6] The "Rebellious Pamphlets" referred to here were those associated with the National Covenant subscribed in Scotland, beginning with the Covenant itself, *The confession of faith of the kirk of Scotland, subscribed by the Kings Majestie and his housholde in the yeare of God 1580 with a designation of such acts of Parlament as are expedient for justefying the union after mentioned, and subscribed by the nobles, barrons, gentlemen, burgesses, ministers, and commons in the yeare of God 1638*, printed at both Edinburgh and Amsterdam, and followed by printed replies to every measure the government of Charles I took against the Covenant, as well as rationales for these responses. In the interest of assuring that "the whole Church of Christ were one as well in forme of publike worship as in doctrine," a new service book based on the Book of Common Prayer was introduced in Scotland in July 1637 after several years of planning and in response to a royal proclamation.[7] The first reading of the new service in St. Giles Cathedral in Edinburgh prompted a riot, which was, according to Peter Donald, "but the tip of the troubles for the king": "As early petitioning followed the advance planning of protest against the liturgy, it was to be argued that, although the Scottish church already had a set form of worship, a new book would in any case require the approval of both general assembly and Parliament, which had presided over past changes."[8] A Supplicant movement emerged in Scotland that questioned the authority of King and bishops to legally impose changes on the Scottish Kirk and that led in February of 1638 to the National Covenant. The Covenant restated the 1581 agreement on the Scottish Kirk reached with James VI. According to Donald Stevenson the Covenant's last section was the most significant. It bound the document's signers to "adhere to and defend the true religion, to forbear the practice of innovations, and not to give approbation to the present government of the kirk until the 'kirkmen' had been tried in free assemblies and parliaments."[9]

As Charles's 1639 Proclamation indicates, the King chose to interpret the acts of the Covenanters as open rebellion against his authority rather than merely a resistance to his religious policies. The proclamation, important as it is as an act of censorship, also offered justification for raising an army to oppose a group of dissident Scots. It actually was drafted as an interim measure until a fuller justification and rationale could be completed. Later in the same year *A large declaration concerning the Late Tumults in Scotland . . . collected out of their owne foule acts and writings* appeared from the press of Robert Young, the King's Printer in Scotland. (Its 420-page length justifies the title's "large.") At the center of both the proclamation and the *Declaration* lies the King's recognition of the power of print. The rebellious Scots, "have endeavoured to poison the hearts of Our good and Loyal Subjects." By producing "the multitude of their printed Pamphlets, or rather infamous Libels ... and spreading of them in divers parts of this our Kingdom" they have sought to "seduce" the English "to the like rebellious courses with themselves."[10] Starting with the *Confession of faith*, the Covenanters had employed the printed word to state their cause to the world. According to Donald, by 1639 when war was looking more likely, the Covenanters produced explicit propaganda which, among objections to Anglicizing the Scottish Kirk, cast aspersions on all those in England who pressed the King towards war, especially the English bishops with their "popish" inclinations.[11] Books on the limit of political obedience like Buchanan's *De Jure Regni Apud Scots* joined these. In addition, editions of Covenanter publications were produced in Amsterdam and Leiden and smuggled into England. From Donald's perspective "foreign versions of the various libels intensified personal hostilities against Laud."[12]

Discussions of Caroline censorship rarely address the last significant effort of the regime to control the printed word. Its four proclamations and two declarations in less than two years far outweigh the 1626 proclamation and 1628 declaration against controversial theology. (The proclamation against de Sales's book pales in significance compared to these.) Charles not only ordered that the 1639 proclamation be read in every church in England at Divine Service, but also commanded that 10,000 copies should be printed. Perhaps more than for any other censored texts, Charles's government engaged in widespread efforts to discover anyone who possessed or traded in Scottish news or books. Searches throughout the provinces for offending texts were carried out – and not by the master and wardens of the Stationers' Company. Regardless of this effort, according to Donald, "the flow of information and deliberate appeals for support, both printed and manuscript, could not easily be stopped."[13]

When the influx of Scottish propaganda would not stop, the King tried another tactic. On March 30, 1640, he issued another proclamation. This one, "against libelous and seditious Pamphlets, and Discourses sent from Scotland," declared

that all and every person and persons of what degree or quality soever, now have or hereafter shall have any such libelous and seditious Discourse or Pamphlet, concerning his Majesties proceedings with his Subjects in Scotland, (other then such Relations and Discources concerning the same, as have been published and printed by his speciall Licence and Authority) and shall not within ten dayes after the date of these presents, bring and deliver the same to one of his principall Secretaries of State; All and every such person and persons shall incur the uttermost of such punishments and penalties as by the Lawes of this Realm are to be inflicted upon those that keep such scandalous and seditious Pamphlets and Papers.[14]

This proclamation is notable not only because it prohibits possession and declares dire penalties, but also because it specifies "every person and persons of what degree or quality soever." In her consideration of the motives for English censorship in the early modern period, Debora Shuger notes a "relatively broad tolerance for dangerous and dirty ideas," especially among what this proclamation described as people of "quality."[15] The government's response to the Covenanter pamphlets evidences clear anxiety about a political ideology that challenges the rights of the monarch and the bishops to institute religious changes without a council or a parliament. Indeed, if the response to the Covenanter pamphlets is placed within the context of the trial of Burton, Bastwick, and Prynne, where Laud objected so vehemently to their charges of innovation in the Church of England, the anxiety may be seen as extending to any mention of "innovations."[16]

While the government feared that the Covenanter pamphlets and manuscript news from Scotland might have a politically destabilizing effect on the English people, actually their effect was on the government. Scottish writing fed government anxieties about English Puritanism. In December of 1637 the London Stationer John Bartlett was summoned before the High Commission for selling schismatic books, including Bastwick's *Letany* and Burton's *Appeal*, and for receiving "Scottish news" and causing copies to be made. Since the Scottish material included letters to the Scottish Privy Council disparaging King Charles, Bartlett was detained in the Fleet for examination by Secretary of State Windebank and the Scottish Secretary of State, the Earl of Stirling. His case was heard before Charles's Privy Council with the King present, instead of in the High Commission. According to Donald, "Laud interpreted the case as signifying the link between Scots and English that he feared."[17] Shortly thereafter Laud and Thomas Wentworth, Earl of Strafford, corresponded about a Puritan plot in which Laud suspected that Bishop John Williams was operating from the Tower prison with contacts in both England and Scotland to work with subversives to summon an English Parliament that would "undo the work of recent years."[18] Even though Charles was intent on isolating the Scottish problem, as the censorship campaign against the Covenanter pamphlets reveals, his refusal to accommodate the Scots may have been driven by fears, like Laud's, of a Puritan plot.

Ironically, Laud's worst fears about an English Parliament were realized but not because of any of Williams's machinations in Scotland. Instead, King Charles's resort to force to tame the rebellious Scots placed so great a strain on financial resources that the King was forced to summon the Parliaments of April and November in 1640. Historians have come to recognize the important role affairs in Scotland had in giving rise to the English Civil War, but few have expressed this understanding as succinctly as David Cressy: "Charles I's misguided attempt to impose prayer-book uniformity on Presbyterian Scotland precipitated the events that led to revolution and civil war. His blind pursuit of conformity proved disastrous for his family, his church, and his realm."[19] King Charles expected the April Parliament to vote subsidies, but instead, he met with its members' insistence on discussing the grievances accumulated for the past eleven years. Widespread dissatisfaction followed the King's dissolution of the Parliament after only three weeks. Even so, the King pursued war with the Scots. By September, however, the Scots occupied England's northeastern region, and the King was forced to summon another Parliament where "he faced not criticism but revolution."[20] Looking back to this time, one royalist historiographer blamed this revolution on the printed word:

I know not any one thing that more hurt the late King then the paper bullets of the press; it was the scandalous and calumniating ink of the Faction that from then blackened him, and represented all his words and actions to the misguided People, who would difficultly have been persuaded to such a horrid Rebellion, if they had not first been prepossessed by the tongues and pens of the Faction ...[21]

It is more likely, I think, that the paper bullets fired from Scotland did far more than Burton, Bastwick, and Prynne ever did to galvanize English support for parliamentary measures to remedy their discontents.

PARLIAMENT AND THE PRESS

The Long Parliament has been the object of intense historical scrutiny, including among historians of print culture. Loewenstein says that the opening years of the Long Parliament "constitute what is perhaps the most notorious moment in early modern English press control."[22] Some of this notoriety derives from John Milton's *Areopagitica*, whose impassioned plea for freedom of the press has indelibly impressed on the historical imagination the evils of both ecclesiastical press controls and the courts that enforced them under the Tudor and early Stuart monarchs; some from the 1643 Licensing Act to which Milton objected; and some from the unprecedented escalation in printed texts. All of these, although important, can best be understood by considering how in its first days and weeks the Long Parliament reinterpreted the practices of Caroline press control and responded to them.

The Long Parliament convened on Tuesday, November 3, 1640.[23] On Thursday the King addressed the Commons, and on Friday the Commons set to the work of creating committees, including one on religion and another on the courts of justice. On Saturday, the petitions of Susannah Bastwick and Sara Burton on behalf of their husbands, John and Henry, were read, and it was resolved that by warrant of the house, the men would be sent for "in safe custody."[24] The rest of the day's business concerned grievances about religious innovation, the new canons, the absence of parliaments, ship money, and monopolies.[25] On the subject of religion some of the speeches sound much like a replay of the parliaments in the 1620s with complaints about the advancement of "Arminians" who were "superstitious, corrupt in their doctrine, and vicious in their lives."[26] Sir Benjamin Rudyard complained of efforts to "quell preaching and draw the religion to old ceremonies" and blamed Peter Heylyn for branding "all good Protestants under the name of puritans."[27] John Pym's objections to the "arbitrary proceedings" in the courts of justice – which ignored law and precedents and denied subjects "all defence" – drew Mr. Bagshaw's pronouncement, "Let them be cut off that frame[d] mischief by law."[28] On Monday the petitions of Alexander Leighton and John Lilburn to have their cases newly prosecuted were heard and granted, and Mr. Rous proposed that Bishop John Williams's cause might be worthy of consideration.[29] By the end of November a subcommittee of the Committee for Religion was charged with enquiring into the "oppressions and sufferings of ministers by reason of any of the ecclesiastical proceedings." They were also called to meet "to examine touching the abuse in licensing books, and for refusing to license other books, and for refusing to give order to ministers, and what questions as have been propounded to ministers upon the same to take orders."[30]

During the month of December this subcommittee took up petitions and complaints about specific texts, including Martin Luther's *Last Divine Discourses*, Samuel Ward's *Dogmatical Theological Questions and Evangelical Essays*, Lancelot Andrewes's *Catechistical Discourses*, "Mr. Doctor Featley's sermons,"[31] and books by William Fenner, John Pocklington, and Richard Sibbes. The committee discovered that at the request of William Bray, Laud's chaplain, thirty sheets were expunged from Daniel Featly's book of sermons, while another Laudian licenser,

Thomas Wykes, required that words favoring bowing at the name of Jesus be added to a book by Sibbes. They also learned that the High Commission had prevented the printing of the *Catechistical Discourses* because it had not received official approbation, and that the master and wardens had surreptitiously entered the title in the Company books. The subcommittee continued its work into the next year, demonstrating that, indeed, Laud's licensers had assured that books which advanced ceremonial innovations were printed, and that books by godly authors like Featly and Sibbes were altered to favor the ceremonies.

Early in December another committee was created to investigate abuses in the courts of High Commission and Star Chamber.[32] Specifically, the committee was asked to consider petitions that had already been received, mostly relating to Burton and Prynne, as well as to "receive all petitions of the like nature: and to consider the jurisdiction of the High Commission Court of Canterbury and York, and of the several abuses committed in those courts . . . and of the jurisdiction of the Court of Star Chamber."[33] Burton's petition complained that his answer in the 1637 Star Chamber trial had been "mutilated and expunged."[34] Prynne's petition recounted the abuses he suffered in the matter of *Histrio-mastix*, when he was first questioned by Attorney General Noy about inoffensive passages, and later condemned through the misreadings Heylyn assigned the text. Shortly after the committee was formed, it received the petitions of Alexander Leighton and John Bastwick. On December 9 the committee proceeded to a hearing on Prynne's complaints. In the course of the proceedings the committee heard Heylyn's testimony that

Mr. Secretary Coke gave him a book called *Histriomastix* and charged him in the kings name to peruse it and to draw out such passages as were scandalous, whereupon he did it; and delivered the notes he had taken, being fair written out, to Secretary Coke aforesaid before the information was put out against Mr. Prynne, and did after deliver the foul original draft to Mr. Attorney Noy.[35]

Following this, one of the committee members observed that if Heylyn had proceeded in a Christian spirit, "he might have prevented Mr. Prynne's punishment by interpreting those places dexterously which he distorted sincerely."[36] (A few months later, it was even proposed that Heylyn should be prosecuted for the injustice he inflicted on Prynne – though this never came to pass.) On December 15 the committee proceeded to the judgment

that all the proceedings in the Star Chamber upon which the sentence February 17 anno 9 Caroli was grounded against Mr. William Prynne were all of them unjust and that the said sentence ought to be reversed. And it was resolved secondly upon the question, that he ought to have reparations made for all his wrongs and losses therein sustained.[37]

A week later the committee considered Burton and Prynne's 1637 trial, and based on irregular procedures that led them to be condemned in Star Chamber *pro confesso*, determined that they had been proceeded against unjustly. The Star Chamber charges were reversed, and the committee proposed that Prynne be "restored to his practice and profession of an utter barrister in Lincoln's [Inn] and to the degree of bachelor of art in Oxford."[38] On May 25, 1641 the restitution was ordered, and on June 8 Burton's license to preach was restored.[39] In January the committee had turned to the High Commission's irregular procedures in imprisoning John Bastwick for his Latin book (previously printed with license and authorization) objecting to the Pope. (The bishops on the High Commission interpreted it as being against their authority.) In February it considered his Star Chamber trial. It also considered Leighton's petition regarding his 1630 Star Chamber trial. On June 11 the Commons ordered restitution to both Leighton and Bastwick for their suffering.[40]

The Commons' readiness not simply to hear the petitions of Leighton, Bastwick, Prynne, and Burton but to vindicate them early in the Long Parliament's first session speaks to the Caroline regime's choice of singling them out for exemplary public punishment rather than to any particular parliamentary umbrage taken to Caroline censorship. The committee that considered their plight was a committee appointed to consider judicial abuse. With the exception of their concern for how Heylyn contributed to manufacturing charges against Prynne out of *Histrio-mastix*, the committee took less interest in the content of the books than in the ways in which the courts took liberties with regularly established procedures. In the 1637 trials of Burton, Bastwick, and Prynne, for example, Star Chamber proceeded *pro confesso*, even though they had entered answers. With the caveat that the illegality of the court's proceedings is still disputable, that in 1640 and 1641 the committee investigating abuses in the Star Chamber chose to focus on these notorious cases testifies to the extraordinary impression they made on the public imagination. When the committee reported its findings to the Commons, it did not contend that the books for which these men suffered were, after all, acceptable books. They stressed, instead, that these men had undergone a miscarriage of justice. They had been denied protections guaranteed to English subjects by Magna Carta. Their studies had been invaded, their books seized, and they had suffered long imprisonment without cause being first demonstrated. Beside exorbitant fines, the punishments they endured deprived them of their means of livelihood. The question of the abuse of justice did not stop with the remedies Parliament offered these men, it extended to the statute they passed against these courts, and, further, to the attainders of treason passed against the Earl of Strafford and Archbishop Laud. Parliament's principal charge against the men who put King Charles's government into jeopardy was that they counseled him to ignore the laws of England.

The Committee for the Jurisdiction of Star Chamber and High Commission was appointed on December 3, 1640, barely a month after the Parliament had convened. We learn something of its concerns from one meeting of the subcommittee appointed to hear Prynne's appeal. According to Simond D'Ewes, in the course of discussing Prynne the committee digressed to a discussion of the origins of the High Commission. In comparing the High Commission under Elizabeth to the Caroline High Commission, they noted that the Elizabethan commission was fairly small in size and had lay members as well as ecclesiastical. The Caroline High Commission was large, had few lay members, and was dominated by the bishops both in number and power. The committee concluded that the Caroline High Commission was not warranted by the Elizabethan statute.[41] The legality of Star Chamber was apparently of less importance than the abusive penalties it imposed. In March 1641 the Committee on Star Chamber and High Commission was ordered to prepare a bill regulating Star Chamber.[42] On June 8, 1641 the Commons approved a bill regulating the Privy Council, abolishing Star Chamber, and another repealing the clause in the Elizabethan statute that called for the creation of a commission to enquire about the ecclesiastical state. After several conference meetings with the House of Lords during which the Lords proposed revisions, the Lords passed the bill on June 26, with the proviso that it would not come into effect until August 1. On July 5, remarking that to approve these statutes would be "no less than to alter, in a great measure, those fundamental laws, ecclesiastical and civil, which my predecessors have established," King Charles, nevertheless, approved the statute.[43]

Looking at the language of both acts explains both the motives that led to abolishing the two courts and the consequences of the abolition. The preamble to taking away Star Chamber essentially looks back to the Five Knights Case and the Petition of Right to argue that the Magna Carta guarantees that no man can be imprisoned without the lawful judgment of his peers and that the common law establishes due process. The common law, the preamble states, redresses all matters that have been examined in

Star Chamber. Furthermore, neither the King nor his council has jurisdiction over a man's estate (16 Charles I, ca. 10). Star Chamber's abolition
clearly addressed much larger issues than censorship. Indeed, the entire
question of Star Chamber jurisdiction over the press was absent from both
the statute and from parliamentary proceedings on the matter. The question of court jurisdiction also arose in the statute repealing the clause in the
Act of Supremacy (1 Eliz., ca. 1) that empowered the monarch to form an
ecclesiastical commission. The preamble explains that the Elizabethan
statute's purpose had been to restore to the Crown the ancient jurisdiction
of the state ecclesiastical and spiritual. In its subsequent history, the High
Commission used fines and imprisonment to exercise authority not
belonging to the Crown's ecclesiastical jurisdiction, and, therefore, the
Caroline statute repeals the clause allowing the monarch to create an
ecclesiastical commission. Although not stated directly, the issue of printing is more relevant here. As we have seen, the High Commission had come
to exercise jurisdiction in patent and Company license disputes in the print
trade – a matter that only rarely had to do with the Crown's ecclesiastical
jurisdiction. Furthermore, after 1590 the High Commission had extended
its jurisdiction from clerical conformity to becoming an ecclesiastical court
of appeals. In 1592 common law judges in Caudry's case had ruled favorably on the High Commission's legitimacy as a court of law, but widespread opposition to its procedures, including the oath *ex officio* continued.
With the escalation of litigation at the end of the sixteenth century in all the
courts, distinctions between secular and religious jurisdiction blurred and
litigants brought cases where they felt they could be best served. Cross-
suiting – entertaining separate or counter-suits in the same or different
courts – became such common practice that actions confined to a single
suit in a single court were exceptions.[44] Common law judges regularly
employed writs of prohibition (orders from a common law court to an
ecclesiastical or Admiralty court to cease a proceeding) to restrict the
"encroachments of High Commission, the Court of Requests, the
Council of the North and the Council of the Marches and Wales."[45]
That the House of Lords added the Councils of the North and of the
Marches and Wales to the High Commission as courts that should be
abolished in 1641 indicates that the old question of judicial encroachment
influenced the move to eliminate the High Commission as much as the
sufferings of Burton and Bastwick.

The decision to eliminate the courts of Star Chamber and High
Commission, although not a direct response to Caroline censorship, did
impact print culture but not quite in the manner Hill and Siebert have

seen. The fall of the High Commission and Star Chamber is usually linked to the end of licensing because they were seen as the principal means to assure its enforcement. For most of its life the Stationers' Company enforced licensing – the Company license and, to lesser degree, ecclesiastical authorization. The only license that the Stationers consistently required was that which identified a member's copy. For most of the Company's life, the master and wardens exercised their judgment in requiring official authorization and in punishing "unauthorized" printing. It was not until the 1630s that Stationers' Company members were prosecuted in High Commission and Star Chamber for "unlicensed" printing. Even then, however, the only unlicensed printing that provoked prosecution was for texts to which the Caroline regime objected – initially books of religious controversy, later books against the bishops. The 1637 Star Chamber decree removed enforcement of both kinds of licensing entirely from the Company court's jurisdiction, but after 1637 neither Star Chamber nor High Commission prosecuted either kind of licensing violation unless it involved books the government deemed offensive. Moreover, the Stationers' court of Assistants was no longer responsible for any licensing enforcement. When printing began to escalate in 1640 – a year before Star Chamber and High Commission were dissolved – the Stationers' Company lacked the authority to act against routinely "illegal" (unlicensed) printing and "illegal" (unregistered) presses, and Star Chamber and High Commission, which had the authority, exercised it only if unlicensed printing was also illegal in the sense of being "scandalous," "schismatic," "seditious," against the doctrine of the Church of England, or printed in violation of the King's Printers' patent. Ironically, the very tool the Stationers had sought to strengthen their monopoly, weakened it and, indeed, nearly destroyed it once Star Chamber and High Commission were outlawed. That the Stationers' Company was astutely aware of this is apparent in their 1643 *Remonstrance* to the Parliament.

The *Remonstrance*, written during the time that Parliament was preparing a bill on printing (which receives consideration below), provides valuable insights into the problems the Company was experiencing in the 1640s. The document usually is interpreted as an effort to assure that the new regulation would protect the Company's printing monopoly.[46] One of the *Remonstrance*'s most significant but rarely considered components, however, addresses the Company's role in enforcement. Prosecution, it says, is "the Life of all Law," and "in matters of the Presse, no man can so effectually prosecute, as Stationers themselves." If they do not currently do so, "it is partly for want of full authority, and partly for want of true encouragement." The power they seek is not to be "solely or confusedly entrusted with the Government of the Presse ... but onely in order to prosecution of Delinquents." The authority they seek "is so farre from an Innovation, that tis the removal of a dangerous innovation."[47] It is telling that the precedents to which the *Remonstrance* appeals are its charter "granted by severall Princes" and the "good Decrees" made in the eighth and twenty-eighth years of Elizabeth's reign, and not the 1637 Star Chamber decree. From the Stationers' perspective most of the abuses in printing, the "exorbitances," would be remedied "were there but a modest limited power in the Stationers."[48] That the radical transformation that occurred in print culture in the 1640s would never have happened at all if the Stationers had retained their customary authority takes their argument too far. The *Remonstrance*, however, makes the very important point that the shift from internal to external regulation that occurred in the print trade during the 1630s had an impact on print culture comparable to abolishing Star Chamber and High Commission. As important as these matters of enforcement were, both the uses for print and the kinds of things printed, as well as the institution of licensing itself, also comprised the "revolution" Cressy has identified in print culture in the 1640s.

Even before the first Parliament convened in 1640, licensing (official approbation) was problematic both in its practice and its perception. The 1637 decree had made obtaining a license both expensive and complicated. Anyone seeking a license first had to pay for two "written" (manuscript) copies of the text. There would be a fee for the official licenser, a fee to the Company for its license, and a fee to the Company's clerk for entering the license in the Register. All this would be in addition to the cost of paying the author for the copy (or paying a publisher to arrange printing), and all the actual printing costs incurred for paper and labor. Besides the expense, the actual activity of procuring a license must have been difficult (and probably intimidating), especially since, outside of the ecclesiastical licensers, the persons issuing licenses were Privy Councillors who met regularly. Perception posed further problems. Whether or not obtaining a license was actually difficult, especially for a religious book, it was perceived to be so. One of the stunning features of the anti-Arminian books in the 1620s was the degree to which they thematized licensing. I would agree with Shuger that for most of the early modern period no one believed censorship (licensing) was a bad idea, but this was not the case after 1626. People who had been part of the religious consensus were now marginalized, and one measure of this was their purported inability to get their books licensed. The same thematization of censorship persisted in the Puritan press in the 1630s. By 1640 plenty of Londoners did believe that ecclesiastical licensing, if not actually a bad idea, certainly was not without a host of problems. This might all have been nothing more than a "troublesome" aspect of life in Caroline England, except that the most outspoken critics of the licensing regime were so publicly (and so brutally) punished by the State. However necessary or just Caroline censorship may have been in practice, public perception saw it differently. And in 1640 perception was everything.

These perceptions about licensing fed objections made to the Long Parliament about the state of religion. On November 23, 1640, speaking to the Committee of the Whole House for Religion, Edward Dering, who chaired the Commons committee on printing, compared recent censorship to the Roman Inquisition's *Index expurgatorius* "whereby they clip the tongues of such witnesses, whose evidence they doe not like." "Licenses for the Presse," according to Dering, were "so handled that Truth is supprest and Popish pamphlets fly abroad *cum privilegio*." The licensers ("the supercilious men of my Lords young Chaplain") have even "growne so bold in this new trade, that the most learned labours of our ancient and best Divines, must bee now corrected and defaced with a *Deleatur*."[49] On December 11, 1640, on behalf of 15,000 Londoners who had signed it, 1,500 persons presented the Commons with a petition that came to be known as "The Root and Branch Petition" because it demanded the abolition of the existing church government "with all its dependencies, roots and branches." Article 9 complained against the bishops' "hindering of godly books to be printed, the blotting out or perverting those which they suffer, all or most of that which strikes either at popery or Arminianism: the adding of what or where pleaseth them, and the restraint of reprinting books formerly licensed, without relicensing."[50] According to Cressy, Parliament also received "some twenty county petitions against episcopacy."[51] One of the few that survives in print, "The Humble Petition of many of the inhabitants within His Majesties Country of Kent," joined with the "Root and Branch Petition" in objecting to ecclesiastical licensing: "They do countenance and have of late encouraged papists, Priests, and Arminian both Bookes and persons," and "They hinder good and godly bookes to be printed: yet they do license to be published, many Popish, Armenian[sic], and other dangerous tenets."[52] This abuse of licensing was also one of the objections the Commons made against Archbishop Laud. On December 18, 1640 the Commons impeached Laud for high treason, although the articles of impeachment were not voted against him until

February 24, 1641. The ninth impeachment article declares that Laud employed as his domestic chaplains men "whom he knew to be notoriously disaffected to the reformed religion" and committed the licensing of books to them, "by which meanes divers falsse and superstitious Books have been published, to the great scandal of Religion."[53]

It was not only the disrepute into which ecclesiastical licensers and licensing had fallen that encouraged unlicensed printing and the proliferation of texts associated with it, but also a fundamental change that had escalated during the 1630s in the way in which print was employed. During this time both Church and State had regularized the use of print to legitimate their actions. Using print to defend his actions did not begin with Charles's *A large declaration concerning the Late Tumults in Scotland . . . collected out of their owne foule acts and writings.* On several occasions the King's Printers had published decisions made in Star Chamber that related to issues as diverse as rates for horsemeat, restrictions on inns and gaming houses, building specifications, and, as we know, printing. One wonderfully titled publication suggests how far-reaching a single effort to govern through print could be: *Certaine statutes especially selected, and commanded by his Maiestie to be carefully put in execution by all iustices, and other officers of the peace throughout the realme with his Maiesties proclamation for further direction for executing the same. Also certaine orders thought meete by his Maiestie and his Priuie Counsell, to bee put in execution, together with sundry good rules, preservatives, and medicines against the infection of the plague, set downe by the Colledge of the Physicians upon his Maiesties speciall command: as also a decree of the Starre-Chamber, concerning buildings and in-mates* (London, 1630). A cursory survey of titles printed in 1640, even before Star Chamber and High Commission fell, shows the rule of print was a practice that Charles continued and Parliament readily adopted. For the King, of course, printed proclamations were always a useful tool. In 1640 Charles used them, among other things, to levy payments for ship money, to declare Scots entering England traitors, and to summon sergeantry and knights to service in Scotland. But he also published a declaration *To All His Loving Subjects, Of the Causes which moved him to dissolve the last Parliament.*[54] As soon as the Long Parliament convened parliamentary business started to appear in print. This ranged from items as perfunctory as *A catalogue of the names of the knights for the counties, citizens, burgesses* or *Order and manner of sitting*, to those of more topical interest like *An order made to a select committee, chosen by the whole House of Commons to receive petitions touching ministers*, parliamentary speeches, and accounts of impeachments like *The accusation and impeachment of Iohn Lord Finch.* What changed in 1640–41 was that members of Parliament were co-opting the rule of print from the King. In 1641 daily publications (diurnals) appeared in print alongside a flood of acts, bills, orders, and articles. By 1642 more than 100 printed speeches naming members of Parliament were in circulation.[55] Not all of these, of course, were official. Sheila Lambert notes that "although it is evident that the parliamentary leaders had a thorough grasp of the importance of printed propaganda and rapidly became expert in its use, it is not so easy to put together a list of publications officially authorized by the Parliament."[56] Even so, both Parliament and Crown stimulated the growth in printing in 1640–41, both by their use of print and by the endorsement of print implicit in this use. Following the government's suit, printed petitions called for parliamentary action, while treatises cautioned and counseled. The tradition of printing while Parliament was sitting was an old one. Indeed, during the *Histrio-mastix* trial, one witness had reported that "Sparks [*sic*] said he would Print any thing in Parliament-time."[57] But never before had Parliament itself been so visible in print.

While both the prevailing disdain for licensing and an implicit endorsement of print as a legitimate political tool may have increased the number of texts printed, neither was probably as significant as the change that was taking place in the market place of print. Historians who have attributed the escalation of printed texts to the fall of Star Chamber and High Commission inevitably point not only to the titles of books that could not have been printed a few years before – the Marprelate tracts, Leighton's *Plea to Parliament*, and godly books that had been held back – but also to the escalation of texts printed with authors' and printers' names withheld. In response to this, Lambert and McKenzie remind us that if press output is measured in sheets printed, technically there was no real explosion in print. For 1644 McKenzie suggest that it is likely that, at the very least, half of the titles printed consisted of single sheets. He also observes that authorial anonymity was a convention, as was withholding the name of printer or bookseller.[58] Most of McKenzie's evidence is directed to disputing the inflated claims made for the fall of censorship, which is, I think, most useful. Besides this, his survey of 1644 titles offers, I think inadvertently, insight into the most revolutionary aspect of the shift in print culture in the 1640s – the development of what he calls "different registers" in ephemeral writing that use print "more generally as if it *were* a public speaking."[59] This is precisely the character of parliamentary speeches and King Charles's declarations. These highly topical publications addressed to the current moment were particularly suited to "short pamphlets with short lives."[60]

Besides changes in the political uses of print, the rise in ephemeral writing also can be attributed to conditions in the London print trade. As we saw in the last chapter, the Star Chamber decree's provisions for journeymen printers made little difference in their condition. In 1640 booksellers dominated the Stationers' Company in both wealth and power. Their decision of whether to withhold or to print stock titles had an enormous impact on employment. If a printer chose to supplement his work, what could be easier than printing a single-sheet pamphlet? If the nature of the pamphlet was as ephemeral as McKenzie has indicated, whether or not it was entered or licensed was irrelevant. A Company license protected a copy owner from another printer "pirating" his copy. Why should a poor printer spend the money for a license for something that was unlikely to be reprinted? Similarly, why bother to "sign" such a text? The signed imprint, although long required by Company ordinance, was, after all, most important for proving copy ownership. As for the Company's enforcement of regulations against "illegal" printing, the Company members in the position of enforcing regulations were precisely those members – the court of Assistants – whose economic interests were least affected by the printing of ephemera that did not compete with their lucrative stock titles.

McKenzie derives his conclusions on the "largely illusory" effects of the lapse on licensing by comparing book production and licensing conformity in 1644 with 1688. From this, he dismisses the notion that books being produced in the 1640s were unusually provocative. While, for the most part, this is a valuable insight, a more accurate sense of the time's tenor might be gained by looking at publications a few years prior to 1644 and comparing them with earlier book production. With the caveat that I appreciate McKenzie's objection that the Thomason catalogue is a poor guide to total production,[61] it is worth noting that for 1641, about one third of the titles give no production information. Given the ephemeral nature of the pamphlets Thomason collected, while this is understandable, this would not have been the case in 1639, when both the Company and the Crown were attentive to printing that was unlicensed, in both senses of the word. Printers' names appeared for 25 percent of the 1641 titles, and all but one of the twenty-two named printers were members of the Stationers' Company. Slightly over 40 percent identified the publisher or bookseller. Of the eighty-eight booksellers' names that appear, 72 percent published only one or two titles. Even with an increase in the number of titles printed in 1641, it does not appear that many publishers made great economic gains – certainly not enough to support making a career in the book trade. It seems much more likely that these were the publishers, along with those

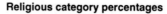

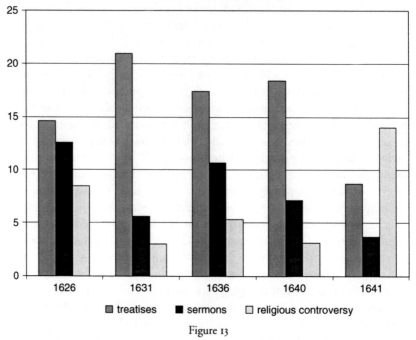

Figure 13

who did not sign their books, that would have taken their printing to the small underemployed printing operations rather than operate presses of their own. The radical pamphleteer, ironmonger-cum-printer, Henry Walker, notorious for his illegal printing, should be seen more as the exception than the rule in this new world of print.[62]

Profiles of pamphlet printers and publishers indicate that in 1641 ephemeral publications were as significant as McKenzie found them to be in 1644. Comparing textual production in 1640 and 1641 to earlier years reveals definite changes in the kinds of things that were printed. The percentage of publications that can be classified as religious, the largest category throughout the period, declined slightly from 39 percent of total titles in 1626 to 33 percent in 1641. The kinds of religious texts published, however, changed significantly. Between 1630 and 1640, religious controversy fell to less than 5 percent of total textual production, from nearly 10 percent in 1626. In 1641 nearly 15 percent of total print production was religious controversy. In 1641 the printing of sermons and religious treatises declined significantly. This kind of writing, most of which had been

Print category percentages

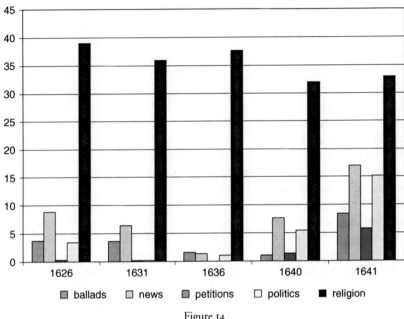

ballads ☐ news ☐ petitions ☐ politics ■ religion

Figure 14

written and licensed before 1625, had been the mainstay of religious publication during the 1630s.

Another area in which significant change occurred was in various forms of political writing. Included here are ballads and broadsheets, something notoriously problematic because of their highly ephemeral quality. The lowest point for broadsheet/ballad production is 1636. The rise in 1641 might be solely attributable to Thomason's collecting, except that in 1626 and 1631 ballad production was fairly constant. The decline in news books in 1636 corresponds to the stay on news books. In 1640 news books return to the levels of 1626 and 1631, around 7 percent. This nearly doubles in 1641 – clearly a sign of the times. Writing on other political topics, nearly non-existent in the 1630s, triples between 1640 and 1641 from 5 to 15 percent.

With the increased interest in news and politics, other reading areas were put aside. That the percentage of literary works published declines from 16 percent in 1636 to 3 percent in 1641 speaks to the anxieties about the times that Cressy has accounted for so well in *England on Edge*. Politics, news, and religion captured the reading public's full attention as England moved towards civil war.

By locating the transformation in print culture in the rise in ephemeral publication, in the government's appeal to print, and in the changing tastes of English readers in the 1640s rather than in the fall of the High Commission and Star Chamber, I do not mean to suggest that England rushed to enthusiastically embrace the principle of a free press. Michael Mendle describes London print culture between 1640 and 1643 as a world of "de facto freedom" and "de facto authority," a characterization that is far more appropriate than Siebert's version of Parliament having to settle down before it could get down to the work of controlling the press. Even so, by subscribing to the view that the Stationers' Company was in partnership with the King and the Church to control the press,[63] Mendle misses an important point. Even though propagandists on one side and show trials on the other had thematized Laudian censorship in the cultural imagination, with only a few recent exceptions, the expression "de facto freedom" applies fairly well to London print culture from 1558 onwards. I suspect that censorship, or the lack thereof, was one of the less important causes of the structural transformation that took place in print culture in the 1640s, one where the printed word became a public venue for restructuring the old regime. The problem was not that the partnership between Parliament, the Church, and the Stationers to control the press broke down, but rather that the nature of authority itself was being radically restructured. Between 1640 and 1649 different parties for different reasons demanded that the press be better regulated, mostly because they feared that the world they saw in print genuinely represented the world in which they lived. McKenzie says that during the 1640s "the interchange of highly topical texts . . . helped to break down the anxiety-provoking distinctions between speech, manuscript and print."[64] While this may be true from the long-range perspective of the major transformation in print culture that occurred in the late seventeenth and eighteenth centuries, for the time being this breaking down of distinctions produced an anxiety of its own about the ephemera that were now being produced. Parliamentary licensing has often been seen as too little too late, a fruitless effort to put the genie back in the bottle.[65] I would suggest, instead, that parliamentary censorship responded to particular local and immediate problems that emerged during a time of considerable cultural unrest.

PARLIAMENTARY LICENSING

On June 14, 1643 the Lords and Commons in Parliament ordered that no parliamentary order or declaration of either House be printed without the express order of both Houses; that no other book, pamphlet, or paper be printed without approval by authority and entered in the Stationers' Register; that anything printed carry the printer's name; that no one print Stationers' Company stock without permission from the Company's officials or print titles belonging to Company members without their express permission. The order also recognizes the Stationers' Company's customary rights of search and seizure for unlicensed printing presses, but likewise confers this right on the Gentleman Usher of the House of Peers and the Sergeant of the Commons. Anyone who resists the searches could be brought before either of the houses or the Committee of Examinations. Mendle says "the new licensing arrangements were as tight as anything the Laudians had devised,"[66] which, as the last chapter showed, was clearly not the case. While the parliamentary order expresses concern for writing that is "false forged, scandalous, seditious," and "to the great defamation of Religion and government,"[67] the characterization of objectionable writing is neither so clearly articulated nor so frequently repeated as in the 1637 degree. By 1643 books had been published that had provoked objections to Parliament, but Parliament had objections of its own. As the 1643 order's provisions suggest, the regulation's central purpose was protecting the Stationers' Company's monopoly, something the Company actively sought. This does not represent a return to a Laudian status quo; indeed, since by 1643 Star Chamber no longer existed, it does not represent a return to the status quo prior to the 1586 Star Chamber decrees. Furthermore, since by 1642 royal authority was an institution under siege, the 1643 orders cannot technically be said to be "returning" to the precedents set by the Elizabethan Injunctions. The 1643 orders essentially rearticulate the terms of the Stationers' Company's charter within the current political circumstances. (They are not even as precise as the charter about rooting out writing contrary to "Mother church.") Outside of the provisions for upholding the Stationers' customary rights as a guild, the principle interests of the orders are preventing printed defamation of the Church and State, as well as parliamentary speeches and orders without Parliament's official approval.

Lambert finds disarray in the Long Parliament's publication of its proceedings in the first few years. Beginning with the Speaker of the House's speech at the opening session, parliamentary speeches were frequently printed – "with or without the consent of the author." Publishing parliamentary proceedings, according to Lambert, violated a long-established convention, and, should members of Parliament have wished to do so, they could have proceeded against their own members for breaching parliamentary privilege. That they refrained from doing so Lambert interprets as either ambivalence or hypocrisy.[68] A. D. T. Cromartie, however, viewing parliamentary privilege differently, sees neither:

> the printing of speeches, even if it was sometimes unexpected, was an accepted extension of manuscript circulation ... Large-scale transmission of news between London and the provinces, including manuscript accounts of speeches, was a well-established phenomenon even of the 1620s. The session was expected to be a long one, and its proceedings were of unparalleled importance and interest. Parliamentary privilege existed to prevent tale-bearers reporting to the court, not M.P.s reporting to their constituents, and the court's power, in late 1640, can rarely have seemed less dangerous. Readiness to publish, and to condone publishing, is perhaps an index of the extent to which members felt secure from pressure, both from above and below.[69]

Even so, Cromartie maintains that based on limits "within the minds of members themselves," MPs did effectively constrain publications of some of their speeches, especially when consensus dissolved during the second session of the Long Parliament.[70] For the speeches that were published, Parliament's greatest concern was over the accuracy of the printed copy. On one of the earliest occasions when the question of printing speeches arose, the objection was made that Solicitor General St. John's speech on ship money was full of errors, and for this, the printer should be punished. In the interest of "the public good," Simond D'Ewes conceded that a new and true version should be desired, but he personally preferred to follow the old parliamentary course to preserve the "*arcana sacra.*"[71]

While MPs' self-censorship may have imposed some limits on what speeches actually given in Parliament should appear in print, fabrications were another matter. The hunger for parliamentary news created an "early Stuart Grub Street," where, according to Cromartie,

> Hack work at half-a-crown led writers to take the line of least resistance. Hatred of prelates, fear of papists, horror of the Irish, were the most important political emotions they recorded. They avoided rational development of any case that outran the movement of popular feeling ... Fabrications were brought out to make money, not to create a stir, but their very production favored the opposition cause.[72]

Cromartie believes that since opposition leaders "gained from any publication that helped sustain popular hysteria, and that directed popular interest in parliamentary events," the House of Commons "lacked both the ability and the will to control the printers."[73] Lambert views this differently.

While Lambert certainly does not envision a system of rigorous parliamentary censorship, she does find an expression of concern for assuring the truth and accuracy of what Cromartie refers to as "authentic" printed parliamentary speeches. "The Beginning of Printing for the House of Commons, 1640–42" details the many occasions of infraction and the efforts made to secure the cooperation of the Stationers' Company in preventing unofficial reports from Parliament. One of the most important responses, she says, was to create a select committee to examine: "all abuses in printing, licensing, importing and suppressing of books of all sorts; and in denying licence to some books, and expunging several passages out of others."[74] This committee had begun as the subcommittee appointed to investigate the abuses in Laudian licensing, but once it was formed, it heard all objections made to the Commons about offensive texts, as well as objections that arose within the House concerning misprinting parliamentary matters. As Lambert observes, matters were frequently referred to the committee for which there is no further record of action. The printing committee, Lambert emphasizes, was not, however, created to draft a licensing act.

It was to the Lords and not the Commons that the Stationers appealed to impose sanctions against illegal presses and piracy. According to Lambert, the occasion on which they briefly imprisoned two non-Company publishers as an example was "prudently chosen" by the Stationers as an occasion where the Lords' privileges were breached.[75] In this incident, I think, we can understand the real impact of abolishing the High Commission. After 1586, as we have seen, as a court of law, the High Commission heard cases where non-Stationers operated presses and printed titles owned by the Company or its members. The 1637 Star Chamber decree had briefly extended this jurisdiction to include the court of Star Chamber and, as we have seen, added to this oversight of authorization, license, and entrance. The abolition of these courts is frequently seen in terms of taking away bodies that imposed regulation from above. The real loss for the Stationers' Company was of a court of law where it could bring suits against non-Stationers, and after the 1637 decree, against its own members who violated the closest thing they had to copyright. This is why, as their 1643 *Remonstrance* made clear, the question of confirming the Company's authority was so important. The 1643 order, while it still confirmed this authority, did not resolve the problems in the printing trade.

In his study of the Stationers' Company during the Civil War years, Cyprian Blagden exposes the fault lines in a Company that was seriously incapable of exercising the kind of authority that it sought to enforce its own monopoly and protect its members' copies.[76] Not all the problem, however, was internal. The 1643 order did not expressly create a legal venue replacing the courts of Star Chamber and High Commission where the Stationers could seek legal redress against violations by non-Stationers. By default, then, Parliament assumed this jurisdiction, but rather than hear cases about illegal presses and patent violations, the Committee of the House of Commons for Examinations had to intervene to help the Company resolve its internal disputes about the Company's government, its properties, and printing both its old stock and its new monopoly for the Bible.[77] When the Company appealed to Parliament, such issues as the hardships imposed on the Company by foreign Bibles, finding the capital to print an English one, and inequities in the Company's governance took precedence over challenging the small fry who were printing and hawking single-sheet pamphlets, even if some were scandalous to the Church and State.

It is not surprising, then, that the 1643 order was not the last word in parliamentary press control. The Journals of both Houses report at least fifty-five occasions between 1643 and 1649 when either offensive books were referred to the Committee on Printing (or later to the Committee on Examinations), or actions were taken against authors or printers.[78] Once King Charles left London for Oxford, the Commons issued an order prohibiting the sale and circulation of books bearing an Oxford imprint. While the 1643 order had instituted parliamentary licensing, and a separate one immediately afterwards appointed official licensers,[79] the occasions of parliamentary censorship mentioned in the Journals do not indicate an effort to enforce licensing. In 1647, in response to publications labeled "Seditious, False, Scandalous" and to the "insufferable reproach of the proceedings of Parliament and the Army," Parliament declared that anyone who was any way involved with these would be fined or committed to jail for up to forty days. Hawkers and pedlars were to be "whipt as a Common Rogue." It gave to the committees for the militia, mayors, and justices of the peace the rights of search and seizure. Those who wrote anything "seditious, treasonable, or blasphemous" were not included; "offenses of the kinde shall be liable to such further penalties as by the Laws of the Land are provided, or by the Authority of Parliament adjudged."[80] In 1649, after the execution of Charles I, Parliament redefined treason as "maliciously or advisedly by Writing, Printing, or Publicly declaring That the Government is Tyrannical, Usurped, or Unlawful: or that the Commons in Parliament assembled are not the Supreme authority of this Nation; or shall Plot, contrive or Endeavor to stir up or raise force against the present Government."[81] Shortly thereafter, it issued a new licensing act that essentially restated the provisions laid out in the 1647 orders.

The 1647 orders, far more than those that had been issued in 1643, reflect an extraordinary transformation in the conceptualization of press control. First, they make no mention whatsoever of the Stationers' Company's license, nor do they look for the Company's aid in seeking out scandalous writing – which the Company rarely actually did. Press control now resided entirely in the government, and public officers were appointed to search for and seize unlicensed and objectionable books. They held authors, and not just printers and publishers, accountable. They placed the prosecution of the authors of "seditious, treasonable, or blasphemous" books within the jurisdiction of the "laws of the land" and Parliament. In his study of censorship in the late 1640s and early 1650s, Jason McElligott observes that "Cromwellian censorship was effective precisely because it chose to pursue and punish only those books and pamphlets which it deemed most dangerous."[82] A complex system of licensing worked because it did not pursue the prosecution of every unlicensed item: "Licensing was not conceived as a Berlin Wall blocking all potentially offensive material, but as a 'Keep off the Grass' sign which would deter most transgressors and allow for the selective punishment of those whom the authorities decided to prosecute."[83] The reason Cromwellian censorship could operate in this way was because, following the 1647 precedent, the law of the land punished sedition, treason, and blasphemy, and licensing infractions were a separate matter.

The kind of press censorship McElligott describes in Cromwell's England, one that is interested in suppressing genuinely dangerous books and one in which licensing sends the message to "keep off the grass," resembles the way press censorship had actually operated in Elizabethan and Jacobean England. In Elizabethan and Jacobean England, however, the mechanisms that controlled the press were as diverse as the motives. Stubbs's 1576 pamphlet against the French marriage was prosecuted in the court of King's Bench under statutory definitions of seditious libel against the monarch. The Privy Council ordered the review and reformation of Holinshed's *Chronicles* for matters about current times that put the state in a bad light. James I publicly burned books with which he disagreed, but took no further action to prevent their circulation. The master and wardens of the Stationers' Company exercised discretion in obtaining ecclesiastical licenses. Ecclesiastical licensers, although they prevented books supporting papal doctrine, permitted the printing of works by continental Protestant theologians. They also allowed controversial works disputing Roman Catholic doctrine that reprinted the texts that were being disputed. The difference between those times and Cromwell's was that by the end of the

1640s – indeed by the end of the 1630s – censorship had become a topic that could be advocated, disputed, and resisted. Along with so many other things in the 1640s it had become part of the public sphere. Throughout the 1620s and 1630s objections first against Arminianism and later against ceremonies impressed on the public imagination the idea that censorship, although not necessarily an evil in itself, could be unjustly and abusively employed. The Star Chamber show trials were seen by many as a confirmation. The publication of the Star Chamber decree, printed for all to see, proposed a system of licensing and the machinery to enforce it that said a great deal more than "keep off the grass." These contributed to the perception of a "culture of censorship" in Caroline England, even at a time when a wider range of books was in the market place.

AREOPAGITICA AND THE LEGACY OF CAROLINE CENSORSHIP

Understanding this "culture of censorship" helps to explain why historians have had such difficulty in assessing the Caroline regime, especially in its relationship with print culture. The "culture of censorship" has been interpreted by some as identical with the practice of censorship: either the myth becomes the reality or the part is taken to represent the whole. This has proven to be a useful error – particularly in cases when the story of Caroline press censorship has been put to the service of arguments for free speech or a free press. The same may be said of John Milton's *Areopagitica*, one of the few surviving products of the English Revolution's "most revolutionary features," the explosion of print in the Long Parliament's opening years. The canonization of Milton's essay has immortalized *Areopagitica*'s arguments against censorship and put them in service of the principles of liberal democracy, even if, as Loewenstein has demonstrated, Milton did not intend an impassioned plea for a free press.[84] Milton's essay actually belongs to the very local contexts that this chapter – indeed this book – has considered. Milton's essay, which is indebted to the campaigns against Arminianism and Laudianism in the 1630s and 1640s, shows the powerful effect these campaigns had in impressing censorship on the cultural imagination, an impression kept alive for generations by Milton's essay. This warrants a closer look at the ways in which *Areopagitica* participates in its particular cultural moment.

First of all, Milton, like Featly, Burton, and Prynne (and the Elizabethan reformers before them), affirms the desirability, indeed the necessity of debate: "For this is not the liberty which we can hope, that no grievance ever should arise in the Commonwealth – that let no man in this work expect but when complaints are freely heard, deeply considered and speedily reformed, then is the utmost bound of civil liberty attained that wise men look for."[85] Although Milton may not be arguing for freedom of the press, he is making a powerful appeal for an intellectual practice deeply rooted and only recently denied in England.

When Milton refers to ecclesiastical licensing, he appears in particular to be identifying it as a tool of popery in much the same way that Burton and Prynne did: "this project of licensing crept out of the Inquisition, was catched up by our prelates, and hath caught some of our presbyters."[86] Milton insists that he is not interested in the licensing practices of the Stationers' Company, "But that other cause of licensing books, which we thought had died with his brother *quadragesimal* and *matrimonial* when the prelates expired, I shall now attend with such a homily, as shall lay before ye, first, the inventors of it to be those whom ye will be loath to own ..."[87] It is not all ecclesiastical licensing against which Milton makes his case but that of "our late prelates and their chaplains," whose "five Imprimaturs are seen together dialogue-wise in the piazza of one title-page, complimenting and ducking each to other with their shaven reverences."[88] (Title-page imprimaturs were a Laudian creation.) Milton argues that the new parliamentary licensing similarly derives from the desire to control religious "orthodoxy," and in doing so, merely replaces one kind of authority with another: "it cannot be guessed what is intended by some but a second tyranny over learning: and will soon put it out of controversy, that bishops and presbyters are the same to us, both name and thing."[89] The first tyranny over learning came in the 1620s when, Burton contended, "the case" was "altered." The renewal of the prelatical tyranny, from Milton's perspective, was not what the recent reformation in the Church had intended:

This is not, ye Covenants and Protestations that we have made! This is not to put down prelacy; this is but to chop an episcopacy; this is but to translate the Palace Metropolitan from one kind of dominion into another; this is but an old canonical sleight of commuting and penance ... While things are yet not constituted in religion, that freedom of writing should be restrained by a discipline imitated from the prelates and learnt by them from the Inquisition, to shut us up all again into the breast of a licenser, must needs give cause of doubt and discouragement to all learned and religious men.[90]

Instead, the promise of England is to fulfill the Reformation, not by looking to past Reformers, but by pursuing religious truth, indeed possibly a new truth anchored in the gospel, that a new regime of licensing will curtail:

It is not the unfrocking of a priest, the unmitring of a bishop, and the removing him from off the Presbyterian shoulders, that will make us a happy nation. No, if other things as great in the Church, and in the rule of life both economical and political, be not looked into and reformed, we have looked so long upon the blaze of Zuinglius and Calvin hath beaconed up to us, that we are stark blind. There be who perpetually complain of schisms and sects, and make it such a calamity that any man dissents from their maxims ... Why else was this nation chosen before any other, that out of her, as out of Sion, would be proclaimed and sounded forth the first tidings and trumpet of Reformation to all Europe? ... She needs no policies, nor stratagems, nor licensings to make her victorious; those are the shifts and the defences that error uses against her power.[91]

Milton's vision of England as a new Sion participates in precisely the vision of the Church of England that dominated English Calvinism during the reign of James I and which was kept alive by London printers in the 1630s. In this imaginary of a great Protestant nation whose Church fulfills the Reformation's highest ideals being placed at risk by "prelatical licensing" Milton reenacts precisely those anxieties about "the strange alteration of these times within this 7 yeares" Burton expressed in 1628.[92] Whether or not he intended it, Milton's *Areopagitica*, like the stories told about censorship and a repressive Caroline regime, have inspired principled arguments for free speech, a free press, and the separation of Church and State. Perhaps some measure of the recognition bestowed on Milton for this should also go to the likes of Daniel Featly, Francis Rous, Henry Burton, and William Prynne.

Notes

I CENSORSHIP AND THE LAW: THE CAROLINE INHERITANCE

1. Annabel Patterson, *Censorship and Interpretation: The Conditions of Writing and Reading in Early Modern England* (Madison, 1984), p. 10.
2. Jody Greene, *The Trouble with Ownership: Literary Property and Authorial Liability in England, 1660–1730* (Philadelphia, 2005), p. 220, n. 6.
3. Frederick Seaton Siebert, *Freedom of the Press in England 1476–1776: The Rise and Decline of Government Controls* (Urbana, 1952), p. 126.
4. *Ibid.*, pp. 123–24.
5. Kevin Sharpe, *The Personal Rule of Charles I* (New Haven, 1992), p. 758.
6. Patterson, *Censorship and Interpretation*, p. 45.
7. *Ibid.*
8. *Ibid.*, p. 11.
9. *Ibid.*, p. 46.
10. *Ibid.*, p. 107.
11. Sharpe, *Personal Rule*, pp. 758–65.
12. *Ibid.*, p. 758.
13. *Ibid.*, p. 579.
14. *Ibid.*, p. 758.
15. *Ibid.*
16. Debora Shuger, *Censorship and Cultural Sensibility: The Regulation of Language in Tudor–Stuart England* (Philadelphia, 2006), pp. 223, 225.
17. *Ibid.*, pp. 223–24. Shuger here repeats the error in the trial date that appears in the account in T. B. Howell, *A complete collection of state trials and proceedings for high treason and other crimes and misdemeanors from the earliest period to the present time, with notes and other illustrations* (London, 1811–1826). The trial actually took place in February 1633/34.
18. Shuger, *Censorship and Cultural Sensibility*, p. 229. "Devil's Chapels" refers to playhouses.
19. *Ibid.*, p. 25.
20. *Ibid.*, p. 42.
21. David Cressy, *Travesties and Transgression in Tudor and Stuart England: Tales of Discord and Dissension* (Oxford, 2000), p. 214.
22. *Ibid.*, pp. 213–14.

23. *Ibid.*, p. 218.
24. *Ibid.*, p. 216.
25. *Ibid.*
26. *Ibid.*, p. 219.
27. *Ibid.*
28. *Ibid.*, p. 221.
29. *Ibid.*, p. 214.
30. I am following Peter Blayney in employing "authorization" to refer to the official vetting of text prior to print, and "license" to refer to the proprietary right in a title conferred by the Stationers' Company on its members. In some places where because of source material I have to refer to official pre-print scrutiny as "licensing," I employ "official licensing" or "ecclesiastical licensing." For full rationale and discussion of practices, see pp. 31–40.
31. Charles M. Gray, "Parliament, Liberty, and the Law," *Parliament and Liberty from the Reign of Elizabeth to the English Civil War*, J. H. Hexter, ed. (Stanford, 1992), pp. 155–200: p. 185.
32. Richard Atkyns, *The Original and Growth of Printing: Collected out of the History and Records of this Kingdome. Wherein is also demonstrated that Printing appertaineth to the Royal Prerogative* (1664), B1v.
33. *Ibid.*, C3r–v.
34. Adrian Johns, *The Nature of the Book* (Chicago, 1998), p. 338; Siebert, *Freedom of the Press*, p. 21.
35. G. R. Elton, *The Tudor Constitution: Documents and Commentary* (Cambridge, 1960), p. 17.
36. *Ibid.*
37. *Ibid.*
38. *Ibid.*, p. 20.
39. Alternatively, the imprint might also be *cum privilegio regali*. Henry VIII's 1538 proclamation that demanded that all printed books receive pre-print approval (license), also specified that having obtained a license to print, printers could not use the words *cum privilegio regali* without adding *ad imprimendum solum*. The inclusion of book licensing and the imprint language for privilege vexed the new bibliographers, who regarded the imprint as indication of license rather than privilege, an interpretation to which Joseph Loewenstein subscribes (*The Author's Due* [Chicago, 2002], pp. 79–81). In an English Short Title Catalogue (ESTC) survey of title-page imprints after 1638, I only rarely find the words *cum privilegio* on books that are *not* printed under a royal patent. Existing bibliographical evidence challenges Loewenstein's assertion that "by the second half of the [sixteenth] century it [*cum privilegio*] functions as a general warrant of propriety, signifying approval by the licensing authorities, allowance by the Stationers' Company, and, occasionally, the protection of the king's privilege" (p. 112).
40. For a discussion of Jacobean patents, see Cyndia Susan Clegg, *Press Censorship in Jacobean England* (Cambridge, 2001), pp. 41–60 (hereafter cited as *Jacobean England*).

41. Some insight can be gained into the importance of a trade being formally recognized as a guild or company, if we remember that for anyone not of the nobility or a nobleman's household to be a citizen of London, city ordinances required that he be either free of a London company or an apprentice.

42. Cyprian Blagden gives a fuller description of the Company and its composition in *The Stationers' Company: A History 1403–1959* (London, 1960), chapter 2. For an interpretive account, see also Johns, *Nature of the Book*, chapter 3. Johns reliably accounts for the court of Assistants' practices, but curiously models his description of the Company on Continental guilds and largely neglects the sixteenth century. The strength of Johns's work lies in his knowledge of printing history after the Civil War.

43. The custom of the city allowed men free of one company to engage in the trade of another.

44. I discuss the formation and governance more fully in *Press Censorship in Elizabethan England* (Cambridge, 1997), pp. 14–25 (hereafter cited as *Elizabethan England*).

45. Further, Mary's charter to the Company included in its allowance of searches to enforce the Company's regulations the right "to seize, take, hold, burn ... all and several those books and things which are or shall be printed contrary to the form of any statute, act, or proclamation." In Edward Arber, *A Transcript of the Registers of the Company of Stationers of London*, 5 vols. (London and Birmingham, 1875–94), vol. I, pp. xxviii–xxxii.

46. *Ibid.*, vol. I, p. xxx.

47. The statutory grounds for press censorship were primarily concerned with treasonous writing, that is, writing or printing texts denying the monarch's ecclesiastical and temporal authority, advocating the rights of anyone else to that authority, advocating rebellion, calling the monarch a heretic or usurper, "compassing" bodily harm, slandering, or defaming the monarch; attacks on the Crown's authority came within the compass of high treason. Actual trials for treasonous writing were few in Tudor England; possessing books which did any of these things, however, often became part of the evidence rather than the cause itself in treason trials. Trials for high treason were held before special commissions of *oyer* and *terminer* called for the express occasion. Lesser treason cases were tried at the assizes. The text of the statutes depends on *Statutes of the Realm* (London, 1812), and will be cited hereafter, throughout the book, by regnal year and chapter rather than by volume and page number.

48. Elton, *Tudor Constitution*, p. 22.

49. *Ibid.*

50. Paul L. Hughes and James F. Larkin, *Tudor Royal Proclamations*, 3 vols. (New Haven and London, 1964), vol. I, p. xxvi.

51. *Ibid.*, vol. I, pp. 181–86.

52. *Ibid.*, vol. I, p. 194.

53. *Ibid.*, vol. I, p. 375.

54. *Ibid.*, vol. I, p. 517.

55. *Ibid.*, vol. II, p. 90.

56. *Ibid.*, vol. II, p. 6.
57. *Ibid.*, vol. II, pp. 57–60.
58. *Ibid.*, vol. II, p. 312.
59. *Ibid.*, vol. II, pp. 347–48.
60. *Ibid.*, vol. II, pp. 501–02.
61. *Ibid.*, vol. III, p. 34.
62. For full accounts of the books that incited these proclamations and the conditions of their writing, publication, and censorship, see Clegg, *Elizabethan England*, chapters 3, 4, and 8.
63. Debora Shuger sees seditious libel – or slander – as the principal focus of Elizabethan censorship, a matter I will discuss more fully below. See Shuger, *Censorship and Cultural Sensibility*, pp. 14–27.
64. Elton, *Tudor Constitution*, p. 17.
65. James F. Larkin and Paul L. Hughes, *Stuart Royal Proclamations*, 2 vols. (Oxford: 1973) vol. I, p. 243 (hereafter cited as *Stuart Proclamations*). For a full account of the circumstances, see Clegg, *Jacobean England*, pp. 137–43.
66. *Stuart Proclamations*, vol. I, p. 497.
67. *Ibid.*, vol. I, p. 583. The 1586 decrees, which will be considered below, specified that no one should print or allow his press to be used for printing any kind of text "Except the same book, work, coppye, matter, or any thinge, hath been heretofore allowed, or heareafter shall be allowed … according to the order appointed by the Queenes maiesties Iniunctyons" (Arber, vol. II, p. 810). James did not discriminate between the Company's license and official authorization.
68. W. W. Greg, *Companion to Arber* (Oxford, 1967), pp. 226–29.
69. SP 14/165, art. 53, Public Record Office, National Archives, Kew Gardens, London. Hereafter cited throughout the book as PRO.
70. Thomas Smith, *De Republica Anglorum*, quoted in Elton, *Tudor Constitution*, p. 19.
71. Elton, *Tudor Constitution*, p. 18.
72. Shuger, *Censorship and Cultural Sensibility* p. 275.
73. *Ibid.*, p. 77.
74. *Ibid.*, p. 69.
75. *Ibid.*, p. 272.
76. Indeed, some of the oppositional writing, like William Allen's *A true sincere and modest defence of English Catholiques that suffer for their faith both at home and abrode* (1584) (and, indeed, most of his books), although condemned, criticizes English religious policy in an entirely moderate fashion.
77. For the scope of such actions, see Clegg, *Jacobean England*, chapter 2, "Burning Books as Propaganda."
78. Rev. Joseph Mead to Sir Martin Stuteville in Thomas Birch, *The Court and Times of James I*, 2 vols. (London, 1848), vol. II, 266.
79. Mark Kishlansky, "Tyranny Denied: Charles I, Attorney General Heath, and the Five Knights' Case," *The Historical Journal*, 42.1 (1999), 53–83: p. 79.
80. John Baker, *The Oxford History of the Laws of England*, vol. VI (Oxford: Oxford University Press, 2002), p. 201.

81. *Ibid.*, p. 202.
82. Cyndia Susan Clegg, ed., *The Peaceable and Prosperous Regiment of Blessed Queene Elisabeth: A Facsimile from Holinshed's Chronicles (1587)* (San Marino, 2005). Debora Shuger uses the Holinshed censorship to argue for a necessary theorization of censorship because for acts of censorship "history usually leaves few traces and so can only be *conjecturally* reconstructed." If this censorship were politically motivated, why, she asks, would the censors have left "untouched the hard-to-miss opening sentence of the chapter on Parliament with its (one would think) incendiary assertion that Parliament held 'the most high and absolute power of the realm ... ' "? (Shuger, *Censorship and Cultural Sensibility*, p. 2). Textual evidence is but one of the many kinds of available evidence that allow the history of censorship to be far more than conjecture.
83. *Acts of the Privy Council*, ed. John Roche Dasent, 32 vols. (London, 1890–1907), vol. XXX, p. 328.
84. *Ibid.* Thomas Egerton, Lords Nottingham and Buckhurst, Robert Cecil, and Attorney General John Popham were the only councilors present.
85. *Ibid.*, vol. XXX, p. 499.
86. See, for example, Richard Dutton, " 'Buggeswords': Samuel Harsnett and the Licensing, Suppression and Afterlife of Dr. John Hayward's *The first part of the life and reign of Henry IV*," *Criticism*, 35 (1993), 305–40, p. 316. Dutton says Hayward was tried in Star Chamber for writing *Henrie IIII*, but this appearance before members of the Privy Council bears no resemblance to trials in Star Chamber. Hayward certainly was not tried and sentenced for treason since Star Chamber did not conduct treason trials, nor does it appear that he was tried and sentenced for libel (a Star Chamber matter). No indictment was entered by Attorney General Coke as was customary for State-initiated actions in Star Chamber.
87. Elton, *Tudor Constitution*, p. 228.
88. Brackets appear in the original text.
89. Charles Henry Parry, *Parliaments and Councils of England* (London, 1839), p. 247.
90. *Ibid.* The book in question was *A discourse plainely prouing the euident vtilitie and vrgent necessitie of the desired happie vnion of the two famous kingdomes of England and Scotland* (1604).
91. *Ibid.*
92. *Calendar of the Patent Rolls, Elizabeth I* (London, 1939), vol. I, p. 118.
93. Alternatively, permission to print might be sought from the Queen (in writing), by six Privy Councilors, or the chancellors of the universities.
94. See Clegg, *Elizabethan England*, p. 44–46.
95. Philip Tyler, "Introduction," Roland Usher, *The Rise and Fall of the High Commission* (London, 1913 [reprinted 1968]), pp. xxviii–xxix.
96. John Guy, *Tudor England* (Oxford and New York, 1988), pp. 292–93.
97. Philip Tyler maintains that the High Commission derived its procedures from older-established ecclesiastical courts: evidence was written; the ex

officio oath obliged the accused to answer a libel of articles that he had not previously seen; the service of neither advocate nor proctor was necessarily granted; and judgment was summary (Tyler, "Introduction," *The Rise and Fall of the High Commission*), pp. xxviii–xxix.

98. Brian P. Levack, *The Civil Lawyers in England 1603–1641* (Oxford, 1973), p. 84.

99. *Ibid.*, p. 73. Common law judges issued prohibitions, orders from the judges of the civil law or prerogative courts not to hear a case, when they perceived a violation of common law jurisdiction. Judges from both sides would then confer and determine the jurisdiction.

100. The struggle over the High Commission between the common law lawyers and the King/Church alliance was but one act in the dramatic confrontation between rival authorities that played out during James's reign. For a more detailed assessment of the rivalries that emerged between the common law lawyers, Parliament, and the alliance of Church and Crown, see *Jacobean England*, chapter 4.

101. Kenneth Fincham, *Prelate as Pastor: the Episcopate of James I* (Oxford, 1990), p. 50.

102. J. P. Kenyon, *The Stuart Constitution, 1603–1688* (Cambridge, 1966), pp. 181–85.

> we ... do by these letters patent under our Great Seal of England give and grant full, free and lawful power and authority unto you ... to inquire as well by examination of witnesses or presentment as also by examination of the parties accused themselves upon their oath ... of all and singular apostacies, heresies, great errors in matters of faith and religion ... and also of all blasphemous and impious acts and speeches, scandalous books, libels and writings against the doctrine of religion, the Book of Common Prayer, or ecclesiastical state or government now established in the Church of England ... And also we ... do give ... authority unto you ... to inquire and search for ... all heretical, schismatical and seditious books, libels and writings, and all makers, devisers, printers and wilful dispersers of any such ... books ... and their procurers, counsellors and abettors, and the same books ... and the printing presses themselves likewise to seize, and so to take, apprehend and imprison ... the offenders in that behalf. (*Ibid.*, pp. 182–83)

103. Clegg, *Jacobean England*, pp. 50–57.

104. *Ibid.*, pp. 190–96.

105. SP 14/159, art. 41, PRO. While the High Commission may have been prepared to be lenient with the printer and give him his liberty, King James intervened. Having learned the printer had gained £1,000 by selling the pamphlet, the King demanded the man be returned to prison and pay a £1,000 fine. Apparently James also sent an emissary to France to have these pamphlets' author, the merchant John Reynolds, discovered and returned to England. Upon his return, Reynolds "for his wellcome was clapt into close prison" (SP 14/159, art. 41, PRO).

106. SP 14/130, art. 132; SP 14/157, arts. 40–41, PRO.

107. Arber, *Transcript*, vol. III, p. 230.

108. Stanley Rypins estimates that the several 1603 editions of the book comprised 10,000 copies. ("The Printing of Basilikòn Dôron, 1603," *The Papers of the Bibliographical Society of America*, 64 [1970], 393–417: p. 400.)

109. William A. Jackson, *Records of the Court of the Stationers Company* (London, 1957), pp. 3, 5.

110. Ellesmere 2652 and Ellesmere 2768, Huntington Library. According to John Guy, these summaries were prepared by the clerical staff of the court of Star Chamber for the consideration of the chancellor and "were collected as much as anything in the quest for precedents affirming Star Chamber's jurisdiction, which Egerton was anxious to defend" (John Guy, *The Court of Star Chamber and Its Records to the Reign of Elizabeth I* [London, 1985], p. 8, n. 669).

111. Siebert, *Freedom of the Press*, p. 29.

112. Johns, *Nature of the Book*, p. 251.

113. Baker, *Oxford Laws of England*, p. 195.

114. *Ibid.*, pp. 196–97.

115. Hargreave 26, British Library.

116. Thomas G. Barnes, "Star Chamber Litigants and their Counsel, 1596–1641," *Legal Records and the Historian*, J. H. Baker, ed. (London, 1978), pp. 7–28, p. 13.

117. Additional MS 48057, British Library.

118. Thomas G. Barnes, "Star Chamber Mythology," *The American Journal of Legal History*, 5 (1961), p. 4.

119. *Ibid.* p. 5.

120. *Ibid.*, pp. 9–10.

121. *Ibid.*, p. 6.

122. *Ibid.*, p. 7. Debora Shuger mistakes this kind of punishment as hinging on contrition rather than guilt and in doing so argues that Star Chamber participates in a kind of "penitential" judicial process that secures "absolution" for the offender (*Censorship and Cultural Sensibility*, p. 112–13.)

123. Stowe 418, f. 103, British Library.

124. Arber, *Transcript*, vol. II, p. 753.

125. *Acts of the Privy Council*, vol. VII, pp. 188–89, 277–78.

126. Arber, *Transcript*, vol. II, p. 753.

127. None of these cases concerns itself with government suppression of religiously or politically unacceptable printed materials – that is, with materials traditionally considered likely candidates for censorship. Since the court of Star Chamber was the regular venue for printing disputes, it was not at all unusual that it should have heard a number of printing cases between 1577 and 1586 that arose from a challenge posed not only to the Stationers' Company's powers but to the printing privileges extended by the Queen.

128. Wolfe, a member of the Fishmongers' Company, served as an apprentice to a Stationers' Company member, John Day, between 1562 and 1572, though he did not complete his apprenticeship. For full account of this assault, see Harry R. Hoppe, "John Wolfe, Printer and Publisher, 1579–1601," *The Library*,

4th ser., 14 (1933), 241–74. For further information about Wolfe's position in the London book trade, see Clifford Chalmers Huffman, *Elizabethan Impressions: John Wolfe and his Press* (New York, 1988).

129. Later on, Wolfe made further demands of Barker, insisting upon work, a loan, and an allowance of apprentices beyond the Stationers' Company's usual allotment of one to three, and while Barker agreed to help Wolfe, they still didn't reach an agreement.

130. Arber prints the copy of the Star Chamber decree contained in SP 12/190 art. 48, PRO. Other copies exist in SP 12/171 art. 48, PRO and Lansdowne 280, British Library.

131. Arber, *Transcript*, vol. II, p. 810.

132. *Ibid.*

133. Such a case may be seen in 1598 when the Stationers brought a suit against the Drapers which alleged that they violated the Star Chamber decree by publishing and selling books. The court found in favor of the Stationers, which effectively extended the Stationers' monopoly from printing to selling books. See Gerald D. Johnson, "The Stationers Versus the Drapers: Control of the Press in the Late Sixteenth Century," *The Library*, 6th ser., 10 (1988), 1–17.

134. Martin Ingram, *Church Courts, Sex and Marriage in England, 1570–1640* (Cambridge, 1987) pp. 292–96.

135. Ronald Marchant, *The Church Under the Law: Justice, Administration and Discipline in the Diocese of York, 1560–1640* (Cambridge, 1969), p. 61.

136. Laura Gowing, "Language, Power and the Law: Women's Slander Litigation in Early Modern London," *Women, Crime and the Courts in Early Modern England*, Jennifer Kermode and Garthine Walker, eds. (Chapel Hill and London, 1994), pp. 26–47.

137. Richard Crompton, *Star-Chamber Cases* (1630), p. 10.

138. Shuger's argument about legal interest in defamatory language depends upon the model of *iniuria* whose precedents appear in Roman law and which, she contends, is transmitted into English common law and common law practice through medieval canon law. One thread of her argument depends upon her contention that Star Chamber "defamation procedures" are consistent with the church courts. According to Shuger, "Star Chamber defamation procedure, like that of the church courts, sought 'to permit the removal of unjustly incurred *infamia*' through 'a public declaration of innocence'." As the Star Chamber's "stress on confession, amends, and communal solidarities indicates, its perspective is that of Christian justice – the same perspective that informs the handling of transgressive language in the English church courts and in the *ius commune*" (*Censorship and Cultural Sensibility*, p. 113). Such an understanding of the court of Star Chamber and its procedure is misleading at best.

139. Earlier Tudor monarchs had established pre-print authorization by their proclamations, which became null at their deaths, and by statutes that were subsequently rescinded by their heirs. See Clegg, *Elizabethan England*, chapter 1.

140. Johns, *Nature of the Book*, p. 230.

141. *Ibid.*

142. *Ibid.*, p. 190.

143. Loewenstein, *Author's Due*, p. 28.

144. According to John Feather, "Although an entry was the only *proof* of own-ership, it is important to recognize that the Register was merely a record of established rights; an entry could not, by itself, confer those rights." John Feather, *Publishing, Piracy and Politics: An Historical Study of Copyright in Britain* (London, 1992), p. 27.

145. Arber, *Transcript*, vol. II, p. 477

146. *Ibid.*, p. 823.

147. Peter Blayney, "The Publication of Playbooks," *A New History of Early English Drama*, John D. Cox and David Scott Kastan, eds. (New York, 1997), pp. 383–422.

148. *Ibid.*, pp. 400–01.

149. *Pollard and Redgrave's A Short-Title Catalogue of Books Printed in England, Scotland, and Ireland and of Books Printed Abroad, 1475–1640*, 3 vols. (1986, 2nd edn.). Hereafter referred to or cited as *STC*.

150. Arnold Hunt, "Licensing and Religious Censorship," Andrew *Literature and Censorship in Renaissance England*, Andrew Hadfield, ed. (Houndmills, Basingstoke, 2001), pp. 127–46: p. 128.

151. Loewenstein believes "That it was normal company policy to enter only copies that had been approved by a reputable licensing authority is implied by occasional entries in the Stationers' Register indicating the exceptional and grudging registration: copies 'tolerated unto' their owners and those to be printed 'at the peril' of the registrant" (*Author's Due*, p. 29). Shuger generally assumes that licensing was a successful representation of the values of a Christian culture.

152. In calculating this, I have omitted ballad entries, since both entry and authorization were highly irregular. Also since so few ballads survived, and so many were printed, their presence distorts statistical evidence.

153. Hunt, "Licensing and Religious Censorship," p. 128.

154. Anthony Milton, "Licensing, Censorship, and Religious Orthodoxy in Early Stuart England," *The Historical Journal*, 41 (1998), 625–51: pp. 631, 645.

155. Shuger, *Censorship and Cultural Sensibility*, p. 258.

156. *Ibid.*

157. Shuger finds "Featly's account" as being "of the true sweetness of Jacobean censorship" (*ibid.*, p. 252). Truly an imaginative reading, Shuger is wrong in so many ways. She reads the account as Featly's defense of a benevolent censorship system that "endeavors to reconstruct an actual event" as "an ideal – as the ideal of censorship" (p. 252). What appears as *Cygnea Cantio* was actually a letter from Featly to the Dean of Winchester, which, when it was forwarded to King James, the King proclaimed should be printed. The letter's interest was in "relating divers difficult points, and remarkeable directions to Students in Divinity, delivered by King James our late Soveraigne of blessed memory"

(Daniel Featly, *Cygnea Cantio* [London, 1639], B2). The King's interest in seeing it printed was undoubtedly to clarify his theological objections to William Crompton's *Saint Austens Summes*, whose publication was not restrained, though Shuger indicates that it along with Elton's *Gods Holy Mind* and perhaps a third book, was burned (*Censorship and Cultural Sensibility*, p. 230, p. 313, n.61). (For what was burned, see Stephen B. Lewkowicz, "Elton's *An Exposition of the Ten Commandements of God* [1623]: a Burnt Book?" *PBSA*, 77 [1977]: 201–08.) Shuger accepts without question Featly's claim that Elton's book, also the subject of the interview, was printed without license, even though it was entered in the Stationers' Registers under Featly's hand. Furthermore, she dismisses manuscript evidence that indicates that Laud and Neile called attention to Crompton's book to cause trouble on the grounds that it disagrees with Laud's diary, which she misreads (*Censorship and Cultural Sensibility*, p. 314, n.85). According to Shuger, Laud's diary indicates that Crompton gave a manuscript presentation copy of his book to Buckingham, who showed it to the King. When the King found fault with several passages, Crompton promised to revise it, and on December 21, 1624, Laud returned the manuscript to Crompton. However, Laud's diary for December 21 reads:

Mr. *Crompton* had set out a Book, called *St: Augustins Summe*. His Majesty found fault with divers passages in it. He was put to recall some things in Writing. He had Dedicated this Book to my Lord Duke of *Buckingham*. My Lord sent him to me to overlook the Articles, in which he had recalled and explained himself; that I might see, whether it were well done, and fit to shew the King. This day Mr. Crumpton [*sic*] brought his Papers to me.

The matter continued on December 31:

Friday, His Majesty sent for me; and delivered unto me Mr. Crumpton's [*sic*] Papers, the second time (after I had read them over to himself) and commanded me to correct them, as they might pass in the Doctrine of the Church of England.
(*Diary* [1695], p. 14)

The documents in question are not a presentation manuscript, but articles in which Crompton "recalled and explained himself," and there is nothing in Laud's diary to indicate what might have initiated the demand for this explanation, though it would not have been unlikely for the King to have Laud look at an explanation in a matter in which Laud himself had raised objections.

158. Featly, *Cygnea Cantio*, B3v, B4.
159. SP 12/275, f. 31, PRO.
160. Jackson, *Records*, p. 85.
161. Add. MS 4378, f. iv. British Library.
162. Add. MS 27,936, f. 62, British Library.
163. *Ibid.*, f.64.
164. Featley, *Cygnea Cantio*, C2v–C3.

165. Shuger, *Censorship and Cultural Sensibility*, p. 242.
166. Andrew Marvell, *The Rehearsal-Transposed* (1672), quoted in W. W. Greg, *Licensers for the Press* (Oxford, 1962), p. 101.
167. Kenneth Fincham, "Prelacy and Politics: Archbishop Abbot's Defense of Protestant Orthodoxy," *Historical Research*, 61 (1988), 36–69: p. 60.
168. The multiple interests that affected official and ecclesiastical "licensing" during the reign of James clearly created a system – if it may even be called a system – that operated very differently than that described by Siebert. According to Siebert, "Founded on the king's prerogative power, administered by the archbishop and his subordinates, and operated with the assistance of the Stationers' Company, the licensing system continued as the basic printing regulation during the early Stuart period" (*Freedom of the Press*, p. 141).
169. Glynn Wickham, *Early English Stages, 1300–1576*, 3 vols. (1959–81), vol. II, p. 94.
170. Baker, *Oxford Laws of England*, chapter 25.
171. David J. Seipp, "The Structure of English Common Law in the Seventeenth Century," *Legal History in the Making: Proceedings of the Ninth British Legal History Conference, Glasgow 1989*, W. M. Gordon and T. D. Fergus, eds. (London, 1991), pp. 61–83: pp. 61–62.
172. Baker, *Oxford Laws of England*, p. 469.
173. *Ibid.*, p. 470.
174. Shuger, *Censorship and Cultural Sensibility*, p. 5.
175. William Camden, however, did record the event in *Annales rervm Anglicarvm et Hibernicarvm regnante Elizabetha*, published in Latin in 1615 and in English in 1625.

2 PRINT IN THE TIME OF PARLIAMENT: 1625–1629

1. Henry Burton, *A tryall of Private Devotions or A Diall for the Houres of Prayer* (1628), A2.
2. I purposely here address the question of factions rather than invoking the language of Calvinism/anti-Calvinism or Arminianism/Calvinism, though I will address these issues more fully below.
3. James F. Larkin, C.S.V., *Stuart Royal Proclamations*, vol. II. (Oxford, 1983), p. 92.
4. *Journals of the House of Commons* (1830), vol. I, p. 805. Hereafter cited as *CJ*. For a discussion of the writing and publication of these two works and their rhetorical strategies, see Cyndia Susan Clegg, *Press Censorship in Jacobean England* (Cambridge, 1992), pp. 197–200, 208–15.
5. *CJ*, vol. I, p. 808.
6. Larkin, *Stuart Royal Proclamations*, vol. II, p. 92. Nicholas Tyacke maintained that the proclamation effectively outlawed Calvinism on a national basis ("Puritanism, Arminianism and Counter Revolution," *The Origins of the English Civil War*, Courad Russell, ed. [New York, 1973], pp. 119–43: p. 132).

7. Nicholas Tyacke, "Puritanism, Arminianism and Counter Revolution," expanded in *Anti-Calvinists* (Oxford: Clarendon, 1987).
8. Peter White, *Predestination, Policy and Polemic: Conflict and Consensus in the English Church from the Reformation to the Civil War* (Cambridge, 1992), p. 2.
9. Beza is the anglicized version of Théodor de Bèze, a French Protestant theologian and scholar who was a disciple of John Calvin and lived most of his life in Switzerland.
10. Jacobus Arminius was a Dutch theologian who opposed the tenets of Calvinism. He held that God's election is conditional on and follows faith in Jesus, that Jesus' atonement was for all people (and not just the elect as Calvin maintained), that faith is an act of man's free will not God's irresistible grace, and that salvation, since it is dependent on faith, can be lost. Conrad Vorstius and Petrus Bertius, both Dutch theologians, subscribed to the teachings of Arminius.
11. White, *Predestination, Policy and Polemic*, p. 312.
12. In addition to Tyacke, see: Kenneth Fincham, "Prelacy and Politics: Archbishop Abbot's Defence of Protestant Orthodoxy," *Historical Research*, 61 (1988), 36–69; Kenneth Fincham and Peter Lake, "The Ecclesiastical Policy of James I," *Journal of British Studies*, 24 (1985), 169–207; and Patrick Collinson, *The Religion of Protestants: The Church in English Society 1559–1625* (Oxford, 1982).
13. Julian Davies, *The Caroline Captivity of the Church: Charles I and the Remoulding of Anglicanism, 1625–1641* (Oxford, 1992); Kevin Sharpe, *The Personal Rule of Charles I* (New Haven, 1992).
14. The theological divide between Durham House and the Abbot circle has received notable attention but remarkably little has been said of the personal rivalry of their principals, Richard Neile and George Abbot, something I have considered at length in *Press Censorship in Jacobean England*, chapter 6.
15. Tyacke, *Anti-Calvinists*, p. 109.
16. Fincham, "Prelacy and Politics," p. 42.
17. John Cosin, *Correspondence* (London, 1869), vol. I, pp. 32, 34, 40.
18. Correspondence of Daniel Featly, Rawlinson D.47, Bodleian Library. Samuel Ward's correspondence is included in Tanner 72–74, Bodleian Library.
19. Fincham, "Prelacy and Politics," p. 41.
20. *Articles Agreed Upon by the Archbishops and Bishops* (1628), B1.
21. The *STC* and Harvard University's catalogue say this appears on Harvard's Houghton Library copy, but it does not appear on the Houghton copy (14454.140.5). Houghton, like the British Library, identifies the author as John Rhodes.
22. SP 16/142 art. 22, PRO.
23. J[ohn] R[ussell], *The Spy discovering the danger of Arminian heresie and Spanish trecherie* (Strasburgh [i.e. Amsterdam: By the successors of Giles Thorp], 1628), †2.
24. David Colclough, *Freedom of Speech in Early Stuart England* (Cambridge, 2005), p. 118.

25. Russell, *Spy*, †2v.
26. *Ibid.*, A1.
27. Since Durham House used the word "Calvinist" to describe their opponents and the Calvinists used the word "Arminian" to refer to Durham House, I am going to use this language – even if, as White contends, it is not precisely accurate.
28. Russell, *Spy*, A3v.
29. *Ibid.*, A4v.
30. *Ibid.*, B1.
31. For a discussion of this propaganda campaign in relationship to the tradition of counseling the monarch, see David Colclough, *Freedom of Speech in Early Stuart England*. For its relationship to Jacobean press censorship see Clegg, *Press Censorship in Jacobean England*, chapter 5.
32. Russell, *Spy*, B3v.
33. *Ibid.*, B4r–v.
34. Theodore Beza, *The Treasure of Truth* (1581).
35. Russell, *Spy*, B4v.
36. *Ibid.*, C2r–v.
37. Edward Coke, "The Case *de Libellis famosis*, or of Scandalous Libels," in *The Reports of Sir Edward Coke, in English*, 7 vols. (London, 1776–77), p. 125. David Colclough offers a useful discussion of the implications of this case in *Freedom of Speech in Early Stuart England*, pp. 217–19.
38. Russell, *Spy*, C1v.
39. *Ibid.*, C2.
40. SP 16/30, art. 72, PRO.
41. Russell, *Spy*, C2.
42. *Ibid.*, C4.
43. *Ibid.*, E3v.
44. *Ibid.* E4.
45. *Ibid.*, E3v–E4.
46. *Collegiat suffrage of the divines of Great Britain, concerning the five articles controverted in the Low Countries* (1629), B1.
47. *Ibid.*, G2.
48. *Ibid.*, S3.
49. White, *Predestination, Policy and Polemic*, p. 230.
50. White, however, dismisses the moderation expressed in many of these writings as a pose assumed to strengthen the parliamentary campaign against Montagu (*ibid.*, p. 232).
51. George Carleton, *An Examination of those Things wherein the Author of the Late Appeale Holdeth the Doctrines of the Pelagians and Arminians to be the Doctrine of the Church of England* (1626), E2v–E3. White says that George Carleton "saw Rome as the real issue" (*Predestination, Policy and Polemic*, p. 184), but the *Examination* is solely concerned with taking Montagu to task for his doctrinal positions on predestination and perseverance.
52. Carleton, *Examination*, B3.

53. *A Joynt attestation, avowing that the discipline of the Church of England was not impeached by the Synode of Dort* (1626), A4v. The STC attributes this to Gwalter Balcanquhall. Its final page is subscribed as follows:

> Georgius Cicestriensis Episcopus.
> Johannes Sarisburiensis Episcopus [Davenant]
> Gualterus Balcanquall Decan. Ross
> Samuel Ward Pub. profess. Theol in Acad. Cant. & Col. Sid Praefect.
> Thomas Goad Sacre Theol. Doctor.

54. The five articles addressed the theological differences between the Arminians and the established churches on: (1) God's predestination; (2) Christ's death and suffering for man's redemption (justification); (3) man's free will after the Fall; (4) the irresistibility of God's grace; and (5) the perseverance of the Saints (the Elect). The English delegation concurred with the findings of the Synod against the doctrine of the Arminians, and maintained that the Synod's findings were consistent with scripture and the doctrine of the Church of England. In 1619 the Synod's findings, *The judgment of the Synode of Dort, concerning the five articles*, appeared from the English press of John Bill. The actual opinions of the English delegation did not appear until 1626, *Suffragium Collegiale Theologorum Magnae Britanniae*, in Latin from the press of Robert Milbourne, who published one third of the 1626 books opposing Montagu's *Appello Caesarem*. It was reprinted in 1627, again in Latin, and in 1629 appeared in an English translation with the title *Collegiat suffrage of the divines of Great Britain, concerning the five articles controverted in the Low Countries*.

55. *A Joynt attestation*, B4.

56. Anthony Milton, *Catholic and Reformed: The Roman and Protestant Churches in English Protestant Thought, 1600–1640* (Cambridge, 1995).

57. *Ibid.*, p. 18.

58. Matthew Sutcliffe, *A brief censure upon an appeale to Caesar* (1626). According to White, "All surviving copies are imperfect. The attribution to Sutcliffe rests on the *Diary of John Rous*, ed. M. A. E. Green. Camden Society. 66 (1856), p. 5" (White, *Predestination, Policy and Polemic*, p. 231, n. 90).

59. Sutcliffe, *A brief censure upon an appeale to Caesar*, D4r–v.

60. White, *Predestination, Policy and Polemic*, p. 222.

61. Arnold Hunt, "Featly, Daniel (1582–1645)," *Oxford Dictionary of National Biography*, Oxford, 2004; online edn., 2006 [www.oxforddnb.com/view/article/9242, accessed December 31, 2006].

62. John Yates, *Ibis ad Caesarem* (1626), Fff2-v.

63. According to Kenneth Gibson, Burton lost his living at St. Matthew's, Friday Street because of his letter to Charles accusing Bishop Richard Neile and William Laud of popish leanings ("Burton, Henry (*bap.* 1578, *d.* 1647/8)," *Oxford Dictionary of National Biography*, Oxford, 2004; online edn., 2006 [www.oxforddnb.com/view/article/4129, accessed December 31, 2006]). In *A Plea to an Appeale*'s dedication to King Charles, Burton's reference to his own poverty and "the very scares of his late disgrace with so gracious a Maister"

(1626, ¶2v) suggests he had been dismissed. In October 1628, however, an article objected by the Commissioners for Causes Ecclesiastical identifies Burton as "Clerk, Parson of St. Matthew's, Friday Street, London" (*Calendar of State Papers for the Reign of Charles I. Addenda, March 1625–January 1649*, William Douglas Hamilton and Sophia Crawford Loma, eds. [London, 1897, p. 299]; hereafter cited as *CSPD*). Gibson also mentions that Burton was cited before the High Commission for writing his response to Montagu, although no proceedings followed. The High Commission action against Burton was not until 1628, and it was for writing the following anti-Arminian books against Charles's 1626 proclamation: *Israel's Fast, The trial of Private Devotions, A Plea to an Appeal, The Bayting of the Popes Bull, The Seven Vials*, and "sundry other books of the like titles" (*CSPD*, Addenda, p. 299.) Since Burton answered the articles against him, we may presume that proceedings did, indeed, follow, although no action may have been taken. For a discussion of the High Commission's action against Burton, see chapter 3.

64. Burton, *A Plea to an Appeale*, B2.
65. *Ibid.*, B4v.
66. Milton, *Catholic and Reformed*, p. 116.
67. Colin Burrow, "Rous, Francis (1580/81–1659)," *Oxford Dictionary of National Biography*, Oxford, September 2004; online edn., 2006 [www.oxforddnb.com/view/article/24171, accessed December 31, 2006].
68. Francis Rous, "Epistle Dedicatory," *The Arte of Happiness* (1619), A3.
69. Burrow, "Rous, Francis (1580/81–1659)."
70. Francis Rous, *Testis Veritatis* (1626), M1–2.
71. William Prynne, *The Perpetuitie of a Regenerate Mans Estate* (1626), ¶2v.
72. *Ibid.*, **1v.
73. Colclough, *Freedom of Speech in Early Stuart England*, p. 97. John Donne twice preached admonitory sermons that considered the necessity and the proper means of the free and open speech of counsel.
74. *Ibid.*, p. 77.
75. *Ibid.*, p. 81.
76. Prynne, *Perpetuitie*, ¶ 2.
77. Rous, *Testis veritatis*, M2-v.
78. For excellent discussions of the role linking the Pope to Antichrist played in the English Protestant imagination, see Anthony Milton's *Catholic and Reformed*, chapter 2, and Peter Lake and Michael Questier, *The Antichrist's Lewd Hat* (New Haven, 2002).
79. And, notoriously, Peter White has concluded they do not, and Nicholas Tyacke that they do.
80. See Charles Hardwick, *A History of the Articles of Religion* (London, 1888).
81. Charles I, *By the King a proclamation for the establishing of the Peace and Quiet of the Church of England* (1626). Reprinted in Larkin, *Stuart Royal Proclamations*, vol. II, p. 92.
82. *Ibid.*
83. *Ibid.*

84. *Ibid.*
85. Laud placed "O" next to the names of Church of England clerics in his diary. (William Laud, *The Works of William Laud*, W. Scott and J. Bliss, eds. [Oxford, 1847–60]).
86. Throughout the reign of Elizabeth, divines in the Church of England had readily engaged their opponents on both sides in print. Even for texts they deemed seriously dangerous to the established religion – texts that were suppressed – respondents printed the error along with the controversialist's response. This was done with writings in the Admonition Controversy, in response to the Marprelate tracts, and in response to Catholic Continental writings, especially by Bishop John Jewel. See Cyndia Susan Clegg, *Press Censorship in Elizabethan England* (Cambridge, 1997), chapters 4 and 8.
87. Tyacke, *Anti-Calvinists*, pp. 154, 157.
88. Joseph Mead to Martin Stuteville, Harley MS 390, f. 83r, British Library. Quoted in White, *Predestination, Policy, and Polemic*, p. 246, n. 37.
89. Sheila Lambert, "Richard Montagu, Arminianism, and Censorship," *Past and Present*, 124 (1989), 36–68: p. 62.
90. *Ibid.*, p. 59.
91. *Ibid.*
92. *Ibid.*, p. 60.
93. Daniel Featly, *A Second Parallel together with a Writ of Error Sued against the Appealer* (1626), Mm4.
94. Rous, *Testis veritatis*, A2. The marginal note reads: "Doctor Baleanquell [Balcanquhall] in the prefaces of his Concie ad clerum. Febr. 7."
95. Henry Wotton, *Reliquiae Wottonianae* (4th edn., 1685), p. 321. I am indebted to David Cressy for this reference.
96. Prynne, *Perpetuitie*, **3.
97. Mark H. Curtis, "William Jones: Puritan Printer and Propagandist," *The Library*, 5th ser., 19 (1964), 38–66.
98. Prynne, *Perpetuitie*, ¶2-v. Lambert dismisses Prynne's allegations of anti-Calvinist censorship – perhaps understandably since they dominate his account of the trial of Laud, *Canterburies Doome* (1646).
99. Featly, *Second Parallel*, Ff2v.
100. *Ibid.*, Ff3.
101. Burton, *A Plea to an Appeale*, ¶3.
102. White, *Predestination, Policy and Polemic*, pp. 245–46.
103. Bishops George Montaigne (London), Richard Neile (Durham), Lancelot Andrewes (Winchester), William Laud (St. David's) and John Buckeridge (Rochester) to the Duke of Buckingham, January 16, 1626, Harleian 7000, f. 193, British Library.
104. *Ibid.*
105. Sue Ellen Towers concludes that official licensing practices seem to indicate that "the policy itself was unclear" and "from these results [licenses] it remains difficult to determine whether the Proclamation of 1626 was directed at Armininian or Calvinist books or both and how successful it was" (*Control*

of Religious Printing in Early Stuart England [Woodbridge, Suffolk, 2003], p. 188).

106. Not all titles entered, however, were approved by the ecclesiastical authorizers. My statistics are based on my database of the Stationers' Registers.
107. White, *Predestination, Policy and Polemic*, p. 246, n. 40.
108. William Gouge, *The Worke of William Gouge* (1627), a5r–v.
109. Peter Lake, *Moderate Puritans and the Elizabethan Church* (Cambridge; New York, 1982), p. 2.
110. *CSPD, Addenda*, p. 341.

[April] Petition of Michael Sparke, Stationer, now prisoner in the Fleet to the Council. That alighting upon a book of sermons upon the temptation of Christ, printed above 30 years since [published in 1592] by a printer who had it allowed and entered by the Stationers' Company, the same being reputed to be the work of [Lancelot Andrews], late bishop of Winchester, but now out of print, he was induced to reprint it; before, however, it could come out, the press was stayed for a while by command of the bishop of London, upon the information of some who labour to have the printing of the whole of the late bishop's works. Hearing no more of this business for nine weeks, and pressed to pay for the paper, and being in much want of money, he disposed of these books for which he is committed to the Fleet Prison by your Lordships. This being his first fault in this kind, and ignorant of the gravity of the offence, he prays you to commiserate his poor estate, and give order for his enlargement.

111. George Montaigne to Lord Conway, January 22, 1627, SP 16/51, art. 6, PRO.
112. *Ibid.*
113. *Ibid.*
114. Lancelot Andrewes, *XCVI Sermons* (1629), A2.
115. *Ibid.*
116. *CSPD, Addenda*, p. 341.
117. Peter McCullough, "Making Dead Men Speak: Laudianism, Print, and the Works of Lancelot Andrewes, 1626–1642," *The Historical Journal*, 41 (1998), 401–24: p. 402. This provides an excellent account of the use of print to advance Laud's vision of the Church of England – even if it misunderstands the licensing history of the Sparke–Cotes edition of *Seven Sermons*.
118. *Ibid.*, p. 406.
119. Thomas Jackson, *A treatise of the holy catholike faith and Church*, 1627, D1.
120. For discussion of nature and manifestations of the debate on the visible and true Church, see Milton, *Catholic and Reformed*, chapter 3.
121. Wotton, *ReliquiaeWottonianae*, p. 321.
122. John Dod and Robert Cleaver, *Brief dialogue concerning preparation for the worthy receiving of the Lords Supper* (1627).
123. William Bradshaw, *A preparation to the receiving of Christs body and Blood* (1627), D4, D7.
124. John Carter, *A plaine and compendious exposition of Christs Sermon in the Mount* (1627), p. 31.

125. I have made the identification of Fredrich van Hulsius as the author of *The character of a Christian* (1627) based on the statement on page 177 that the author also wrote *Rome's Ruine* (1624).
126. Van Hulsius, *The character of a Christian* G6v.
127. Henry Burton, *The Bayting of the Popes Bull* (1627), ¶4.
128. *Ibid.*, **1v.
129. *Ibid.*, **2.
130. *Ibid.*, **3.
131. *Ibid.*, ***4r–v.
132. SP 16/54, art. 4, PRO.
133. SP 16/43, art. 5, PRO.
134. Kevin Sharpe, *Sir Robert Cotton, 1586–1631* (Oxford, 1979), pp. 237–30.
135. Sheila Lambert, "Committees, Religion, and Parliamentary Encroachment on Royal Authority in Early Stuart England," *English Historical Review*, 33 (January, 1990), 60–95.
136. White, *Predestination, Policy and Polemic*, p. 218.
137. Conrad Russell, *Parliaments and English Politics 1621–1629* (Oxford, 1979).
138. According to Russell,

> From the very beginning of the Parliament, the plague, as well as the projected war, contributed to the growing alarm felt about what seemed to be incipient toleration of Catholic recusants. Sandys reacted by moving for a committee to draft a petition showing, article by article, how to "strengthen our own religion and weaken theirs" . . . The petition, which was ultimately drawn by Pym and Sandys, thus covered ways of repressing recusancy, and ways of revitalizing the Church of England.
> (*ibid.*, pp. 229–30)

139. *Ibid.*, p. 207.
140. *Ibid.*, p. 247.
141. *CJ*, vol. 1, p. 807.
142. Russell, *Parliaments and English Politics*, p. 64.
143. SP 16/47, art. 40, PRO.
144. Robert Sibthorpe, *Apostolike Obedience* (1627), p. 3.
145. Russell, *Parliaments and English Politics*, pp. 343–44.
146. *Ibid.*, p. 345.
147. SP 16/78, art. 19, PRO. The document, sent to Secretary Conway by Francis Nethersole, is calendared as "Observations on Dr. Cosin's Book of Hours of Prayer, principally with respect to the publication of a reprint of a first impression" (*The Calendar of State Papers for the Reign of Charles I, 1627–28*, John Bruce, ed. [London, (1859), p. 342]). The document, however, is clearly focused on informing Conway that the first edition, only 200 of which had been printed, clearly had to have been imprinted in violation of the initial suppression.
148. John Cosin, *A Collection of Private Devotions* (1627), a1r–v.
149. Burton, *A tryall of Private Devotions* ¶2.
150. *Ibid.*, A1v.

151. *Ibid.*, A2v.
152. *Ibid.*, B3.
153. *Ibid.*, F3.
154. *Ibid.*, D2.
155. *Ibid.*, D2r–v.
156. William Prynne, *A Briefe Survay and Censure of Mr Cozens his Couzening Devotions* (1628), ¶2.
157. *Ibid.*, ¶2.
158. *Ibid.*, ¶¶2v–¶¶3. This corresponds to a similar account of the publishing circumstances in Prynne's testimony at Laud's trial, published as *Canterburies Doome*, except that the trial testimony says that Prynne ultimately obtained license for his book from Featly.

> In the Yeare 1627. Doctor Cosens published a Booke intituled, A Collection of private Devotions, Or, the houres of Prayer, fraught with Popery, and Popish Superstitions, which gave great offence; whereupon, at the importunity of diverse well affected persons, he [Prynne] Writ a Refutation threof, intituled; A Briefe Survey and Censure of Master Cosens his Cosening Devotions; which by this Bishops meanes and his Confederates was refused License, at London House; but afterwards licensed at Lambeth House by Doctor Featly, and printed sitting the Parliament, in the Yeare 1628, for writing which Booke only against Doctor Cosens his Popery, hee was immediately after the Parliament ended, questioned in High Commission by the Bishops procurement, and thence delivered by a Prohibition, to the Bishops great Griefe. (p. 185)

I can find nothing to corroborate the claim that Featly licensed Prynne's book.

159. SP 16/108, art.75, PRO. *The Calendar of State Papers for the Reign of Charles I, 1628–29*, John Bruce, ed. (London, 1859), p. 87, dates this June despite an endorsement that says April.
160. SP 16/102, art. 38, PRO.
161. Jeremiah Dyke, *A Sermon Preached at the Publicke Fast to the Commons House of Parliament, April 5th 1628* (1628), E1.
162. *Ibid.*, F3v–F4.
163. *Ibid.*, G2.
164. *Ibid.*, G2–G3v.
165. *Articles Agreed upon by the Archbishops and Bishops of both Provinces, and the whole Cleargie: In the Convocation holden at London, in the yeere 1562* (1628), A1–B1.
166. Indeed, when the 1625 Parliament moved towards censuring Montagu, his position figured more prominently than predestination among their concerns. See *Cobbett's Parliamentary History* (London, 1807), p. 7.
167. Tyacke, *Anti-Calvinists*, 148.
168. Joseph Hall, *The Olde Religion: A Treatise, Wherin is laid downe the true state of the difference betwixt the Reformed, and Romane Church; and the blame of the schisme is cast upon the AUTHORS. Serving for the vindication of our innocence, for the settling of wavering minds for a preservative against Popish insinuation* (1627), ¶4.

169. *Ibid.*, B2v–B3.
170. Henry Burton, *Seven Vials* (1628), A4v.
171. *Ibid.*, D4v
172. *Ibid.*, F4v.
173. Joseph Hall, *The Reconciler* (1629, censored), p. 8.
174. Henry Burton, *Babel no Bethel* (1629), **3v.
175. *Ibid.*, **4v.
176. *Ibid.*, ¶2v–¶3.
177. Thomas Spencer, *Maschil Unmasked* (1629), ¶¶v.
178. *Ibid.*, ¶2r–v.
179. SP 16/141, art.17, PRO.
180. Joseph Hall, *The Reconciler* (1629), A1v.
181. Bishop Hall wrote to Turner to allow him to omit "certain passages" of his letter and the letter of Bishop Davenant because they contained "certain strong declarations" of the Church of England's anti-Arminianism. Hall consented to suppressing "passages" so as not to "draw blame" on Turner, but Turner must have cut more than Hall intended (SP16/136, art.82, PRO).
182. SP 16/142, art. 22, PRO.
183. *Ibid.*
184. Burton, *Seven Vials*, ¶2v.

> Yea though I was told Your Majesty was lately offended with me. But I answered, No; I had no reason to believe it. For first, I knew well the gentle disposition of your royall breast, guided by such a dextrous iudgment, is not easily incensed, where there is no just cawse. And I am sure I daily injoy the influence of your favour, though not the gratious aspect of your face ... And as I told my Lord of London, at my first examination about *Israels Fast*, All that I had done, was for Gods glory, the service of my King & Country, & the Church of England, whereof wee were members; and for which I was ready (if need were) to lay downe my life.

185. SP 16/135, art. 40, PRO. Wallace Notestein, *Commons Debates for 1629* (Minneapolis, 1921), p. 58.
186. *An Appeale of the Orthodox Ministers* (1629), c3.
187. *Ibid.*, d3.
188. *Ibid.*, e1.
189. *Ibid*, f2v.
190. William Prynne, *The Church of Englands Old Antithesis to the New Arminianism* (1629), A2. This title is shortened to "*Anti-arminianisme,*" in contemporary sources, a practice I will use throughout this study.
191. *Ibid.*, A2.
192. *Ibid.*, B2.
193. *Ibid.*, ¶4v.
194. SP 16/138, arts. 10 and 23, PRO.
195. Alexander Leighton, *An Appeal to the Parliament; or Sions Plea aginst the Prelacie* (1629), A3.

196. *Ibid.*, B3.
197. *Ibid.*, M3v.
198. For a full discussion of these circumstances, see pp. 116–19 following.
199. Leighton, *An Appeal*, Xx1r–v.
200. Prynne, *Anti-arminianisme*, **4v.
201. Prynne, *Perpetuitie*, **4v–A1.
202. *The Seconde parte of a register: being a calendar of manuscripts under that title intended for publication by the Puritans about 1593, and now in Dr. Williams's Library, London*, Albert Peel, ed. (Cambridge, 1915), pp. 13–14.
203. Burton, *A tryall of Private Devotions*, F3.
204. William Prynne, *Church of England's Old Antithesis* (2nd edn., 1630), ¶¶¶2v. Also contemporarily referred to as *Anti-arminianisme*.
205. *Ibid.*, B2–B2v.
206. Henry Burton, *Israels Fast. Or, A Meditation Upon the Seventh Chapter of Joshuah: A faire Precedent for thee times* (1628), A2v.
207. Daniel Featly, *Cygnea Cantio* (1629), p. 5.
208. David Cressy, *Travesties and Transgression in Tudor and Stuart England: Tales of Discord and Dissension* (Oxford, 2000), p. 225.

3 TRANSFORMATIONAL LITERALISM: THE REACTIONARY
REDEFINITION OF THE COURTS OF HIGH COMMISSION AND
STAR CHAMBER

1. Richard Atkyns, *The Original and Growth of Printing* (1664), B1v.
2. *Ibid.*
3. Charles Howard, Earl of Berkshire, *A true copy of the Lord Andevers speech to the Parliament, Concerning the Star-Chamber* (1641), Thomason Tract, E 196, p. 40.
4. Maija Jansson, ed. *Proceedings of the Opening Session of the Long Parliament* 7 vols. (Rochester, NY, 2000–07), vol. 1, p. 37.
5. *Ibid.*, p. 483.
6. Harold Weber, *Paper Bullets: Print and Kingship under Charles II* (Lexington, KY, 1996), p. 151.
7. According to Sheila Lambert, "the notion that there was strict state control of the press continues to win the day, because it is such a useful concept, to be invoked to cover everything from poor standards of printing, to failure to look with sufficient care for evidence of dissent" ("State Control of the Press in Theory and Practice," *Censorship and the Control of Print in England and France 1600–1910*, Robin Myers and Michael Harris, eds. [Winchester, 1992], pp. 1–32: pp. 1–7). F. S. Siebert (*Freedom of the Press in England* [Urbana, 1952]) proposes a Whig historical progression from repression to enlightenment which locates the height of censorship in the Star Chamber Decrees of June 23, 1586 which he regards as "the most comprehensive regulation of the press of the entire Tudor period," and as Elizabeth's answer to "insufficient efforts" of "government

officials, ecclesiastical licensers, and Stationers' Company searchers" to suppress opposition literature (p. 61).

8. Philip Hamburger, "The Development of the Law of Seditious Libel and the Control of the Press," *Stanford Law Review*, 37 (1985), 661–762.

9. *Ibid.*, p. 667. The law of seditious libel does not emerge, he maintains, until the eighteenth century, when Parliament failed to renew seventeenth-century licensing statutes.

10. Lambert, "State Control," p. 9.

11. Lambert, "The Printers and the Government, 1604–1637," *Aspects of Printing from 1600*, Robin Myers and Michael Harris, eds. (Oxford, 1987), pp. 1–29.

12. Thomas G. Barnes, "Star Chamber Litigants and their Counsel, 1596–1641," *Legal Records and the Historian*, J. H. Baker, ed. (London, 1978), pp. 7–28: p. 7.

13. SP 16/102, art. 38, PRO.

14. SP 16/153, arts. 44, 51, PRO.

15. SP 16/158, art. 18, PRO.

16. Roland G. Usher, *The Rise and Fall of the High Commission*, with a new Introduction by Philip Tyler (Oxford, 1968), p. 323. Usher's conclusion have been born out by the work of Philip Tyler (appended to the 1968 edition of Usher's book), by Kenneth Fincham's *Prelate as Pastor* (Oxford, 1990), and by Ronald A. Marchant's *The Church under the Law* (Cambridge, 1969).

17. William Laud to Buckingham, November 18, 1624, Harleian MS 7000, f. 166v, British Library.

18. Usher, *High Commission*, p. 344.

19. *Ibid.*, p. 254.

20. Charles I, *By the King a proclamation for the establishing of the Peace and Quiet of the Church of England* (1626). Reprinted in James F. Larkin and Paul L. Hughes, *Stuart Royal Proclamations*, 2 vols. (Oxford, 1973), vol. II, p. 92.

21. SP 16/529, art. 30, PRO.

22. *Ibid.*

23. *Ibid.*

24. Edward Arber, ed., *A Transcript of the Registers of the Company of Stationers of London*, 5 vols. (London and Birmingham, 1875–94), vol. II, p. 810.

25. W. W. Greg and E. Boswell, eds. *Records of the Court of the Stationers' Company* (London, 1930).

26. Larkin and Hughes, *Stuart Royal Proclamations*, vol. I, pp. 583–84.

27. While the High Commission may have been prepared to be lenient with the printer and give him his liberty, King James intervened. Having learned the printer had gained £1,000 by selling the pamphlet, the King demanded the man be returned to prison and pay £1,000 fine.

28. Larkin and Hughes, *Stuart Royal Proclamations*, vol. I, pp. 583–84.

29. Charles I, *By the King a proclamation signifying his maiesties pleasure, that all the men being in office of government . . . shall so continue* (1626).

30. On March 28, 1625, Privy Council business included a "general proclamation" to support "proceedings for preservacion of peace, administration of justice in

the government of the state," but this appears not to have survived (J. V. Lyle, ed. *Acts of the Privy Council.* 40 vols. [London, 1934], vol. XL, p. 4).

31. SP 16/119, art. 58, PRO.
32. SP 16/140, art. 17, PRO.
33. SP 16/140, art. 15, PRO.
34. SP 16/142, art. 22, PRO.
35. SP 16/141, art. 81, PRO.
36. *Calendar of the Patent Rolls, Elizabeth I*, vol. I (London, 1939), p. 118.
37. SP 16/142, art. 40, PRO. The books to which Burton refers are Hugh Cholmely's *The state of the now-Romane Church. Discussed by way of vindication of the Right Reverend Father in God. The Lord Bishop of Exceter, from the weak cavils of Henry Burton* (1629); and Robert Butterfield's *Maschil, or a Treatise to Give Instruction Touching the state of the Church of Rome since the council of Trent* (1629).
38. *Christ's confession and complaint: concerning his kingdom and seruants; conuincing Iewes of obstinacie, Romish Catholickes of conspiracie, seducers of sedition, Arminians of apostacie, and diuers others of coldnes, schisme, treachery and hypocrisie.* / By J. P. (1629). *STC* identifies this as having been printed abroad.
39. SP 16/158, art. 49, PRO.
40. SP 16/162, arts. 12, 20, PRO.
41. For a discussion of the positions expressed in *Christ's Confession and Complaint*, see chapter 2.
42. SP 16/161, art. 39, PRO.
43. *Ibid.*
44. SP 16/205, art. 102, PRO.
45. SP 16/161, arts. 176, 181, PRO.
46. SP 16/324, art. 7, PRO.
47. SP 16/214, art. 34, PRO.
48. Kevin Sharpe, *The Personal Rule of Charles I* (New Haven, 1992).
49. The standard work on sedition and libel has long been W. S. Holdsworth, *A History of English Law*, 9 vols. (Boston, 1926). Roger Manning's "The Origins of the Doctrine of Sedition," *Albion*, 12 (1981): 99–121) offers a valuable and concise redefinition. Philip Hamburger provides a useful counter to Holdsworth and a valuable account of the development of the law of seditious libel in the late seventeenth and eighteenth centuries, although he overstates the case for the efficacy of state licensing in the late sixteenth and early seventeenth centuries.
50. Edward Coke, *The First part of the Institutes of the laws of England* (1629), Third Institute, chapter 14.
51. See especially, *Star Chamber Cases Shewing What Causes Properly Belong to the cognizance of that court* (1641). This was first published in 1630, and it is a compilation in English of sections on Star Chamber that appeared in Richard Crompton, *L'authoritie et jurisdiction des courts de la majestie de la roygne* (1594). According to Crompton, "Libellers be oftentimes dealt with in Star

Chamber, as offenders not sufficiently provided by the lawes otherwise" (English translation, 1641, B1v) and "If a man speake slanderous words of Noblemen . . . he shall have an action upon the Stat. de *Scandal. Magnat.* But the Defendant shall be punished in this Court" (1641, D2v).

52. Edward Coke, *Reports* (London, 1658), p. 228.
53. *Ibid.*, p. 489.
54. Holdsworth, *History of English Law*, vol. VIII, pp. 337–38.
55. Siebert, *Freedom of the Press*, p. 119.
56. Hamburger, "Seditious Libel," p. 665.
57. Hamburger, however, is wrong in his contention that the government of Elizabeth was unsatisfied with prosecutions under *Scandalum Magnatum*, namely against John Stubbs for writing *A Gaping Gulf* in 1579. Stubbs was actually tried under a Marian statute (1 Phil. & Mar., ca. 3) that deemed writing against the Queen and her husband seditious. Hamburger is likewise altogether wrong when he says that in the Martin Marprelate controversy and the Essex rebellion of 1601 the Crown sought harsh penalties "and the satisfaction of prosecuting the culprits for the contents of their writings" ("Seditious Libel," p. 677). John Hayward was never prosecuted for the book that has generally (and incorrectly) been associated with the Essex rebellion, *The First Parte of the History of Henry IIII* (1599), and the author of the Marprelate tracts was never found.
58. Hamburger, "Seditious Libel," p. 673.
59. *Ibid.*, p. 678.
60. *Cobbett's Parliamentary History of England: from the Norman Conquest, in 1066, to the year 1803*, vol. II (London: 1806), pp. 488–90.
61. Conrad Russell, "Eliot, Sir John (1592–1632)," *Oxford Dictionary of National Biography*, Oxford, 2004; online edn., 2006. [www.oxforddnb.com/view/article/8630, accessed March 6, 2007].
62. T. B. Howell, *A Complete Collection of State Trials*, 10 vols. (London, 1811–26), vol. II, pp. 235–38.
63. *Ibid.*, vol. II, p. 239.
64. *Ibid.*
65. SP16/530, art. 52, PRO; Russell, "Eliot, Sir John."
66. Howell, *State Trials*, vol. II, p. 242.
67. *Ibid.*, vol. II, pp. 267–68.
68. *Ibid.*, vol. II, p. 249.
69. *Ibid.*, vol. II, p. 252.
70. John Rushworth, *Historical Collections*, part 2, (1680) p. 56.
71. *Ibid.*, p. 56.
72. Howell, *State Trials*, vol. II, p. 398.
73. *Ibid.*, vol. II, p. 387.
74. *Ibid.*, vol. II, p. 562.
75. Coke, *Reports*, p. 227.
76. Lambert, "State Control of the Press," p. 7.
77. Siebert, *Freedom of the Press*, p. 2.

78. Thomas G. Barnes, "Star Chamber Mythology," *The American Journal of Legal History*, 5 (1961), 4.
79. *Ibid.*, p. 5.
80. During the forty-five years of Elizabeth's reign there were twenty-three actions taken to suppress objectionable books, bring court cases against their authors, or order a search for illegal materials; during the twenty-two years of James I's reign, there were twenty-five instances. During the fifteen years between 1625 and 1640, the government engaged in seventy acts of censorship.
81. Christopher Hill, "Censorship and English Literature," *The Collected Essays of Christopher Hill*, 2 vols. (Brighton, 1985), pp. 32–70: pp. 32–33.
82. David Cressy, *Travesties and Transgression in Tudor and Stuart England: Tales of Discord and Dissension* (Oxford, 2000), pp. 213–33.

4 CENSORSHIP AND THE PURITAN PRESS

1. Thomas Gataker, *A Discours Apologetical, wherein Lilies lewd and lowd Lies . . . are cleerly laid open* (1654), p. 26.
2. *Ibid.*
3. Brett Usher, "Gataker, Thomas (1574–1654)," *Oxford Dictionary of National Biography*, Oxford, 2004; online edn., 2006 [www.oxforddnb.com/view/article/10445, accessed January 4, 2007].
4. Peter Heylyn, *Cyprianus Anglicus* (1668), p. 517.
5. Debora Shuger, *Censorship and Cultural Sensibility* (Philadelphia, 2006), p. 4.
6. *Ibid.*
7. *Ibid.*, pp. 272, 275.
8. See *ibid.*, especially, pp. 232–33, in which she observes that Gataker's desire for "more charity and less presumption" and his effort to instill this in the godly community is "spoken like a true Laudian."
9. *Ibid.*, p. 3.
10. Christopher Hill, "Censorship and English Literature," *The Collected Essays of Christopher Hill*, 2 vols. (Brighton, 1985), pp. 32–70: p. 34.
11. Arnold Hunt, "Licensing and Religious Censorship," *Literature and Censorship in Renaissance England*, Andrew Hadfield, ed. (Houndmills, Basingstoke: 2001), p. 127.
12. Anthony Milton, "Licensing, Censorship, and Religious Orthodoxy in Early Stuart England," *The Historical Journal*, 41 (1998), 625–51: pp. 626–27.
13. *Ibid.*, p. 627.
14. Peter Lake, "The Laudian Style: Order, Uniformity and the Pursuit of the Beauty of Holiness in the 1630s," *The Early Stuart Church, 1603–1642*, Kenneth Fincham, ed. (Stanford, 1993), pp. 161–85. Lake is charting a course that cautiously avoids the ongoing debate about whether Laud's reforms were initiated out of his own interest or whether he was merely implementing King Charles's vision. See, for example, Kevin Sharpe, *The Personal Rule of Charles I* (New Haven, 1992) and Kenneth Fincham, "The Restoration of Altars in the 1630s," *The Historical Journal*, 44 (2001), 919–40.

15. Lake, "Laudian Style," p. 162.
16. *Ibid.*, p. 165.
17. *Ibid.* p. 166.
18. Edward Boughen, *A Sermon concerning decency and order in Church* (1638), quoted by Lake, "Laudian Style," p. 167.
19. Lake, "Laudian Style," p. 171.
20. *Ibid.*, p. 172.
21. Kenneth Fincham, "Clerical Conformity from Whitgift to Laud," *Conformity and Orthodoxy in the English Church, c. 1560–1660*, Peter Lake and Michael Questier, eds. (Woodbridge, Suffolk, 2000), pp. 125–58: p. 146.
22. Kenneth Fincham, "Episcopal Government, 1603–1640," Fincham, ed., *The Early Stuart Church*, p. 79.
23. *Ibid.*, p. 80.
24. *Ibid.*, pp. 88–89.
25. George Abbot to the King, January 2, 1632, MS 945, f. 105, Lambeth Palace Library.
26. William Laud to the King, January 2, 1634, MS 945, fos. 251–55. See also MS 945, fos. 261–63, Lambeth Palace Library.
27. Tom Webster, *Godly Clergy in Early Stuart England: The Caroline Puritan Movement, c. 1620–1643* (Cambridge, 1997), p. 4. Webster provides insight into the communities of godly clergy that arose in the English countryside through seminaries and patterns of clerical associations. Its focus on clergy, while excellent, is not as useful as Lake's for defining Puritanism more generally.
28. Peter Lake, *The Boxmaker's Revenge* (Stanford, 1998) pp. 53, 69.
29. *Ibid.*, p. 74
30. *Ibid.*, p. 202.
31. See, for example, Susan Holland, "Archbishop Abbot and the Problem of 'Puritanism'," *The Historical Journal*, 37 (1994), 23–43.
32. *Ibid.*, pp. 31–30. See also, Webster, *Godly Clergy*, especially chapters 7 and 8.
33. Webster, *Godly Clergy*, p. 167
34. Heylyn, *Cyprianus Anglicus*, p. 364.
35. Milton, "Censorship in Early Stuart England," pp. 628–33.
36. *Ibid.*, p. 645.
37. *Ibid.*, pp. 645–46.
38. *Ibid.*, p. 641.
39. *Ibid.*, p. 647.
40. *Ibid.*, p. 629.
41. Lake, *Boxmaker's Revenge*, p. 404.
42. Hunt, "Licensing and Religious Censorship," p. 143.
43. *Ibid.*, p. 141.
44. *Ibid.*, p. 142.
45. Shuger seriously misrepresents both Hunt and Milton in her claim that they have shown that "Laudian censorship concerned the suppression of hate speech" (*Censorship and Cultural Sensibility*, pp. 231–33).
46. Hunt, "Licensing and Religious Censorship," pp. 143–44.

47. For a discussion of the order's implementation, see Franklin B. Williams, Jr., "The Laudian Imprimatur," *The Library*, 5th ser., 15 (1960), 96–104.
48. Milton, "Censorship in Early Stuart England," p. 645.
49. See Cyndia Susan Clegg, *Press Censorship in Elizabethan England* (Cambridge, 1997) and *Press Censorship in Jacobean England* (Cambridge, 2001).
50. Peter White, *Predestination, Policy and Polemic* (Cambridge, 1992), pp. 250, 298–99, 304.
51. Williams, "Laudian Imprimatur," p. 66–7.
52. Sheila Lambert, "Richard Montagu, Arminianism, and Censorship," *Past and Present*, 124 (1989), 36–68: p. 67; Milton, "Censorship in Early Stuart England," p. 627.
53. Maureen Bell and John Barnard, "Provisional Count of *STC* Titles 1475–1640," *Publishing History*, 31 (1992), 46–66.
54. My calculations depend on my database that records all entries in the Stationers' Register for the reign of Charles. My analysis corrects for the large number of entries for titles in part because ballads were not entered regularly but instead an entry might be made retrospectively for several years – in part because survival rates make it difficult reliably to determine whether or not entered titles were actually printed.
55. My statistics employ Dr. Maureen Bell's estimates based on the STC and my own database of the Stationers' Company's Registers.
56. Hunt, "Licensing and Religious Censorship," pp. 128–29.
57. Gataker, *A Discours Apologetical*, p. 53; Lake, *Boxmaker's Revenge*, pp. 87–88. Lake provides a solid account of the efforts of Durham House to discredit Featly and thereby Abbot over this incident. I have also considered this in *Press Censorship in Jacobean England*, pp. 216–17. The manuscript upon which both Lake and I depend for our understanding of the events is MS 38.34, Dr. Williams's Library, a manuscript of John Quick's "Icones Sacrae Anglicanae Volume I," which Quick was preparing for publication. Shuger dismisses this account because it was "written at a considerably later date" (*Censorship and Cultural Sensibility*, p. 314, n. 85). John Quick (bap. 1636, d. 1706), was a Puritan clergyman who was ejected at the Restoration. Since he had been working on "Icones" only a generation after the events he described, and since he very likely traveled in circles where Featly would have been well known, the manuscript should be accepted as a valid witness.
58. Brian Quintrell, "Juxon, William (*bap.* 1582, *d.* 1663)," *Oxford Dictionary of National Biography*, Oxford, 2004; online edn., 2006 [www.oxforddnb.com/view/article/15179, accessed December 31, 2006].
59. Heylyn, *Cyprianus Anglicanus*, p. 362
60. Sheila Lambert, "State Control of the Press in Theory and Practice: the Role of the Stationers' Company before 1640," *Censorship and the Control of Print in England and France 1600–1910*, Robin Myers and Michael Harris, eds. (Winchester, 1992), pp. 1–32: p. 22.
61. Featly, *Cygnea Cantio* (1629).
62. SP 16 190, art. 109, f. 40, PRO.

63. Giles Widdowes, *The schysmaticall puritan* (1630), C2v.
64. *Ibid.*, B2v.
65. *Ibid.*, C1.
66. William Prynne, *Anti-Arminianisme* (1630), Oo*2.
67. *Ibid.*, Pp*2.
68. *Ibid.*, Qq*2.
69. Giles Widdowes, *A Lawlesse Kneelesse schismatical Puritan* (1620), A1.
70. *Ibid.*, M1v–M2.
71. William Prynne, *Lame Giles His Haultings* (1630), A1.
72. *Ibid.*, 9A2v.
73. *Ibid.*, A1v.
74. *Ibid.*, A2.
75. William Page, *Treatise on Justification* (1631), R1v-R2.
76. SP 16 188, art. 18, f. 13, PRO.
77. SP 16 190, art. 96, fos. 35, 39, PRO.
78. For a discussion of this see W. W. Greg, *A Companion to Arber* (Oxford, 1967), pp. 269–73.
79. William Baker to William Page, May 31, 1631, MS 945, f. 27, Lambeth Palace Library.
80. Henry Burton, *The Opinion, Judgement, and Determination of two reverent, learned and conformable Divines* (1632), D8v.
81. J. A. Robinson, ed., "Documents of the Laudian Period," *Collectanea: A Collection of Documents from Various Sources*, T. E. Palmer, ed., Somerset Record Society, vol. XLIII (1928), pp. 183–90: pp. 183, 190.
82. See especially, chapter 12, "The Battle of the Altars: Turning the Tables and Breaking the Rails," in David Cressy, *Travesties and Transgression in Tudor and Stuart England: Tales of Discord and Dissension* (Oxford, 2000), pp. 186–209.
83. Cressy says that this was Williams's treatise *Holy Table, Name and Thing* (*ibid.*, p. 192), but given the way the printed treatise relates to Heylyn's *Coale*, it seems more likely the Williams's actual letter to the vicar was what was actually being circulated.
84. John Hacket to William Laud, 1635, Codice 1030, item 65, f. 111, Lambeth Palace Library.
85. Brian Quintrell says this was done to cause problems for Williams during Star Chamber proceedings against him. Quintrell does an excellent job at sorting out the complicated proceedings (Brian Quintrell, "Williams, John (1582–1650)," *Oxford Dictionary of National Biography*, Oxford, 2004; online edn., 2006 [www.oxforddnb.com/view/article/29515, accessed December 31, 2006]).
86. Peter Heylyn, *Coale from the altar* (1636), D1v.
87. Jasper Fisher to Archbishop William Laud, 1633, Codice. 1030, item 58, f. 96; Lambeth Palace Library. The unnamed archdeacon was actually John Hacket, a moderate Calvinist and a royal chaplain. Hacket's remarks at the Visitation prompted a rebuke from Laud, to which Hacket responded with a letter of prostrate apology: "If I have offended, no Divine in the world shall be more

heartily sorry . . . How modestly I spoke upon the booke called the Holy Table name and Thing, I hope all can testify." He then explains his remarks about *Coale from the Altar*, adding "God know my hart if I had known then, or could have imagined that that book had been acceptable to the higher persons, I would have sooner lost my hand than have railed against it" (John Hacket to Archbishop Laud, 1637, Codice 1030, item 65, f. III, Lambeth Palace Library).

88. Fisher to Laud, item 58, f. 96.
89. William Prynne, *A Quench-coale* (1637), Yy2v.
90. *Ibid.*, Tt2v.
91. SP 16/364, art. 180, PRO.
92. John Williams, *Holy Table, Name and Thing* (1636), A1.
93. *Ibid.*, A4v.
94. Tanner 67, fos. 61–63, Bodleian Library.
95. *Ibid.*, f. 62.
96. T. B. Howell, *A Complete Collection of State Trials*, 10 vols. (London, 1811–26), vol. III, pp. 771–72.
97. John Williams's submission to King Charles (1637), Codice 1030, item 93, f. 159, Lambeth Palace Library.
98. William A. Jackson, *Records of the Court of the Stationers' Company* (London, 1957), p. 299. In a note Jackson comments, "The book bears a licence from Bishop Williams for the Diocese of Lincoln but apparently was not otherwise licensed or entered. It was evidently not a fast selling book and it is probable that not all the editions were printed for Bourne" (p. 299, n.2).
99. Edward Brerewood, *A Treatise of the Sabaoth* (1630), I2. Not all copies have both the treatise and the reply to Byfield, though they were printed at the same time, with a continuous signature – A–H for the treatise, I–O for the reply.
100. Richard Byfield, *The Doctrine of the Sabbath Vindicated, In confutation of a treatise of the sabbath written by M Edward Breerwood against M. Nic Byfield* (1631), A2v.
101. *Ibid.*, Aa3.
102. SP 16 269, Acts of the High Commission, f.68, PRO.
103. Milton, "Censorship in Early Stuart England," p. 646. Prideaux's treatise is printed in forty-one pages, twenty-six lines per page. Heylyn's introduction consists of fifteen pages at thirty-two lines per page.
104. John Prideaux, *The Doctrine of the Sabbath* (1634), D4.
105. Milton, "Censorship in Early Stuart England," p. 648.
106. *A soveraigne antidote against sabbatarian errours. Or, A decision of the chiefe doubts and difficulties touching the Sabbath* (1636), A4v. This was not entered in the Stationers' Register.
107. Henry Burton, *A brief answer to a late Treatise of the Sabbath day* (1635), A1v.
108. *Ibid.*, D3v.
109. Francis White, *An examination and confutation of a lawlesse pamphlet, intituled, A briefe answer to a late treatise of the Sabbath-day: digested dialogue-wise betweene two divines* (1637), A2v.

110. *Ibid.*, A4v.
111. Henry Burton, *A Divine Tragedie Lately Acted* (1636), H2.
112. Letter from E. R., January 4, 1637, Harleian 7000, f. 387v, British Library.
113. Milton, "Censorship in Early Stuart England," pp. 647–49.
114. Charles I, *Proclamation for the establishing of the Peace and Quiet of the Church of England* (1626).
115. Cressy, *Travesties*, p. 218.
116. Actually neither Gardiner not the manuscript he prints records the date of the initial day of the trial, but it does give February 15 as the second day.
117. John Rushworth, *Historical Collections*, part 2 (1680), A1v.
118. *Ibid.*, A2v.
119. *Ibid.*, B1c.
120. Tanner 299, fos. 123–36, Bodleian Library; Stowe 159, fos. 45–73, British Library; ENG 835, Houghton Library; HM 80, Huntington Library. (In further citations as in the narrative of my text I refer to ENG 835 as "Houghton," and HM 80 as "Huntington.")
121. Huntington, f. 14.
122. *Ibid.*, f. 14.
123. *Ibid.*, f. 19.
124. *Ibid.*, fos. 46–47.
125. As much as possible, I am relying on evidence outside of the trial proceedings.
126. SP 16/231, art. 77, PRO. According to Allestree's *Almanack* (1632), Michaelmas Term ended on December 28 in 1632.
127. Burton, *A Divine Tragedie*, H1; William Prynne, *A New Discoverie of the Prelats Tyranny* (1641), B1.
128. In a letter dated January 3, 1632/3 John Pory wrote Sir Thomas Puckering that "on wednesday next the Queens pastorall is to be acted in the lower court of Denmark house ... No great lady shall be kept out, though shee have but mean apparell and a worse face. And no inferior lady or woman shall be let in, not such as have extra brave apparel and better faces" (MS Harleian 7000, f. 349, British Library). Pory wrote on a Thursday.
129. John Pory to Sir Thomas Puckering, January 24, 1633, Harleian 7000, f. 350, British Library.
130. George Gresley to Sir Thomas Puckering, January 31, 1633, Harleian 7000, f. 464v, British Library.
131. SP 16/242, art. 6, PRO.
132. SP 16/246, art. 108, PRO. This is calendared conjecturally at September. Given that Prynne says in it that he has been in the Tower for thirty-four weeks, some time in September would be correct.
133. SP 16/240, art. 120, PRO.
134. Prynne, *New Discoverie*, B2.
135. George Gresley to Sir Thomas Puckering, January 31, 1633, Harleian 7000, f. 464v, British Library.
136. Howell, *State Trials*, vol. III, p. 563.
137. Huntington, fos. 1–3.

138. Howell, *State Trials*, vol. III, pp. 569–70.
139. *Ibid.*, p. 574.
140. *Ibid.*, p. 573.
141. *Ibid.*, p. 574.
142. *Ibid.*
143. S. R. Gardiner, ed., *Documents Relating to the Proceedings Against William Prynne, in 1634 and 1637* (London, 1877), p. 24.
144. *Ibid.*, p. 25.
145. Huntington, IIv.
146. *Ibid.*, f. 16.
147. *The Calendar of State Papers for the Reign of Charles I. Addenda, March 1625–January 1649*, William Douglas Hamilton and Sophia Crawford Loma, eds. (London, 1897), p. 465.
148. SP16/534, art. 71, f. 153, PRO.
149. *Ibid.*, fos. 150–01.
150. *Ibid.*, fos. 153v.
151. *Ibid.*, f. 154.
152. *Ibid.*, f. 154v.
153. *Ibid.*, f. 152v.
154. *Ibid.*
155. Howell, *State Trials*, vol. III, p. 572.
156. *Ibid.*, pp. 572–73.
157. Cressy, *Travesties*, p. 222.
158. Huntington, f. 53.
159. Gardiner, *Documents*, p. 57. Prynne's letter is printed in full in *ibid.*, pp. 32–56.
160. Burton, *A Divine Tragedie*, H1.
161. *Ibid.*, H1r–v.
162. Prynne, *New Discoverie*, B1v.
163. SP 16/261, art. 178, PRO.
164. SP16/33, art. 140, PRO.
165. Prynne, *New Discovery*, B3v.
166. *Ibid.*, B4v. On February 20, 1636, the High Commission called upon John Wragg to search private houses not only for conventricles, but also for any unlicensed and unlawful books and papers. Along with the warrant is a notation that by virtue of such warrants the books of Mr. Burton and Mr. Prynne were taken, but it gives no dates for these seizures (SP 16/214, arts. 34 and 36, PRO).
167. Egerton 3383, British Library.
168. The first two are Cressy (*Travesties*, p. 223), the last is Sharpe (*Personal Rule*, p. 759). That both essentially agree attests to the genuinely transgressive nature of these books.
169. In addition to Prynne's *A New Discoverie*, see Sharpe, *Personal Rule*, p. 760. Sharpe bases his account on Rawlinson C.827, Bodleian Library.
170. Henry Burton, *An Apology of an Appeale* (1636), D2v3.

171. Cressy, *Travesties*, pp. 226–27.

172. *Ibid.*, p. 224.

173. SP 16/362, art. 42, PRO. Reprinted fully in Gardiner, *Documents*, pp. 86–90 and partially in Cressy, *Travesties*, p. 225.

174. Paul Seaver, *The Puritan Lectureships: The Politics of Religious Dissent, 1560–1662* (Stanford, 1970).

175. For a detailed account of the alterations in both the 1616 and 1637 editions, see N. W. Bawcutt, "A Crisis of Laudian Censorship: Nicholas and John Okes and the Publication of Sales's *An Introduction to a Devout Life* in 1637," *The Library*, 7th ser., 1 (2000), 406–22: pp. 406–10, 421–22.

176. For an account of the problems discerning whether Nicholas or John printed the 1637 edition, see *ibid.*, pp. 411–13.

177. James F. Larkin, *Stuart Royal Proclamations*, vol. 11 (Oxford, 1983), p. 557.

178. William Prynne, *Canterburies Doome* (1646), p. 187.

179. Bawcutt, "Crisis," p. 410.

180. *Ibid.*, p. 414.

181. *Ibid.*, p. 406.

5 THE PRINTERS AND PRESS CONTROL IN THE 1630S

1. *A decree of Starre-Chamber, concerning printing made the eleuenth day of Iuly last past* (1637). Reprinted in Edward Arber, ed., *A Transcript of the Registers of the Company of Stationers of London*, 5 vols. (London and Birmingham, 1875–94), vol. IV, pp. 529–36.

2. Joseph Loewenstein, *The Author's Due: Printing and the Prehistory of Copyright* (Chicago, 2002), p. 63.

3. Ian Gadd, "'Being Like a Field': Corporate Identity in the Stationers' Company 1557–1684," DPhil dissertation, 1999, Oxford University. I am indebted to Dr. Gadd for providing me with an electronic file of his dissertation, which, because it is electronic, may differ slightly in pagination from the copy on file.

4. *Ibid.*, p. 4.

5. *Ibid.*, p. 4.

6. *Ibid.*, p. 92.

7. *Ibid.*, p. 26.

8. *Ibid.*, p. 192.

9. Sir Francis Nethersole to Elizabeth, Queen of Bohemia, February 1, 1629, SP 16/135, art. 40, PRO.

10. Report on the petition of the journeyman printers, 1635, SP 16/301, art. 105, PRO. In response to the petition from the journeymen, the Privy Council appointed six Stationers to investigate; this is their report.

11. SP 16/339, art. 89, PRO.

12. Michael Sparke, *Scintilla* (1641).

13. SP 16/170, art 54; SP 16/246, art. 56, PRO.

14. SP 16/261, Acts of the High Commission, fos. 197a-98a, PRO. Reprinted in W. W. Greg, *A Companion to Arber* (Oxford, 1967), pp. 307–09.
15. Anthony B. Thompson, "Licensing the Press: The Career of G. R. Weckherlin during the Personal Rule of Charles I," *The Historical Journal*, 41 (1998), 653–678: p. 665.
16. Fritz Levy, "The Decorum of News," *News, Newspapers and Society in Early Modern Britain*, Joad Raymond, ed. (London and Portland, OR, 1999), pp. 12–38: p. 33.
17. In addition to *ibid.*, see Folke Dahl, "Amsterdam – Cradle of English Newspapers," *The Library*, 5th ser., 4 (1949–50), 171–73; T. C. Cogswell, "England and the Spanish Match," *Conflict in Early Stuart England*, Richard Cust and Ann Hughes, eds. (London, 1988), pp. 118–23; T. C. Cogswell, *The Blessed Revolution: English Politics and the Coming of War, 1621–1624* (Cambridge, 1989); Sheila Lambert, "Coranto Printing in England: The First News Books," *Journal of Newspaper and Periodical History*, 8 (1992), 3–18; Richard Cust, "News and Politics in England," *Past and Present*, 112 (1995), 60–90.
18. The end of his licensing career did not lead to the falling away of entering news books in the Stationers' Register, as Sheila Lambert says ("Coranto Printing," p. 9). In 1625 news book entries identified Featly, Goad, and Worrall as licensers.
19. Trumbull, vol. xviii, f. 82, British Library.
20. Thompson, "Licensing the Press: Weckherlin," p. 664. Unless otherwise indicated, my account of Weckherlin's licensing practices relies on Thompson's well-researched article.
21. *Ibid.*, p. 664.
22. *Ibid.*, p. 665.
23. Harleian, 390/263, British Library, quoted in Thompson, "Licensing the Press: Weckherlin," p. 666.
24. Trumbull, Misc. Corr., xix, f. 16, British Library. Quoted in Thompson, "Licensing the Press: Weckherlin," p. 668.
25. Thompson, "Licensing the Press: Weckherlin," p. 668.
26. Weckherlin memo, February 8, 1632, Trumbull, Misc. Corr., xlii, f. 35, British Library, reprinted in Thompson, "Licensing the Press: Weckherlin," p. 668.
27. Thompson, "Licensing the Press: Weckherlin," p. 669.
28. Lambert, "Coranto Printing," p. 12.
29. *A decree of Starre-Chamber*, A3r–v.
30. Lyman Ray Patterson, *Copyright in Historical Perspective* (Nashville, 1960), p. 125, quoted in Loewenstein, *The Author's Due*, p. 160.
31. Frederick Seaton Siebert, *Freedom of the Press in England 1476–1776: The Rise and Decline of Goverument Controls* (Urbana, 1952), p. 142.
32. Peter Heylyn, *Cyprianus Anglicus* (1668), Aaa3.
33. *Ibid.*, Aaa2.
34. *Ibid.*, Aaa3v.

35. Sheila Lambert, "State Control of the Press in Theory and Practice: the Role of the Stationers' Company before 1640," *Censorship and the Control of Print in England and France 1600–1910*, Robin Myers and Michael Harris, eds. (Winchester, 1992), pp. 1–32: p. 22.

36. Cyprian Blagden, *The Stationers' Company: A History 1403–1959* (London, 1960). See also Donald W. Rude and Lloyd E. Berry, "Tanner Manuscript No. 33: New Light on the Stationers' Company in the Early Seventeenth Century," *The Papers of the Bibliographical Society of America*, 66 (1972), 105–34.

37. Sheila Lambert, "The Printers and the Government, 1604–1637," *Aspects of Printing from 1600*, Robin Myers and Michael Harris, eds. (Oxford, 1987), pp. 1–29: p. 4.

38. *Ibid.*, pp. 5–8.

39. *Ibid.*, p. 7.

40. *Ibid.*, p. 1.

41. Arber, *Transcript*, vol. IV, p. 535.

42. *Ibid.*, p. 534.

43. See Greg, *Companion*, pp. 310–18.

44. See Gerald D. Johnson, "The Stationers Versus the Drapers: Control of the Press in the Late Sixteenth Century," *The Library*, 6th ser., 10 (1988), 1–17.

45. Arber, *Transcript*, vol. IV, p. 535.

46. *Ibid.*, p. 531.

47. *Ibid.*

48. Gadd, "Corporate Identity," p. 44, n. 43.

49. Adrian Johns, *The Nature of the Book* (Chicago, 1998), pp. 193–97.

50. Arber, *Transcript*, vol. IV, p. 529.

51. Lambert, "Printers," p. 1.

52. *Ibid.*, p. 7.

53. PC 2, 44, p. 123. "Acts of the Privy Council" for 1631–37 are available by a photographic reproduction (microopaque cards) issued 1962.

54. See Greg, *Companion*, pp. 253–65, 305–69.

55. Arber, *Transcript*, vol. IV, p. 529.

56. *Ibid.*, p. 531.

57. *Ibid.*, p. 535.

58. *Ibid.*, p. 529.

59. *Ibid.*, p. 530.

60. *Ibid.*

61. *Ibid.*, p. 533.

62. John Lilburn, *The Christian Mans Trial* (1641), A1v–A3.

63. Following Philip Hamburger, ("The Development of the Law of Seditious Libel and the Control of the Press," *Stanford Law Review*, 37 [1985], 661–762), D. F. McKenzie incorrectly takes the case of Lilburn as evidence that authors, printers, publishers, and booksellers of seditious books were prosecuted for licensing charges ("The London Book Trade in 1644," *Bibliographia: Lectures 1975–1988 by Recipients of The Marc Fitch Prize for Bibliography*, John Horden, ed. [Oxford, 1992], pp. 130–52).

6 THE END OF CENSORSHIP

1. David Cressy, *England on Edge: Crisis and Revolution, 1640–1642* (Oxford, 2006), p. 282.
2. *Ibid.*, p. 293.
3. Christopher Hill, "Censorship and English Literature," *The Collected Essays of Christopher Hill*, 2 vols. (Brighton, 1985), vol. 1, p. 40; Keith Thomas, "The Meaning of Literacy in Early Modern England," *The Written Word: Literacy in Transition*, Gerd Baumann, ed. (Oxford, 1986), pp. 97–131: p. 120.
4. Fredrick Seaton Siebert, *Freedom of the Press in England 1476–1776* (Urbana, 1952), p. 166.
5. D. F. McKenzie, "The London Book Trade in 1644," *Bibliographia: Lectures 1975–1985*, John Horden, ed. (Oxford, 1992); Sheila Lambert, "State Control of the Press in Theory and Practice," *Censorship and the Control of Print in England and France 1600–1910*, Robin Myer and Michael Harris, eds. (Winchester, 1992), pp. 1–32.
6. Charles I, *A proclamation and declaration to inform our loving subjects of our kingdom of England of the seditious practices of some in Scotland, seeking to overthrow our regall power under false pretences of Religion* (1638).
7. *The Booke of Common Prayer* (Edinburgh, 1637), a3r.
8. Peter Donald, *An Uncounselled King: Charles I and the Scottish troubles, 1637–1641* (Cambridge, 1990), p. 45. Donald provides a useful account of the larger differences between Charles I and Scotland that climaxed in the crisis over the service book.
9. Donald Stevenson, *The Scottish Revolution 1637–44: The Triumph of the Covenanters* (New York, 1973), p. 84.
10. Charles I, *A proclamation and declaration to inform our loving subjects of our kingdom of England of the seditious practices of some in Scotland*, A1.
11. Donald discusses some of the books, including *Short Relation of the State of the Kirk of Scotland* (1638) and *Information to All Good Christians within the Kingdome of England* (1639) as well as the scale of the propaganda campaign in *An Uncounselled King*, chapter 5.
12. *Ibid.*, p. 189.
13. *Ibid.*
14. Charles I, *A Proclamation against libelous and seditious Pamphlets, and Discourses sent from Scotland* (London, 1640), A1.
15. Debora Shuger, *Censorship and Cultural Sensibility* (Philadelphia, 2006), pp. 63–68.
16. Laud's speech in the Star Chamber at Burton, Bastwick, and Prynne's trial, which vehemently disclaims against their charges of innovation, was published by the King's command in 1637 (*A speech delivered in the Starr-Chamber, on Wednesday, the XIVth of Iune, MDCXXXVII. at the censure, of Iohn Bastwick, Henry Burton, and William Prinn; concerning pretended innovations in the Church. By the most Reverend Father in God, VVilliam, L. Archbishop of Canterbury his Grace*).

17. Donald, *Uncounselled King*, p. 180.
18. *Ibid.*, p. 185.
19. Cressy, *England on Edge*, p. 69
20. *Ibid.*, p. 73.
21. John Nalson, *An Impartiall Collection of the Great Affairs of State* (London, 1682), vol. II, p. 809.
22. Joseph Loewenstein, *The Author's Due: Printing and the Prehistory of Copyright* (Chicago, 2002), p. 161.
23. Maija Jansson, ed., *Proceedings of the Opening Session of the Long Parliament.* 7 vols. (Rochester, NY, 2000–07). My account depends on this volume for the events and dates. I will give page citations only for quoted proceedings beyond dates and commonly known events.
24. *Ibid.*, vol. I, p. 28.
25. "Ship money" referred to the taxes Charles I levied to pay the costs of war. While there was precedent in England for monarchs to levy these extra-parliamentary taxes in wartime, in the 1630s, during peacetime, Charles's levies were perceived by many to be illegal. The "new canons" refers to the canons drafted by Laud and approved by the bishops, that made Laudian ceremonialist practices part of canon law. These contained an oath of allegiance to uphold the Church of England's episcopal governance and to oppose all doctrinal innovations.
26. Jansson, *Proceedings*, vol. I, p. 32.
27. *Ibid.*, vol. I, p. 34.
28. *Ibid.*, vol. I, p. 41.
29. *Ibid.*, vol. I, p. 64.
30. *Ibid.*, vol. I, p. 260.
31. Jansson's note (vol. I, p. 410, n. 156) citing the *Dictionary of National Biography*, identifies this as John Featley "chaplain to King Charles." According to the note, "Three of his sermons were printed: *The Honor of Chastity* (London, G. Purslow f. Bourne, 1632), *STC* 10741; *Obedience and Submission* (London, Badger, 1636), *STC* 10742; *A Sermon Preached at S. Buttolphs* (London, Bourne, 1629), *STC* 10743)." The Featly in question here, however, is Daniel Featly, whose collection of sermons, *Clavis Mystica*, was heavily censored by William Bray.
32. Jansson, *Proceedings*, vol. I, p. 483.
33. *Ibid.*
34. *Ibid.*, vol. I, p. 440.
35. *Ibid.*, vol. I, p. 527. This is almost certainly the document, "Passages extracted from Prynne's work entitled 'Histrio-Mastrix'," SP16/534, art. 71, PRO, which I discuss in some detail in chapter 4.
36. Jansson, *Proceedings*, vol. I, p. 527.
37. *Ibid.*, vol. I, p. 604.
38. *Ibid.*, vol. II, p. 23.
39. *Ibid.*, vol. IV, p. 46, vol. V, p. 25. The House of Commons determined that since this was not actual legislation, these actions could be taken without sending the proposal to the House of Lords.

40. *Ibid.*, vol. V, p. 25.
41. *Ibid.*, vol. II, pp. 281–82.
42. *Ibid.*, vol. II, p. 772.
43. *Ibid.*, vol. V, p. 505.
44. Tim Stretton, *Women Waging Law in Elizabethan England* (Cambridge, 1998), p. 12.
45. J. P. Kenyon, *The Stuart Constitution, 1603–1688* (Cambridge, 1966), p. 91.
46. See, for example, Loewenstein, *Author's Due*, pp. 166–68.
47. *To the High Court of Parliament: The humble Remonstrance of the Company of Stationers, London* (1643), A2r–v.
48. *Ibid.*, A3.
49. *A Collection of Speeches made by Sir Edward Dering, Knight and Baronet in matter of Religion* (1642), A4.
50. Henry Gee and William John Hardy, eds., *Documents Illustrative of English Church History* (New York, 1896), p. 549.
51. Cressy, *England on Edge*, p. 184.
52. *Speeches of Sir Edward Dering*, B3.
53. *The Speech or declaration of John Pymm, Esq. To the Lords of the upper House, upon the delivery of the Articles of the Commons assembled in Parliament, against William Laud, archbishop of Canterbury . . . together with a true Copie of the said Articles* (1641), B4v.
54. Charles I, *His Majesties Declaration: To All His Loving Subjects, Of the Causes which moved him to dissolve the last Parliament* (1640).
55. A. D. T. Cromartie, "The Printing of Parliamentary Speeches November 1640–July 1642," *The Historical Journal*, 33 (1990), 23–44: p. 23.
56. Sheila Lambert, "The Beginning of Printing for the House of Commons, 1640–42," *The Library*, 6th ser., 3 (1981), 43–61: pp. 44–45.
57. John Rushworth, *Historical Collections*, part 2 (London, 1680), p. 224.
58. McKenzie, "London Book Trade," pp. 135–37.
59. *Ibid.*, p. 141.
60. *Ibid.*, p. 142.
61. *Ibid.*, p. 134.
62. Cressy, *England on the Edge*, p. 294
63. Michael Mendle, "De Facto Freedom, De Facto Authority: Press and Parliament, 1640–1643," *The Historical Journal*, 38 (1995), 307–32: p. 309.
64. McKenzie, "London Book Trade," p. 142.
65. Mendle, "De Facto Freedom," pp. 331–32.
66. *Ibid.*, p. 330.
67. *Journals of the House of Commons* (1830), vol. II, p. 743.
68. Lambert, "Beginning of Printing," pp. 43–44.
69. Cromartie, "Printing of Parliamentary Speeches," p. 26.
70. *Ibid.*, pp. 27, 33.
71. Jansson, *Proceedings*, vol. 2, p. 382.
72. Cromartie, "Printing of Parliamentary Speeches," p. 39.
73. *Ibid.*, pp. 38–39.

74. *Journals of the House of Commons*, vol. II, p. 79, cited in Lambert, "Beginning of Printing," p. 43.
75. Lambert, "Beginning of Printing," pp. 47–48.
76. Cyprian Blagden, "Stationers' Company in the Civil War Period," *The Library*, 5th ser., 13 (1958), 1–7.
77. *To all Printers, Booke-sellers, Booke-binders, Free-men of the Company of Stationers* (1645).
78. Any effort to obtain a precise count, as Lambert reminds us, is hindered by the fact that the journal of neither House is perfect ("Beginnings of Printing," p. 45).
79. C. H. Firth and R. S. Rait, eds., *Acts and Ordinances of the Interregnum, 1642–1660*, 3 vols. (London, 1911), vol. I, p. 186.
80. *Ibid.*, vol. I, p. 1023.
81. *Ibid.*, vol. II, p. 120.
82. Jason McElligott, "'A Couple of Hundred Squabbling Small Tradesmen'? Censorship, the Stationers' Company, and the State in Early Modern England," *Media History*, II (2005), 87–104: p. 98.
83. *Ibid.*, p. 99.
84. While Joseph Loewenstein has disabused us of an impassioned plea for a free press, he has attended more closely to Milton's imaginative ties to issues of licensing as monopoly rather than as a tool to enforce a particular version of religious truth.
85. John Milton, *Areopagitica, John Milton: Complete Poems and Major Prose*, Merritt Y. Hughes, ed. (New York, 1957), p. 718.
86. *Ibid.*, p. 720.
87. *Ibid.*, pp. 719–20.
88. *Ibid.*, p. 724.
89. *Ibid.*, p. 738.
90. *Ibid.*
91. *Ibid.*, p. 742.
92. Henry Burton, *A tryall of Private Devotions or A Diall for the Houres of Prayer* (1628), A2.

Bibliography

PRIMARY

An Appeale of the Orthodox Ministers. 1629.

Articles Agreed upon by the Archbishops and Bishops of both Provinces, and the whole Cleargie: In the Convocation holden at London, in the yeere 1562. 1628.

Atkyns, Richard. *The Original and Growth of Printing: Collected out of the History and Records of this Kingdome. Wherein is also demonstrated that Printing appertaineth to the Royal Prerogative.* 1664.

Balcanqual, Walter, *et al. A Joynt attestation, avowing that the discipline of the Church of England was not impeached by the Synode of Dort.* 1626.

Bastwick, John. *Elenchus papisticaae religionis in quo probatur neque apostolicam, neque Catholicam, imo neque Romanam este/authore Iohanne Bastuuick . . .; accedit ad calcem, ejusdem authoris exercitatio quedam theologica ad versus episcoporum papalium usurpationem.* Amsterdam, 1634.

The letany of John Bastvvick. [Leiden], 1637.

Beza, Theodore. *The Treasure of Truth, touching the grounde worke of man his salvation.* 1581.

The Booke of Common Prayer. Edinburgh, 1637.

Boughen, Edward. *A Sermon concerning decency and order in Church.* 1638.

Bradshaw, William. *A preparation to the receiving of Christs body and Blood.* 1627.

Brerewood, Edward. *A Learned Treatise of the Sabaoth.* Oxford, 1630.

A Second Treatise of the Sabbath. Oxford, 1632.

Burton, Henry. *An Apology of an Appeale.* 1636.

Babel no Bethel. 1629.

The Bayting of the Popes Bull. 1627.

A brief answer to a late Treatise of the Sabbath day. [Amsterdam, 1635].

A Divine Tragedie Lately Acted. [Amsterdam and London], 1636.

For God and the King. [Amsterdam], 1636.

Israels Fast. Or, A Meditation Upon the Seventh Chapter of Joshuah: A faire Precedent for thee times. 1628.

The law and the gospel reconciled. 1631.

The Lords day, the Sabbath day. 1636.

A Plea to an Appeale. 1626.

Seven Vials, or a briefe and plaine exposition on the 15: and 16: chapters of Revelation. 1628.

A tryall of Private Devotions or A Diall for the Houres of Prayer. 1628.

Butterfield, Robert. *Maschil, or a Treatise to Give Instruction Touching the state of the Church of Rome since the council of Trent.* 1629.

Byfield, Richard. *The Doctrine of the Sabbath Vindicated, In confutation of a treatise of the sabbath written by M. Edward Breerwood against M. Nic Byfield.* 1631.

Camden, William. *Annales rervm Anglicarvm et Hibernicarvm regnante Elizabetha.* 1615, English edition 1625.

Carleton, George. *An Examination of those Things wherein the Author of the Late Appeale Holdeth the Doctrines of the Pelagians and Arminians to be the Doctrine of the Church of England.* 1626.

Carter, John. *A plaine and compendious exposition of Christs Sermon in the Mount.* 1627.

Charles I. *By the King a proclamation signifying his maiesties pleasure, that all the men being in office of government . . . shall so continue.* 1626.

A proclamation and declaration to inform our loving subjects of our kingdom of England of the seditious practices of some in Scotland, seeking to overthrow our regall power under false pretences of religion. 1638.

A Proclamation against libelous and seditious Pamphlets, and Discourses sent from Scotland. 1640.

Cholmely, Hugh. *The state of the now-Romane Church. Discussed by way of vindication of the Right Reverend Father in God, The Lord Bishop of Exceter, from the weak cavils of Henry Burton.* 1629.

Coke, Edward. *The First part of the Institutes of the laws of England.* 1629.

The Reports of Sir Edward Coke. 1658.

Collegiat suffrage of the divines of Great Britain, concerning the five articles controverted in the Low Countries. 1629.

Cosin, John. *A Collection of Private Devotions, or the Houres of Prayer.* 1627.

Crompton, Richard. *L'authoritie et jurisdiction des courts de la majestie de la roygne.* 1594; English translation, 1641.

Crompton, William. *Saint Austens Summes. Printed and bound with Alexander Cooke, Saint Austins Religion.* 1625.

A decree of Starre-Chamber, concerning printing made the eleuenth day of Iuly last past. 1637.

Dering, Edward. *A Collection of Speeches made by Sir Edward Dering, Knight and Baronet in matter of Religion.* 1642.

Dyke, Jeremiah. *A Sermon Preached at the Publicke Fast to the Commons House of Parliament, April 5th 1628.* 1628.

Elton, Edward. *An Exposition of the Ten Commandements of God.* 1623.

Gods Holy Mind touching matters moral. 1625.

Featly, Daniel. *Ancilla Pietatis.* 1639.

Cygnea Cantio. 1629.

A Second Parallel together with a Writ of Error Sued against the Appealer. 1626.

Gataker, Thomas. *A Discours Apologetical, wherein Lilies lewd and lowd Lies . . . are cleerly laid open.* 1654.

Gouge, William. *The Worke of William Gouge.* 1627.

Hall, Joseph. *The Olde Religion: A Treatise, Wherin is laid downe the true state of the difference betwixt the Reformed, and Romane Church; and the blame of the schisme is cast upon the* AUTHORS. *Serving for the vindication of our innocence, for the settling of wavering minds for a preservative against Popish insinuation.* 1627.

The Reconciler. 1629.

Heylyn, Peter. *Antidotum Lincolniense.* 1637.

Coale from the Altar. 1636.

Cyprianus Anglicus. 1668.

Howard, Charles, Earl of Berkshire. *A true copy of the Lord Andevers speech to the Parliament, Concerning the Star-Chamber.* 1641.

Hulsius, Fredrich van. *The character of a Christian: As Hee is distinguished from all Hypocrites and Hereticks. With the freedome of the faithful: As they are proposed by our Saviour in the words of the Gospel.* 1627.

Romes ruine. 1624.

Information to All Good Christians within the Kingdome of England. 1639.

Jackson, Thomas. *A treatise of the holy catholike faith and Church.* 1627.

The judgment of the Synode of Dort, concerning the five articles. London, 1619.

Laud, William. *The history of the troubles and tryal of the Most Reverend Father in God and blessed martyr, William Laud, Lord Arch-Bishop of Canterbury wrote by himself during his imprisonment in the Tower; to which is prefixed the diary of his own life.* 1695.

A speech delivered in the Starr-Chamber, on Wednesday, the XIVth *of Iune,* MDCXXXVII. *at the censure, of Iohn Bastwick, Henry Burton, & William Prinn; concerning pretended innovations in the Church. By the most Reverend Father in God, VVilliam, L. Archbishop of Canterbury his Grace.* 1637.

Leighton, Alexander. *An Appeal to the Parliament; or Sions Plea aginst the Prelacie.* 1629.

Lilburn, John. *The Christian Mans Trial.* 1641.

Marvell, Andrew. *The Rehearsal-Transposed.* 1672.

Nalson, John. *An Impartiall Collection of the Great Affairs of State.* London, 1682.

P., J. *Christ's confession and complaint: concerning his kingdom and seruants; conuincing Iewes of obstinacie, Romish Catholickes of conspiracie, seducers of sedition, Arminians of apostacie, and diuers others of coldnes, schisme, treachery & hypocrisie.* 1629. STC identifies this as having been printed abroad.

Page, William. *A treatise or justification of bowing at the name of Jesus.* Oxford, 1631.

Prideaux, John. *The Doctrine of the Sabbath.* 1634.

Prynne, William. *A Briefe Survay and Censure of Mr Cozens his Couzening Devotions.* 1628.

Canterburies Doome. 1646.

The Church of Englands Old Antithesis to the New Arminianism. 1629, 1630.

God: no impostor, nor deluder. 1629.

Histrio-mastix. 1633.

Lame Giles His Haultings. 1630.

A New Discoverie of the Prelats Tyranny. 1641.

Newes from Ipswich. Ipswich, 1636.

The Perpetuitie of a Regenerate Mans Estate. 1626.

A Quench-coale. Amsterdam, 1637.

Pym, John. *The Speech or declaration of John Pymm, Esq. To the Lords of the upper House, upon the delivery of the Articles of the Commons assembled in Parliament, against William Laud, archbishop of Canterbury . . . together with a true Copie of the said Articles.* 1641.

Rous, Francis. *The Arte of Happiness.* 1619.

Testis Veritatis. 1626.

Rushworth, John. *Historical Collections,* part 2. London, 1680.

R[ussell], J[ohn]. *The Spy discovering the danger of Arminian heresie and Spanish trecherie.* Strasburgh (i.e. Amsterdam: By the successors of Giles Thorp), 1628.

Sibthorpe, Robert. *Apostolike Obedience.* 1627.

A soveraigne antidote against sabbatarian errours. Or, A decision of the chiefe doubts and difficulties touching the Sabbath. 1636.

Sparke, Michael. *Scintilla.* 1641.

Spencer, Thomas. *Maschil Unmasked.* 1629.

Star Chamber Cases Shewing What Causes Properly Belong to the cognizance of that court. 1641.

Stationers' Company. *To the High Court of Parliament: The humble Remonstrance of the Company of Stationers, London.* 1643.

Suffragium Collegiale Theologorum Magna Britannae. London, 1627.

Sutcliffe, Matthew. *A brief censure upon an appeale to Caesar.* 1626.

To all Printers, Booke-sellers, Booke-binders, Free-men of the Company of Stationers. 1645.

Warriston, Archibald Johnson, Lord. *Short Relation of the State of the Kirk of Scotland.* [Edinburgh], 1638.

White, Francis. *An examination and confutation of a lawlesse pamphlet, intituled, A briefe answer to a late treatise of the Sabbath-day: digested dialogue-wise betweene two divines.* 1637.

Williams, John. *Holy Table, Name and Thing.* 1636.

Yates, John. *Ibis ad Caesarem.* 1626.

SECONDARY

Arber, Edward, ed. *A Transcript of the Registers of the Company of Stationers of London.* 5 vols. London and Birmingham, 1875–94.

Baker, John. *The Oxford History of the Laws of England,* vol. vi. Oxford, 2002.

Barnes, Thomas G. "Star Chamber Litigants and their Counsel, 1596–1641." *Legal Records and the Historian.* Ed. J. H. Baker. London, 1978, pp. 7–28.

    "Star Chamber Mythology." *The American Journal of Legal History,* 5 (1961), 1–11.

Bawcutt, N. W. "A Crisis of Laudian Censorship: Nicholas and John Okes and the Publication of Sales's *An Introduction to a Devout Life* in 1637." *The Library*, 7th ser., 1 (2000), 406–22.

Bell, Maureen and John Barnard. "Provisional Count of *STC* Titles 1475–1640." *Publishing History*, 31 (1992), 46–66.

Blagden, Cyprian. "Stationers' Company in the Civil War Period." *The Library*, 5th ser., 13 (1958), 1–7.

The Stationers' Company: A History 1403–1959. London, 1960.

Blayney, Peter. "The Publication of Playbooks." *A New History of Early English Drama*. Ed. John D. Cox and David Scott Kastan. New York, 1997, pp. 383–422.

Bliss, James, ed. *The works of the Most Reverend Father in God, William Laud, DD*. London, 1847–60.

Burrow, Colin. "Rous, Francis (1580/81–1659)," *Oxford Dictionary of National Biography* Oxford, September 2004; online edn., 2006 [www.oxforddnb.com/view/article/24171, accessed December 31, 2006].

The Calendar of State Papers for the Reign of Charles I, 1627–28. Ed. John Bruce. London, 1859.

The Calendar of State Papers for the Reign of Charles I, 1628–29. Ed. John Bruce. London, 1859.

The Calendar of State Papers for the Reign of Charles I. Addenda, March 1625–January 1649. Ed. William Douglas Hamilton and Sophia Crawford Loma. London, 1897.

Clegg, Cyndia Susan. *Press Censorship in Elizabethan England*. Cambridge, 1997.

Press Censorship in Jacobean England. Cambridge, 2001.

Cobbett's Parliamentary History of England: from the Norman Conquest, in 1066, to the year 1803. 1806–20.

Cogswell, T. C. *The Blessed Revolution: English Politics and the Coming of War, 1621–1624*. Cambridge, 1989.

"England and the Spanish Match." *Conflict in Early Stuart England*. Ed. Richard Cust and Ann Hughes. London, 1988, pp. 118–23.

Colclough, David. *Freedom of Speech in Early Stuart England*. Cambridge, 2005.

Collinson, Patrick. *The Religion of Protestants: The Church in English Society 1559–1625*. Oxford, 1982.

Cosin, John. *The Correspondence of John Cosin, D. D., Lord Bishop of Durham*. 2 vols. London, 1869–1872.

Cressy, David. *England on Edge: Crisis and Revolution, 1640–1642*. Oxford, 2006.

Travesties and Transgression in Tudor and Stuart England: Tales of Discord and Dissension. Oxford, 2000.

Cromartie, A. D. T. "The Printing of Parliamentary Speeches November 1640–July 1642." *The Historical Journal*, 33 (1990), 23–44.

Curtis, Mark H. "William Jones: Puritan Printer and Propagandist." *The Library*, 5th ser., 19 (1964), 38–66.

Cust, Richard. "News and Politics in England." *Past and Present*, 112 (1995), 60–90.

Dahl, Folke. "Amsterdam – Cradle of English Newspapers." *The Library*, 5th ser., 4 (1949–50), 171–73.

Dasent, John Roche, ed. *Acts of the Privy Council*. 32 vols. London, 1890–1907.

Davies, Julian. *The Caroline Captivity of the Church: Charles I and the Remoulding of Anglicanism, 1625–1641*. Oxford, 1992.

Donald, Peter. *An Uncounselled King: Charles I and the Scottish Troubles, 1637–1641*. Cambridge, 1990.

Dutton, Richard. " 'Buggeswords': Samuel Harsnett and the Licensing, Suppression and Afterlife of Dr. John Hayward's *The first part of the life and reign of Henry IV.*" *Criticism*, 35 (1993), 305–40.

Elton, G. R. *The Tudor Constitution: Documents & Commentary*. Cambridge, 1960.

Feather, John. *Publishing, Piracy and Politics: An Historical Study of Copyright in Britain*. London, 1992.

Fincham, Kenneth. "Clerical Conformity from Whitgift to Laud." *Conformity and Orthodoxy in the English Church, c. 1560–1660*. Ed. Peter Lake and Michael Questier. Woodbridge, Suffolk, 2000, pp. 125–58.

"Prelacy and Politics: Archbishop Abbot's Defense of Protestant Orthodoxy." *Historical Research*, 61 (1988), 36–69.

Prelate as Pastor: the Episcopate of James I. Oxford, 1990.

"The Restoration of Altars in the 1630s." *The Historical Journal*, 44 (2001), 919–40.

Fincham, Kenneth, ed. *The Early Stuart Church, 1603–1642*. Stanford, 1993.

Firth, C. H. and R. S. Rait, eds. *Acts and Ordinances of the Interregnum, 1642–1660*. 3 vols. London, 1911.

Foster, Stephen. *Notes from the Caroline Underground: Alexander Leighton, the Puritan Triumvirate and the Laudian Reaction of Nonconformity*. Hamden, CT, 1978.

Gadd, Ian. " 'Being Like a Field': Corporate Identity in the Stationers' Company 1557–1684." DPhil dissertation, Oxford University, 1999.

Gardiner, S. R., ed. *Documents Relating to the Proceedings Against William Prynne, in 1634 and 1637*. London, 1877.

Gee, Henry and William John Hardy, eds. *Documents Illustrative of English Church History*. New York, 1896.

Gibson, Kenneth. "Burton, Henry (*bap.* 1578, *d.* 1647/8)," *Oxford Dictionary of National Biography*, Oxford, 2004; online edn., 2006 [www.oxforddnb.com/view/article/4129, accessed December 31, 2006].

Gowing, Laura. "Language, Power and the Law: Women's Slander Litigation in Early Modern London." *Women, Crime and the Courts in Early Modern England*. Ed. Jennifer Kermode and Garthine Walker. Chapel Hill, NC and London, 1994, pp. 26–47.

Gray, Charles M. "Parliament, Liberty, and the Law." *Parliament and Liberty from the Reign of Elizabeth to the English Civil War*. Ed. J. H. Hexter. Stanford, 1992, pp. 155–200.

Greene, Jody. *The Trouble with Ownership: Literary Property and Authorial Liability in England, 1660–1730*. Philadelphia, 2005.

Greg, W. W. *A Companion to Arber: Being a Calendar of Documents in Edward Arber's "Transcript of the Registers of the Company of Stationers of London, 1554–1640" with Text and Calendar of Supplementary Documents.* Oxford, 1967.

Licensers for the Press. Oxford, 1962.

Greg, W. W. and E. Boswell, eds. *Records of the Court of the Stationers' Company.* London, 1930.

Guy, John. *The Court of Star Chamber and Its Records to the Reign of Elizabeth I.* London, 1985.

Tudor England. Oxford and New York, 1988.

Hamburger, Philip. "The Development of the Law of Seditious Libel and the Control of the Press." *Stanford Law Review,* 37 (1985), 661–762.

Hardwick, Charles. *A History of the Articles of Religion.* London, 1888.

Hill, Christopher. *The Collected Essays of Christopher Hill.* 2 vols. Brighton, 1985.

Holdsworth, W. S. *A History of English Law.* 9 vols. Boston, 1926.

Holland, Susan. "Archbishop Abbot and the Problem of 'Puritanism'." *The Historical Journal,* 37 (1994), 23–43.

Hoppe, Harry R. "John Wolfe, Printer and Publisher, 1579–1601." *The Library,* 4th ser., 14 (1933), 241–74.

Howell, T. B. *A Complete Collection of State Trials.* 10 vols. London, 1811–26.

Huffman, Clifford Chalmers. *Elizabethan Impressions: John Wolfe and his Press.* New York, 1988.

Hughes, Merritt Y., ed. *John Milton: Complete Poems and Major Prose.* New York, 1957.

Hughes, Paul L. and James F. Larkin, *Tudor Royal Proclamations.* 3 vols. New Haven and London, 1964.

Hunt, Arnold. "Featly, Daniel (1582–1645)," *Oxford Dictionary of National Biography,* Oxford, 2004; online edn., 2006 [www.oxforddnb.com/view/article/9242, accessed December 31, 2006].

"Licensing and Religious Censorship." *Literature and Censorship in Renaissance England.* Ed. Andrew Hadfield. Houndmills, Basingstoke, 2001, pp. 127–46.

Ingram, Martin. *Church Courts, Sex and Marriage in England, 1570–1640.* Cambridge, 1987.

Jackson, William A. *Records of the Court of the Stationers' Company.* London, 1957.

Jansson, Maija, ed. *Proceedings of the Opening Session of the Long Parliament.* 7 vols. Rochester, NY, 2000–07.

Johns, Adrian. *The Nature of the Book.* Chicago, 1998.

Johnson, Gerald D. "The Stationers Versus the Drapers: Control of the Press in the Late Sixteenth Century." *The Library,* 6th ser., 10 (1988), 1–17.

Kenyon, J. P. *The Stuart Constitution, 1603–1688.* Cambridge, 1966.

Kishlansky, Mark. "Tyranny Denied: Charles I, Attorney General Heath, and the Five Knights' Case." *The Historical Journal,* 42 (1999), 53–83.

Lake, Peter. *The Boxmaker's Revenge.* Stanford, 1998.

"The Ecclesiastical Policy of James I." *Journal of British Studies* 24 (1985), 169–207.

"The Laudian Style: Order, Uniformity and the Pursuit of the Beauty of Holiness in the 1630s." *The Early Stuart Church, 1603–1642*. Ed. Kenneth Fincham. Stanford, 1993, pp. 161–85.

Moderate Puritans and the Elizabethan Church. Cambridge and New York, 1982.

Lake, Peter and Michael Questier. *The AntiChrist's Lewd Hat*. New Haven, 2002.

Lambert, Sheila. "The Beginning of Printing for the House of Commons, 1640–42." *The Library*, 6th ser., 3 (1981), 43–61.

"Committees, Religion, and Parliamentary Encroachment on Royal Authority in Early Stuart England." *English Historical Review*, 33 (1990), 60–95.

"Coranto Printing in England: The First News Books." *Journal of Newspaper and Periodical History*, 8 (1992), 3–18.

"The Printers and the Government, 1604–1637." *Aspects of Printing from 1600*. Ed. Robin Myers and Michael Harris. Oxford, 1987, pp. 1–29.

"Richard Montagu, Arminianism, and Censorship." *Past and Present*, 124 (1989), 36–68.

"State Control of the Press in Theory and Practice: the Role of the Stationers' Company before 1640." *Censorship and the Control of Print in England and France 1600–1910*. Ed. Robin Myers and Michael Harris. Winchester, 1992, pp. 1–32.

Lamont, William M. *Marginal Prynne 1600–1669*. London, 1963.

Larkin, James F. *Stuart Royal Proclamations*, vol. II. Oxford, 1983.

Larkin, James F. and Paul L. Hughes. *Stuart Royal Proclamations*. 2 vols. Oxford, 1973.

Levack, Brian P. *The Civil Lawyers in England 1603–1641*. Oxford, 1973.

Levy, Fritz. "The Decorum of News." *News, Newspapers and Society in Early Modern Britain*. Ed. Joad Raymond. London and Portland, OR, 1999, pp. 12–38.

Loewenstein, Joseph. *The Author's Due: Printing and the Prehistory of Copyright*. Chicago, 2002.

Lyle, J. V., ed. *Acts of the Privy Council*. 40 vols. London, 1934.

Manning, Roger. "The Origins of the Doctrine of Sedition." *Albion*, 12 (1981), 99–121.

Marchant, Ronald. *The Church Under the Law: Justice, Administration and Discipline in the Diocese of York, 1560–1640*. Cambridge, 1969.

McCullough, Peter. "Making Dead Men Speak: Laudianism, Print, and the Works of Lancelot Andrewes, 1626–1642." *The Historical Journal*, 41 (1998), 401–24.

McElligott, Jason. "'A Couple of Hundred Squabbling Small Tradesmen'? Censorship, the Stationers' Company, and the State in Early Modern England." *Media History*, 11 (2005), 87–104.

McKenzie, D. F. "The London Book Trade in 1644." *Bibliographia: Lectures 1975–1988 by Recipients of The Marc Fitch Prize for Bibliography*. Ed. John Horden. Oxford, 1992, pp. 130–52.

Mendle, Michael. "De Facto Freedom, De Facto Authority: Press and Parliament, 1640–1643." *The Historical Journal*, 38 (1995), 307–32.

Milton, Anthony. *Catholic and Reformed: The Roman and Protestant Churches in English Protestant Thought, 1600–1640*. Cambridge, 1995.
"Licensing, Censorship, and Religious Orthodoxy in Early Stuart England." *The Historical Journal*, 41 (1998), 625–51.
Notestein, Wallace. *Commons Debates for 1629*. Minneapolis, 1921.
Parry, Charles Henry. *Parliaments and Councils of England*. London, 1839.
Patterson, Annabel. *Censorship and Interpretation: The Conditions of Writing and Reading in Early Modern England*. Madison, 1984.
Patterson, Lyman Ray. *Copyright in Historical Perspective*. Nashville, 1960.
Quintrell, Brian. "Juxon, William (*bap.* 1582, *d.* 1663)," *Oxford Dictionary of National Biography*, Oxford, 2004; online edn., 2006 [www.oxforddnb.com/view/article/15179, accessed December 31, 2006]
Robinson, J. A., ed. "Documents of the Laudian Period." *Collectanea : A Collection of Documents from Various Sources*, Somerset Record Society, vol. XLIII (1928), pp. 183–90.
Rude, Donald W. and Lloyd E. Berry. "Tanner Manuscript No. 33: New Light on the Stationers' Company in the Early Seventeenth Century." *The Papers of the Bibliographical Society of America*, 66 (1972), 105–34.
Russell, Conrad. "Eliot, Sir John (1592–1632)," *Oxford Dictionary of National Biography*, Oxford, September 2004; online edn., 2006 [www.oxforddnb.com/view/article/8630, accessed March 6, 2007].
Parliaments and English Politics 1621–1629. Oxford, 1979.
Rypins, Stanley. "The Printing of Basilikòn Dôron, 1603." *The Papers of the Bibliographical Society of America*, 64 (1970), 393–417.
Seaver, Paul. *The Puritan Lectureships: The Politics of Religious Dissent, 1560–1662*. Stanford, 1970.
The Seconde parte of a register: being a calendar of manuscripts under that title intended for publication by the Puritans about 1593, and now in Dr. Williams's Library, London. Ed. Albert Peel. Cambridge, 1915.
Seipp, David J. "The Structure of English Common Law in the Seventeenth Century." *Legal History in the Making: Proceedings of the Ninth British Legal History Conference, Glasgow 1989*. Ed. W. M. Gordon and T. D. Fergus. London, 1991, pp. 61–83.
Sharpe, Kevin, *The Personal Rule of Charles I*. New Haven, 1992.
Sir Robert Cotton, 1586–1631. Oxford, 1979.
Shuger, Debora. *Censorship and Cultural Sensibility: The Regulation of Language in Tudor–Stuart England*. Philadelphia, 2006.
Siebert, Frederick Seaton, *Freedom of the Press in England 1476–1776: The Rise and Decline of Government Controls*. Urbana, IL, 1952.
Stevenson, Donald. *The Scottish Revolution 1637–44: The Triumph of the Covenanters*. New York, 1973.
Stretton, Tim. *Women Waging Law in Elizabethan England*. Cambridge, 1998.
Thomas, Keith. "The Meaning of Literacy in Early Modern England." *The Written Word: Literacy in Transition*. Ed. Gerd Baumann. Oxford, 1986, pp. 97–131.

Thompson, Anthony B. "Licensing the Press: The Career of G. R. Weckherlin during the Personal Rule of Charles I." *The Historical Journal,* 41 (1998), 653–78.

Towers, Sue Ellen. *Control of Religious Printing in Early Stuart England.* Woodbridge, Suffolk, 2003.

Tyacke, Nicholas. *Anti-Calvinists: The Rise of English Arminianism c. 1599–1640.* Oxford, 1987.

"Puritanism, Arminianism and Counter Revolution." *The Origins of the English Civil War.* Ed. Conrad Russell. New York, 1973, pp. 119–43.

Usher, Brett. "Gataker, Thomas (1574–1654)." *Oxford Dictionary of National Biography,* Oxford, 2004; online edn., 2006 [www.oxforddnb.com/view/article/10445, accessed January 4, 2007].

Usher, Roland. *The Rise and Fall of the High Commission.* London, 1913 (reprinted Oxford, 1968), Introduction by Philip Tyler.

Weber, Harold. *Paper Bullets: Print and Kingship under Charles II.* Lexington, KY, 1996.

Webster, Tom. *Godly Clergy in Early Stuart England: The Caroline Puritan Movement, c. 1620–1643.* Cambridge, 1997.

White, Peter. *Predestination, Policy and Polemic: Conflict and Consensus in the English Church from the Reformation to the Civil War.* Cambridge, 1992.

Williams, Franklin B., Jr. "The Laudian Imprimatur," *The Library,* 5th ser., 15 (1960), 96–104.

Index

Lightning Source UK Ltd.
Milton Keynes UK

172836UK00009B/59/P